Special Operations and Strategy

Fed by layers of official secrecy, personal memoirs of operators, and hundreds of units and campaign histories, the mystique surrounding special operations forces has been enhanced by their success in Afghanistan and Iraq. Despite this wealth of literature special operations forces have been prone to misuse or misapplication: in particular how strategic operations achieve their strategic effects has not been well understood.

This book examines how special operations, in conjunction with more conventional military actions, can achieve and sustain strategic effect(s) over time and argues that the root of their effectiveness lies in understanding the relationship that exists between moral and material attrition at the strategic level through an examination of strategic theory and case studies.

A pioneering work on special operations forces, this book uses two concepts from classic works of strategy, strategic paralysis and attrition, as a method of examining the effectiveness of special operations within a theoretical context. However, James Kiras argues that the path to strategic success is rarely so direct as a number of elements outlined by Clausewitz, including friction, fog of war, and uncertainty, conspire to prevent individual actions, however audacious, from achieving their desired effects. In particular the author reassesses the famous "Dambusters" raid and its strategic effects on Nazi Germany and the Allied war effort and examines why the Special Air Service (SAS) was not used to greater effect in the Normandy campaign. In addition to these two historical case studies, this volume draws upon numerous special operations examples, both contemporary and historical, to illustrate how the unlikely pairing of special operations and attrition offers a better explanation of how strategic effects caused by special operations occur.

This book will be of interest to policymakers and practitioners in the special operations community, as well as advanced undergraduate and postgraduate students of military affairs and strategic studies.

James D. Kiras is assistant professor at the School of Advanced Air and Space Studies, Maxwell Air Force Base, Alabama, where he teaches on the subjects of terrorism and insurgency. He is also an Associate Senior Fellow of the Strategic Studies Division of the Joint Special Operations University, Hurlburt Field, Florida and has worked on a number of US special operations policy efforts since 2001. He was awarded a PhD from the University of Reading in 2004—this book is based on his doctoral thesis.

Cass Series: Strategy and History
Series Editors: Colin Gray and Williamson Murray
ISSN: 1473-6403

This new series will focus on the theory and practice of strategy. Following Clausewitz, strategy has been understood to mean the use made of force, and the threat of the use of force, for the ends of policy. This series is as interested in ideas as in historical cases of grand strategy and military strategy in action. All historical periods, near and past, and even future, are of interest. In addition to original monographs, the series will from time to time publish edited reprints of neglected classics as well as collections of essays.

1. **Military Logistics and Strategic Performance**
   Thomas M. Kane

2. **Strategy for Chaos**
   Revolutions in military affairs and the evidence of history
   Colin Gray

3. **The Myth of Inevitable US Defeat in Vietnam**
   C. Dale Walton

4. **Astropolitik**
   Classical geopolitics in the space age
   Everett C. Dolman

5. **Anglo-American Strategic Relations and the Far East, 1933–1939**
   Imperial crossroads
   Greg Kennedy

6. **Power and Policy in the Space and Information Age**
   Pure strategy
   Everett C. Dolman

7. **The Red Army, 1918–1941**
   From vanguard of world revolution to US Ally
   Earl F. Ziemke

8. **Britain and Ballistic Missile Defence, 1942–2002**
   Jeremy Stocker

9 **The Nature of War in the Information Age**
  Clausewitzian future
  David J. Lonsdale

10 **Strategy as Social Science**
   Thomas Schelling and the nuclear age
   Robert Ayson

11 **Alexander the Great**
   Lessons in Strategy
   David J. Lonsdale

12 **Disarmament of Germany after World War I**
   The diplomacy of arms inspection 1920–31
   Richard Shuster

13 **Military Transformation in East Asia**
   Technology, warfare and future security
   Malcolm Davis

14 **The German 1918 Offensives**
   A case study of the operational level of war
   David Zabecki

Special Operations and Strategy
From World War II to the War on Terrorism

James D. Kiras

LONDON AND NEW YORK

First published 2006
by Routledge
2 Park Square, Milton Park, Abingdon, Oxon, OX14 4RN

Simultaneously published in the USA and Canada
by Routledge
270 Madison Ave, New York NY 10016

*Routledge is an imprint of the Taylor & Francis Group,
an informa business*

Transferred to Digital Printing 2007

© 2006 James D. Kiras

Typeset in Times by
GreenGate Publishing Services, Tonbridge, Kent

All rights reserved. No part of this book may be reprinted or reproduced or
utilized in any form or by any electronic, mechanical, or other means, now
known or hereafter invented, including photocopying and recording, or in
any information storage or retrieval system, without permission in writing
from the publishers.

British Library Cataloguing in Publication Data
A catalogue record for this book is available
from the British Library

Library of Congress Cataloging in Publication Data
Kiras, James.
Special operations and strategy from World War II to the War on Terrorism /
James D. Kiras.
　　p. cm. – (Strategy and history, ISSN 1473-6403 ; 17)
　　Includes bibliographical references and index.
　　ISBN 0-415-70212-7 (hardback)
　　1. Special operations (Military science) I. Title. II. Strategy and history
(Routledge (Firm)); 17.

U262.K58 2006
356'.1609045–dc22

2005030697

ISBN10: 0-415-70212-7 (hbk)
ISBN10: 0-415-45949-4 (pbk)
ISBN10: 0-203-96964-2 (ebk)

ISBN13: 978-0-415-70212-6 (hbk)
ISBN13: 978-0-415-45949-5 (pbk)
ISBN13: 978-0-203-96964-9 (ebk)

Dedication

For Michelle
You make it all worthwhile

Contents

	List of illustrations	x
	Foreword	xi
	Preface	xiii
	Acknowledgments	xiv
	List of abbreviations	xvi
1	Special operations and great raids	1
2	"Seeing 'black lights' before sinking into oblivion": theories of strategic paralysis	16
3	"A dark picture of destruction": special operations, the persistence of ideas, and dambusting	35
4	Death by a thousand cuts: special operations, attrition, and the nature of warfare	58
5	"Looting a burning house": the SAS in the campaign of attrition in Normandy, 1944	83
6	Conclusion: special operations and the nature of strategy	112
	Notes	118
	Bibliography	195
	Index	224

Illustrations

Figures

2.1	Fuller's unity of the principles of war	18
2.2	Warden's five-ring model	25
2.3	Boyd's OODA loop	30
3.1	How Upkeep worked	49
3.2	Dam types	51
4.1	Delbrück's forms and poles	66
4.2	Typologies of strategy and war	72
5.1	Pre-D-Day German force disposition and *maquis* strength estimates	97
5.2	SAS operations: code names, locations, and drop dates	100

Tables

3.1	RAF WA Plans	44

Foreword

Dr James Kiras has written a book for which we have long been waiting. For the better part of two decades, those of us who have sustained or developed a serious interest in Special Operations Forces (SOF) and Special Operations (SO) have complained about the near total absence of a genuinely strategic literature on the subject. Well, now, in Dr Kiras's powerful analysis, we have the potent beginnings of just such a literature.

Some readers may find it hard to believe that a subject as popular among military authors and journalists as SOF and SO, and especially their equipment and tactical methods, should be close to naked of strategic analyses. This absence is especially striking in the case of SOF, but this is just an extreme example of a general condition, an inability, unwillingness, or simply a failure to understand the critical importance of strategy. The key question for the strategist is "So what?" You can regale an audience with extraordinary tales of bravery, skill, and even self-sacrifice by SOF, but, at the end of the day, as the cliché directs our thoughts, what difference did those deeds make to the course, outcome, and possibly the consequences of war? This view may appear callous, cynical, dismissive of the all-important human factor. It is nothing of the kind. Indeed, quite to the contrary, relentless posing of the "So what" question helps ensure that brave, skilled, and relatively rare special warriors are not committed to, or expended in, strategically futile operations. A particular glory of Dr Kiras's book is that he succeeds magnificently not only in explaining the nature of SOF and SO, though that alone is a notable achievement, given that both are somewhat contestable topics to some. What this book does in addition is to explore conceptually and empirically the necessary relations among war, strategy, and SO. In other words, Dr Kiras gives us context. This is always useful, if not vital, but in the case of SOF it is far more than merely useful, it is literally essential. The reason why this should be so lies in the very nature of SOF and SO. Because SOF are super-elite soldiers, and therefore very few in number, they can only be employed with surprise in brief bursts of action. Or, if in an intelligence-gathering role, they must be deployed only very stealthily. Not unreasonably, perhaps, one might ask, "What can a few elite soldiers accomplish?" Well, what is the historical context? In a war of nations, with literally millions engaged, what, if any, are the roles worth performing by SOF? Note that Dr Kiras's two case studies are both drawn from the most total of the wars of the industrial age, the Second World War.

The temptation to seek spectacular missions which could have strategically extraordinary consequences is well nigh irresistible. Inadvertently, I myself may have encouraged this Hollywood perspective on SOF when I entitled an article in 1999, "Handfuls of Heroes on Desperate Ventures" (*Parameters*). Probably the spirit of this approach to SOF is best captured in those often-quoted words attributed to the Mongol warlord, Yasotay: "When the hour of crisis comes, remember that forty selected men can shake the world."

Dr Kiras tells a different story. One, I regret to say, that is far more plausible. He argues persuasively that although SOF can do many things in many contexts, their principal value is to contribute usefully, sometimes even significantly, to the material and especially the moral erosion of an enemy's ability and willingness to fight in a lengthy war of attrition. In some ways, this book is almost as much a disquisition on the nature and character of war and strategy, as it is on the relationship of SOF to those central matters. All too often, Dr Kiras argues, SOF employment is guided by no theory of their expected strategic effectiveness. It follows inevitably that even SO that are tactical triumphs are essentially a waste of effort. They have no wider meaning.

It is necessary to remember that strategy is the bridge between policy and military power, including SOF. Only if that bridge is in good repair, and if policymakers and soldiers conduct a constant dialogue, albeit an unequal one privileging the politicians, as Eliot Cohen reminds us (in his *Supreme Command*, 2002), will military effort be purposefully directed. SOF, alas, face a double peril. First, they share the risk common to all soldiers of being misemployed by a war effort that lacks coherent strategic guidance. Recall Vietnam! Second, because of their unusual character, with its contestable "specialness," they will always be at risk to misuse both by policymakers who want quick results on the cheap, and by more regular soldiers who will try to control them for immediate tactical purposes. Dr Kiras's case studies illustrate these dangers perfectly.

This book is a singular achievement. Now, at last, we have the first glimmer of a worthy literature on the roles and value of SOF and SO in contemporary war. Given the new-found popularity of SOF today, Dr Kiras's study could hardly be timelier. I hope that it is read widely, deeply, and is inwardly digested by those many people who are genuinely confused about the roles and utility of SOF.

Colin S. Gray

Preface

I am heartened to see this comprehensive and scholarly work by Dr James Kiras. Only a few talented academics can bridge the gap between theory and practice as Dr Kiras has done in recent years.

After 11 September 2001 he contributed substantially to policy developed in this Pentagon office and was a principal author of a study that detailed the implications for employing special operations forces (SOF) as a centerpiece for the Global War on Terrorism (GWOT). He continues to work with the special operations community on some of our most vexing problems. Few academics know the modern aspects of special operations better than Dr Kiras.

Dr Kiras marshals an impressive array of evidence to demonstrate how throughout history SOF have achieved strategic effects. He makes an unconventional argument that is sure to generate scholarly and professional debate—attrition is a strategic concept that is not particularly well understood and its association with special operations is counterintuitive.

Dr Kiras nevertheless manages to link convincingly this theoretical concept with the sustained use of special operations as a method to explain how SOF achieve their strategic effects. He takes issue with the notion that special operations can inflict strategic paralysis on an adversary. Through his examination of the Dambusters Raid conducted in 1943, he demonstrates that SOF are rarely a quick fix to strategic problems

Even when special operations are integrated into a larger campaign plan with attrition as its main goal, Dr Kiras reminds us in his case study on the use of the Special Air Service in Normandy that a number of aspects endemic to strategy—personalities, competing organizations, command structures, and friction—can complicate or derail even the best laid plans.

Given the nature of the war we will fight for years to come, the issues Dr Kiras raises will be mandatory reading for today's policymakers as well as generations of successors.

Robert Andrews
Principal Assistant Secretary of Defense
Special Operations and Low Intensity Conflict

Acknowledgments

It is fitting, if not a touch ironic, that a work that discusses the strategic concept of attrition should have a prolonged development. Simply put, this work would not have been completed without the assistance of a number of organizations and individuals along the way.

To begin, the generous financial support of the H.B. Earhart Foundation assured study time in England as well as the resources to conduct research into many a dark corner. The dedicated staffs of several archives and libraries have my sincere gratitude for pointing out additional reference material and answering my endless string of questions. In particular, I wish to thank the staffs of: the Liddell Hart Military Archives at King's College, London; the National Archives/Public Records Office, Kew; the National Archives at College Park, MD; the Interlibrary Loan staff of the University of Hull; the library staff of various departments of the Air University; the Public Affairs Office of the United States Special Operations Command, Tampa, FL; and, to Cathy Murphy at Canadian Forces Command and Staff College in Toronto, Ontario, Canada for all of her assistance during the early years. My sincere appreciation goes to Lt. Col. (retd) Keith Edlin, MBE, of the Special Air Service Regimental Association for reviewing part of the manuscript, correcting a few sins of commission, and kindly granting permission to reproduce the copyrighted image on the book cover.

It has been my good fortune to be surrounded by colleagues, coworkers, and friends whose knowledge, acumen, and motivation have set very high standards that I have striven to meet. First and foremost on the list are the students, staff, and fellow professors at the School of Advanced Air and Space Studies (SAASS) at Maxwell Air Force Base, Alabama. There is no better environment in professional military education in which to work and I am astounded by the insights I glean from my colleagues and the students daily. Two individuals in particular, Dr Edward Westermann and Dr Scott Gorman, deserve special mention for agreeing to slog through the manuscript and offer insights and criticism of the most constructive kind. In addition, the Commandant of School, Dr Thomas Griffith, has been nothing but supportive in authorizing the time and resources required to rework my PhD dissertation into book form.

Other fellow travelers during the lifespan of this project deserve special mention. While on the road to the PhD and their own subsequent careers Dr C. Dale

Walton, Dr Brian Auten, and Dr John Sheldon have stayed the course and reviewed this work throughout its lifespan, sharpening its focus, and improving its quality tremendously without unduly straining our friendships. Matthew J. Springer offered contributions too numerous to name for which I am truly grateful. Two "true believers," Scott Moore and Kevin Baugh, were tireless champions for the completion of this work during the tumultuous life of the Directorate of Strategy, Concepts, and Initiatives in the Office of the Assistant Secretary of Defense for Special Operations and Low Intensity Conflict and continue to be sources of insight and wisdom. John Warden, Glenn Harned, and John Collins provided thoughtful responses to a seemingly endless array of questions. Many thanks are in order to the members of my viva committee, Dr Duncan Anderson of the Royal Military Academy, Sandhurst, and Dr David J. Lonsdale of the University of Reading. And last, but certainly not least, to Professor Colin S. Gray I owe intellectual and professional debts that a lifetime of effort could not possibly repay. He has been the paragon of what an intellectual mentor, advisor, and colleague should be.

Andrew Humphrys and Marjorie Francois of Taylor and Francis are the epitome of professionalism in the Malthusian world of publishing and I appreciate all of their efforts to get this work into print. The staff of GreenGate Publishing provided first rate editing and typesetting of the manuscript. In particular, Anna Carroll kept the production schedule on track in a firm but friendly manner and Adele Brimacombe provided attentive and detailed copyediting comments that saved me from a few potential embarrassments. Any remaining mistakes or oversights are mine and mine alone.

My family members have been as much a part of this work as anyone, if not more. They include my parents, Chester and Doris Kiras, my sister and brother-in-law, Cheryl and Peter Berg, and my grandparents, Jim and Mary Buchan. To them I give my heartfelt appreciation and I hope that they see their contributions hidden in the pages of this work. Last, but certainly not least, I dedicate this work to Michelle, whose convictions and support, not to mention companionship, have made it all worthwhile.

Abbreviations

AFSOC	Air Force Special Operations Command
CINCPAC	Commander-in-Chief, Pacific
CENTCOM	Central Command
CFLN	*Comité Français de la Libération Nationale*
COSSAC	Chief of Staff to Supreme Allied Commander
EMFFI	*Etat-major des Forces Français de l'Intérieur*
EMP	Electromagnetic Pulse
EO	Executive Order
GWAPS	Gulf War Air Power Survey
LD	Line of Departure
LRDG	Long Range Desert Group
MACV-SOG	Military Assistance Command, Vietnam, Studies and Observation Group
NATO	North Atlantic Treaty Organization
NDU	National Defense University
OODA Loop	Observation, Orientation, Decision, Action Loop
OSS	Office of Strategic Services
PIAT	Projector, Infantry, Anti-Tank
POE	Port of Embarkation
POL	Petroleum, Oil, and Lubricants
POW	Prisoner of War
RAF	Royal Air Force
SAS	Special Air Service
SBS	Special Boat Section/Squadron
SD	*Sicherheitsdienst*, or Security Service
SEAD	Suppression of Enemy Air Defenses
SEAL	Navy Sea, Air, and Land Commandos
SFHQ	Special Forces Headquarters
SHAEF	Supreme Headquarters Allied Expeditionary Forces
SIG	Special Interrogation Group
SO	Special Operations
SOE	Special Operations Executive
SOF	Special Operations Forces

sPzAbt	*schwere Panzer Abteilung*, or heavy tank unit
SS	*Schutzstaffeln*
UCAV	Unmanned Combat Aerial Vehicle
USAAF	United States Army Air Force
USAWC	United States Army War College
USSOCOM	United States Special Operations Command
WA Plans	Western Air Plans

1 Special operations and great raids

> Mount a sudden strike on their doubts. Attack their haste. Force them to constrict their deployment. Launch a sudden strike against their order. Take advantage of [their failure] to avoid harm. Obstruct their strategy. Seize their thoughts. Capitalize on their fears.
>
> (*The Methods of the Ssu-ma*[1])

On the evening of 27 February 1943, six Norwegian saboteurs infiltrated the Norsk Hydro plant near the town of Vemork and demolished the only equipment in Europe capable of producing heavy water in quantity. Originally utilized in the plant as a more efficient means of producing fertilizer, heavy water was also essential for atomic fission research. The action against the Norsk Hydro plant, better known to history as "the Telemark raid," has all the hallmarks of a quintessential special operation. It prevailed where conventional force could not be applied, in the case of the Royal Air Force (RAF), or had failed previously. The raid also was approved at the highest policy or strategic decision-making levels. In addition, using minimal force and guile, the saboteurs efficiently and economically succeeded in denying German access to resources central to atomic bomb research. The strategic effects of the raid have been couched in unequivocal counterfactual terms: had the plant not been so severely damaged during the raid, the Nazi atomic bomb program might have unlocked the secrets to nuclear fission before the Allies. According to at least one author "the very course of history depended on whether or not the mission succeeded."[2]

Yet the raid was only one action among many designed to deny the Germans their source of this material. Within five months of the attack, the equipment destroyed during the Telemark raid was repaired or replaced and Norsk Hydro resumed production of heavy water. In mid-November 1943, a wave of mixed US Army Air Force (USAAF) heavy bombers visited the target, disrupting heavy water production but not destroying available stocks. The final German attempt to acquire heavy water from Norway was denied on 20 February 1944 on Lake Tinn, where Norwegian saboteurs sank a ferry that was transporting heavy water and production equipment to Germany. Other events affected Nazi attempts to develop the atomic bomb, including the haphazard manner in which the German atomic research program led by Walter Heisenberg was conducted, the decision in that program that graphite was an impractical moderator for neutrons, and accidents that occurred during experiments with heavy water reactors.[3] Placed in its context, the Vemork raid was a paragon of courage and military prowess but was not, in and of itself, independently decisive.

This work argues that the root of strategically effective special operations is an appreciation for how special operations forces (SOF) perform in extended campaigns by inflicting moral and material attrition in conjunction with conventional forces. For a variety of reasons, special operations and how they achieve strategic effects have not been well understood. Special operations are often discussed in campaign or general military histories as a footnote to the major battles. The few works that examine the effects of special operations at the strategic level are prone to limit their investigation of the subject to one type of activity: individual direct action missions, or raids. Focusing on "great raids" makes sense methodologically as they are overt events of limited duration, meaning that source material is often plentiful and well defined.[4] Although useful in understanding the details of individual events, such studies do little to explain how a number of different special operations, in relation to other more conventional political and military actions, achieve and sustain strategic effect(s) over time. In addition, a majority of authors have made exaggerated claims regarding the strategic effect and outcome of the specific special operation.[5] Strategic effect results from success in overcoming improbable odds to accomplish a difficult, but important, single mission. The mission's importance, reflected in approval from cabinet or executive level authorities or the character of the target itself, is proof positive that strategic effects are intended and achieved. In contrast, where special operations fail or have been chronically misused, the culprit is identified as "limited" conventional minds unable to grasp the value and limitations of a significant and finite resource as SOF. Direct causal linkages are sound logically but undercut the complex interaction among and between the moral and material factors that comprise strategy.

Special operations, including "great raids" or "decapitation" strikes, have been depicted as individual actions designed to end hostilities in one blow. In addition to being "self contained acts of war," special operations are also postulated as independently decisive acts as well. Lengthy and costly attacks against the fielded forces of an adversary are replaced by direct targeting against a discrete "center of gravity" of an enemy. The complex interrelationships that comprise strategy, including the dynamics that exist within and between competing systems, are simplified to a metaphorical "shot to the brain" delivered by special operators and/or the latest technology. In fact, special operations could be considered the ultimate realization of doctrine of preemptive war if the "shot to the brain" is done early enough. The author of a draft paper on the future roles and missions of the Special Air Service (SAS), written at the end of the European campaign, suggests for example that: "it might be considered politic (if Foreign Office diverged from its present appeasement policy) to cause future Hitlers and Mussolinis to disappear before they became a public nuisance."[6] Decapitation strikes are appealing precisely because they compress the vertical and horizontal dimensions of strategy into a single flat line in which actions, unburdened by friction or imperfect knowledge and unimpeded by political considerations, achieve their effects against an enemy system in a preordained manner. Special operations misuse has resulted, in large part, because political and/or military leaders could not resist the appeal of an apparently simple, direct and low-cost solution to difficult strategic problems. Combined with the lure of a "free lunch,"[7] the danger of theories such as "strategic paralysis" is that sometimes they get put into practice. As in the case of the famed "Dambusters Raid," more than half of the attacking force, including a number of veteran aircrews, did not return from the mission because a group of Air Staff planners viewed the German war industry in terms of "critical nodes" whose destruction would cause the entire system to collapse. This is not to say that individual audacious acts should not be undertaken but that a coherent framework that guides their use, one that capitalizes on their intended and unintended consequences as well as their limitations, be developed that accounts for the enduring nature and changing character of strategy.

The key to understanding how special operations improve strategic performance resides in the concept of strategic attrition. To comprehend strategic attrition, one must understand that the nature of strategy consists of complex moral and material interactions that exist between two or more competing, adaptive adversaries. Theories of annihilation, or strategic paralysis, suggest avoiding prolonged material damage and inflicting moral damage through indirect strikes or maneuver against an identifiable center of gravity. Attrition, in contrast, is widely understood only as the extended material erosion of combat power in sustained offensives over time. As with strategy in general, however, attrition also contains a moral dimension. Although special operations are useful tactically in the whittling away of adversary material resources, their strategic impact will be negligible if this is the only purpose for which they are used. SOF exist only in limited quantities, and often fight against vastly numerically superior forces, so they are in danger of losing a struggle based entirely on material attrition. Special operations can inflict disproportionate moral damage, in conjunction with strikes against material resources, by virtue of their ability to accomplish what was previously thought impossible. This can take the form of improving conventional military performance or eroding the moral resolve of adversaries through material strikes against lines of communications and/or sanctuaries. The cumulative effect of a number of special operations focused against an enemy's moral and material vulnerabilities, in conjunction with conventional operations, is a more rapid and less costly dissolution of an enemy's will to fight than by conventional means alone.

Understanding the theory behind a complex phenomenon such as strategy is relatively simple compared to implementing it in practice. By extension, knowing how special operations improve strategic performance does not translate into immediate and continuous special operations success. Even in a campaign of attrition such as the one waged in Normandy during the Second World War, where the purpose to which armed forces were used was well understood, special operations played a marginal role despite considerable success elsewhere. Factors such as personalities, internal bureaucratic competition, shifting operational and political priorities, and the actions of the enemy contribute to the uncertainty and friction that can thwart even the best-laid plans or immaculate strategic vision. The "art" of strategy for the practitioner is incorporating all instruments of military power, including special operations, into a sufficiently flexible approach to achieve political goals as efficiently as possible. In order to be used more effectively, however, special operations must be better understood within the context of the nature of strategy.

Definitions

A primary reason why special operations have not been well understood historically is definitional in nature. Defining special operations appears to present few challenges, as one can start by describing the characteristics of "regular" operations and then compare the differences.[8] Special operations can be viewed as a subset of regular operations[9] or anything beyond conventional operations, as in "that class of military (or paramilitary) actions that fall outside the realm of conventional warfare during their respective time periods."[10] Too broad a definition, however, opens the door for gross interpretation. For example, given the criteria above, the activities of the *SS Einsatzgruppen* in occupied areas of Europe during the Second World War could be considered "special operations." Their atrocious activities, as well as those of their associated *Sonderkommando* (or special commandos),[11] were paramilitary in nature and certainly "outside the realm of" regular military operations in this century (or any other).

In other works, special operations have been characterized to suit the case studies discussed. For example, the definition "[a] special operation is conducted by forces specially trained, equipped, and supported for a specific target whose destruction, elimination, or rescue (in the case of hostages), is a political or military imperative"[12] unduly limits discussion to individual direct action missions, or "great raids," whose strategic effects tend to be overstated.[13] There is no scope in this definition for any other type of special operation, including counterinsurgency activities, much less the cumulative effect of different types of special operations over time. Tailoring the definition of special operations to case studies can be taken to the extreme, especially when the term "strategic" is added to lend weight:

> [S]uch strikes can be called strategic special operations. These are secret military or paramilitary strikes, approved at the highest level of the US government after detailed review. Executed in limited time and with limited resources, they seek to resolve through the sudden, swift, and unconventional application of force major problems of US foreign policy.[14]

Although this definition seems innocuous enough, it was constructed to allow discussion of the 1962 Central Intelligence Agency-sponsored "Bay of Pigs" with military special operations.[15] Therefore, almost all covert and clandestine direct action activities of intelligence agencies or other paramilitary forces also must be considered as special operations.[16]

Special operations are not merely unconventional in character. Another defining trait, beyond unorthodox approaches, is that special operations fill a void that is unachievable conventionally and there is an elevated political or military risk associated with their failure.[17] In addition, special operations should be defined according to their intended effect: improving conventional military performance. Although special operations have been called "self-contained acts of war,"[18] their primary military utility is to improve the military performance of conventional forces while achieving other strategic effects by targeting enemy vulnerabilities. Special operations are therefore defined throughout this work as:

> Unconventional actions against enemy vulnerabilities in a sustained campaign, undertaken by specially designated units, to enable conventional operations and/or resolve economically politico-military problems at the operational or strategic level that are difficult or impossible to accomplish with conventional forces alone.

For the purposes of this study, the actions that comprise the spectrum of special operations conform to four of the nine "tasks" identified by the United States Special Operations Command (USSOCOM):

- Counterterrorism (CT), offensive measures taken to prevent, deter, preempt, and respond to terrorism ... missions include, but are not limited to intelligence operations, attacks against terrorist networks and infrastructure, hostage rescue, recovery of sensitive material from terrorist organizations, and non-kinetic activities aimed at the ideologies or motivations that spawn terrorism;
- Special reconnaissance (SR), reconnaissance and surveillance actions conducted as special operations in hostile, denied or politically sensitive environments to collect or verify information of strategic or operational significance, employing military capabilities not normally found in conventional forces;
- Direct action (DA), the conduct of short-duration strikes and other small-scale offensive actions conducted as a special operation in hostile, denied, or politically sensitive environments to seize, destroy, capture, exploit, recover, or damage designated targets of strategic or operational significance, employing specialized military capabilities. Direct action difffers (sic) from conventional offensive actions in the level of physical and political risk, operational techniques, and the use of discriminating force to achieve specific objectives; and
- Unconventional warfare (UW), or military and paramilitary operations, normally of a long duration ... conducted by, with, or through indigenous or surrogate forces who are organized, trained, equipped, supported, and directed in varying degrees by an external source ... [and] includes guerrilla warfare and other direct offensive, low-visibility, covert, or clandestine

operations, as well as the indirect activities of subversion, sabotage, intelligence activities, and unconventional assisted recovery.[19]

The phrase "specially designated units" is useful in distinguishing conventional forces who have performed missions similar to special operations from those trained, equipped, and designated to do so. Special operations skills are highly perishable and require constant training and education to maintain at the peak of efficiency. The training is performed jointly on a small scale to ensure that the various service components understand each other's unique methods of operation and requirements. Historically, conventional forces see specially designated units as a threat to their own budget and prestige and have been instrumental in disbanding or neutering special force capabilities.[20] Although conventional units have conducted actions that appear to be special operations, there are differences between special operations carried out by specially trained units of selected personnel and conventional raids-in-force.

An associated categorization related to special operations and special designation is that of *corps d'elite*. Some authors are inclined to divide special and elite forces neatly along task orientation lines while insisting that all operations are equally "special."[21] In other words, the conventional and costly amphibious assault carried out by the elite US Marines at Tarawa in 1943 is the equivalent to the measured, economical, and highly unorthodox operations of the Long Range Desert Group (LRDG) and SAS in the Western Desert theater outlined in Chapter 5. Attempting to distinguish between special and elite forces does not suggest that actions conducted by *corps d'elite* cannot have operational and strategic effect, but merely that they are not considered special operations for the purposes of this work.

The primary differences between *corps d'elite* and SOF are functions of status, selection, and size. *Corps d'elite* often receive their designation on the basis of unusually effective performance against the enemy; therefore any unit, special or otherwise, can be considered elite if it performs well.[22] A more important distinction is in the selection phase of SOF training. Not all military units perform identical training; in order to serve in a special force candidates must pass a selection phase in which a premium is placed on physical stamina and psychological stability under extreme duress. Failure rates among these candidates are high as the primary trait required is an ability to operate independently in the face of adverse odds.[23] As mentioned previously, some special operations can be undertaken by elements of conventional units or *corps d'elite*. These elements, however, become de facto SOF if they receive special designation for the mission, intensive pre-mission training, and greater-than-average technical support. Although comprised of elite paratroops, the members of *Sturmabteilung Koch*, for example, were separated from their parent units and sequestered for six months while they trained in special assault tactics and weapons designed specifically for the task of seizing and holding the Belgian fortress of Eben Emael in May 1940. After successfully performing the mission, the unit was disbanded and the survivors returned to their original units.[24] By definition, SOF perform special operations but on numerous occasions they have been squandered in unsuitable conventional missions to perform the tasks better suited to conventionally equipped or organized *corps d'elite*.[25] A crucial difference between special forces and *corps d'elite* is that the former operate in small units relative to their conventional brethren and lack the organic support of the latter.[26] Finally, possessing SOF that are trained and equipped to perform special operations avoids one of the major reasons for their abuse: having an existing special operations capability when a crisis occurs, as opposed to cobbling together an untested capability as the crisis is unfolding, which has historically been disbanded once the need has passed, only to be required later.[27]

As mentioned previously, the potential utility of special operations derives primarily from their strategic impact. Special operations are not independent war-winners but achieve their strategic effects in other ways. As Colin Gray points out, strategy is first and foremost a bridge between the means used and the ends to be achieved; it is neither policy nor battle.[28] That bridge is not linear nor is the outcome of a strategy assured. Operational skill, exceptional planning, and a just cause may contribute to strategic effect but not strategic success. The reason for this apparent contradiction, or "paradoxical logic,"[29] is that strategy involves a struggle of wills between two competing adversaries.[30] The arbiters of strategy are human beings and any realm of human activity, especially one based on competition between thinking, adapting adversaries, is governed ultimately by uncertainty, friction, and chance.[31]

In addition to the complexities associated with the human aspect of the subject, strategy is multidimensional, involving inputs from a range of moral and material sources.[32] Therefore attempts to reduce strategy to a quantifiable formula, much less predict outcome with any certainty, are destined to fail. As the French officer and theorist André Beaufre points out, "strategy cannot be a single defined doctrine; it is a *method of thought*, the object of which is to codify events, set them in order of priority and then choose the most effective course of action [emphasis in original]."[33] That course of action must be tailored to fit the specific situation within its own context. The character of war often changes and although strategies can be similar, no combination of military, political, social, and economic conditions is exactly alike.[34] Dogmatically reproducing strategies, or even operational plans, without understanding the unique circumstances of the present conflict almost invariably leads to disaster, unless one's adversary is especially brittle or incompetent.[35]

Despite its complexity, strategy is ultimately doable. The elements of strategy have been understood well enough throughout the ages for political and military leaders to achieve their desired goals. Successful strategy depends in large part on strategic performance. As one author judiciously points out, "Strategic effect is the impact of strategic performance upon the course of events."[36]

Strategic performance is related to, but does not necessarily result from, military performance at the operational and tactical levels of war.[37] Overall strategic performance will be meager if tactical or operational virtuosity contradicts, cannot achieve, or does not relate to the broader political goals. For example, Field Marshal Erwin Rommel's inspired operational and tactical acumen is undisputed.

8 *Special operations and great raids*

Rommel, however, could not reconcile his operational plans with Germany's strategic requirements, much less the culminating point of his logistics chain.[38] As a result, he exceeded his initial orders, consistently outran his supply lines, and eventually engaged in a seesaw campaign against logistically superior, but tactically and operationally inferior, Commonwealth, Free French, and American forces. The Third Reich, however, was still on a peacetime economic footing[39] and could ill afford to support additional ground offensives in another theater during the run-up to *Unternehmen Barbarossa*, the invasion of the Soviet Union.[40] The end result was an unanticipated drain of resources that could, in theory, have altered German strategic performance by turning the tide on the Eastern Front.[41] A victory over the Soviet Union would have had a tremendous strategic, grand strategic, and geopolitical effect for Nazi Germany and changed tectonically the global balance of power.

Special operations and the linkages to strategy

Much like intelligence and espionage, the realm of special operations is a problematic area for serious scholarly inquiry. Special operations can consist of highly sensitive activities whose details remain classified for extended periods of time.[42] Despite these restrictions, the number of published works on or relating to the subject is prodigious although these works range dramatically in scope and quality. It is not necessary to review every work written on the subject, and broad categories within the literature illustrate the point. A more comprehensive listing of sources is contained in the bibliography.

Given the political risks associated with special operations, it is unsurprising that a number of works have focused on the factors that contributed to a perceived misuse of SOF capabilities.[43] Political embarrassment, especially in the wake of clandestine special operations that received considerable press attention, such as the aborted Iran hostage rescue mission in 1980 or the SAS use of deadly force on Gibraltar in 1988, has driven a number of inquiries. The purpose of such works is functional in nature, mainly to identify the contributing factors and propose solutions or safeguards to ensure that failures or excesses do not occur again.[44] Closely associated with this literature on SOF is a subcategory focused on institutional changes designed to prevent failure. Written on the basis of recollections, interviews, and available documentation, such works outline the methods used by individuals to institutionalize SOF capabilities within ponderous bureaucracies.[45] Works on institutional change, however, offer little in the way of insights on the strategic effects generated by or application of special operations. The literature relating to the conditions for special operations success is limited and is discussed in the section on strategic utility of SOF below.

Despite the volume of works written about special operations and SOF, including battle narratives, unit campaign histories, and biographies,[46] the strategic aspects of the subject are barely mentioned. When the term "strategic" has been used in such works, it has been done so liberally without reference to how performance is improved or effects are achieved, as in Andy McNab's assertion that the

SAS are "strategic troops, so what we do behind enemy lines can have serious implications."[47] When associating special operations with their strategic effects, there appears to be little middle ground; some authors make grossly exaggerated and unsubstantiated claims of their effects while others ignore or completely marginalize them. Authors who overreach suggest that special operations can be decisive in and of themselves. In the case of one work on the SAS, the author attempts a conceptual bridge too far when he suggests that British special operations were the primary instruments of British grand strategy during the Cold War. Ken Connor maintains that SOF allowed Britain to maintain its geopolitical link with the United States and sway defense and natural resource contracts in its former colonies.[48] It is one thing to suggest that special operations have effects on decision making, but quite another to propose that SOF were the most important method used by Britain to punch above its political weight. Other authors make even more sensational claims: special operations are responsible for altering history or saving Western civilization.[49] Reductionists, on the other hand, are critical or dismissive of the contributions made by special operations during a campaign. They have used the following arguments individually or in combination: special operations do not matter, because conventional forces and big battles do;[50] special operations are no substitute for diplomacy;[51] special operations are a drain on scarce resources that could be used better elsewhere;[52] special operations are nothing more than glorified light infantry actions;[53] and, special operators undermine the cornerstone principles of democracy by institutionalizing elites and advocating covert action.[54]

When the strategic aspects of a special operation are discussed in detail in the literature, the significance of the action is overstated the closer in detail it is explored. The special operation to neutralize the Belgian frontier fortress of Eben Emael on 10 May 1940 is an exemplary case in point. The operation was a prodigious feat of arms: "[s]ixty-nine German glidermen engaged and soundly defeated a Belgian force ten times their size protected by the largest fort of its day."[55] James Mrazek claims that "warfare had forever changed in character"[56] by making vertical envelopment a military reality.[57] More arguable is his claim that had the fortress not fallen, the Allied armies of France, Britain, and Belgium would have had the time to redeploy and defeat the German panzer thrusts.[58] William McRaven echoes this assessment and adds that Eben Emael was "one of the most decisive victories in the history of special operations."[59] Scant attention is paid in either work to other special operations in support of the offensive or the broader German concept of operations;[60] Mrazek goes so far as to suggest that fall of Eben Emael itself was the psychological blow that precipitated Belgian collapse.[61]

The speed with which the Germans crossed water barriers and attacked in depth, including the use of airborne forces in the operational rear, did more than anything to dislocate the Belgian defense and lend a degree of imperative to Anglo-French counterstrokes. German operations in Belgium and the Netherlands were designed to play on Allied preconceptions; the thrusts were a diversion designed to deceive the Allies into mobilizing their forces northward into the Low Countries, as codified in the Dyle Plan, and away from the German main thrust through the Ardennes forest.[62] The German concept of operations included several special operations to seize and hold objectives that would enable the panzer and infantry forces of the Sixth Army to advance as quickly as possible across Dutch and Belgian waterways. The operational feint convinced the French high command that the Germans were attempting a repeat of the so-called "Schlieffen Plan" from 1914: a long "left hook" around the Ardennes forest, through the Low Countries, with Paris as the goal. The French Dyle Plan committed Allied forward forces into an attack northwards to counter the anticipated German sweep. The individual records of German special operations in this campaign are varied but those operations succeeded in their cumulative goal: levering the obstacles confronting regular forces and enabling those forces to complete their task as part of a broader plan. Perhaps the most sober assessment of the effect that special operations had during the summer of 1940, placed in the context of the overall campaign, is contained in the history published by the *Militärgeschichtliches Forschungsamt*:

> The special operations, on whose preparation Hitler has spent so much time, had only been partially successful. In Maastricht the Dutch managed to blow up the bridges in good time, before the German commandos arrived. The deception based on faked Dutch uniforms proved useless. The two operational squads of counter-intelligence came under fire and suffered considerable losses. Even so, only one bridge over the Albert Canal escaped the German coup, and at Gennap members of the Construction Training Battalion 800 [the Brandenburgers] succeeded in capturing a bridge over the Meuse. Elimination of Fort Eben-Emael by the air-landed Koch Assault Detachment was very largely successful. In consequence it was possible, despite a 24-hour hold-up in Maastricht, to burst through a defence system which could not have been overcome so quickly by traditional means. At the same time these spectacular special operations concealed the real main effort of the German operation.[63]

In other words, the effect of these German special operations was to enhance German military performance during 1940.[64]

Much like the record of German special operations in the French campaign in 1940, the few attempts to explore in detail the strategic dimensions of special operations in the literature have had mixed results. Some authors are prone to delineate too sharply and artificially the different levels of war when assessing the strategic aspects or effects of an individual mission: "there has been dialogue about how to employ SOF" but not "if and when to employ SOF strategically."[65] Although the author, Gregg Jones, concludes that "SOF strategic employment, as represented by the operations examined, has been mostly effective" the basis for that assessment is tactical success.[66] Therefore, the raid on St Nazaire on 28 March 1942 was a strategic success because the primary mission was accomplished; the larger question of strategic effectiveness remains unanswered. By the time that the raid, codenamed "Operation Chariot," was conducted, the German leadership no longer required the use of the Normandie dock facilities; destroying the docks did not "neutralize" the threat presented by the *Tirpitz*.[67]

In lieu of a theory of special operations, William McRaven is absolutely correct when he asserts that the theoretical concept of "friction" is the key to understanding the strategic performance of special operations. Strategic and operational performance flows from tactical success. He argues that SOF can suspend temporarily the effects of friction and achieve relative superiority over more numerous foes but the focus of his work is almost entirely on tactical indicators.[68] When relative superiority is lost, SOF lose the initiative and are overwhelmed. McRaven codifies principles for special operations which allow relative superiority to be achieved.[69] According to the author, his theory is "a powerful tool to explain victory and defeat," at least from a tactical perspective after the fact, but it misses a fundamental point: when Clausewitz was discussing friction, he envisioned it as a factor that affects both sides in a conflict.[70] Human nature dictates that any organized effort, especially one involving life-and-death struggle, is prone to friction. Clausewitz placed emphasis on the willpower of the commander as a crucial element in the inevitable presence of friction—not in creating or suspending its effects.[71]

Among the works devoted to various other aspects of special operations, only a handful examine the strategic aspects of special operations in detail.[72] Colin Gray, who has written extensively on the strategic utility of SOF, suggests that existential and cultural factors are the key to understanding the effectiveness of special operations. Special operations are subject to their nature that is "qualitatively different from regular warfare" but equivalent in strategic impact to other applications of force.[73] Organizational culture and national style can be key determinants for the successful or unsuccessful use of special operations, even if the nature of special operations cannot be changed by cultural or historical context.[74] Although Gray provides "[f]indings on the military utility of special operations," this and subsequent discussions of special operations nevertheless contain shortcomings. The lack of distinction between strategic utility and strategic effectiveness, as well as the identification but not discussion in depth of how strategic effect is achieved, are the problematic aspects of his *Explorations in Strategy*.[75] The examples of special operations Gray draws upon suggest that most unconventional military operations are special operations. For example, the Allied raid on Dieppe (19 August 1942) and the operations of Wingate's Chindits in Burma (Operations Longcloth and Thursday, 1943–4) are used as examples to illustrate several points but they can hardly be considered as special operations given their scope and size of the forces committed relative to the task at hand.[76]

Methodology

From the preceding discussion it is clear that no theory exists which explains how special operations achieve strategic effects. This work is designed to accomplish three goals: impose a level of academic rigor on a subject dominated by mass market works that capitalize on the mystique of SOF; expand the definition of special operations used in literature beyond direct action raids, to include counterinsurgency actions, attempts to topple regimes, and special intelligence-gathering activities of SOF; and elevate discussion of the effects generated by special operations from the tactical to the operational and strategic realm.

A number of mitigating factors drive the methodological approach to this study. The argument outlined in previous pages, namely that special operations achieve their strategic effects through attrition, is a counterintuitive one. Given that this study links special operations practice with theory, a mixture of analysis of strategic theoretical concepts and historical case studies is used. The concepts underpinning strategic paralysis and attrition theory are assessed in detail. Examples of and from specific special operations are used to illustrate theoretical points. The major themes developed in the theory chapters on strategic paralysis and strategic attrition are explored in detail in the case studies.

The covert nature of the bulk of special operations work presents its own methodological problems for case studies. As mentioned previously, much information related to special operations over the past three decades remains sensitive and highly classified. The exception to this general rule occurs in Western democracies, where success has focused attention on the achievements of a specific special operation, often in order to increase a unit's or a country's prestige or political/financial access, or where failure merits public scrutiny to determine what went wrong and who should accept blame. Rather than dwell on incidents already explored in considerable detail in other works, such as Operations Jonathan (the rescue of Israeli hostages from Entebbe, Uganda in 1976), Nimrod (the rescue of hostages from the Iranian Embassy in London in 1980), and Eagle Claw (the attempted rescue of American hostages held in Tehran, Iran in 1980), among others, this study uses archived official documents, including documentation declassified under the Freedom of Information Act, first-person accounts, memoirs, and interviews, as well as available secondary source material, to review in detail the assumptions behind and effects of two little-studied special operations: the Dambusters Raid of 16/17 May 1943 and the use of the SAS in support of the Normandy invasion from June until September 1944. Although other case studies in different conflicts could have been examined, including the use of special operations in the Korean (1950–3), Malayan (1950–8), Vietnamese (1965–75), and Falklands (1982) conflicts, those from the Second World War allow a comprehensive examination of the roots, assumptions, planning factors, and execution of operations in unprecedented detail. The use of two British case studies from the Second World War, as well as the "form" of war in which they took place (i.e. global conventional war versus a colonial counterinsurgency campaign), is not limiting for another substantive reason: the nature of strategy.

This study is built upon the theoretical foundation that the nature of strategy is unchanging. As such this work draws heavily upon the theory developed by Prussian theorist Carl von Clausewitz. Although *On War* contains numerous structural limitations and flaws, as is to be expected of a work uncompleted before the author's death, it nevertheless remains an unmatched investigation into the nature and mechanics of both war and strategy. War has been, and remains, the use of organized violence between two or more actors for the purpose of imposing their will upon one another in order to fulfill the goals of policy. Given this nature, the interplay and net effect of human emotions and foibles at all decision-making levels, imperfect knowledge, systemic, individual and resource limitations, organizational dynamics, as well as internal and external competition, strategy remains a complicated undertaking that defies attempts to impose absolute order upon it. If this study contains an aphorism, it is that strategy contains no shortcuts.

Chapter 2 examines theories that offer strategic shortcuts to victory. New means, including special operations and/or emerging technologies, purportedly allow users to avoid the difficulties posed by the nature of strategy and sizeable enemy armies. Experience with the material component of attrition has led these theorists to the "holy grail" of operational art: achieving victory in a bloodless fashion. At the heart of strategic paralysis theory is the concept of the "strategy of annihilation" in its purest conceptual form: the delivery of a crippling moral blow that makes extended material struggle unnecessary. Much like the misconceptions surrounding special operations, strategic paralysis theory is an appealing "economy of force" option provided that everything works as anticipated when put into practice. Strategic paralysis theory attempts to separate artificially the moral and material aspects of strategy. More pointedly, paralysis theory assumes that the complexities of strategy, including the moral resilience of an adversary, can be overcome by superior military skill (in the case of special operations), technology (the tank in J.F.C. Fuller's estimation, and airpower in John Warden's), or process (according to the theories of John Boyd), in effect fusing tactical and strategic actions into a single, decisive blow.

The case study in Chapter 3 explores how the assumptions behind one variant of strategic paralysis theory fared against the enemy when put into practice on 16/17 May 1943. The irrationalities and inconsistencies of human behavior that shape strategy, in this case the unwavering belief that a moral critical node existed in the German war economy and that airpower could annihilate it, persisted long after evidence was available to the contrary. The idea that the German war economy and the will of the leadership of the Third Reich could be induced to collapse by simultaneously destroying the dams of the Ruhr river estuary, depriving industry of power and forcing Hitler to sue for peace, stemmed from the optimism of Royal Air Force planners faced with the task of putting airpower theory into practice after decades of inadequate preparation. Optimism for the success of the plan overruled significant informational gaps in how the German war economy operated as a system, much less the moral value structure of Adolf Hitler and other senior leaders of the Third Reich. Having temporarily abandoned strikes on the Ruhr dams for lack of effective resources, the idea was revived with the invention of the "bouncing bomb" and the means to deliver it. Despite three years of evidence as to the moral effects of bombing, the adaptability of the German civilian population and industry, and the previously underestimated complexity of the

German war economy, enthusiasm for the plan to deal a single debilitating blow to the Third Reich gained increasing political and military importance as well as a momentum of its own. The heroic effort in the special operation conducted by the men of 617 Squadron had little impact on the Third Reich as plans for it reduced the moral component of strategy to a tangible center of gravity, overestimated the moral effects of a single strike, and misjudged the material complexity of the German industrial system, not to mention the moral resilience of the leadership and population.

The relationship between the moral and material aspects of strategy, as well as unique ability of special operations to inflict disproportionate moral damage by performing the unthinkable, is the subject of Chapter 4. In their quest to expand upon the relationship identified by Clausewitz regarding the moral and material dimensions of strategy, interpreters were inclined to emphasize one or the other in support of their argument for either attrition or annihilation. Along the way, as these arguments were put into practice, the debates increasingly became operational in character and distinction between the two even more polarized. The strategy of annihilation was interpreted as the epitome of pure military skill, relying on qualitative and/or quantitative superiority in organization, equipment, and maneuver until the decisive blow could be struck. Attrition, in turn, was associated with positional warfare devoid of movement and relying exclusively on superior numbers to bleed an adversary white and eventually break their will. Theories of irregular warfare, developed from the position of military weakness and looking to defeat a stronger adversary by any and all means available over time, reconstituted the balance between the moral and material dimensions of attrition that exists at the strategic level. Special operations have a unique relationship with attrition at the strategic level. As individual acts, the moral effect of "performing the impossible" in a special operation can perturb adversaries and cause them to lose the initiative or divert attention elsewhere. The difficulty with special operations lies in conducting a sustained campaign, in conjunction with conventional forces, to extend and expand upon the moral and material effects they both generate cumulatively, although not always sequentially, at the strategic level.

Chapter 5 demonstrates the difficulties in integrating special operations with conventional forces in a campaign of attrition. Such difficulties reflect not only the differences between special operations and conventional ones but also those elements that make strategy difficult to execute in practice. One of the guiding principles in the lead up to the invasion of Normandy on 6 June 1944 was that the *Wehrmacht* stood between the Allied armed forces and the unconditional surrender of Nazi Germany. One method of weakening the German *Seventh Army* prior to, during, and after the invasion was to channel and focus the energy of the various French resistance groups in order to divert German attention, delay counterattacking reinforcements, and demoralize German fighting forces. The SAS, expanded to brigade size and looking to participate in the invasion after successes in North Africa and Italy, was expected to play a major role in keeping the Germans off-balance by wreaking havoc in their rear areas while they faced Allied attacks to break out of the beachhead. Competing interests between different SOF organizations, the rapid expansion of the SAS, dysfunctional command arrangements, political constraints, friction, and German adaptation ensured that the SAS played a marginal role in eroding German moral or material reserves. Instead of focusing on a phased effort designed to disrupt the *Seventh Army's* moral and material logistics lifeline to Germany, whose character changed throughout the campaign and whose constriction could have speeded German moral collapse, SAS teams were instead scattered throughout France to conduct the tactical attrition of German reserves and rear area security units.

2 "Seeing 'black lights' before sinking into oblivion"[1]
Theories of strategic paralysis

> The concept of center of gravity suggests that a nation's ability to fight can most readily be unhinged by seeking out the one pivotal element of its force that, if destroyed, would cause all of its force to collapse.
>
> (Robert Scales, Jr, *Certain Victory*[2])

Operation Iraqi Freedom involved the most unprecedented use of SOF historically. According to press accounts, more than 10,000 special operators from the United States, the United Kingdom, Australia, and Poland took part in missions ranging from securing airfields, oil fields, and other high value targets, designating targets for coalition aircraft, tying down numerous Iraqi units in the north and west of the country, and even assuming operational control of a conventional armored and airborne task force.[3] The coalition effort in Iraq in 2003 was also unique from another special operations perspective. It saw an attempt to end the war in a single strike before the conflict began in earnest. Much press speculation surrounds the opening shot of Operation Iraqi Freedom, on 20 March 2003, in which information allegedly provided by SOF or paramilitary sources enabled the B-1 precision strike against a bunker complex believed to contain Saddam Hussein and other senior regime officials.

The German special operations expert of the Second World War, Otto Skorzeny, not only would have recognized but also approved of attack against the Dora Farms complex designed to decapitate the Iraqi regime. To him, the linkage between the armed forces, population, and leadership of an enemy is clear. Destroying the leadership, or "carving out the brains" using special operations, severs the link between the brain and the body.[4] In Skorzeny's estimation removing the most senior leaders, while inflicting overwhelming shock in key areas throughout rest of the system, will cause paralysis and collapse at the strategic level. The Soviet Union implemented Skorzeny's theory and it earmarked its *Spetsnaz* forces to assassinate key military and political personnel within the North Atlantic Treaty Organization during the opening blows of any invasion of Western Europe.[5] The Soviets put the theory to the test in Afghanistan in December 1979, where their SOF seized key facilities in Kabul and killed Afghan Prime Minister Hafizullah Amin.[6] The target of a devastating blow to cause paralysis need not be leadership only. As the next chapter demonstrates, some Air Staff planners of the Royal Air Force believed that the key to collapsing German industry, and with it both the means and the will to prosecute war, lay in the simultaneous destruction of the Ruhr valley dams—that could be achieved through a special operation.

Theories of strategic paralysis are not new.[7] The motivation behind paralysis theory is almost as old as warfare itself: "attaining one hundred victories in one hundred battles is not the pinnacle of excellence. Subjugating of the enemy's army without fighting is the true pinnacle of excellence."[8] If this cannot be achieved, the next best thing is inflicting a crippling, decisive blow to win an ideal victory. Given the increasing scale and complexity of war, as well as the resilience and diversity of adversaries, dealing such a blow has become much more difficult. The ascent of new technologies, superior decision making, and/or improved military means and methods such as special operations has led some theorists to conclude that the obstacles endemic to war and strategy are not only surmountable but irrelevant. In the same way that some equate the tactical success of an individual special operation with grossly disproportionate strategic effects, advocates of strategic paralysis assume that an identifiable center of gravity can be struck tactically with cascading effects that culminate in strategic collapse. This chapter reviews the major works on strategic paralysis, traces their evolution, and assesses their assumptions and conclusions.

Although the theories of John Frederick Charles Fuller, John Warden, and John Boyd advocate different methods to achieve the goal of strategic paralysis, they share a number of similarities. Each author was motivated to find a better method of waging war that eschewed the tactical attrition they had observed. All three theories were initially developed to account for phenomena observed at the tactical level and evolved to accommodate the strategic level of war without revisiting their underlying assumptions. When such theories are elevated to the strategic level, however, the direct linkages of action and effect oversimplify the intangible factors of strategy such as friction, adaptability, and political will. In paralysis theory, superior technology, combat skill (in the form of special operations), or process cuts through the potentially dislocating effects of friction to strike directly at the center of gravity of an adversary. Material struggle, in the form of tactical attrition, is unnecessary as striking the center of gravity sets in motion a chain of predictable events leading to the moral collapse of an adversary. As the attempted strikes on Saddam Hussein and Ali Hassan al-Majid (nicknamed "Chemical Ali") suggest, overwhelming material and technology supremacy does not guarantee that friction will not obstruct the most determined attempts to inflict strategic paralysis, by special operations or other means.[9]

Strategical paralysis[10] and tanks

The grandfather of twentieth-century paralysis theory is John Frederick Charles (J.F.C.) Fuller. His stamp is noticeable on many aspects of post-Second World War Western military thought, from air and space power theory to nuclear strategy.[11] Yet few authors pay intellectual tribute to Fuller as a pioneer when discussing

18 Theories of strategic paralysis

their own theories of paralysis.[12] Fewer still have analyzed in depth the assumptions behind strategic paralysis, including the role that technology and military skill play in improving strategic performance. Theories, however, are not formulated in a vacuum. Fuller's ideas relating to the strategic effects of technology had their roots in tactical observations made regarding the moral shock that tanks could inflict. Before exploring the evolution of Fuller's notion of strategic paralysis, it is important to place the individual within his historical context. Fuller was a theorist who influenced the development of German armored warfare doctrine prior to the Second World War,[13] Soviet thinking regarding "Deep Battle" and the use of special operations,[14] and the formative conceptual thinking of his peer and eventual rival, Basil Liddell Hart.[15]

J.F.C. Fuller eventually retired at the rank of Major General after a tempestuous career in the British Army that began as a "gentleman cadet" at Sandhurst in 1897.[16] Never one to suffer fools lightly, he was a voracious reader on subjects as diverse as military history, political and scientific theory, literature, and the occult.[17] His bookishness, combined with an irascible temperament and espousal of unconventional ideas, ensured ostracism from his conservative fellow officers.[18] In addition, Fuller was prone to writing excessively dense prose and expressing his ideas in baffling visual and qabbalistic form (see Figure 2.1 below).[19]

Aside from his more curious diversions, such as dabbling in mysticism and with fascism,[20] Fuller was nevertheless one of the most influential theorists of his

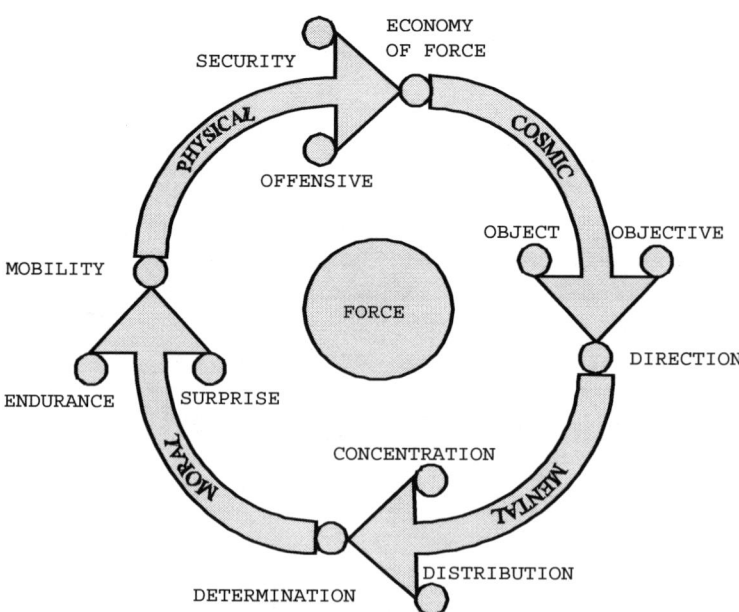

Figure 2.1 Fuller's unity of the principles of war

day. Two themes run through Fuller's works over 58 years: a desire to see warfare humanized and waged as efficiently as possible, in contrast with his experiences in the Boer and First World Wars;[21] and, the belief that technology could transform warfare.[22]

Tactical paralysis: plan 1919

A considerable source of tension between Fuller and Liddell Hart in later years was their professional rivalry. Each wanted to be seen as *the* influential theorist of their generation. Both authors were shameless self-promoters but differed considerably in their approach,[23] especially regarding their perceived influence on the famous commanders of the Second World War.[24] Liddell Hart maintained that he viewed mechanized warfare strategically whereas Fuller was only talking about the subject tactically.[25] Fuller refuted that claim, although the criticism has some validity in his earliest work.[26] "Plan 1919" was a concept of operations designed to break the stalemate of trench warfare by combining the strengths of the various branches of the British Army and applying them in a coordinated fashion.[27] More importantly, the plan was embryonic articulation of what became known as strategical paralysis. Its initial goals were modest and Plan 1919 was decidedly tactical in scope.

Plan 1919 sets out the material requirements for the offensive and suggests how best to take advantage of the tank's evolving capabilities. In his earlier briefing papers, Fuller took into account the limitations of the tank in its infant stages: offensive penetrations would be limited to a maximum of six miles on a broad or narrow front.[28] The goal expressed in "Tank Operations Decisive and Preparatory" is a tactical one: the envelopment and destruction of the German reserves followed by a vigorous pursuit of remaining forces.[29] The following year Fuller envisioned inflicting *operational* disruption upon the German Army similar to that experienced by the British during the German offensives in 1918. The potential deployment of the Medium "D" tank could extend the range of penetration to 100 miles.[30] This could be accomplished only with support, in the form of interdiction, strikes, and aerial resupply, from the nascent Royal Air Force.[31] The *schwerpunkt* of a British armored attack, or the point of focus, concentration, and effort, would be the Imperial German Army general headquarters. According to Fuller, the cohesion of the army would be annihilated in one blow through focused tactical action at the operational center of gravity of the Imperial German Army.[32]

The technical performance of contemporary tanks was only one element that shaped Plan 1919. The plan reflected other pressing political and military requirements, including a manpower crisis in the British Army. Fuller developed the plan as a way of increasing mobility on the battlefield while simultaneously reducing the requirements on British manpower. Britain had maintained historically a small standing army that expanded exponentially and suffered galling casualties in five years of war.[33] By 1918, even with substantial recruitment drives and volunteers from the colonies, the British Army was in the grip of a manpower crisis.[34] Through Plan 1919, this problem could be addressed. The British Army could field fewer troops yet possess significantly greater offensive power by mechanizing.[35]

The basis for Fuller's subsequent thought on strategical paralysis was laid in Plan 1919. Variations of the plan emphasized different technologies or methods of approach.[36] Regardless of the iteration, the goal of Fuller's strategical paralysis remained the same: exploiting mechanized forces to bypass the main line of resistance and induce collapse. Focused use of technology that avoided engaging the enemy in breadth, and struck indirectly at a vulnerable enemy center of gravity, would be a more economical use of force. Fuller used diverse analogies to explain how mechanized forces should be armed and organized. Early on in his writings, Fuller hit upon an analogy that other theorists have periodically resurrected: as machine power was replacing muscle power, brain warfare would replace body warfare.

Body and brain warfare

Fuller ruminated on the performance of the British Army after the end of the Great War. In his eyes, the emphasis on the grand infantry marches of envelopment in August 1914 was foolish in the face of repeating, magazine rifles, and machine guns.[37] Defense had been the dominant form of warfare and Imperial Germany was isolated from its allies and drowned in a sea of industrial output and manpower at great material cost to the Entente. Planning prior to the First World War assumed the equipping, fielding, transporting, and sustaining of "the nation in arms."[38] Victory would go to the side outlasting the other by inflicting "a succession of slight wounds which would eventually cause [them] to bleed to death."[39] To paraphrase a Fullerian metaphor, the last man standing in the boxing ring of body warfare would be the victor.

This view of warfare, according to Fuller, was both misguided and uneconomical. Looking historically, he discerned a continuous struggle between offense and defense on the battlefield.[40] The obvious solution to the dominance of missile weapons, such as the longbow and machine gun, lay in mobility and protection.[41] How could industrial nations protect their soldiers while restoring primacy of the offense? Fuller reasoned that an industrial-age problem required an industrial-age solution: the internal combustion engine provided the means to propel armor and men quickly and safely through "the perfect storm of shrapnel."[42] Once clear of the front lines, tanks could have a considerable impact by disrupting the vulnerable rear areas that linked the enemy's army with its means of command and supply.

Although Fuller toyed with the idea of a fleet of tanks specialized along the line of naval vessels, as well as with the concept of the armored personnel carrier, he rejected them in the zeal to promote the potential effects of the main battle tank.[43] Supporting arms would play a secondary role in Fuller's scheme. Infantry would fix the adversary's army in place and mop up whatever resistance remained, while artillery would open the initial breach for the tanks.[44] Airplanes could serve several useful purposes: reconnaissance, deep strike, command and control, close air support, and resupply.[45] Chemical weapons were added to Fuller's concept of war later; aircraft and tanks could spread incapacitating chemical weapons allowing armored forces to reach command centers that much quicker.[46]

Fuller the military officer and technology enthusiast was not content merely to see tanks driving in an enemy's rear area causing havoc. As the developer of the principles of war for the British Field Services Regulations (vol. II) in 1924, mechanized forces had to have an objective upon which they would converge when the enemy line of resistance was penetrated.[47] Fuller settled on a metaphor to describe where the nascent armored forces should concentrate their effort. Taking a conceptual leaf out of Spenser Wilkinson's influential *The Brain of an Army*,[48] Fuller adopted the human body as an allegory for an army. Each army had functions roughly equivalent to nerves, a stomach, arms, and a brain.[49] Referring in this case to the chief of general staff, instead of the lower level command centers described by Fuller, Wilkinson describes the fragility of the military "brain":

> Every day (the armies are manoeuvring to contact) brings its surprises, even to the best informed and best prepared headquarters. The strategist's equilibrium must be disturbed as little by unexpected events as by the throbs of national emotion ... the strategist's judgement must work smoothly and easily, like the compass in a storm, with no derangement of its delicate equipoise.[50]

The fragile brain of an army was the place where Fuller deduced tanks should concentrate their energy to disturb its equilibrium. To extend the alliteration, mechanized forces would distract, distend, dislocate, and disrupt an adversary.[51] By concentrating on this target armored forces would act as a metaphorical "shot through the brain" paralyzing the enemy army.[52] Without its major command functions, an army would have no option but to submit to a technologically superior, mobile, armored force.[53] Military effort would be maximized and more effective, in Fuller's estimation, than shooting an adversary elsewhere in the "body."[54] A campaign in which one's army was victorious but as battered as its foe could be avoided altogether. In other words, paralysis for Fuller would be the ultimate expression of the principle of war of "economy of force."[55] Just as strategic effect should not be mistaken for effectiveness, the next chapter demonstrates that economy of force with respect to special operations has been translated as a cheap and easy solution to complicated and niggling strategic problems.

In addition to providing the attacker with economy of force, the tank would be the dominant instrument with which to humanize warfare—science and technology could make war less barbarous.[56] Tanks alone, however, could not induce collapse. The virtuoso score embodied in the concept of strategical paralysis required a virtuoso conductor to orchestrate it. Fuller tackled the problem of conducting the *coup de main* of collapsing an adversary. He understood that a "great captain" such as Napoleon or Alexander could easily undertake the task; such leaders, however, were all too rare historically. Fuller's solution was to create a new breed of military specialist specially selected and trained to instill *coup d'oeil* by embracing mechanization and its scientific study.[57] This "special force," comprised of "scientists of war," could then realize the potential of strategic paralysis and return speed, economy, and decision to warfare.[58]

Technology and center of gravity

Fuller understood that the object of any military campaign is to impose one's will upon an adversary.[59] Will, or moral force, was the true center of gravity in his estimation. Emerging technologies promised the means to avoid a prolonged battle of attrition. Tanks could pass through lines of resistance and aircraft could fly over them:

> If the shield is, however, not hacked to pieces, what shall we see? While the axe is being wielded against it, aircraft, like arrows, will speed over it; and fast moving tank forces, like javelins, will shiver past its flanks, and these will transfix the civil brains of the enemy with terror.[60]

Mechanized power could compress the time required for decisive military operations.[61] Strategical paralysis would result from a combination of direct attacks against military leadership and civilian population targets in a short period of time. In other words, Fuller was making a direct correlation between will and time:

> Bearing in mind such rapidity of movement, it becomes almost a certainty that, in the next great war, the endurance of civil moral will be in direct proportion to the speed of the war machines used; consequently, the duration of wars will be short.[62]

The quicker an enemy could be struck in depth, therefore, the faster an adversary's morale would shatter. Fuller assumed that an adversary could not recover from the initial shock of the speed of advance. More importantly, he suggested that political and military leadership was the decisive point against which maximum effort should be made. In keeping with his fascistic beliefs,[63] systemic shock would occur when the general population and military were deprived of their leadership. After all, without proper leadership, the masses were little more than herd animals: "most men are sheep, their opinions are more often than not mere bleatings."[64]

Military operations during the Second World War proved that a number of Fuller's assumptions about technology and paralysis were misguided. Populations did not collapse when bombed from the air. After initial panic, civilians responded to continued bombardment with a combination of ambivalence, fatalism, stoicism, and/or acceptance.[65] Chemical weapons were deemed unsuitable for technical and political reasons.[66] Deft armored maneuver by technologically superior forces could be offset by unrealistic strategic goals, defense in depth, geography, the weather, and poor support services.[67] Menacing army headquarters could create confusion but fielded forces often continued to fight, even when surrounded.[68] In the face of the evidence presented during the course of the Second World War, Fuller abandoned his idea of strategical paralysis and with it, the annihilation of enemy morale and cohesion in a single blow.[69] The lure of a potential military quick fix, in the form of new technologies or covert special operations, has proven too appealing to abandon entirely. Two decades after Fuller's death, the concept of strategic paralysis would be revived in modified form. This time, instead of tanks, airpower alone would strike the decisive blow leading to systemic collapse.

The air campaign and John Warden III

John Warden was arguably the one of the most prominent airpower theorists of the late twentieth century. His ideas influenced the planning and conduct of the Gulf War air campaign dubbed "Instant Thunder" and according to at least one author, "If indeed Carl Builder is correct when he argues that the Air Force has lost its doctrinal roots, he should be gratified to know that Warden has stirred things up to stimulate a rediscussion of the purpose of that institution."[70] His theory of airpower is taught throughout US military professional military education and current American aerospace doctrine is steeped in Warden's theory of strategic paralysis, or "parallel attack" as it more popularly known.[71] At least one of his colleagues on the Checkmate planning staff for the Gulf War air campaign has used the idea of parallel warfare as the theoretical vehicle behind arguments for the preeminence of the US Air Force in the Revolution in Military Affairs.[72] In addition, the conduct of American air campaigns since the Gulf War has been criticized for not conforming to Warden's concept of parallel attack.[73] Much like Fuller, the seed of parallel attack was planted in Warden's own experience with attrition-based warfare in Vietnam. Looking for a more efficient way to apply airpower, Warden's concept of parallel attack has evolved into a means to annihilate effortlessly the control functions of any adversary of the United States.

As with many officers of his generation, the conduct of the air campaign in the Vietnam War motivated Warden to seek more effective application of the unique characteristics of airpower.[74] The United States used airpower incrementally in an attempt to coerce the North Vietnamese government by striking infrastructure targets.[75] A number of vital targets in North Vietnam were proscribed for political reasons and the President and Secretary of Defense personally approved target sets.[76] Only later in the war, after a change in administration, was an intensive bombing campaign attempted.[77] A completely different, and in some aspects much more problematic air war was waged in South Vietnam. Given US air supremacy in South Vietnam and the form of conflict there, namely a prolonged irregular war, airpower was used predominantly for combat support purposes.[78]

After the Vietnam War, Warden gained valuable operations and planning experience with the Air Force Staff as well as at US Central Command (CENTCOM).

But he was still dismayed by what he saw as "deployment plans without any linkage to how the war could or should be fought."[79] Planning and gaming exercises for war in Europe confirmed Warden's suspicions. He concluded that "it was clearly nonsensical to pit ourselves in an attrition contest with a larger enemy who had a demonstrated record of disregard for losses."[80] These experiences, combined with a natural academic curiosity, led Warden to research the conduct of historical air campaigns while at the National War College.[81] His written and published product, *The Air Campaign*, contains the first iteration of what later became known as parallel warfare.

The Air Campaign is the first attempt to develop a unifying theory for the planning and conducting of an air campaign at the operational level of war.[82] Warden's theory is unique in that it attempts to bridge the divide between two schools of airpower thought: the tactical school, which argues that airpower is most useful in support of land and sea power through close air support and aerial interdiction;[83] and, the strategic school, whose most vocal advocates have suggested that airpower is an independent, war-winning instrument.[84] In Warden's estimation, airpower would achieve its results not just by striking the center of gravity; coordinated attacks would ensure that the blows would have a decisive outcome.[85]

As with Fuller's initial writings that contain the kernels of his later theory, *The Air Campaign* discusses elements for the successful use of airpower within a theater of operations.[86] Conditionals and caveats temper his assertions and suggest comprehension of the nuances of strategy.[87] Warden understood that warfare is complicated and cannot be reduced to a single theorem of success. He depicts strategy as a continuum; strategic actions have an impact on operations and tactics and vice versa.[88] War is a human endeavor, prone to the effects of friction and the fog of war, in a competitive struggle between two adversaries to impose their will upon each another.[89] Although *The Air Campaign* was written about the use of airpower, Warden is careful to state that airpower is not dominant. He argues that air superiority is a precondition for military victory and that the air force may be the "key force" in the campaign. Warden, however, does not explicitly suggest that the airpower can win independently.[90] One of the few nods to visionary theories of strategic airpower he makes is the brief mention of "panacea" targets: "the place where an investment in attack will yield the greatest return."[91]

From air superiority to five rings

A subtle but significant shift occurred in Warden's thought after the publishing of *The Air Campaign*. The concept of center of gravity was the linchpin of the air campaign; at the operational level, any one of a number of target sets could be the center of gravity.[92] At the strategic level, however, Warden posited that the strategic utility of airpower was being able to directly influence, or coerce, the decision-making "core" of an organization.[93] From this starting point, Warden considered whether there might be other strategic centers of gravity that protected the leadership and were vital to the state.[94] The result was the "enemy as a system" concept known colloquially as "the five-ring model."[95]

The five-ring model postulates that all organizations are comprised of elements that fit into general categories: leadership, organic essentials, infrastructure, population, and fielded forces (see Figure 2.2 below). Warden knew when he initially developed the five-ring model that it had limitations; its primary utility, however, would be in distilling a complex argument about how systems functioned to a more basic level.[96] Fielded forces protect the population, infrastructure, organic essentials, and leadership from attack. The traditional method of imposing one's will on an adversary was to breach each layer, individually or in tandem, to reach the leadership "core."[97] In the Second World War, for example, the Allies engaged in a prolonged battle of production and strategic attrition by grinding down the *Luftwaffe*, the *Heer*, and the *Kriegsmarine* while simultaneously striking the other rings using airpower.[98] Limitations in aerial bombing accuracy meant that population centers had to be bombed in order to reach infrastructure and organic essential targets. Both methods, involving prolonged attrition, were wasteful and destructive according to Warden—there simply had to be an easier, more effective way of waging war.[99]

The assumption underpinning the five-ring model is that fielded forces could be bypassed and enemy leadership pressured more directly.[100] Warden hypothesized that the target rings were more sensitive to influence the closer one approached to the center of the model. For example, one bomb dropped on fielded forces would result in little change. Hitting a hydroelectric plant, or a leadership center, would have a much greater effect in theory.[101] Warden concluded that the most expeditious method of bypassing fielded forces was through the use of airpower. Technology, however, would enable airpower to fulfill political requirements, inflict shock, and realize its potential as the premier element of military power.

Unlike Fuller, Warden had an opportunity to put his theory into almost immediate practice. The crisis precipitated by Iraq's invasion of Kuwait found Warden in the right place at the right time. He was intimately familiar with CENTCOM

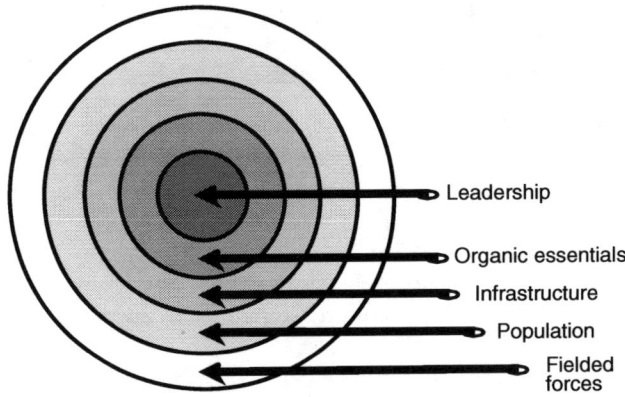

Figure 2.2 Warden's five-ring model

contingency plans, having contributed to their development. As the Deputy Director of Plans for Warfighting Concepts, Warden had the opportunity to expand upon his "enemy as a system" concept. When the Air Force Vice-Chief of Staff was requested to brief General Norman Schwarzkopf on available airpower options, Warden and the Checkmate staff amalgamated the five-ring model with the political imperatives outlined by President George Bush.[102] Iraq was to be evicted from Kuwait as quickly as possible with minimal loss of friendly lives; almost as important was that little damage be done to the infrastructure of both Iraq and Kuwait to minimize the requirement to rebuild after the war.[103]

In Warden's estimation, emerging technologies would not only allow the United States to achieve its goals efficiently, they would also permit airpower to be a swift executioner's sword rather than a bludgeoning cudgel. Airpower could bypass Iraq's ground forces and strike at the heart of the Iraqi regime.[104] Attacking Saddam Hussein directly presented legal and technical challenges;[105] if the Iraqi leadership could be severed instead from the other rings, by hitting its communications links and damaging critical infrastructure, the Iraqi state "system" would theoretically cease to function.[106] In order to achieve the quick and judicious application of force from the air, Checkmate planners sought out the "key nodes" of the Iraqi system.[107]

From five rings to systemic collapse

The details of the military campaign of the Gulf War are well known; the role airpower played in winning the conflict, however, is still the subject of much debate.[108] The planning for the air campaign was a Pyrrhic victory for Warden. Although personally frustrated and physically removed from the theater due a clash of personalities with a senior officer, Warden believed that his concept was validated by subsequent events.[109] He expanded upon the "enemy as a system" model and hypothesized that systems could be struck swiftly in parallel. When the five-ring model was applied to strategic centers of gravity, and an air campaign planned accordingly, the resulting effect would be strategic paralysis and collapse.

In reasoning hearkening back to Fuller, Warden suggested that the enemy's system could be equated to the human body. The five rings translated to body functions: the leadership ring was the brain, eyes, and nerves; organic essentials were the food/oxygen powering the vital organs; infrastructure was equivalent to vessels, bones, and muscles; the population were individual cells; and the fighting forces were leukocytes that defended the body from illness and infection.[110]

For Warden the "brain" was an irresistible target: isolating it from the rest of the system would bring about paralysis of an enemy state, obviating the need for the commitment of ground forces or the destruction of enemy fielded forces.[111] If the brain could not be located, Warden suggested striking targets in the next closest ring. The result would not be as quick as "decapitating" the system, but it would be just as effective: "this paralysis in one part of the strategic system is likely to cause much of the rest to atrophy and become ineffective."[112]

The five-ring model morphed from a planning tool for operational air campaigns into a universal tool to explain organizational vulnerability in a deterministic manner: "every life-based system is organized about the same way. Only the details vary."[113] In order to cause a system to collapse, planners unimpeded by deception and with knowledge of how enemy systems work need to identify the critical junctures or the centers of gravity within centers of gravity.[114] Warden postulated that the five-ring model was the most useful tool "to categorize information and to understand the importance of any particular bit."[115] The task is relatively simple:

> States have a small number of vital targets at the strategic level—in the neighborhood of a few hundred with an average of perhaps 10 aimpoints per vital target ... If a significant percentage is struck in parallel, the damage becomes insuperable.[116]

The five-ring model offers military planners and civilian policymakers the correct way, in Warden's view, to view the adversary: instead of a bottom-up assessment, starting from the tactical level of fielded forces, planners and policymakers will think strategically and operationally about how to affect enemy decision making from the top down.[117]

According to Warden, what he characterized as the Clausewitzian paradigm of attrition warfare, or struggle aimed exclusively at the destruction of fielded forces, was rendered obsolete by the performance of airpower in the Gulf War.[118] American comprehension of the Iraqi centers of gravity, and the ability of airpower to strike them, led to the annihilation of will in the month preceding ground operations. Little else could explain one of the shortest military ground offensives, 90 hours, in the history of warfare. The engine driving the change in warfare was the technological revolution in military affairs (RMA). The destruction of armies is no longer necessary, as information is the key to an RMA that enables precision-guided munitions, superior command and control systems, and superlative, stealthy platforms to function together seamlessly—a form of conflict that Warden classifies as hyperwar.[119] Information provides perfect situational awareness, from which accurate target sets within the five rings can be drawn. This information, passed to platforms and weapons systems, allows fewer aircraft to destroy more targets more precisely. When these aircraft are coordinated through information, target sets can be struck nearly simultaneously.

Simultaneous strikes have a compounding effect that leads to instantaneous systemic shock. The innermost ring, the enemy's leadership, cannot make informed decisions or exert control, as its communications have been severed.[120] The destruction of organic essentials and infrastructure isolates the leadership, fielded forces, and the population from one another. Deprived of control mechanisms and without the means to coordinate or sustain action, the system goes into shock until such functions can be restored.[121] Paralysis will be achieved when it is "physically impossible for [the enemy] to oppose us."[122] The alternatives to paralysis are imposing incremental costs on an adversary through escalating coercive

28 *Theories of strategic paralysis*

strikes or a destructive campaign akin to Second World War area bombing that Warden dismisses as untenable politically.[123]

Warden believes that technology has made warfare predictable.[124] Predictable war, executed by airpower, renders previous forms of warfare such as linear and area warfare obsolete.[125] The primary instruments of those forms of warfare, armies and navies, can be scrapped. Airpower is dominant for the foreseeable future and US global air supremacy is a reality. Half of the US Air Force's combat platforms can be retired, as unmanned combat aerial vehicles (UCAVs), merged with sensors and precision-guided munitions, will carry out sorties without risking American lives.[126]

Warden suggests airpower can serve a higher purpose through the reality of parallel attack and strategic paralysis—as a strategic deterrent.[127] No rational leader would want to challenge the United States, as the result would be decisive attack, systemic collapse, and potential loss of political power.[128] Should the use of force be required, parallel attack makes warfare more humane: the lives of airmen will not be put at risk; the lives of civilians will be spared as only those objects that sustain the system will be attacked; the target is moral (i.e. the leader's will) and not physical; once the leader has been deposed, the state can return to working order in a short period of time with little reconstruction; and non-lethal weapons can be used with impunity.[129] Technology will not only enable airpower to become the decisive instrument of strategy; airpower can serve a higher purpose than war. In the ultimate expression of technology humanizing war, or forging the sword into a ploughshare, the elements of parallel attack can be used to revolutionize humanitarian missions through precision-guided aid delivery.[130]

Technology facilitated the predominance of first armor, and then airpower, according to Fuller and Warden. Both theorists were pragmatic enough to recognize that technological change is constant. Indeed, Fuller and Warden understood the constant struggle between offense and defense that drives the development of military technology. One day new technology would render first the tank, and the airplane, obsolete.[131] Yet they both believed that technology provided the means to induce paralysis on an adversary by disrupting their command facilities in different ways: Fuller by direct attack against the brain, and Warden by coercing the brain by depriving it of its senses and support. Technology, operating with the restrictions of systemic friction or imperfect knowledge, allows smaller military forces to have unprecedented strategic performance by striking the source of cohesion and will within an enemy system. As with technology, special operations present decision makers with an appealing, low-cost option to solve strategic problems. When combined with strategic paralysis theory, the allure of a special operation designed to end hostilities is difficult to resist, as the next chapter demonstrates. Not all theorists, however, believe that technology or special operations are necessary to inflict strategic paralysis. For John Boyd, the annihilation of enemy will and resolve is not a function of the means but rather in the way that strategy is executed.

John Boyd and air kill ratios

No discussion of twentieth-century theories of strategic paralysis would be complete without including the work of John Boyd. In Boyd's estimation, technology can be an enabler of strategy but the key to strategic performance, and inflicting paralysis, is superior information processing, system performance, and decision making. For Boyd, the psychological and managerial aspects of strategy are crucial and if a system cannot maintain the pace of competition, it will inevitably collapse due to its own imperfections. This section explores the development of Boyd's theory from an explanation of a tactical phenomenon to a universal theory of strategic competition. Boyd's ideas will not be discussed in the same detail as those for Fuller and Warden for several methodological reasons: unlike Fuller and Warden, Boyd published few articles detailing his theory;[132] the body of his theory exists as slides to accompany several lengthy briefings he gave;[133] he left behind almost nothing in terms of personal correspondence discussing his ideas and the only archival material available is in the form of margin notes from his book collection;[134] and, as Boyd passed away in March 1997 and did not leave a substantive archive, questions regarding his theories can only be answered second-hand by his interpreters.[135]

The genesis of Boyd's theory was an attempt to explain how the US Air Force achieved high aircraft kill ratios over Korea.[136] The intuitive answer was superior American training, pilot skill, and aircraft technology. A problem with this answer, however, was that American pilots were flying at a technological disadvantage. During the Korean conflict Communist aviators used an aircraft with handling characteristics superior to that of the US F-86 Sabre.[137] A sizeable number of the "Korean" pilots were skilled Russian veterans of the Second World War, or Chinese trained by the Russians, and roughly equal to or in some cases more skilled than their American counterparts.[138] Boyd discovered the answer in an unlikely place: cockpit design, canopies, and hydraulics.

Boyd found that the superior performance of the Soviet aircraft was offset by the ability of American pilots to make faster transient maneuvers. Put simply, American pilots had a wider, clearer field of vision resulting from their larger canopies; they were more aware of their surroundings. Hydraulic controls in the American aircraft meant that pilots could react more quickly than their Soviet counterparts.[139] Boyd reasoned that success in fighter combat stemmed from superior maneuver, or agility, rather than advanced technology alone. His theories of energy maneuverability suggested that as long as you remained agile, and therefore reacted more adroitly to your opponent's moves, you could win any engagement regardless of initial advantage or disadvantage.[140]

Over the course of a quarter century Boyd worked on variations of his theory of fighter tactics.[141] He also applied his ideas to fighter and simulator design. Not everyone was enamored with the man or his ideas; Boyd used his theories to challenge the rationale underpinning at least one high-profile and expensive Air Force procurement program, the FX (which became the F-15).[142] While working on a fighter simulator for the National Aeronautics and Space Administration in 1976,

30 Theories of strategic paralysis

Boyd developed the crux of his strategic theory: "Idea of <u>fast transients</u> suggests that—in order to win or gain superiority—we should operate at a <u>faster tempo</u> than our adversaries or inside our adversaries [sic] <u>time scales</u> (underlining in original)."[143]

From Immelmanns to OODA loops

If fighter combat was nothing more than a competition at the simplest level, Boyd reasoned that his theory could have wider application. After all, individual aircraft actions only comprise a fraction of the overall strategic competition. As war is similar conceptually to a duel, conducted between two thinking adversaries, Boyd examined inductively and deductively how complex systems such as military organizations act and respond to internal and external stimuli.[144] The result of this work would consume Boyd for the next two decades as he refined, rethought, and expanded upon the initial idea of "the OODA loop."

The OODA loop is a simple decision model demonstrating how complex systems gather information, assess it, and respond. A "dialectic engine," prompted by changing conditions of the environment that reflected actions and reactions between adversaries, drives the OODA process.[145] The four letters comprising the "OODA" section correspond to four separate phases of the process "loop": observation; orientation; decision; and action. A graphic representation of the relationship between, and elements within, one phase of the loop is depicted in Figure 2.3.[146]

The OODA loop charts an individual system responding to information changing constantly as a result of decisions made and actions taken. Each loop represents a "slice" of time that can be broken down in its component phases.

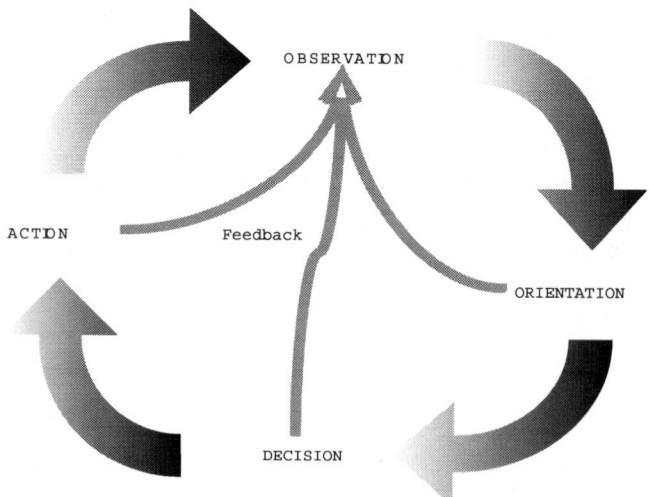

Figure 2.3 Boyd's OODA loop

External and internal inputs, as well as the level of competition, determine how quickly the cycle is completed.[147] Adding a second loop to represent an adversary provides a basic model of warfare. As war is perhaps the ultimate expression of human competition, involving bloodshed and destruction,[148] Boyd suggested that the OODA loop model can be applied to all levels of conflict, from tactics to grand strategy.[149]

Like Clausewitz, Fuller, and Warden, Boyd relied upon scientific theory and concepts to provide the foundations of his theory. Clausewitz merely utilized physical science concepts to convey the essence of his argument. Boyd, Fuller, and Warden, however, attempted to apply scientific laws, principles, and theories to explain their models. Boyd and Warden, in particular, drew heavily upon the second law of thermodynamics, which states that entropy expands in a closed system.[150] Entropy is a continuous process that cannot be reversed; excess energy is dissipated and matter decays. Some systems suffer more from the effects of entropy than others. A system's entropy could be magnified, in a method hearkening back to Sun Tzu, by attacking an enemy's plans and

> severely disrupting the adversary's combat operation process used to develop and execute his initial and subsequent campaign plans ... multiple events, compressed in time, will quickly generate mismatches, or anomalies between those actions the opponent believes to threaten his survival and those which actually do.[151]

Those systems that cannot sustain the tempo of operations set by their adversary will become progressively less effective until they collapse.[152] Although they are describing the same phenomenon, namely friction, Boyd and Clausewitz are looking at it through different lenses.[153]

Boyd hypothesized that paralysis and collapse would be the outcome of a competition in which one side continuously completed the cycle faster than its adversary. Speed, which yields savings in time, is essential to induce paralysis.[154] As war is ultimately a human enterprise, technology plays an enabling role by shortening processing and reaction times.[155] Faster processing and reaction is problematic as adversaries are often equally matched. Equality in this sense does not mean parity and is a relative term; no two adversaries are identical. Historically adversaries balance weaknesses in one category with offsetting strengths in another unless they are completely outmatched or incompetent.[156] Something was required to break the hypothetical OODA deadlock or the result would be attrition warfare.[157]

From his reading of military history and theory Boyd settled on the dependent variable that would create the conditions for paralysis: an unorthodox mindset.[158] By doing the unexpected and achieving surprise, one could disorganize an adversary and disrupt their functions. Given their unorthodox approaches to military problems, it is unsurprising that Boyd saw an integral role for SOF in gaining early advantage over an adversary:

Special seizure/disruption teams infiltrate (by air and other means) enemy rear areas where, with agents already in place, they: seize bridges and road crossings, sever communications, incapacitate or blow-up power stations, seize or blow-up fuel dumps ... as well as sow confusion/disorder via "false messages and fake orders".[159]

Exploiting the initial disruption to his planning and action cycle would cause one's adversary to fall further behind in the competition over time. One method of achieving this is to keep the opponent guessing as to the true focus of one's own effort.[160] Continually confused and disrupted, an adversary's decision cycle would fly apart from the centrifugal forces of attempting to keep pace in a losing effort. The end result of command collapse would be strategic paralysis.[161]

The theoretical nexi of paralysis: friction and center of gravity

The theories of strategic paralysis discussed above hinge on circumventing or increasing endemic friction and striking a center, or multiple centers of gravity. Prussian soldier-scholar Carl von Clausewitz developed both concepts. Friction, according to another scholar, guarantees Clausewitz a "place among the heroes in the Valhalla of strategic theory."[162] The concept reflects the difficulties associated with the nature of war, and in particular the human aspects and the role played by luck and chance, that permeates strategy.[163] Examples of friction include: the loss or misinterpretation of orders,[164] weather and geography upsetting plans,[165] technology not working as anticipated,[166] an enemy that does not conform to expectations,[167] and individuals exerting disastrous influences for seemingly incomprehensible reasons.[168] Those stresses distress even the most carefully developed plans once they are set in motion.[169] Friction is an inescapable reality of warfare that contributes significantly to unintended consequences and uncertain results: "The good general must know friction in order to overcome it whenever possible, and in order not to expect a standard of achievement in his operation which this very friction makes impossible."[170] In other words, war is the realm of the unexpected and unanticipated.

Similar admiration for conceptual clarity and vision, however, cannot be awarded to Clausewitz for his discussion of center of gravity. Clausewitz refers to center of gravity as "the hub of all power and movement, on which everything depends. That is the point against which all our energies should be directed."[171] In other sections, he refers to centers of gravity within enemy forces.[172] The concept of center of gravity remains the subject of considerable debate.[173] The confusion regarding center of gravity stems, in part, from the character of Clausewitz's work. *On War* is not only an unfinished body of work that contains inherent contradictions but it also demands careful consideration of the level of war to which Clausewitz is referring.[174] Inattentive readers are apt to miss the distinctions between the levels of wars and whether or if Clausewitz is referring to operational centers of gravity or a single strategic center.[175] Most importantly, the terms of reference within which one chooses to view center of gravity establish its relative value.

Theories of strategic paralysis 33

Center of gravity can be viewed in descriptive or predictive terms. When used descriptively, theorists define arbitrarily a perceived center of gravity in a previous conflict. Once identified, the specific center of gravity is placed in the context of the conflict. Scholars rarely agree, however, on which center of gravity is the most important, reflecting the "inherent contradiction" of both the concept as well as uncertainty in strategy. Two examples illustrate these points. The center of gravity of the German Third Reich has been depicted as the *Wehrmacht*, Adolf Hitler, Berlin, the territory of the *Reich* itself, the will of the German people, and the German war economy.[176] Indeed, as the next chapter depicts, the view within some circles of the RAF was that the war economy was the center of gravity of Germany's warmaking potential. This view led directly to a special operation designed to paralyze German will to continue the war in one blow. Alternatively, popular lore holds that the United States during the war in Vietnam had only one apparent center of gravity: US domestic support for the war effort. The North Vietnamese are assumed to have targeted primarily the will of the American public during the 1968 Tet Offensive and they were therefore considerably more adept strategically than their American counterparts.[177]

Disputes on what constitutes the center of gravity in conflicts past are of little interest or value to the modern military planner. If the concept of center of gravity serves any purpose in the planning context, it is as an assessment and resource management tool. As in Warden's theory, successive concentric ring diagrams can "model" centers of gravity from the grand strategic to the tactical level and assist in developing target sets.[178] It is doubtful, however, that Clausewitz ever intended center of gravity to be used as a functional planning aid; like Sun Tzu, Clausewitz's observations are designed to condition the mind, military or otherwise, to think about war at a level beyond battlefield movements.[179]

In paralysis theory, the center of gravity serves both descriptive and predictive functions. In descriptive terms, it provides a focus for strategic efforts. Strategy, however, must ultimately be executable and center of gravity provides the predictive function of allowing the least amount of force to be used to achieve for the greatest strategic effect in the shortest amount of time. By isolating and striking the hub, wars characterized by attrition are replaced by ones in which a single blow annihilates enemy will or ability to continue. The theories of strategic paralysis discussed above share common assumptions regarding center of gravity and friction. These assumptions include: a center of gravity is a vulnerability only, not a source of strength; friction is not an absolute and therefore an adversary's friction can be intensified; a center of gravity can be identified and struck directly or influenced indirectly; a direct correlation exists between striking/influencing a center of gravity and shock; and shock can be maintained through unrelenting strikes until collapse occurs. Underpinning these assumptions is the belief in unequivocal technological superiority and/or dominance that allows for superior information processing and planning, based on a near-perfect understanding of how the enemy system functions.

In a perfect world, systems would function as designed and adversaries would behave as anticipated. Unfortunately, the reality of strategy is that environmental factors, compounded by the flaws of human nature and the stresses of mortal competition, can upset even the most clever and meticulous plans. In attempting to reduce the functioning of an adversary's systems into its component weaknesses, or exploitable seams and joints, paralysis theorists paper over those problematic aspects of strategy that make the conduct of war such a difficult and complicated undertaking. As the next chapter demonstrates, those factors played a predominant role in the assumptions behind, planning for, imperative for, and conduct and results of, an attempt during the Second World War to use a special operations direct action to inflict strategic paralysis, and annihilate German will to continue, by striking at a "panacea target"—their war economy.

3 "A dark picture of destruction"[1]
Special operations, the persistence of ideas, and dambusting

> It is possible, however, that the economic conditions in the German Reich have been so vastly modified by the territorial conquests made in the present war that some pre-war reasons [to attack the dams] are no longer valid, with the consequence that a dam, at one time indispensable, may now have a somewhat reduced value.
>
> ("Air Attack on Dams", 5 February 1943)

The preceding chapter has argued that problems related to the nature of strategy have been assumed away or understated in the formulation of strategic paralysis theory. In particular, such theories suggest that the striking of a defined and discrete center of gravity will lead to moral collapse as effects cascade throughout the enemy system in a predictable way. The enemy center of gravity compresses strategic vulnerability and moral fragility into a tactical, material target set. Enemy moral and material resilience can be annihilated by the surprise of the flawless and audacious "great raid" conducted by special operations or overwhelming technological superiority. Moral attrition, and therefore subsequent attack and prolonged conflict of attrition, is unnecessary. Victory is theoretically achievable in a bloodless fashion. For special operations, the implication of paralysis theory is clear—attack the center of gravity in a single, audacious strike to induce strategic collapse and the need for conventional forces is obviated.

Strategy in practice differs from strategy in theory. Strategy in theory can be conducted in a vacuum unconstrained by political, geographic, economic, and social considerations. When attempting to develop and execute strategy in practice, or bridge the gap between desired ends with available means, a range of behavioral factors and inhibitors exacerbate the friction resident in all systems. These factors and inhibitors include cultural aspects and personal idiosyncrasies, as well as the political considerations that are magnified during the competition between organizations and individuals for resources and status that shape the resulting actions.

The limitations of paralysis theory, reflecting the practical factors outlined above and described in detail in the preceding chapter, are evident in Operation Chastise, conducted on 16/17 May 1943. Chastise, better known to history as "the Dambusters Raid," targeted the dams that supplied power and water to the factories at the heart of the German war industry. The raid was conceived in the belief that destruction of the dams would shut down the Ruhr valley factories. Striking the center of gravity and depriving factories of power to build war materials would have disproportionate effects up to the leadership of Nazi Germany. With the means to sustain the conflict removed, some Air Staff planners of the Royal Air Force believed that Nazi will to continue hostilities would evaporate. Yet the RAF at the beginning of the war could not destroy the dams. In 1943 all of the elements were in place to conduct a special operation to put the Air Staff theory of strategic paralysis to the test.

Operation Chastise offers much material for study. It is an example of how a special operation becomes shrouded in the myth of the "great raid." The "great raid" myth holds that heroism against considerable odds, based on inspired and audacious plans, has strategic effect by virtue of these qualities. The raid was immortalized on film and its details, as well of those of the lives of the major participants, have been covered in detail elsewhere.[2] The operation yields other valuable material as well. This exploration departs from previous works by demonstrating that Operation Chastise was an inevitable extension of British expectations about the paralytic value of airpower that resulted from the First World War.[3] In particular, this chapter directly challenges Anthony Verrier's assertion that:

> the raid on a complex of dams in the Ruhr valley on 16–17 May was not directly a reflection of the "precision" lobby or the "panacea" mongers, but from the particular heroism with which it is carried out and in the apparent success which attended it has come something of a legend that was war in the third dimension at its most gallant, resourceful and effective.[4]

This chapter argues that British belief in the ability of airpower to achieve strategic paralysis, reinforced by air policing experience in the colonies, Sir Hugh Trenchard's influence, and optimism for economy of force options in times of severe resource constraints, culminated in a special operation designed to crush the will of Nazi Germany in one material blow.

Only once it was clear that the British aerial deterrent against Germany failed in the late 1930s did members of the RAF Air Planning Staff develop targeting plans designed to have the greatest effect on Germany with scarce British strategic bombing resources. Key individuals within the Air Planning Staff, such as Richard Saundby and Charles Portal, believed that German industry in the Ruhr Valley was the most important strategic center of gravity of the Third Reich. If the manufacturing capability of the Nazi state could be seriously crippled, the Planning Staff members assumed that Hitler might be induced to sue for peace. Should that crucial segment be hit in one daring strike, German war production might be dislocated sufficiently to induce political surrender and prevent the large-scale deployment of British troops. Demonstrating the influence that human idiosyncrasies have on the development and conduct of strategy, the plans to destroy the Ruhr dams were resurrected long after its rationale had faded, despite substantial changes to the German war economy brought on by conquests in Europe. Common elements of special operations misuse, such as inflexibility of thought, inability to anticipate circumstances, and unrealistic expectations of the outcome, directly resulted in considerable casualties among valuable veteran RAF crews with little effect on German industry or will.

Dambusting: raid or special operation?

The relationship between aerial operations and special operations is ambiguous in the few works published on the subject. Authors are prone to include all "strategic air raids" and special operations support missions or ignore aerial operations altogether. The command historian of the United States Air Force Special Operations Command (AFSOC), for example, suggests that form and classification follows function. Any overt, covert, or clandestine missions performed by AFSOC, including personnel recovery and "tactical" air support and interdiction in Laos and Cambodia, are considered special operations by virtue of organizational affiliation.[5] Some of the confusion in delineating what constitutes an aerial special operation is related to the "strategic" aspects of airpower. In particular, individual perceptions and biases on the utility and the strategic effects of airpower frame that subject in one of two ways.[6] In one camp, some authors regard airpower only as a useful adjunct to land and sea power.[7] In their estimation, air combat support is a force multiplier, or merely an enabler of other instruments of military power, but does not constitute a "special" operation.[8]

Advocates counter such arguments by suggesting that precision technology resulting from the information technology revolution has made airpower decisive in and of itself; they point to interpretations of results achieved from air campaigns in the Gulf War (1990–1), Bosnia (1995), and Kosovo (1999).[9] According to this line of logic, adversaries were coerced into taking desired courses of action primarily or exclusively by airpower.[10] In particular, the coercive value effect of airpower results from the ability to strike at what decision makers value. The precise target for attack, as well as mechanism by which airpower can or cannot coerce, remain the subject of debate. What is clear, however, is that historically the ability of airpower to coerce was limited for technological reasons. Numerous aircraft were required to drop tons of bombs in order to have a reasonable chance of destroying a single target.[11] Specialists have played a subordinate and supporting role in assuring that the bomber gets to its target, delivers its payload, and returns home safely. In other words, the nature of "strategic" airpower is to mass available forces and coerce by striking key enemy targets. Special operations, in contrast, are economy-of-force actions consisting of limited strikes by small numbers of specialists.

Further confusion results from the terminology used to describe airpower. Individual missions attacking a particularly unique or valuable target have been classified historically as "raids."[12] The term "raid" has utility in describing the physical qualities of airpower. A raid differentiates between an individual operation in an unrelenting bombing campaign, the requirement to fight and maintain air superiority, and the inability of aircraft to maintain constant presence over enemy airspace. A few air raids have been classified as special operations, often on the basis of their audacity as well as the effects achieved after the fact, rather than the anticipated outcome or qualities of the forces involved.[13] For example, the Doolittle Raid on Tokyo in 1942 had unintended strategic consequences beyond its punitive purpose and therefore merits distinction in at least one work as a special operation.[14] The logical corollary is that missions that possess the qualities of special operations but fail are only considered as raids.[15]

Based on the definition of special operations outlined in Chapter 1, Operation Chastise merits distinction as a special operation. The operation was unconventional in a number of aspects, including the use of heavy bombers delivering their payload at extremely low altitude and the deployment of an unusual weapon, the bouncing cylindrical "Upkeep" bomb.[16] Although the members of 617 Squadron did not pass through a peacetime selection system as is common in established SOF today, they did pass through a far more rigorous and unforgiving selection process: in addition to being volunteers, most crew members had to be veterans of at least two operational tours.[17] The squadron received special designation given their heavily modified aircraft, the nature of their task, and the desire to maintain operational security in order to preserve the element of surprise. Finally, Operation Chastise was conceived from the beginning as a mission using few resources to achieve grossly disproportional effects. Nineteen modified Lancasters, each with a single bomb, would strike five sizeable dams in the Ruhr Valley whose destruction was intended to paralyze German industry—and to perform by annihilation what four years of repeated bombing raids over cities had failed to do. In contrast, the conventional approach to destroying the Ruhr Valley industries involved repeated raids on area targets to shut down German armaments production.

Ascribing the arc: from "air policing" to the "knockout blow"

To understand why the Ruhr dams were targeted, it is necessary to frame the development of British airpower theory. An enduring criticism of airpower is that the results have never fulfilled its promise. Even before the development of formal airpower theory, or in some cases before the creation of the actual instruments themselves, science fiction writers discussed the effects of airpower.[18] H.G. Wells, in his *War in the Air*, paints a picture of the collapse of civilization brought on by aerial bombardment.[19] But Wells was skeptical of the decisive value of airpower:

> [W]ith the flying machine war alters its character; it ceases to be an affair of "fronts" and becomes an affair of "areas"; neither side, victor or loser, remains immune from the gravest injuries, and while there is a vast increase in the destructiveness of war, there is also an increased indecisiveness.[20]

The collapse of civilization, he presaged, was caused as much by political, social, and economic shortcomings of modern Western society as it was by the destruction wrought by airpower.[21] The earliest iterations of airpower theory were depicted in terms of inflicting swift, crippling punishment on the civilian willpower and military industries of a warring state.[22] Initial civilian reactions to aerial bombardment during the First World War seemed to confirm the effects of airpower on civilian will.[23] These observations, as well as dramatic improvements in the range and lift capabilities of aircraft, led some advocates to suggest as early as 1917 that airpower could be independently decisive.[24]

After the First World War ended, visionaries within the RAF sold the concept of strategic bombing to civilian decision makers using a number of selective, but empirically questionable arguments. The argument that appealed most to civilian members of government was the economic value of airpower. In many respects the political ground within Britain was fertile for an alternate and cost-effective method of using "force to compel our enemy to do our will."[25] Britons had relied on a small standing army for almost four centuries;[26] the social and economic cost of a mobilized citizen army in the face of industrialized methods of war had been extremely burdensome.[27] In addition, although British policymakers did not question the necessity of having a navy, they did raise concerns over the need to maintain a peerless, expensive fleet that fought rarely during the war and demonstrated little value in protecting vulnerable sea lines of communication from the predations of German U-boats and commerce raiders.[28] British imperial defense was further complicated by the addition of colonial territory formerly under the control of Imperial Germany as well as the last remnants of the Ottoman Empire. Airpower provided an appealing alternative to British politicians and civil servants keen to reduce the burden on the Treasury.

To deal with uprisings in far-flung colonies, punitive action need no longer be limited to costly land campaigns. Recalling some of the arguments put forth by J.F.C. Fuller in the preceding chapter, sizeable overseas garrisons of troops would not be required and considerable savings realized in not having to transport by sea ground forces for retaliatory actions. As airpower advocates were quick to point out, bombing missions, or "air policing," appeared remarkably effective in quelling uprisings or punishing raiding tribes. Among the instances in which air policing proved its value were the bombing of Kabul (1919), the suppression of the Mad Mullah's rebellion in Somaliland (1920), and punitive actions against tribes in Iraq and the Transjordan (1922).[29] Indeed, a key selling point of aerial bombardment as the future force of choice was exaggerated claims to both precision and "moral effect." For example, in at least one case:

> The (Colonial Office) Resident in Waziristan maintained that the bombers had picked out "not only the villages of the guilty but the very houses of those most deeply concerned, leaving untouched the property of the well-disposed," a claim that was repeated almost verbatim by the Air Staff before the Committee of Imperial Defence in July 1930.[30]

Wars against rebellious colonials could only be of limited duration, and prolonged conflict avoided, as native hostility would evaporate once the bombs first started falling.

The primary architect of the strategic bombing role for the RAF, Sir Hugh Trenchard, required some form of leverage in order to assure institutional survival and independence from the other services. The British experience with air policing seemed to provide the evidence that demonstrated the power, unique qualities, and efficiency of airpower.[31] Although David Omissi has demonstrated effectively that there was little direct influence between air policing experience and the development of British airpower *doctrine* for dealing with future continental European adversaries, the same cannot be said regarding British *strategic theory* regarding airpower.[32] Trenchard adopted almost any argument that would allow the RAF to survive, including claims to the economic value of airpower in terms of blood and treasure relative to the costs of mounting a land or naval campaign.[33] In addition, Trenchard backed arguments in support of the precision of strategic bombardment and the moral effect of bombing population and industrial centers.[34] J.F.C. Fuller characterized succinctly, if somewhat petulantly, the "moral effect" argument:

> All military power is finally dependent on the civil will. It is the nation and not its army which makes war, consequently as the movement of air forces cannot to any great extent be restricted by armies and navies, the civil population can now be directly attacked and terrorized into submission.[35]

Trenchard also cleverly made use of contrary viewpoints during the RAF's bureaucratic fight for survival.[36] Some RAF officers, as well as key officials in the Army and Royal Navy, were cautious to the point of outright skepticism in their evaluation of the effects of airpower, moral or otherwise.[37] RAF Air Marshal John Salmond, for example, hypothesized that airpower only achieved its coercive effects over time through the gradual attrition of will among the civilian populations. The basis for his argument was the rapid adaptation of indigenous peoples to new methods of war.[38] Trenchard skillfully adopted the so-called "three phase" theory to bolster his moral effect argument and lobby for resources adequate to grind down civilian morale.[39]

Trenchard and the Air Staff won the battle for the continued existence and independence of the RAF using selective interpretation of events and arguments to reinforce unproven assumptions about the effects of strategic bombing. Where data was unavailable from which to draw conclusions, Trenchard opted instead to develop his own: "At present the moral effect of bombing stands undoubtedly to the material effect in a proportion of 20:1."[40] Despite these exceptions, however, Trenchard and the Air Staff were careful to temper their vision of airpower on occasion to fit within the construct of interservice cooperation in time of war.[41] Although Trenchard was keen to guarantee the survival of his service, he appreciated the reality of the influence of the RAF against the established army and navy lobbies in Whitehall and on the Thames. A number of internal and external factors, however, perpetuated and exacerbated the faith in effects of strategic aerial bombardment: the air disarmament movement, which reflected the general disarmament zeitgeist of the 1920s, sought to reduce or eliminate entirely air armaments based on their projected terror value and the immorality of bombing civilian populations;[42] a vocal minority of commentators who molded public awareness about what strategic bombing could accomplish;[43] the paucity of professional officer higher education and development,[44] especially among the Air Staff, in addition to a reliance on rhetorical rather than critical methods of teaching and assessment;[45] the retirement of Trenchard in 1929 and his subsequent replacement by a number of bureaucratically competent, but unimpressive successors;[46] and the untrammeled acceptance of the offensive value of airpower, based in part on British awareness of their own vulnerability to strategic bombing, which led to the adoption of a faulty deterrence strategy based on airpower.

Turning the corner: planning the "knockout blow"

For over a decade, British planners and policymakers were content to view airpower as a powerful deterrent to whatever threat might come from continental Europe. France was considered the obvious threat during the 1920s and early 1930s; with the rise of Adolf Hitler to power and the stated German intention to rearm, however, that threat perception changed. Malcolm Smith argues that the British aerial deterrent was intellectually fulfilling but deeply flawed:

> The threat of an overwhelming pre-emptive strike, or of what later came to be known as "massive retaliation," seemed to offer British diplomats a new and effective reinforcement in negotiation, if only the force could be built to give substance to that threat ... British vulnerability to air attack produced a paradox in British rearmament in the early 1930s, the creation of an air-strike force projected at home and abroad as a deterrent, but one which was never intended to and was never capable of carrying out the threat that deterrence implied.[47]

British perceptions on how the future air war would be fought were related intimately to the aim of airpower once the deterrent failed. The aim changed little from Trenchard's articulation in 1928: "to paralyse from the very outset the enemy's productive centres of munitions of war of every sort and to stop all communications and transportation."[48] Paralysis achieved by airpower resonated deeply with the British, reflecting their understanding of the vulnerability of their own country to aerial attack. If aircraft could avoid fighting through the main lines then they could also surmount Britain's historical and geographical insulator from wars on the continent: the English Channel. Indeed, given advances in aircraft and engine design, London was less than 15 minutes' flight from bases on the French coast, and the industrial heartland of England was well within the range of marauding bombers.[49] Increased engine performance also meant that aircraft could carry heavier bombloads. The mystique surrounding modern aircraft and strategic bombing led a Labour Party member to suggest to his parliamentary colleagues that a mere 20 aircraft could raze London to the ground.[50]

British awareness of their vulnerability to continental airpower led to consideration of the steps required to protect themselves against attack. One group suggested that passive and active defenses could whittle down the numbers of incoming bombers, provided enough fighter aircraft could be coordinated, although such views were decidedly a minority within the RAF.[51] The more prevalent view espoused within Bomber Command suggested that defending against bombers was a futile exercise. This view was captured so markedly by Prime Minister Stanley Baldwin in his famous speech to Parliament:

> I think it well also for the man in the street to realize there is no power on earth that can protect him from bombing, whatever people may tell him. *The bomber will always get through* [italics added], and it is very easy to understand if you realize area and space.[52]

Within the preceding paragraph of this speech, however, Baldwin states the argument for the *offensive* use of bombing forces espoused by Bomber Command:

> In the next war you will find any town within the reach of an airdrome can be bombed within the first five minutes of war to an extent inconceivable in the last war and the question is whose morale will be shattered quickest by preliminary bombing.[53]

In other words, the best defense against enemy bombers was not merely a good offense; what mattered most was using that offensive capability first to cripple one's adversary. Precisely how much effect Baldwin's speech, and the more strident claims of Bomber Command's representatives, influenced the British public, its decision-making elites, and the policies of its future allies, is beyond the scope of this work.[54] Nevertheless, the doctrine of "first use" helped sell the concept of an aerial "knockout blow" to the Cabinet. As Bomber Command approached the Second World War, armed with the view that disarmament was impractical at best and foolish at worst, the prevalent belief within the Command was

> that the next war would start with an air attack, that the key to victory would be enemy morale, and that one could destroy enemy morale through strategic air attack; therefore, the RAF must have a large, constantly alert, offensive force.[55]

Trenchard, the Air Staff, and ultimately Bomber Command, however, sold the Cabinet a bill of goods that it could not possibly deliver.

The efficacy of Britain's aerial deterrent was called into question by Nazi German rhetoric and actions, including territorial demands, the renouncing of Versailles Treaty arms limitations, and expanded rearmament policies. The British aerial deterrent hinged on the stated policies of massive aerial retaliation and the maintenance of numerical parity with the Germans.[56] Numerical parity without technological improvement ultimately compromised the ability of the

RAF to strike a fatal blow on German industry.[57] A number of factors eroded the feet of clay on which the British aerial deterrent was based. The first was Adolf Hitler's uncanny understanding of the mindset of his Western European counterparts prior to 1939, which in turn undermined British and French attempts to pose credible threats to the Reich. The second factor was the cumulative effect of the "locust years" of British defense spending in which little investment was made in the armed forces. John Ferris notes that:

> It took the catastrophic breakdown of the international economic system in 1929–30 to destroy the possibility that a stable world might follow from the Washington Conference and the Locarno Pact and to unleash the dangerous forces which British (sic) had always known existed in other states. Even then it still had a warning period of seven years to improve its position. However, this analysis led British governments to take a strategic gamble, which they lost. Between 1926 and 1933 they cut first their projected and then their actual service spending … they deferred programmes for Britain's security until threats actually became imminent.[58]

Finally, there was the blind faith in both the accuracy and overwhelming destructiveness of airpower prevalent in both civilian and military circles. A battle of attrition in the air would be unlikely for these reasons. As a result, the belief persisted within segments of the RAF that airpower would annihilate German will to continue the struggle. Such beliefs not only colored British strategic bombing planning that began in 1937 but they carried through until the special operation to crack the dams was launched in 1943.

When circumstances forced the Air Staff to put their ideas of strategic bombing into the realities of a planning context, substantial questions were raised about how the "knock-out blow" would be implemented against Germany specifically. The Chiefs of Staff—Joint Planning Committee handed Air Staff planners a list of ten categories of plans that included considerations of the Army and the Navy. From those ten categories, the Air Staff developed initially 14, and eventually more than 16 "Western Air Plans" as shown in Table 3.1.

Before the start of hostilities in 1939, three of the WA Plans were completed.[60] The first plan was a counterforce option (WA1), striking directly at the German air arm should Nazi Germany begin a strategic bombing campaign. The second was an interdiction option (WA4) to disrupt German supply and mobility should France and the Low Countries be invaded. The third was the strategic bombing campaign long advocated by Trenchard and the Air Staff and embodied in WA5, directed at aluminum, electricity, and oil industries.[61]

The "knock out blow" and "moral effect" arguments tilled the conceptual field for the special operation against the Ruhr dams, but WA Plans 5(a) and 5(c) were the seeds of Trenchard's legacy that were nurtured and continued to grow. If excessive optimism and enthusiasm drove the "moral effect" argument, then economy of effort was both the main theme and source of contention between those who argued for bombing specific sectors of the German war industry.

Table 3.1 RAF WA Plans[59]

Index no.	Subject
WA1	Plans for attack on the German Air Striking Force, and its maintenance organisation (including aircraft industry)
	1(b) Action against certain major aerodromes in the North West corner of Germany
WA2	Plans for reconnaissance with the navy in Home Waters and the Eastern Atlantic
WA3	Plans for close co-operation with the Navy in convoy protection in Home Waters and the Eastern Atlantic
WA4	Plans for the attack of German military rail, canal and road communications
	4(a) Attack on rail and road communications in W. Germany in a concentration period
	4(b) Attack to delay a German invasion of Southern Holland, Belgium and France
WA5	Plans for attacking German manufacturing resources
	5(a) The attack on German war industry
	5(b) The attack of the RUHR and its effect on the military lines of communication in Western Germany
	5(c) Attack on Germany's war resources of oil
WA6	Plans for attacking Italian manufacturing resources
WA7	Plans for counter offensive action in defence of seaborne trade in co-operation with the Navy, i.e. attack on the Fleet or on the bases of enemy surface, submarine and air forces operating against our trade
	7(a) Attack on WILHELMSHAVEN
	7(b) Limited attack with air forces alone on WILHELMSHAVEN
WA8	Plans for attack on specially important depots or accumulations of warlike stores other than air, in enemy country
WA9	Plans for putting the Kiel Canal out of action
WA10	Plans for the destruction of enemy shipping and facilities in German mercantile ports—precedence to be given to the Baltic
WA11	Plans for attack on forests
WA12	Plans for attacking the German Fleet or a section thereof at sea
WA13	Plans for attack on enemy's headquarter and administrative offices in Berlin and elsewhere
WA14	Plans for dropping propaganda leaflets
WA15	Plans prepared in concert with the Naval Staff for operations against enemy shipping by 'M' Mine
WA16	Buoyancy mine attack against German waterways

Relative weakness and limited resources of the bombing force, plus the beliefs in the effect of strategic bombing, drove planners to identify critical vulnerabilities of the Nazi German state. In order to cripple Germany's war industries, planners looked beyond individual armaments factories and focused instead on critical sectors that supported production. For example, rather than bombing every target associated with German steel production, planners sought to disable production by hitting vulnerable segments of the steel production process: mining, raw material transportation methods, coking plants, electricity generation, and water supply.[62] Of all the targets, though, oil and electricity were the most appealing. Refined petroleum was a key component of the Nazi German war machine, oil products also helped sustain German industry, and petroleum products are highly flammable and therefore easily destroyed.[63] Electricity generating plants, on the other hand, were alluring to planners for other reasons: their core components, such as turbines and transformers, were vulnerable to destruction and relatively difficult to replace; the targets were easily identifiable by air; most of the targets that supported German industry in the Ruhr Valley were within range of British bombers; and, most importantly, the moral and physical effects of depriving German industry and citizens of electricity were perceived to be wider ranging than bombing oil targets.[64]

The members of the Air Targets Sub-Committee of the Bombing Committee further refined their target planning against the German electrical grid.[65] They quickly focused on the next higher level of supply in the electricity generating chain that supported the Ruhr industries: the dams of the Ruhr and Weser Rivers.[66] The dams included the Sorpe (72 million m^3 water volume) and Möhne (134 million m^3 water volume) dams on the Ruhr Catchment and the Eder (202 million m^3 water volume) dam on the Eder and Diemel Catchment.[67] The Ruhr dams fit the Air Staff's axiom:

> whatever may be the intrinsic value of an objective, however much its destruction or dislocation would embarrass the enemy or assist ourselves, it is only suitable as a target for air attack if it can be destroyed or dislocated *economically*, i.e., without undue expenditure or effort [emphasis in original].[68]

The dams fit this description as they supported German industry in numerous ways. In addition to providing the water for hydro-electric power generation, most dams also supplied water for commercial and civilian use, including supplying cooling water for thermal electric plants.[69] Enthusiasm for and analysis supporting the bombing of the dams, however, was not matched by RAF capabilities. Although the dams had been under British scrutiny as targets since 1938, the problem of how to destroy them seemed beyond the means of the RAF even three years into the war.

46   *Special operations, the persistence of ideas, and dambusting*

Struggling to maintain lift: the means and method of a special operation

Economy of force was more than just a planning watchword for the RAF in 1937; it was a reflection of a "strategic" bombing force that had assets barely capable of battlefield interdiction. In terms of strategic bombing capability, by 1939 "the necessary elements to translate theory into operational plans were virtually non-existent."[70] In addition to a dearth of useful air intelligence on all aspects of the German economy, which exacerbated assumptions about the linkages between sectors of the German war industry and economy,[71] the RAF was pitifully trained and woefully equipped. Lack of realistic training exercises or appreciable doctrine before the war translated into lessons learned and skills bought at a heavy cost in equipment and personnel losses. For example, loss rates as high as 50 percent of the attacking force in unescorted daylight bombing missions convinced those within the Air Ministry to shift instead to night raids.[72] Night bombing required the development of entirely new sets of skills and doctrine to find, mark, and bomb targets with reasonable accuracy, as well as conduct battle damage assessment.[73]

The tools with which to paralyze Germany industry into submission were similarly deficient. On the eve of the war, the core of the RAF strategic bombing force was comprised of twin-engine medium bombers: Vickers Wellingtons, Bristol Blenheims, Whitworth Whitleys, and Handley-Page Hamptons.[74] These models, while relatively fast by 1938 standards, were nevertheless inadequate in range, bomb payload, and defensive armament.[75] The qualities of these aircraft resulted, in part, from parsimony of the Treasury and the pace of aircraft technology development during the 1930s. More importantly, however, the state of the British bomber force directly reflected the inability of the Air Staff to view aircraft design, development, and tasking holistically. As Scot Robertson observed: "the Air Staff failed to appreciate the dialectical nature of the problem. Instead of considering each piece of equipment as part of a weapons system, they chose to focus on individual equipment considerations in isolation."[76] The same factors influenced the quality and quantity of the "cash" element of strategic bombing commercial transaction: the bombs themselves. Although tests had been conducted in 1930 with bombs as heavy as 1,500 pounds, several elements limited the destructiveness of weapons available to the RAF: the belief in the Air Staff that the General Purpose 250-, 500-, and 1,000-pound bombs were the right tools for the job; and the insistence on a 1:4 ratio of explosive to ballistic casing to improve the bomb's flight stability at the expense of destructive power.[77]

Given the methods available to the RAF at the start of the air war, there was little probability of bombers flying at high altitude destroying hardened point targets such as a catchment dam, making a special operation necessary. Low-level missions had proven vulnerable previously to intercept and ground-based anti-aircraft artillery.[78] Even if bombers could place armor-piercing ordinance on the face of the dam, such bombs would do little damage to the sturdy masonry or even bounce off its surface. Masonry dams, such as those servicing the Möhne and Eder basins, were over 34 meters in width at the base and 40 meters high. An alternate approach was to crack the dams by detonating a charge below the water's surface close to the dam wall. Causing an explosion underwater magnifies the explosive effect, creating a wave of hydrostatic pressure. Should either the pressure wave or tamped explosives[79] create sufficient fissures, water pressure on the dam wall would expand them and cause the masonry to collapse. The Germans had anticipated underwater attack using torpedoes and had placed booms, or suspended nets, in the basin.[80] The dams were such lucrative targets that "gentleman amateurs" independently formulated schemes for their destruction in plans that ranged from the visionary to the incomprehensible.[81]

One solution to destroying the dams was developed in May 1940 by part-time inventor Wing Commander C.R. Finch-Noyes.[82] His "short range high capacity torpedo" had a number of iterations but all sought the same result: placing approximately 20,000 pounds of explosives on the face of the dam under water. Rather than using conventional torpedoes with 440-pound warheads, Finch-Noyes envisioned a torpedo with a 2,000-pound warhead.[83] In order to overcome the boom and anti-aircraft defenses erected by the Germans, Finch-Noyes and his colleague Noel Pemberton suggested that the torpedo either "glide" to target from a stand-off distance, or propel itself across the surface of the water.[84] The "hydroplane skimmer" would be propelled by either "rocket under water plus steam jet propulsion," or "automatic gun (say 20 mm) firing blanks in a tube … firing astern."[85] Despite the promise that "such a unit [to conduct attacks using the short range high capacity torpedo] should in six months from the word 'Go' have effected its objects if given the necessary priority,"[86] the program faltered due to difficulty in delivering the weapon precisely enough. An alternate plan involved using explosives on hand, namely "M" Mines, in sufficient quantity to breach the dam wall. Precise placement was again the problem. There was simply no way to deliver the mines and detonate them simultaneously to destroy the dam. One Air Vice-Marshal simply concluded that "The practical difficulties of this method are considered to be insuperable at present."[87]

The difficulties in destroying the dams may have been insuperable but they did not dissuade Air Staff planners from believing that the weak links in the German war machine were the dams that powered and supplied industry. Shortly after Finch-Noyes began his work, Air Marshal Charles Portal wrote that:

> I am given to understand that almost all the industrial activity of the RUHR depends upon the water contained in and supplied by this dam, and that if it were destroyed not only would most of the industry of the RUHR be brought to a standstill but very great havoc would be wrought throughout the length of the water course. It appears to me that, though difficult, the task is by no means impossible provided the correct weapons are available.[88]

Despite programmatic delays and failures, the RAF Group Captain, Operations, was confident a year later that "The destruction of the MOHNE DAM which feeds the Ruhr would paralyze its industry."[89] As analysts within various British agencies began to understand better the linkages between sectors of German industry, they began to challenge the assumption of the importance of the Möhne dam within it. At this juncture, however, Barnes Wallis was perfecting the means to crack a dam with a single bomb and the theory that airpower could inflict industrial paralysis gained a new lease on life.

The story of the development of Upkeep, the cylindrical "bouncing bomb," is already well known and therefore only the pertinent details will be sketched.[90] Barnes Wallis, an engineer with Vickers-Armstrong, initially focused his efforts on developing a bomb capable of achieving supersonic velocity and delivering seven tons of explosives. Seven tons, approximately 16,000 pounds, was capable of causing structural failure in any masonry dam then in existence.[91] By burrowing underground, the bomb would cause a tremendous underground shock wave that would shake structures apart at their foundations. The bomb did not need to be delivered precisely; the most pressing question was how to deliver a weapon that clearly exceeded the payload capacity of any bomber then in existence. On the basis of the tremendous research and development costs, not to mention the resources required, the Air Staff determined that the project was infeasible.[92]

Precisely how Wallis came up with the idea for the bouncing bomb is unclear but he tested both spherical and cylindrical models. By delivering the weapon at a set altitude and speed, a bomb could be made to skip across the surface of the water rather than immediately sinking below it. American, Australian, British, and German aviators had developed this method of attack to extend the range and increase the accuracy of their attacks against shipping.[93] Not surprisingly, the initial support for Upkeep came from the Admiralty, which was interested in developing a stand-off capability to sink German capital ships to replace torpedoes delivered by slow Fairey Swordfish biplanes.[94] A series of controlled experiments determined the following characteristics for Upkeep: it should have a backspin of 500 revolutions per minute, to ensure that it stayed in contact with the face of the dam once it hit and sank, enhancing its explosive effect (see Figure 3.1); it should contain between 6,000 and 7,000 pounds of explosive; it should be no more than 7 feet long, to fit underneath a heavily-modified Avro Lancaster, the only British bomber with sufficient range and payload to carry the weapon; and it should be delivered from 60 feet at approximately 220–40 miles per hour to guarantee accurate placement.[95]

Historians have overlooked Wallis's other contribution to the planning and conduct of Operation Chastise; he was not merely a weapons designer. Wallis not only played a role in selection of targets against which Upkeep would be employed, including the Eder Dam, but he was also a strong advocate of the concept of strategic paralysis.[96] How and why Wallis adopted the theory of strategic paralysis is unclear. There is the possibility that Wallis merely used paralysis theory as a way to sell his ideas and inventions to the Air Staff. In any event, Wallis's understanding of the effect of bombing specific sectors of the German economy might have been influenced by the ideas of Trenchard and Air Staff:

> coalfields, oil fields and districts suitable for development as hydro-electric catchment areas and underground storage tanks for oil … are impossible to

Special operations, the persistence of ideas, and dambusting 49

disperse ... If their destruction or paralysis can be accomplished *THEY OFFER A MEANS OF RENDERING THE ENEMY UTTERLY INCAPABLE OF CONTINUING TO PROSECUTE THE WAR.*[97]

Wallis then linked the ends of paralysis to his suggested means:

these stores of energy are vulnerable to very large bombs; by sterilising their Stores of Energy the Industries of Germany and Italy can be quickly paralysed; the very large bomb and appropriate bomb carrying aircraft are practicable and can be produced in this country.[98]

Barnes Wallis's appearance was serendipitous for the Air Staff advocates of industrial paralysis theory. Without adequate intelligence, Air Staff planners "mirror imaged" their adversary and assumed that German industry operated in the same way that British industry did.[99] The Air Staff planners were fixated on the Möhne Dam since 1938 given its size and perceived importance. Air Marshal Sir Charles Portal, Chief of Staff and a key figure behind the establishment of Air Attacks on Dams Committee in 1941, once quipped "if you want to win the war bust the dams."[100] Paralysis theory, and more specifically the Dams Raid itself, faced mounting opposition from two sources: Arthur "Bomber" Harris and the Ministry of Economic Warfare. Harris believed that the only way to bring Germany to its knees was a sustained area bombing campaign of German industry and population centers to overcome inaccurate methods of bomb delivery and target dispersal, an effort requiring all available resources.[101] Any diversion of precious

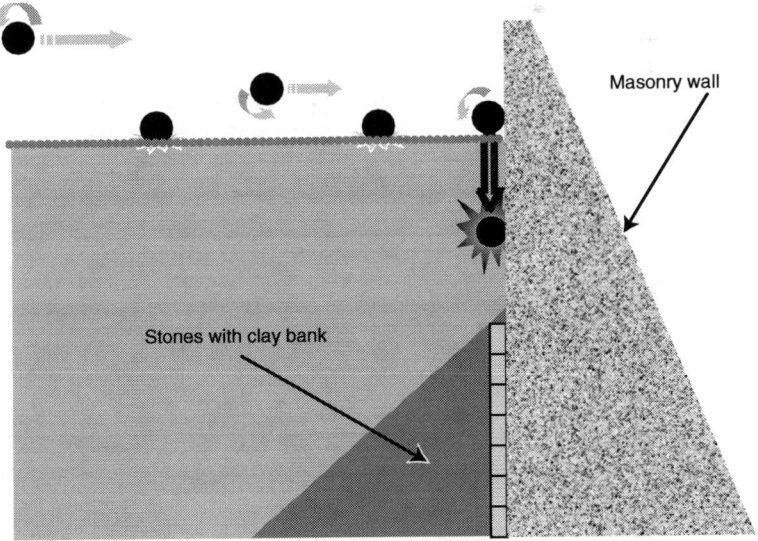

Figure 3.1 How Upkeep worked

RAF assets, especially to attack "panacea" targets,[102] was futile in Harris's view.[103] Eventually, however, Harris grudgingly approved crews and aircraft largely due to pressure from Wallis and supporters such as Portal, Frederick W. Winterbotham,[104] Henry Tizard,[105] and Winston Churchill.[106]

Criticism from the Ministry of Economic Warfare had less to do with strategic bombing catechism than it did with a growing understanding of how the German industrial "system" worked. More specifically, the commentary of the Ministry of Economic Warfare on an Air Staff report on the effects of destroying the dams was both supportive and skeptical:

> both the physical and moral effects of the flood which would be produced are likely to be sufficiently great to justify this operation in themselves, even if there were no other significant effects … the destruction of [the Möhne] dam would not necessarily have any large or immediate effect on the supply of industrial and household water in the Ruhr area.[107]

This evaluation stands in muted contrast to an enthusiast report submitted by the Air Staff just days before:

> The destruction of the Sorpe Dam which together with the Möhne would account for 75% of the water supplies available to the Ruhr, would if effected at the same time as the Möhne Dam, produce a paralysing effect upon the industrial activity of the Ruhr and would result in a still further lowering of morale.[108]

By February 1943 Wallis supported the Air Staff plan to attack more than just the Möhne Dam:

> It is possible, however, that the economic conditions in the German Reich have been so vastly modified by the territorial conquests made in the present war that some pre-war reasons are no longer valid, with the consequence that a dam, at one time indispensable, may now have a somewhat reduced value.[109]

Despite acknowledging that Germany controlled almost all of the resources of Europe, Wallis upheld the Air Staff view of the collective value of the dams, explaining the "immense increase in demand that must have occurred during the three years of war development."[110] He subsequently suggested that primary targets should be the Möhne, Eder, and Diemel Dams.[111] Absent from the list, however, was the Sorpe Dam. Constructed using a method different from that of a gravity dam (see Figure 3.2), the Sorpe Dam consisted of a thin concrete core 68 meters high packed on both sides with ramps of gravel, rubble, stones, and loam.[112] Although Wallis was skeptical that Upkeep could do significant damage against a dam constructed in this fashion, he did not argue against Air Staff plans that listed the Sorpe Dam as the second target in order of importance after the

Special operations, the persistence of ideas, and dambusting 51

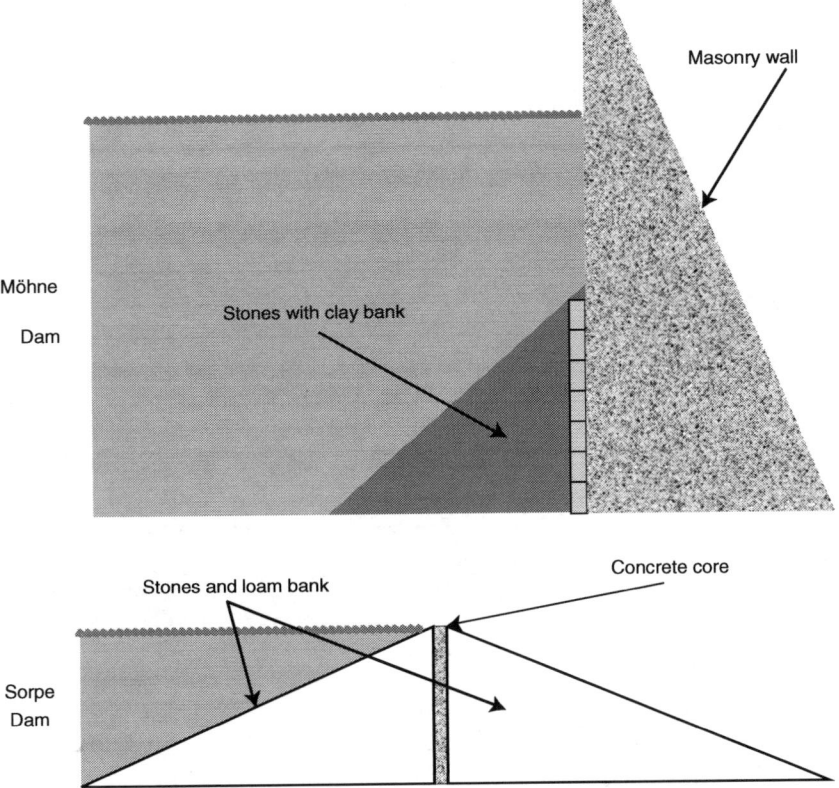

Figure 3.2 Dam types

Möhne Dam.[113] With the means developed to crack one type of dam, a special operation designed to strike at the moral heart of Germany and end the war was one step closer to reality.

Coming full circle: the attempted "knockout blow"

By March 1943, Operation Chastise had assumed a life of its own for a variety of the reasons dismissed by paralysis theorists and outlined in the preceding chapter. Key among the reasons for the enthusiasm to conduct Chastise were the personalities who were convinced of the merits of the plan. Various high-ranking civilian and military leaders, including Winston Churchill and Arthur Harris, had been won over by Barnes Wallis's presentation through formal and informal channels.[114] Churchill was a firm supporter of special operations and raids against Germany. Such audacious attacks served a number of Churchill's strategic goals including: demonstrating British competence to allies, Commonwealth partners, and the public; highlighting German vulnerability and eroding the myth of the

Nazi invincibility; seizing and maintaining the initiative from the Germans; acquiring critical technological information on German defensive systems and preparations, such as the seizure of German radar components at Bruneval; inflicting damage on key German industrial and population sectors in retaliation for attacks on British cities; and, perhaps most importantly, maintaining British influence among two increasingly powerful allies, namely the United States and the Soviet Union.[115] "Bomber" Harris lent his support for Operation Chastise after his initial suspicions were put to rest. If Harris was forced to divert almost two dozen of his prized Lancasters, as well as the personnel to support and fly them, at least they would be operating in support of his sustained bomber offensive recently begun against the industries of the Ruhr Valley.[116]

Other factors influenced the decision to go ahead with the special operation in May 1943. The Admiralty was keen to deploy Highball against a number of targets, including U-Boat pens, current and anticipated German surface threats such as the battleship *Tirpitz* and aircraft carrier *Graf Zeppelin*, as well as the remnants of the Italian fleet.[117] As Highball and Upkeep worked on similar principles, however, operational security considerations, not to mention unresolved technical issues and insufficient numbers of converted Mosquito aircraft, stymied Admiralty plans to use Highball immediately.[118] It did not prevent the Admiralty from pressuring Bomber Command into using Upkeep as soon as practicable.[119] In addition to Admiralty pressure, those who had championed both industrial paralysis theory and Barnes Wallis's invention had their personal reputations at stake. Calling off the attack was simply not an option for Air Marshal Charles Portal, Air Marshal Robert Saundby, Air Chief Marshal Ralph Cochrane, or other supporters on the Air Staff.[120] Having sacrificed much to have their theory of paralysis finally tested operationally, there was little room for doubt now in their minds that the means and methods for destroying the dams were coming together.[121] Although Sir Charles Portal began to downplay the anticipated effects a little over a month before the attacks, both he and Cochrane faced the daunting prospect of calling off the operation to their respective superiors, Churchill and Harris.[122] Both Churchill and Harris could deliver withering criticism if they felt that subordinates were indecisive and/or incompetent.

Material factors also ensured that Operation Chastise would take place. On 21 March 1943 Squadron "X," later renamed 617 Squadron, was established on paper with Wing Commander Guy Gibson commanding.[123] Gibson was given demanding orders: the squadron was to commence flying in four days' time, practicing low-level nighttime bomb delivery.[124] The introduction to Gibson's speech to his new unit leaves little doubt that it was developed to conduct a special operation:

> You're here to do a special job, you're here as a crack squadron, you're here to carry out a raid on Germany which, I am told, will have startling results. Some say it may even cut short the duration of the war. What the target is I can't tell you. Nor can I tell you where it is. All I can tell you is that you will have to practise low flying all day and all night until you know how to do it with your eyes shut.[125]

Squadron members and outside experts solved a number of problems quickly and efficiently through a mixture of determination, adaptability, and innovation.[126] A month after having been established on paper, 617 Squadron had already dropped 1,016 practice bombs and made hundreds of low-level mock attack runs over English dams.[127] The specially selected and trained men, flying heavily modified machines and delivering unique bombs, were ready for the mission.

The final factor driving the special operation was a factor that no amount of planning could avoid: geography and climate. In order to have the greatest destructive effect, Operation Chastise would have to be conducted when the dams contained their maximum level of water. According to calculations derived from scientific observation, domestic expertise, and available sources, the window for attacking the dams shrank to full-moon nights in mid-May.[128] The Möhne dam alone would contain an estimated 134 million tons of water during this crucial time.[129] By 15 May 1943, the special operation designed to collapse German industry had surmounted all challenges but one: contact with the enemy.

The attacks on the Ruhr Valley dams have been outlined in considerable detail in a number of sources.[130] Nineteen modified Type 464 Provisioning Lancasters departed at staggered times from RAF Scampton in three separate attack waves. The aircraft flew at extremely low altitude to avoid radar and circumvent known heavy flak concentrations and fighter bases. Two aircraft ended the mission early due to damage sustained, including an aircraft that flew so low it struck the ground and lost its weapon, while a third aborted due to mechanical failure. Of the sixteen remaining aircraft, eight failed to return. Five aircraft commenced attacks on the Möhne Dam in the face of heavy anti-aircraft defenses that became increasingly accurate as individual aircraft made repeated passes on the dam. After two near misses and one overshoot, two 617 Squadron Lancasters succeeded in placing their Upkeep bombs on target.[131] The Möhne Dam crumbled apart from the middle as anticipated by Wallis. Three aircraft, whose attacks were coordinated by Gibson, proceeded onto the Eder Dam where two of them succeeded in delivering their weapons. The Eder Dam breached as the last attacking aircraft was climbing away. Two aircraft bombed the Sorpe Dam but failed to breach it;[132] Upkeep was designed specifically to crack gravity dams. The remaining aircraft dropped its weapon on either the Ennepe or Bever Dam;[133] in any event both of these dams were still standing when dawn broke the following morning.

In addition to killing just over 1,300 people, the attacks caused initial panic among the local population and anger among senior German leaders.[134] As the damage done during the operation was put into context, Hitler and Propaganda Minister Josef Goebbels shifted focus on and affixed blame for the devastation caused by the raid to their preferred, racial-hatred-based scapegoats: the Jews.[135] In their eyes, a weapon so insidious must have been devised by someone of Jewish descent.[136] Albert Speer, Hitler's Minister of Armaments, recognized the significance of the British special operations effort, as he had put forward a similar idea weeks before:

On April 11, 1943, I proposed to Hitler that a committee of industrial specialists be set to determining the crucial targets in Soviet power production. Four weeks later, however, the first attempt was made—not by us but by the British air force—to influence the course of the war by destroying a single nerve center of the war economy. The principle followed was to paralyse a cross section, as it were—just as a motor can be made useless by the removal of ignition. On May 17, 1943, a mere nineteen bombers of the RAF tried to strike at our whole armaments industry by destroying the hydroelectric plants of the Ruhr.[137]

In a very limited respect the Air Staff planners had been vindicated; the destruction the Möhne and Eder dams had paralyzed certain sectors of German industry within the Ruhr Valley. In the short term, according to Speer, "industry was brought to a standstill" in the Ruhr for a few days but normal production resumed two weeks after the attack.[138] The *United States Strategic Bombing* Survey noted that flooding of the Koepchenwerk plant for three months caused "the impossibility to regulate voltage in the Ruhr area. The conditions in this area, therefore, became much worse."[139] One author summarized the damage as: "A hundred and twenty-five factories were either destroyed or badly damaged, nearly 3,000 hectares of arable land ruined, 25 bridges had vanished, and 21 more were badly damaged. The livestock losses were 6,500 cattle and pigs."[140] Looking over the longer term, however, Operation Chastise had little overall impact on German armaments production.

The unintended strategic effects of operation Chastise

Operation Chastise caused considerable damage but it did not accomplish its intended strategic effects of inducing German industrial paralysis and compelling the Germans to sue for peace. There were two primary moral effects of the special operation on the Germans. The first was to flame the desire for revenge against the British population in an equally spectacular way. Instead of annihilating German industrial capacity, production figures actually increased during the period.[141] As a result, the air war over Germany continued to be one of tactical attrition and area bombing for another 24 costly months. With few exceptions,[142] the unwavering focus of British bombing efforts from May 1943 until May 1945 was the nocturnal battering of German cities from the air. The second moral effect was to increase the sense of vulnerability that the Nazi leadership had regarding the network of dams that existed throughout occupied Europe. The war diary of the headquarters of the *Wehrmacht* noted with concern that some 227 other dams were vulnerable to attack and virtually undefended.[143]

The primary value of this specific special operation strategically, however, stemmed from its unintended consequences. The first and most important unintended consequence was the swaying of American public opinion. The breaching of the Möhne and Eder Dams provided Winston Churchill with an unequivocal demonstration of British courage, daring, and ingenuity at a crucial junction in Allied grand strategic discussions. At issue was the continued primacy of the

Pacific or European theater of war and the leadership role of Great Britain after the war was finished.[144] American political and military leaders were skeptical of British motives during discussions of grand strategy, especially when post-war political aspects were raised.[145] Within the American public there was the perception that Albion was seeking perfidious advantage at the expense of their blood and treasure, or that the British were playing an ancillary role in the war. According to a contemporary British assessment memorandum written for the War Cabinet in the year before Operation Chastise, the author noted that

> During 1940 British prestige stood very high in America. In the last twelve months it has greatly declined ... Unless facts are given more plainly now, the political consequences of the underestimation of Britain's part in the war may be serious in America.[146]

The success of the special operation provided Churchill with a timely, sensational example with which to bolster American public support for Britain.[147] In his speech to the US Congress on 19 May, the day after the raid, Churchill outlined the contributions that Britain was making to win the war, emphasizing the defeat of the *Afrika-Korps* in Tunisia and the impact of Operation Chastise:

> The condition to which the great centres of German war industry, and of particularly the Ruhr, are being reduced, is one of unparalleled devastation. You have just read of the destruction of the great dams which feed the canals, and provide power to the enemy munitions works. That was a gallant operation, costing eight out of the nineteen Lancaster bombers employed, but it will play a very far-reaching part in reducing German munitions output.[148]

Just months before the raid, a senior British official summarized the strategic value of any British military action against the Axis, including special operations, on the population of the United States: "The best ~~publicity~~ propaganda of all is a big and successful attack on Germany or Italy" (correction in document).[149] Operation Chastise suited this purpose admirably and had the additional effect of bolstering British morale at home.

Churchill's speech to Congress alluded to another unintended consequence of this special operation. One consequence was the diversion of substantial military and civilian resources to defend and fix the dams.[150] At the time of the attack only the Möhne Dam was defended to any extent. After the raid the equivalent of a division's equivalent of troops, or some 15,000 personnel with their equipment, were tasked exclusively with the protection of the dams of the Ruhr and Wupper rivers.[151] In addition, 7,000 *Organisation Todt* workers were diverted from construction work on the Atlantic Wall to conduct repairs.[152] The work was only completed in September and required the Germans to scavenge all available generators from surrounding factories.

Finally, Operation Chastise had a strategic effect that has been overlooked by previous authors, namely that it was one of the catalysts for diverting substantial

German resources to, and spurring the production of, the so-called "wonder weapons," or *Wunderwaffen*. Since 1942 Adolf Hitler had been obsessed with retaliatory strikes against British cities in response to increasingly destructive raids by Bomber Command, especially after the massive devastation and loss of life caused during raids on Hamburg from 24/25 July until 3 August 1943. The breaching of the Möhne Dam was more than just an audacious special operation; it was also a shocking blow to prestige that had also killed numerous Germans.[153] In fact, the raid resulted in the deaths of almost 1,300 persons which the Bomber Command War Diary noted "was a new record for a raid on Germany, easily exceeding the 693 people killed at Dortmund in a raid earlier in May in which 596 aircraft took part!"[154] Although the actual number of Germans killed in the raid was less than half the number of total casualties, with the bulk comprised of Russian and East European prisoners of war in a camp near the Eder river,[155] the Dambusters raid nevertheless made an impression on the senior Nazi leaders for the scale of destruction caused by so few aircraft.

Nazi Germany, however, possessed few military responses that could strike Britain in an equally audacious way. Given the defeats at Stalingrad and Tunisia in previous months, the gap between official statements of revenge and a lack of capability became a real concern to German decision makers.[156] In terms of retaliatory capabilities, German losses in night raids over England, for example, had been prohibitive and the much-anticipated four-engine "strategic" bomber, the He-177 *Greif*, continued to have considerable design and testing difficulties.[157] One promising technology pursued by German scientists was jet and rocket propulsion. Captain Walter Dornberger and Wernher von Braun had been developing the first ballistic missiles for the German *Heer* since the early 1930s. Although it is difficult to determine precisely how influential the Dams Raid were in Hitler's decision-making calculus, they directly or indirectly spurred his interest in and involvement with the development of the "V-weapons" in the following ways: by confirming to him that Hermann Göring was incapable of managing a Luftwaffe that was increasingly unable to defend Germany or destroy important targets in Britain or the Soviet Union, even though the development of the Fi-103 "Cherry Stone" (V-1 "buzzbomb") was proceeding;[158] by reinforcing Albert Speer's growing conviction that Germany should have the means to conduct attacks on "bottleneck" targets of the Allies;[159] and, most importantly, by translating Speer's conviction into engaging Hitler more directly in the V-2 program in early July 1943.[160]

Although Hitler had been briefed by the members of the Peenemünde staff previously, and apparently did not understand some of the basic characteristics of the system, he now gave the V-2 the highest priority in the list of Reich production efforts.[161] Although more indicative of his leadership style, Hitler nevertheless imposed directives on the most insignificant production details for the weapon, such as the location of production facilities and the ethnic composition of the production workers.[162] More importantly, Hitler believed that he had found a solution to Allied quantitative superiority in weapons such as V-2: "This is the decisive weapon of the war, and what is more it can be produced with relatively small resources."[163] He interpreted the *Wunderwaffen* as the salvation for the Reich; once unleashed in quantity, the Allies would have no other choice but to request peace terms favorable to Germany. Scarce resources were increasingly diverted to support the development and production of a mind-boggling array of improved systems and new technologies that would turn the tide of the war.[164] Due in no small part to Hitler's personal interest in the *Wunderwaffen*, as well as his belief in their decisive effects, the vast majority were deployed too late to have a strategic impact on the outcome of the war.[165] Only in June 1944, for example, did Hitler retaliate against London for the mounting blows to German pride, including Operation Chastise.[166]

Although Operation Chastise had been an exemplary display of British special operations skill that produced a number of unintentional consequences, it failed in its anticipated goal: shutting down the factories of the Ruhr valley and depriving the Nazi leaders of their industrial capacity to make war. As an individual action, the special operation had temporary strategic effect but it did not enhance the military or strategic performance of the Allies. During prolonged engagements, the challenge for special operations is to inflict moral and material damage on an adversary, in conjunction with conventional forces, in a coordinated manner to improve the military and strategic performance of both. As Chastise demonstrated, however, there was a considerable disconnect between the material damage that the Air Staff planners sought to inflict and the moral effects they actually achieved. Understanding the relationship that exists between the moral and material aspects of strategy is crucial in utilizing special operations in the most effective manner strategically.

4 Death by a thousand cuts
Special operations, attrition, and the nature of warfare

> It is not war that has failed to effect its purpose. It is the negation of skilful warfare—the war of exhaustion—which has revealed its essential senselessness.
>
> ("The Failure of the War of Exhaustion")[1]

For the men of 617 Squadron, Operation Chastise and subsequent attacks against the Dortmund-Ems Canal system demonstrated their undoubted courage, as well as the price of valor. The unit was almost rendered combat ineffective due to mounting losses from their low-level attack profile. The Dambusters Raid failed in its penultimate purpose of causing the collapse of German industry. The German industrial system proved to be more complex, flexible, and adaptive in nature than a portion of the Air Staff had originally concluded. A combination of wishful thinking, driven by a desire to achieve the maximum effect for minimal effort that had sustained the Royal Air Force after the First World War, prolonged interest in the destruction of the Ruhr Valley dams long after the senior leaders of Bomber Command were faced with unequivocal proof of the resilience of German industry and civilian morale. Finally, the raid failed in its ultimate goal of influencing the moral resolve of senior Nazi leaders. A single "critical node" that could compel Adolf Hitler and his cabal to surrender, if such a target existed, eluded the Allies for the duration of the war. Despite the results of Chastise and other attempts to inflict strategic paralysis failing to achieve the moral collapse of their adversaries, such theories remain prevalent even today.

This chapter argues that the means to understanding how special operations improve military and strategic performance is embedded within the body of strategic theory that discusses the approaches of annihilation and attrition. In particular, both approaches place different emphasis on the moral and material dimensions of the struggle. Originally seen as complementary means strategically to achieving victory, subsequent interpretations have polarized attrition and annihilation and placed them in opposition to one another. Attrition has been depicted as prolonged tactical erosion devoid of inspiration or meaningful strategic purpose. The pursuit of military excellence in its purest form, the annihilation of the enemy forces through superior maneuver, became distanced and divorced from internal and external constraints that make the practice of strategy difficult.

Practitioners of irregular warfare, when faced with qualitative inferiority and prolonged struggle, restored the linkages between the moral and material components of attrition at the strategic level when they formulated their own theories. When considering the use of special operations for extended periods as adjuncts to, or in concert with, conventional forces, understanding the relationship between the moral and material components of attrition is crucial to prevent their eventual tactical annihilation due to flawed assumptions about the nature of their adversaries and of strategy.

The preceding chapters have demonstrated that faulty conceptualizations of strategy can lead to misguided expectations for special operations. The goal of strategic paralysis is to inflict shock on an adversary, annihilating at a stroke their ability to resist. Suggesting that annihilation is the only route to strategic success can lead to a form of hubris that implies elegance or momentum at the operational level of war can overcome the inhibitors of decisive victory: incompetence, friction, and the fog of war. The assumptions that underpin annihilation's primacy include: confidence in one's own operational infallibility and ability to constantly dominate an adversary; near-perfect knowledge of an adversary's disposition and intentions; a static, non-reactive foe; a seamless sequential flow of actions unimpeded by friction; and operations unconstrained by the tyranny of logistics. Warfare, and by extension strategy, is a competition characterized by ebbs and flows of fortune and opportunity, as adversaries adapt and apply force in order to achieve their conflicting goals.

Attempts to grasp strategy intellectually have been hobbled by the vastness and complexity of warfare. At its most basic level, war involves the organized use of violence to impose the will of one group upon another.[2] Authors have wrestled with various aspects of warfare: its origins, value, specific instruments, character, and nature. Many authors are content to discuss strategy within the context of recent technological developments or the role played by specific branches of the armed services.[3] A few, however, have attempted to articulate more comprehensive theories of strategy and its relationship to warfare. A common trait shared by authors such as Carl von Clausewitz, Hans Delbrück, and Robert Osgood, to name but a few, has been the development of typologies to distinguish between forms of war and relative levels of effort. These forms of war include limited war, total war, absolute war, war in reality, war of annihilation, and war of attrition.

Much like special operations in practice, attrition in theory arguably was one of the most misunderstood strategic concepts of the twentieth century.[4] Some of the confusion can be ascribed to difficulties associated with translating texts. For example, Carl von Clausewitz's term *"verzehrender krieg,"* which has been rendered into English as "war of attrition," is more accurately translated as "war of consumption."[5] Adding to the confusion are different translations of term *"Ermattungsstrategie"* by Hans Delbrück. Some scholars, including Walter Renfroe, suggest that it should be rendered "strategy of attrition" whereas others suggest that "strategy of exhaustion" is more accurate.[6] Finally, a handful of influential theorists, writing in the wake of the First World War, ascribed a pejorative value to the term attrition that continues to influence perceptions today.[7]

Advocating strategic attrition, or strategies of attrition, has become the intellectual equivalent of inflexibly advocating the slaughter practiced by British general officer "butchers and bunglers" during the First World War.[8]

Understanding the relationship between attrition and strategy is further complicated by the different connotations the term "attrition" has to various military and civilian defense professionals. Functionally the term has a specific and quantifiable meaning. Logisticians and those who program military simulations, for example, find the term useful in their attempts to measure the combat effectiveness of forces in the field.[9] In addition, attrition as a functional concept is linked with retention rates of Service personnel.[10] The moral dimension of attrition tends to be ignored at this level. At the strategic level, this chapter argues that attrition describes a method of imposing one's will upon an adversary through both material and non-material means.

Special operators are familiar with the functional aspects of attrition. Perhaps no other military instrument of power is more sensitive to its effects than SOF. Attrition plays a significant role in the selection process for special operators. Rigorous training, tailored to test an individual's psychological and physical boundaries depending on the operating environment, limits the overall number of available special operators.[11] In addition, the equipment used by SOF is tailored to insert them over large distances clandestinely or covertly, into forbidding terrain, in order to gather intelligence, train indigenous forces, and/or gain temporary firepower superiority over larger and more heavily equipped forces.[12] In other words, small numbers of SOF can conduct missions of limited duration until the fielded forces or force pool requires reconstitution or is exhausted due to tactical attrition. The effects of friction, which often have significant force attrition implications, can quickly debilitate the limited forces available to conduct special operations. For example, during the 1982 campaign to retake the Falkland Islands, almost two dozen Special Air Service Regiment operators were lost in a single air crash when a bird struck their helicopter during a routine cross-decking operation.[13] In addition to the immediate effect that the crash had on operations, which included the death of one of the only individuals adequately trained on newly acquired American Stinger anti-aircraft missiles, one author notes that such attrition was "made worse by the seniority of the men involved ... It would take the Regiment a decade and more to replace their accumulated knowledge and priceless experience."[14] Given the finite quantity of special operations resources, the sensitivity of SOF to losses, and the time it takes to develop the relative maturity and experience of a special operator, it is imperative that they are used for missions that promise the maximum strategic return. As discussed in previous chapters, the allure of inflicting paralysis or "shock and awe" upon an adversary, using special operations, is difficult if not impossible to achieve strategically in all but the most atypical circumstances.[15] As planners for the global war on terrorism are discovering, the strategic conundrum of special operations is how to use them for maximum effect in a sustained campaign, and integrating their combined effects with those achieved by conventional forces, without destroying SOF in the process.

One of the reasons that special operations must be planned with care, to achieve significant effect, relates to the unconventional mindset of the operators themselves. Special operators seek to resolve problems judiciously by doing the unexpected, such as operating in forbidding terrain, and they are willing to push themselves and their equipment beyond their performance envelopes. This can lead to equipment losses and fratricide of the type observed in Iraq and Afghanistan. Sometimes this willingness to accept unfavorable odds, and the methods used to motivate SOF, can be their undoing. For example, Egyptian planners harnessed religious elements to motivate their SOF. The *shahid*, or "martyr" complex, was useful to achieve the objectives of single missions but not for sustained action. During the 1973 Arab-Israeli War, for example, "[Egyptian] special operations slowed the Israelis and caused confusion, anxiety, and surprise in the Israeli rear, although at a high cost in lives of highly trained and motivated Egyptian troops."[16]

This chapter posits that the historical misuse of special operations reflects more than just a misunderstanding of their limitations; its roots lie in the difficulty of translating strategy into practice in all of its forms. A key to understanding the translation of strategy into practice, encompassing the mishandling of special operations, is the concept of attrition. Confusion regarding attrition stems in part from an inability to distinguish between tactical and strategic attrition, as well as the dynamic that exists between attrition and its counterpart: annihilation. For example, the *functional* attrition of special or conventional forces is readily understood as it describes a tangible, linear decrease in men and materiel. Strategic attrition, however, is not divorced from this practical dimension of strategy but it encompasses an aspect that complicates linear explanation of strategy: moral attrition, or the erosion of an adversary's will to fight. Tactical annihilation of specific targets, especially by special operators and their allies working in "safe" rear areas, can have a considerable impact on an adversary's morale. When used in conjunction with the repeated blows delivered by conventional forces, and in a non-linear manner that accounts for the complexities of strategy, the desired result of special operations can be the capitulation of the enemy more swiftly and economically. This chapter argues, therefore, that attrition *strategically* is a cumulative phenomenon that must account for both its material and moral aspects. The strategic value of special operations, by extension, lies in the collective weakening of an adversary's combat power and will to fight. Much like anti-submarine warfare, individual successes are important but not decisive; the strategic value of special operations lies in the effect that their contribution makes either to victory or in meeting more limited policy aims.

In order to understand how attrition relates to both special operations and the nature of strategy, various interpretations of the concept will be explored in this chapter. Attrition at the strategic level is a common element of both strategy and special operations. Theorists have stressed the dynamic that exists between attrition and annihilation, as well as the moral and material dimensions of each, in their excursions on strategy. This includes the "conventional" strategic theories of Carl von Clausewitz, Hans Delbrück, and Aleksandr A. Svechin. However, as the two preceding chapters have demonstrated, a number of theoretical and practical interpreters of Clausewitz's and Delbrück's work have emphasized the differences between moral and material aspects of strategy to the point where the annihilation of moral resolve could be accomplished without prolonged effort. Material struggle is the realm of attrition, whereas the acme of skill embodied in inflicting moral collapse through superior skill, technology, and generalship is the realm of annihilation. The relationship between attrition and annihilation at the operational and strategic level was re-examined in the theories of Thomas Edward Lawrence and Mao Zedong, both of whom were irregular warfare practitioners confronted by qualitatively superior adversaries.

Having laid the theoretical foundations of the concept of attrition and annihilation, this chapter suggests that the conceptual prism of non-linearity studies is a useful method of explaining the relationship that exists between attrition, special operations, and strategy. This theory, although useful as a guiding theme, nevertheless has its own limitations. If war is nothing more than a series of disparate, discrete events, one could conclude that strategy cannot be created in any logical fashion whatsoever. Such conclusions miss a fundamental point of strategy. Strategy is the bridge between policy and available means, including the use of military force.[17] Strategies of annihilation, based on a seamless flow of events ending in the collapse, rout, or total destruction of an adversary, do not anticipate or account for non-linear impediments or the "chaotic" implications, or unintended consequences, of their own actions. These strategies are also predicated upon excessively optimistic or unrealistic projections. For example, the various "ideal" plans developed by Alfred Graf von Schlieffen were based on consistent march rates, effective coordination between Corps, and numerous additional reserves to sustain the advance.[18] A series of events, from unanticipated Belgian resistance through to intercepted German communications, conspired to derail the eventual execution of the plan in 1914.[19] A specific strategy, and the planning process associated with it, must be sufficiently flexible to adapt to the non-linear aspects of war that Clausewitz outlined: fog of war; friction; the realm of chance; the culminating point of victory; and the principle of continuity. The artful aspect of strategy, as opposed to the scientific, lies in using special operations to improve military and strategic performance. The challenge is to use special operations, in conjunction with conventional forces, in an unorthodox but sustainable manner over time to wear down the resolve and resources of an adversary over the course of a conflict without one's own forces succumbing to attrition.

Conventional theories of attrition and annihilation

Strategy is based on offense and defense, reflecting the competitive and confrontational nature of war. Put simply, adversaries have choices regarding the course of activity they wish to pursue, based on their aims and available resources. The simplest route to develop a comprehensive strategic theory would be to assess the offensive and defensive options available at the various levels of war—from tactical to strategic.[20] The resulting matrix, while useful from a theoretical perspective, cannot display the contradictions and paradoxes inherent to the diversity, complexity, and number of variables associated with strategy.[21] For example, a theory of warfare would have to explain the reasons why some wars have total destruction as their aim, while others are fought for limited objectives.[22] Additionally, although the defensive is appealing as the stronger form of warfare, it is passive. Defenders surrender the initiative to their adversary, allowing the latter to choose the time and place of the offensive.[23] A number of theorists have spent a lifetime wrestling with these contradictions and have concluded that warfare assumes two base forms: annihilation/destruction, which is characterized by an offensive that crushes the armed forces of an adversary and wins decisive victory; or a more costly, prolonged struggle of attrition which alternates between the offensive and defensive.

Theories of the dual forms of strategy in warfare: Clausewitz, Delbrück, and reflections on military revolutions

Clausewitz developed his theory of war in the wake of a military revolution that changed the face of conflict as preceding generations had known it. The "system" of war utilized to great effect by Napoleon Bonaparte melded a number of elements into an offensive force that outmaneuvered and outfought most of its European adversaries. Prior to the development of the Napoleonic system, the armies of the monarchs of Europe tended to be manned by the dregs of society reinforced by mercenaries.[24] Pay for a soldier was low, training consisted of intricate drills, a military career in the ranks was looked down upon socially, discipline was harshly enforced, and officer commissions could be purchased. Military commanders, who engaged in elaborate maneuvers in preference to decisive clashes of arms, might capitulate if an adversary cut off their lines of communications, or sources of supply, rather than fight their way through. The French Revolution, however, not only deposed the Bourbon monarch but also unleashed a wave of French nationalism that motivated large numbers of conscripts. What the conscripts lacked in training they made up for in enthusiasm and quantitative superiority over their adversaries. In France, military theory and reforms undertaken prior to the Revolution led to the development of a truly formidable military organization whose infantry, artillery, and cavalry could be orchestrated to break the rigid formations of their opponents.[25] Under the control of a dynamic leader such as Napoleon, who created independent combined arms Corps, "decisive" victories such as Austerlitz and Jena/Auerstadt were possible.[26]

From his experiences and studies, Clausewitz developed a theory regarding the nature of warfare and its characteristics, including the offensive and defensive. Embedded within his discussion of offense are two concepts relevant to the subject of attrition and annihilation: the principle of continuity and the culminating point of victory. Put simply, the principle of continuity suggests that once offensive actions are taken they should continue relentlessly until the adversary capitulates. Having achieved surprise and with the initiative firmly in control, an offensive should not offer an adversary any opportunities to regroup, reconstitute, or regain the initiative. The goal of such sustained activity is to annihilate an adversary's will and means to resist. Careless or casual readers of Clausewitz's unparalleled, yet complicated and flawed theory are bound to miss the distinction that the author makes between war in theory and war in practice, just as they are prone to mistake the specific level of war Clausewitz uses to frame his point.[27] The principle of continuity is the ideal to which all practitioners of the art of war should strive; it is nothing more than a form of war posited at the most utopian, abstract level. In reality, however, certain elements of war can thwart even the most carefully planned campaigns.

In the concept of the culminating point of victory, Clausewitz develops his argument for war's form in reality. In its abstract conceptualization war is devoid of elements such as friction, the fog of war, logistical constraints, limited reserves, and attrition. By discussing the reality of warfare that accounts for two or more adversaries pursuing competing goals, Clausewitz highlights one of the many endemic paradoxes of strategy. The more battlefield success an army has, and the farther it advances, the weaker it becomes while the defender retreats closer to his lines of supplies and theoretically becomes stronger.[28] Although the surest way to victory is a relentless offensive, sustaining and controlling nearly continuous offensive operations becomes increasingly difficult through space and over time.[29] Even the most motivated troops cannot maintain the offensive indefinitely. Sooner or later, casualties, equipment and personnel maintenance, lack of sleep, extended supply lines, and security/occupation detachments will sap the strength from an offensive.[30] Other environmental factors play a role as well, including geography, climate, and political relations with coalition partners. Eventually the offensive will weaken to the point that it must halt in order to regain strength and repair damage. During that time, the defender has an opportunity to seize the initiative, restore moral and material losses and go on the offensive until victorious or its forces reach the culminating point.[31]

Clausewitz was suggesting in the principle of continuity that warfare is linear in character in its purest theoretical form. In practice, however, war is characterized by unforeseen or unintended consequences, and enemy adaptation when one accounts for the influence of variables upon the object of war such as political goals, the nature of human beings, and the nature of the struggle itself. Victory in war goes to the side best able to adjust to changing circumstances and achieve its goals *cumulatively*, whether on the offensive, defensive, or a combination of both:

> In this absurd manner it has become a basic assumption that defensive battles are meant merely to repulse the enemy, and not to destroy him. We consider this a most damaging error, in fact a confusion between form and substance. We maintain unequivocally that the form of warfare that we call defense not only offers greater probability of victory than attack, but that its victories can attain the same proportions and results. Moreover, this applies not only to the *aggregate success* of all the engagements that make up a campaign, but to *each individual* battle, provided there is no lack of strength and determination [emphasis in original].[32]

In other words, success in war is dependent on the ability to shift between the offense and defense, for the purposes of attrition or annihilation, as the circumstances dictate so long as the political will and resources exist.

Clausewitz identified two forms of war in his last book of *On War*, where he clearly delineated absolute war from real war. Absolute war had as its objective the total defeat of the enemy; friendly forces should concentrate exclusively on an adversary's centers of gravity and gain victory as swiftly as possible. Real war, on the other hand:

> consists of separate successes each unrelated to the next, as in a match consisting of several games. The earlier games have no effect upon the later. All that counts is the total score, and each separate result makes its contribution toward the total.[33]

Clausewitz suggests that the decision to adopt the methods of absolute or real war depends on a number of factors: quantitative superiority; qualitative superiority; time; political will; achievable goals; and adequate space. Unfortunately for military theorists and strategists, his discussion of the forms of war is incomplete but has been explored by a number of his interpreters.[34]

The most noteworthy heir to Clausewitz's discussion of the forms of war is Hans Delbrück. An historian whose life's work was the study of the art of war, Delbrück's primary academic legacy is a unique approach to military history that he called *Sachkritik*. *Sachkritik* was Delbrück's method of testing the veracity of ancient historical sources. He would walk battlefield sites and compare statistics and locations cited by classical authors with known contemporary scientific quantities such as daily marching rates and span of control of large armies. In a number of cases, he challenged the assertions of authors such as Herodotus and Julius Caesar, proving logically that their works contained sins of commission, omission, or both.[35] Numerous contemporary classics and ancient history scholars were chagrined by Delbrück's conclusions but his work nevertheless remains influential to this day.[36]

Much like Clausewitz, Delbrück grappled with the significance of military revolutions. Along the way he became intrigued with the idea of forms of war. Delbrück emphatically posited that strategy could be reduced to two forms: a war of annihilation and a war of attrition.[37] According to Delbrück, the key components of annihilation are superior numbers and mobility. For political or cultural reasons, those who advocate a strategy of annihilation seek to decide the conflict as quickly and decisively as possible; the consuming focus of annihilation, in consequence, is decisive battle and pursuit until an adversary capitulates. The goals and the process of a strategy of annihilation are linear and uncomplicated. As the preceding chapters have highlighted, proponents of strategic paralysis theory simply took the strategy of annihilation farther, suggesting that a single center of gravity is the moral and material hub of a system, causing collapse if struck or destroyed.

The dynamics of war, however, rarely proceed in a straightforward manner. Political considerations, especially if coalition partners are involved, may demand the pursuit of options less risky than an offensive on which all wagers are placed. A numerically or technologically inferior adversary may choose to refuse battle, and try and sap the will of the enemy to continue to fight, until the odds are more favorable. The goal of a strategy of attrition is to wear down an opponent *morally and materially* so that they abandon the struggle. A crucial consideration while engaged in a strategy of attrition is that "one's own damages must be taken very carefully into account."[38] Delbrück suggests that a strategy of attrition that does not account for the costs relative to the anticipated gains reflects poor judgment and statesmanship. More importantly, such a callous attitude could well ruin a state that sought to achieve limited goals through attrition.[39] A strategy of attrition can be just as risky as a strategy of annihilation, should one lose sight of its purpose.

Another reason for choosing a strategy of attrition, or if circumstances impose the choice, is that forces may not be available in sufficient space or time to conduct the focused offensive. Indeed, Delbrück would agree with Clausewitz's assertion that "the very nature of war impedes the *simultaneous concentration of all forces*."[40] What separates a strategy of attrition from one of annihilation is that the former does not subsume maneuver to battle. Engagements rather exist anywhere along an axis consisting of maneuver at one pole and battle on the other (see Figure 4.1). A strategy of attrition, therefore, is a non-linear approach to achieving one's political goals: it is characterized by shifts between battle and maneuver and utilizes non-military means so that "the outcome of battle can be counterbalanced" when required.[41] In other words, a strategy of attrition is a strategy of choices:

> With limited resources at his disposal, the *Ermattungsstratege* (the practitioner of a strategy of attrition) must decide which of several means of conducting war will best suit his purpose, when to fight and when to maneuver, when to obey the law of "daring" and when to obey that of "economy of force."[42]

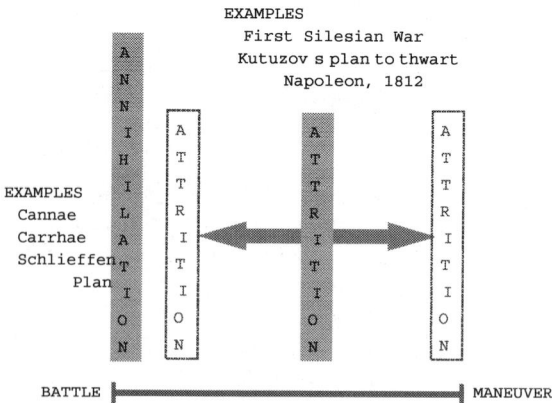

Figure 4.1 Delbrück's forms and poles

There are several implications for special operations in the preceding quote. As great raids, special operations have been viewed as the embodiment of both the law of daring and economy of force. As a result, special operations have been used for or suggested as the arbiters of strategic paralysis theory. As adversaries prove more complex and resilient than initially thought, and conflicts extend in duration, special operations have been used tactically for audacious strikes or to pare down guerrilla infrastructure with little reference towards the principle of continuity. When SOF get closer to the point of combat ineffectiveness or overstretch because they are being used to conduct tactical actions against numerically superior foes, as the next chapter demonstrates, the response historically has been to expand organizations at the expense of overall quality.

Within the strategy of choices, knowing when to make the right choices while being unaware of the adversary's next move at the same time places a tremendous burden upon the commander. A requirement for successful command in the face of these conditions, according to Delbrück, is decisiveness. In conjunction with genius, decisiveness allows a commander to manage the uncertainties inherent in war.[43] The wise commander understands that he is bound by chance, uncertainty, and friction in war but is not paralyzed into inaction by them. Just as political considerations and other elements including friction and the fog of war prevent war from taking its absolute, completely destructive form, such considerations also impose themselves upon decisiveness and genius:

> It was not the battles won by Frederick the Great which made him a great general, but rather his political acumen and the conformity of his strategy with political reality. No strategical system can become self-sufficient; once an attempt is made to make it so, to divorce it from its political context, the strategist becomes a menace to the state.[44]

Politics are not the only influence on the strategic course adopted; social, cultural, and economic considerations play a role as well. As with politics, these considerations can change over time.[45] Although the preemptive campaign against Sicily in 415 B.C. suited the Athenian temperament better than the successful Periclean strategy of attrition used previously,[46] it was a disastrous choice given the political and military climate of the time. In contrast, the seditious counsel provided by the Athenian Alcibiades to Persian monarch Tissaphernes was a judicious rationale for a strategy of attrition that would cost the Persians little and lead to the mutual exhaustion of their Greek enemies.[47]

Delbrück performed a great service for strategists by providing an historical context and expanded discussion of a number of Clausewitz's underdeveloped themes, including the forms of war. Whereas Clausewitz would suggest that the forms of war exist in a flexible continuum, alternating between attrition and annihilation to suit needs and specific circumstances, Delbrück would argue that such forms are exclusive. In Delbrück's view, war is characterized by either attrition or annihilation for individual states at specific times; it is a decision undertaken by a commander based on the internal and external variables outlined above, such as political goals and correlation of forces. In other words, once the decision is made to pursue a linear or non-linear strategy, one is committed to this strategy for the duration of the conflict. Delbrück dismissed suggestions that attrition could be a precursor to a decisive battle of annihilation, much less that an adversary could be annihilated through attrition.[48] The limited goals of attrition do not allow for the annihilation of an adversary; the political rationale for both runs in diametric opposition. As we will see below, irregular warfare practitioners and theorists returned to a construct that resembles Clausewitz's original idea in their own flexible frameworks for understanding strategy and its forms.

Since the First World War, theorists have been using the framework and forms of strategy developed by Clausewitz and refined by Delbrück when advocating force planning requirements in the face of the growing scope and complexity of war. In some cases, the decision has been conscious. Aleksandr Svechin,[49] for example, invoked the strategy of attrition as a counter to the theories of "successive operations"[50] and "deep operations"[51] developed by Vladimir Triandafillov and Mikhail Tukhachevskii respectively. Svechin perceived that "deep operations," which intellectually was related to Fuller's "Strategical Paralysis," was an ideal strategy based on maneuver that focused on annihilation, or destruction of an adversary's army, to the exclusion of all else.[52] Such a strategy, he argued, bore little resemblance to strategy in practice. Svechin acknowledged the unique logic of war that thwarts the most meticulous operational planning:

> With a strategy of destruction, which assigns such unique and overriding importance to an armed clash with the enemy, the situation acquires the characteristics of a kaleidoscopic spectacle: one click of a decisive operation produces a completely new, unexpected picture which is wholly unpredictable. In a strategy of destruction the day after an operation is shrouded in a thick fog.[53]

Destruction could become an *idée fixe* in the mind of the commander, limiting his flexibility through an unhealthy obsession with the programmed "decisive point" of the offensive. Echoing Delbrück, Svechin suggested that attrition placed additional command burdens on the executive in exchange for flexibility of thought and action:

> A strategy of attrition in no way renounces in principle the destruction of enemy personnel as a goal of an operation. But in this it sees only a part of the mission of the armed front rather than the entire mission. Geographical objectives and secondary operations become much more important when a strategy of destruction is rejected.[54]

Svechin did not believe that a strategy of attrition was applicable in all cases. Rather the specific conditions that existed in the Soviet Union in the mid-1920s favored its adoption. Not only did the Soviet Union not possess the required resources for a series of decisive operations, but also the potential costs far outweighed the political or economic gains of a country struggling to industrialize.⁵⁵ Similar arguments linking military means and forms of strategy with desired policy ends have been used by authors alarmed at a lack of national military preparations.⁵⁶

Other theorists have framed discussions of distinct forms of strategy without directly acknowledging the influence of Clausewitz or Delbrück.⁵⁷ American naval officer J.C. Wylie, for example, suggested that strategy consisted of two forms: sequential and cumulative. A sequential strategy is the linear approach to warfighting. Deviation from such a strategy can have significant consequences: "The total pattern of all the discrete or separate actions makes up, serially, the entire sequence of the war. If at any stage of the war one of these actions had happened differently, then the remainder of the sequence would have had a different pattern."⁵⁸ In contrast, a cumulative strategy is non-linear and uses all available options, including psychological or economic warfare, to achieve goals indirectly. The directness of the path to victory does not matter so much as the net effect: "Each individual [action] is no more than a single statistic, an isolated plus or minus, in arriving at the final result."⁵⁹ In the end, the method used matters little to Wylie. The goal of a strategy is to assert control over an adversary; destruction is only one of the methods available.⁶⁰

In addition, other writers have utilized the contrasting strategic forms, first developed by Clausewitz and Delbrück, as a method of explaining why belligerents have adopted specific military courses of action.⁶¹ Distinguishing between forms of strategy is useful intellectually in trying to grasp the complexity inherent in war. The danger, however, as discussed in preceding chapters, is that some observers have attempted to articulate a "pure" form of military strategy, embodied in annihilation and paralysis theory, which achieves desired ends painlessly. Special operations, as exemplars of military skill and puissance, have naturally been linked as the arbiters of such strategies. Theorists of irregular warfare, however, have understood that conflict is most often a protracted struggle, until the weak are sufficiently powerful to challenge the strong. Only by amalgamating forms, for the purpose of strategic attrition and to convince the opponent that the cost of victory is too high, is victory possible. For special operations, which are the application of irregular warfare concepts and principles by conventional military powers, many of the factors associated with prolonged struggle including the principle of continuity apply regardless of technological developments.

Theories of the dual forms of strategy in irregular wars: Lawrence, Mao, and creating the conditions for revolution

Two twentieth-century developments renewed interest in strategies of attrition and annihilation. The first development was the creation, use, and adoption of nuclear weapons. Nuclear weapons, when mated to accurate, long-range missiles, made absolute war a possibility. A strategy of annihilation could theoretically take as little as 30 minutes to implement. The proliferation of nuclear weapons to other major powers such as the Soviet Union and China, as well as international legal restraints on the use of force, complicated the strategic calculus built on decisive battle with an adversary. A strategy of annihilation might result in retaliation in kind; both powers had the capability to destroy each other completely barring the effects of friction and chance. This strategic dilemma persuaded some theorists to re-examine options for the use of nuclear weapons for tactical purposes that did not envision the complete destruction of an adversary.[62] The strategy of attrition appeared in other forms as theories of "limited war."[63]

Presuming adequate numbers and sufficient will to use them, nuclear weapons appeared to allow the concept of annihilation to reach the absolute state that Clausewitz had suggested was unachievable. Achieving limited goals using finite means had been the basis of the strategy of attrition expounded by Clausewitz and Delbrück and this seemed to fit well in an era where assured nuclear destruction was a possibility. Irregular warfare, or the use of organized violence for political purposes by those fighting against vastly qualitatively superior adversaries, exists on the other end of the strategic spectrum. Thomas Edward Lawrence and Mao Zedong both contributed to the theoretical restoration of strategy of attrition that accounts for the moral and material dimensions of conflict. Their ideas are useful in explaining how special operations improve military and strategic performance. Special operations are characterized by the paradoxical combination of numerical inferiority and limited tactical superiority, applied to achieve limited goals, but contributing to strategic success cumulatively.

The theories of irregular warfare developed by Lawrence and Mao share a number of similarities. Both theories, for example, resulted from serious reflection after initial failures.[64] In assessing the reasons for failure, Lawrence and Mao realized that future success is predicated upon building the strength of their own forces, while simultaneously weakening those of their adversary.[65] Their individual strategies had to be tailored to suit a range of local political, military, economic, social, cultural, and environmental conditions.[66] As Mao discovered early in his revolutionary career, merely following other approaches dogmatically without accounting for local conditions was a recipe for failure.[67]

In Lawrence's specific case, he understood that previous British plans to use Arab tribesmen against the Turkish Army were doomed to fail. Nomadic Arab culture was based on raiding, not disciplined fighting against forces advised by the Germans and equipped with the implements of "industrial" war.[68] Using vast areas of desert for cover and mobility, against a Turkish Army sitting in isolated garrisons and dependent on vulnerable rail-borne lines, Lawrence devised a strategy to make the best use of Bedouin cultural traits.[69] His strategy was based on careful consideration of elements within three categories: "the Algebraical element of things, a Biological element of lives, and the Psychological element of ideas."[70] The goal of this strategy, however, was not the annihilation of Turkish forces. Instead, Lawrence wanted to utilize a maneuver-based strategy of attrition: "If we were patient and superhuman-skilled, we could follow the direction of [Maurice de] Saxe and reach victory without battle, by pressing our advantages mathematical and psychological."[71] Pure maneuver, however, would take an inordinate amount of time. In order to accomplish the task quicker, Lawrence suggested attrition that combined battle and maneuver to weaken Turkish garrisons:

We could develop a highly-mobile, highly equipped striking force of the smallest size, and use it successively at distributed points of the Turkish line, to make them strengthen their posts beyond the defensive minimum of twenty men. This would be a short cut to success.[72]

More importantly, Lawrence understood that weakening his adversary prior to the decisive battle, while preserving his own strength, was the key to victory in Palestine.[73] Success in this case was Turkish withdrawal from the Arab lands, to achieve Lawrence's personal goal of freeing those lands from the Ottoman Empire.[74]

Freeing lands is also a major theme of the works of Mao Zedong. More specifically, Mao's political purpose was freedom for China from two different threats. The first was the internal reactionary forces and counter-revolutionary influences that battled with the Communist forces for control of China. These reactionary forces included the Nationalist Chinese and the remaining regional warlords. In 1937, however, invasion by "imperialist" forces from Japan proved to be a greater threat than other Chinese. In any event, the type of threat did not matter to Mao. As with Lawrence, but reflecting fundamental differences in political ideology, Mao initially advocates victory in absolute terms: the total annihilation of reactionary and imperialist forces and influences wherever they exist.[75]

Based on his experiences, Mao outlined a theory with three discrete stages for revolutionary success: the strategic defensive, the stalemate, and the strategic offensive. During the first stage, numerous guerrilla offensive actions at the tactical level seek to wear down, by ambush or battle, the forces of the enemy. Tactical annihilation is preferable to attrition, but the net effect strategically is the reduction or removal of enemy forces from the countryside.[76] The second stage, stalemate, is characterized by attrition focused on the adversary's moral and material strength. Not only are his forces being defeated tactically, but the guerrillas' opponent is progressively forced on the defensive due to a hostile population that supports the guerrillas. Increasingly under siege even in formerly secure areas, the adversary's moral and material strength is whittled away in this prolonged stage of the conflict by guerrilla offensives that grow in size, sophistication, and intensity.[77] Time, secure areas, additional recruits, and the acquisition of increasingly advanced equipment allow the guerrillas to build up a conventional army.[78] Once this army is ready for action, and when the conditions are suitable,[79] the guerrilla commander launches the third and final stage of the campaign: a coordinated strategic offensive designed to annihilate his adversary in a series of decisive battles.[80]

In addition to outlining the stages of a guerrilla war, Mao believed that the further novelty of his theory lay in articulating a new form of war. A mobile war was a war of the offensive; positional war was strictly defensive. Mao suggested that guerrilla conflict was a unique form of war on its own. In the rush to make a distinction between the three forms of war, Mao ascribes features to each:

> But the objective of strategic attrition may also be achieved by campaigns of attrition. Generally speaking, mobile warfare performs the task of annihilation,

72 Special operations, attrition, and the nature of warfare

positional warfare performs the task of attrition, and guerrilla warfare performs both simultaneously; the three forms of warfare are thus distinguished from one another. In this sense war of annihilation is different from war of attrition. Campaigns of attrition are supplementary but necessary in protracted war.[81]

This arbitrary distinction between forms of war stands in stark contrast to the subtle approach Mao takes towards attrition and annihilation elsewhere. In other works, Mao fuses the concepts together into an interdependent whole that accounts for the strategic, operational, and tactical levels of war. Beneath the uncompromising rhetoric of annihilation, and reflecting his Confucian roots, he systematically defines the relationship of attrition, annihilation, offense, and defense at all levels.[82] In Mao's opinion, attrition and annihilation are not the polar opposites expounded by Delbrück. Unlike Delbrück, Mao saw the relationship between individual battles and the strategy as a whole. Although annihilation of the adversary's armed forces remains the objective goal of the strategy, the qualitative and quantitative weaknesses of the guerrilla army make this impossible in the near term.[83] With these intrinsic weaknesses in mind, attrition is the only viable option strategically when confronting a qualitatively superior adversary. Unlike other theorists, however, Mao understood the necessity of attrition as the guiding concept of his strategy. The progressive whittling down of an adversary's moral resolve and material assets, while the guerrillas build their strength, is crucial in order to shift phases to the strategic offensive. In other words, Mao opines that attrition and annihilation are opposing, but complementary, strategic approaches to victory.[84] Reflecting the philosophy of the *I Ching*, Mao's *yin* of attrition at the strategic level is balanced by the *yang* of annihilation at the tactical and operational, or campaign level (see Figure 4.2).[85]

Having suffered sufficient operational and tactical losses, an imperial or counter-revolutionary adversary will either be weakened to the point that the decisive conventional blow can be delivered or they will see that the conflict cannot be won and will capitulate. Mao's ideological preference is to push attrition at the

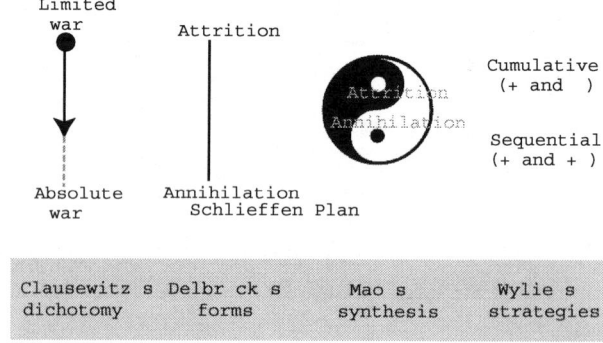

Figure 4.2 Typologies of strategy and war

strategic level to its logical theoretical conclusion and annihilate his adversary. The reality confronting Mao, as Clausewitz argued a century before, was that political considerations constrain war from reaching this point. Mao's goal of annihilating his Nationalist Chinese adversaries was unachievable, as they withdrew to islands off the coast of mainland China and were shielded by the US Seventh Fleet. The political consequences of annihilating his adversaries was not worth war with the Americans in pursuit of his theoretical goal.[86]

Special operations, attrition, and non-linearity

The intuitive conclusion from the preceding discussion is that attrition is the preferred strategy when a weaker power wishes to defeat a stronger adversary by exhausting their will to fight. Within the strategy, the weaker power only seeks battle at a time and place of its choosing to achieve temporary superiority. Through a series of limited tactical and operational offensives, the moral and material strength of the stronger adversary is sapped to the point of either exhaustion or collapse. Numerous examples exist after the Second World War, during the so-called "Wars of National Liberation," when sustained terrorist and guerrilla campaigns led imperial powers to withdraw from former colonies such as Cyprus, Palestine, Indochina, and Guinea-Bissau.[87] By extension this explanation of attrition appears at first glance to explicate the value of special operations strategically.

A number of SOF units were created specifically to take limited offensive action to weaken more powerful adversaries during the strategic defensive phase of a campaign, such as the activities against German forces conducted by the British Special Operations Executive and the Special Air Service detailed in the next chapter. In addition, a significant portion of the history of special operations describes small unit actions in which inferior forces have defeated numerically superior foes. As discussed in Chapter 1, when authors assess the impact of a special operation, they are inclined to link an individual action with direct, grossly disproportionate strategic effects. Examples of the material effects of special operations are limited to the lopsided number of enemy personnel killed or equipment and facilities destroyed by a handful of special operators. An extreme example of directly attributable attrition is made in summarizing the value of the unconventional warfare campaign conducted during the Korean War. Author Ben Malcom states that the return for the investment of the US government in "roughly $100 million" for the Korean partisan movement in 1951–3 was: "4,445 actions throughout North Korea in which 69,000 casualties (dead and wounded) were inflicted, 950 prisoners and 5,000 weapons were captured, 2,700 vehicles and 80 bridges destroyed, and 3,800 tons of food were destroyed or liberated from the North Koreans."[88]

In other cases, a direct correlation is drawn between special operations and their psychological effects.[89] For example, according to one author the failed attempt to rescue US personnel from a prison in North Vietnam in 1970 struck a nerve in the psyche of the North Vietnamese leadership: "the enemy feared

(Brigadier General Donald) Blackburn and (Major General Leroy) Manor's unconventional brand of warfare more than they did an 'invasion' of Cambodia, or some other orthodox military operation."[90] Not content to limit the impact of the special operation to just the North Vietnamese, he suggests that the Son Tay raid instilled fear into the leaders of China and Soviet Russia that their own rear areas were insecure.[91] When viewed as part of a larger campaign over time, however, the contribution of an individual action, or numerous smaller special operations, in improving military or strategic performance is less evident. At the other end of the assessment spectrum, some authors are inclined to dismiss out of hand, or ignore entirely, the contributions made by special operations during the course of a conflict.[92]

The preceding discussion of the relationship between special operations and attrition answers only part of the conceptual equation. The apparent dissonance that exists between special operations and attrition reflects perceptions of their different natures. Special operations are perceived to be bold and audacious actions, undertaken by small groups doing the unorthodox or unexpected. Attrition, however, is understood to be the careful, methodical weakening of an adversary over a prolonged period of time.

For reasons outlined previously, attrition has been characterized pejoratively as the wasteful squandering of resources tactically and thoughtlessly for modest gain. Defining attrition only by its quantifiable elements, or direct *material* costs at the tactical level, runs the risk of severing political imperatives from military ones. Henry Kissinger pointed out where the United States erred in its struggle with Vietnam: "[the United States] fought a military war; [the North Vietnamese] a political one. We sought physical attrition; our opponents aimed for our psychological exhaustion."[93] Clausewitz went one step further when he commented that those who

> exclude all moral qualities from strategic theory, and only examine material factors ... reduce everything to a few mathematical formulas of equilibrium and superiority, of time and space, limited by a few angles and lines. If that were really all, it would hardly provide a scientific problem for a schoolboy.[94]

Attrition cannot be discussed without considering its associated moral component as well. Previous chapters have demonstrated the dangers of an approach that suggests that striking targets with disproportionate moral or systemic value will cause an adversary to collapse. Relying exclusively on either indirect (psychological) or direct (material) attrition alone is to squander resources for little return at best, or to risk defeat at the hands of an adversary willing to pay the price in bloodshed.[95] In undertaking any strategy, a balance is required between attrition and annihilation to achieve what is *politically* feasible with the resources available.

Special operations, in contrast, are often characterized narrowly as bold individual raids whose psychological damage far outweighs the physical destruction, by catching an adversary unawares by their very daring. Although the objectives of such raids are limited to the destruction or recovery of specific equipment or personnel, such as the destruction of the Normandie dock at St Nazaire on 28/29 March 1942,[96] the recovery of Soviet radar components from Green Island during the Israeli attack on 19 July 1969,[97] or the failed hostage rescue attempt that ended in tragedy in the Iranian desert on 25 April 1980,[98] direct action special operations send unequivocal messages to their adversaries. Those messages have been outlined comprehensively elsewhere and include: demonstrating friendly competence and enemy incompetence; exhibiting enemy vulnerability; and raising friendly morale among others.[99] There is a danger, however, in interpreting strategic effects too broadly from specific special operations. Some authors have extrapolated from a single operation strategic effects beyond the scope of the action. For example, the special operation mounted to rescue Israeli citizens in Uganda in 1976, Operation Jonathan, was not only intrepid but it underscored the Israeli policy of not negotiating with terrorists.[100] Yet the operation was not decisive in and of itself.[101] When placed in the context of Israel's prolonged conflict with the Palestine Liberation Organization, or the broader Western war against Marxist-inspired terrorism, Jonathan appears as only one of a number of discrete events.

Some of the tenets of "new sciences," especially non-linearity studies, are useful in explaining conceptually how the discrete events of strategy relate to its nature but they also provide insights into the relationship that exists between special operations and attrition. The key tenet of the theory is that actions taken to alter one aspect of a system often have unanticipated consequences or outcomes.[102] The level of complexity, and inherent unpredictability of a system, increases dramatically as the number of component elements increases and competition between systems is introduced. It is impossible to predict with any degree of accuracy the effects that a single action will have in or on a system, much less how a specific, discrete event affects the outcome. In addition, the relationship between input and output is incalculable and often appears to be paradoxical. For example, nascent information technologies being fielded by the US military are intended to provide individual units with greater "situational awareness," leading to fewer, more lethal units exercising greater flexibility and initiative.[103] Those same technologies, however, may ironically lead to less flexibility and initiative. Fewer available resources translate into higher relative value and greater importance for each. Senior leaders may be unable to resist the urge to "micromanage" and impose instead greater constraints on freedom of maneuver, in the name of preserving resources, limiting individual initiative.[104] There are limitations in the applicability of non-linearity studies to strategic problems. Although useful as a method of comprehending conceptually the complex interactions that comprise strategy, attempts to apply non-linearity theory as a predictive tool to strategy, attrition, and special operations are bound to be frustrated given the number of unquantifiable variables.[105]

The moral attrition achieved by special operations is non-linear in two ways. The first non-linear aspect is causal in nature. As individual acts of war, special operations appear to be the embodiment of Baron Antoine de Jomini's principle of "economy of force." The benefits derived from such actions are grossly disproportionate to the resources committed. There is no way that planners can know ahead of time, however, of the specific moral effects that an individual special operation will achieve even if the tactical objectives are specific. Despite this apparent randomness, special operations are not chaotic in their cumulative attritional effects.[106] Although special operations can have unintended consequences, the net result of numerous discrete "small actions" can be lopsided operational and strategic effects even if the specific returns cannot be calculated in advance. J.C. Wylie, discussed previously, suggested that a cumulative strategy is the non-linear, indirect option that achieves its purpose through discrete "pluses and minuses."[107] Special operations, however, achieve disproportionate psychological results and draw an adversary's attention by repeated and distributed successes. By consistently highlighting the vulnerability of an adversary's prized assets or symbols to tactical destruction, occupation, attrition, or the implied threat to do so, special operations place an adversary on the horns of an operational dilemma. On one hand, an adversary can attempt to ignore these threats and risk having their moral and physical resolve weakened over time. On the other hand, an adversary can respond to the special operations threat and distribute its forces to protect unguarded or poorly guarded areas in which those assets or symbols are located, diverting attention from other areas and weakening the forces available to respond to a coordinated conventional attack.[108] In a limited war designed to achieve limited aims, such as the War of Attrition between Egypt and Israel, special operations were used in a non-linear manner to demonstrate that the costs of continued struggle were too high to bear. Egypt used raids by SOF to offset Israeli conventional superiority, maintain combat below the threshold of conventional war, and to demonstrate its military prowess. Direct action missions by their SOF, however, were not conducted in sufficient depth, breadth, or intensity to attrit Israeli will. By striking deep behind enemy lines, using a combination of SOF and conventional strikes against targets that had both moral and material importance to the Egyptians, the Israelis eventually convinced the Egyptian leadership to abandon the struggle.[109] Announcing the presence of special operations has been used to convey both the resolve of the government to tackle a problem and to begin to erode the will of their adversaries, exemplified by the British policy declaration in January 1976 that elements of the Special Air Service (SAS) would be committed to operations in Northern Ireland.[110] One author suggests that in addition to indirectly signalling a policy shift from passive to active operations in Northern Ireland:

> The bogeyman image of the [SAS] Regiment originally cultivated by the Republicans and their friends for propaganda purposes was now a positive advantage to [Prime Minister Harold] Wilson in his efforts to reassure Loyalists. Since the Republicans believed their own propaganda, this image would prove militarily useful.[111]

The second non-linear facet of special operations and attrition is temporal. Special operations are non-linear in terms of the duration of their effects.

Although special operations can inflict considerable moral shock on an adversary, the nature of war and friction suggests that there is no way of knowing the depth and duration of its effect. Previous chapters have examined the conceptual underpinnings of strategic paralysis and "shock and awe," namely that a center (or centers) of gravity can be struck simultaneously, causing collapse. When the theory has been attempted in practice, and even when special operations have been used as in the case of the Dambusters Raid, paralysis theory has not delivered on its promise. In that specific case, the effects of the "shocking" blow were transitory and not catastrophic. Given that shock is a short-lived phenomenon, special operations campaigns should be designed with two factors in mind. The first is that the strategic rationale behind special operations use is a series of actions designed to weaken the moral and material resolve of an adversary in order to break their will. The process of strategic attrition, which may involve the annihilation of fielded forces or critical infrastructure through skillful and/or economy of force operations at the tactical or operational level, drives the adversary to this point while preserving one's own strength. The second is that although the specific moral effect of an individual special operation cannot be measured, the net effect of discrete, distributed actions against an adversary's vulnerabilities will have unintended consequences that can be exploited to achieve an attritional victory within a shorter period of time using fewer forces.

The conceptual linkage between attrition and non-linearity becomes evident when viewed in the previous discussion on forms of strategy. In the various attempts to demarcate clearly limited war from absolute war, annihilation from attrition, and sequential from cumulative strategy, each theorist has grappled with the contradictions inherent to strategy. The form of strategy adopted to achieve the goal of imposing one's will on an adversary is shaped by the complex interrelationship that exists among the various dimensions of strategy. Endeavors designed to distinguish between forms of strategy, although useful intellectually from a conceptual level, have proven counterproductive when developing and implementing strategy in practice. Strategy in practice is ultimately about the use of force to erode an adversary's will to continue the struggle politically and militarily. Restated in another way, moral and material erosion is attrition at the strategic level directed against an adversary's strengths and weaknesses. When pitting strength against relative strength, the outcome of the conflict has been determined only after prolonged, costly struggle giving attrition its negative connotation. In the case of the First World War on the Western Front, "unflankable" front lines, large manpower reserves, defensive firepower supremacy, national pride, as well as other factors, contributed to both the duration and cost of the war.[112] Although pitting relative strength against an adversary's weaknesses is the preferred course of action, the logic of strategy suggests that unforeseen circumstances including the actions of the adversary will lead to the halt of the offensive during the continual struggle for advantage and the initiative.[113] Strategic attrition, a function related to the costs of sustained struggle and bloodshed, is the process of whittling away the moral resolve and material capacity of combatants until one or more of the parties concludes that continued resistance is no longer worthwhile.

Annihilation, on the other hand, has proven to be impractical historically for a number of reasons.[114] Given that war is filled with uncertainty, fog, and friction, as well as an inability to gauge the effect that operations have on an adversary, most wars last considerably longer than initially anticipated due to unexpected enemy resilience, unanticipated events, and other disruptive elements. The episodic character of war, as well as the principle of continuity and the uncertainty associated with gaining and maintaining the initiative against a reactive adversary, imposes tremendous difficulties in synchronizing the various instruments of national power to achieve the purpose of the struggle. The strategy adopted must be sufficiently flexible to account for these realities, be achievable given various constraints, and not compromise the political objectives for which force was used in the first place.[115] Rather than focus on an elaborate sword stroke designed to decapitate an adversary, the prudent strategist understands how to achieve the strategic sum total required using those elements at his disposal. A sequence of linear inputs, in the form of battles or engagements, will not produce specific outputs despite the best intentions or capabilities.[116] Individual raids or engagements doubtless will achieve some of their objectives. The net *attritional* influence that such inputs have on an enemy system, however, will produce their own unintended consequences to which a sufficiently flexible strategy must adjust.

At the tactical level, the relationship between special operations and attrition is easily understood. From this perspective, the number of enemy killed, vehicles destroyed, and insurgent villages pacified can quantify the attritional effects achieved by an individual special operation. Cumulative totals of such statistics, over the course of a campaign, presumably indicate the net attritional effect of special operations. Special operations, however, are unorthodox military actions by specially selected and trained personnel designed to achieve more than just the material whittling away of enemy forces. They are also intended to have moral effects at the operational and strategic level of war. It is the moral, or non-kinetic component of special operations that gives their material, or kinetic actions such impact. By doing that which an adversary thought was unachievable, and complicating their ability to conduct coordinated activities, special operations can have tremendous disruptive psychological value. Combined with unexpected conventional actions, the results on an adversary appear to create the conditions for quick, decisive victory.[117] One of the reasons that the moral aspects of special operations are avoided or overlooked is that unlike material elements, their effects are hard to objectively quantify.

As preceding chapters have demonstrated, the "shock" value of special operations is difficult if not impossible to sustain long enough for organizations and societies to collapse. As the next chapter demonstrates, the unanticipated setbacks embodied in the fog and friction of war can change the conditions on which the use of special operations was predicated, upsetting the assumptions, timing, and sequencing of future operations. This may be problematic given how SOF train for success. Special operations success in direct action missions is based on repetitive training and perishable intelligence. The quick reaction of SOF, due in part to this training, information, and an unorthodox approach to the problem, allows temporary surprise and shock that offsets their quantitative inferiority. When military action cannot achieve the goals of policy, or unforeseen complications arise, there is a danger of conducting the same mission set repeatedly over time in the hope of eventual success. Doing so allows an adversary to determine the pattern of operations and adapt to them. This can have disastrous consequences for SOF. Somali Habr Gidr militiamen adapted their response to a pattern of special operations raids conducted to capture General Mohamed Farah Aideed and other clan leaders.[118] Although the SOF mission template was changed continually, Somali militia understood that unarmored ground vehicles were vulnerable in Mogadishu's maze of narrow streets, and helicopters had to hover to insert or extract troops and their prisoners. In the words of a Somali "Colonel" who engaged the US forces: "If you use a tactic once, you should not use it a third time. And the Americans had already basically done the same thing six times."[119] Although tactically defeated during the street battles of 3–4 October 1993, the Habr Gidr stressed several pillars of the strategic bridge between the intended policy goals and the military instrument to the point that the President of the United States ordered the withdrawal of all US forces from the Horn of Africa. As conditions on the ground alter, current and future special operations must change with them. Repetitive and unimaginative use of special operations leads inexorably to significant combat losses of a finite, perishable resource.

Special operations are useful adjuncts to conventional forces but are rarely, if ever, decisive in and of themselves. That does not mean that special operations do not possess considerable value and strategic merit. The primary utility of special operations is to improve overall strategic performance. Special operations improve performance by increasing the military effectiveness of friendly forces, accomplishing political and military objectives in a timely, economic manner, but also upsetting the adversary's strategic and operational calculus. A key distinction related to the last point is that special operations do not, however, generate friction in an enemy's system. Friction, as Clausewitz suggested, has an absolute value, based on the uncertainties of war and the difficulties associated with human nature, group dynamics, as well as the stresses inherent in imperfect (and contradictory) information and life-threatening situations. SOF do not create friction, but rather increase its effects on an already burdened decision-making and combat system. For example, special operations can compel an adversary to divert resources to protect high-value targets or, by doing the unanticipated or the seemingly impossible, challenge the basis of strategies and military plans. In addition to adding to an adversary's woes, special operations enable friendly forces to do their job in a much more efficient manner, by providing timely intelligence reflecting changing realities on the ground, harnessing local resistance and indigenous defense forces, improving the accuracy of munitions, and seizing key objectives such as bridges, airfields, and/or important infrastructure. Finally, special operations are also used against targets that conventional forces cannot reach, strike, or influence for a variety of military or political reasons. The following example from the Normandy campaign demonstrates how SOF were able to destroy judiciously a specific objective that had severe operational restraints placed upon it for political reasons:

> Information had been received that the Germans had a refinery for making synthetic petrol near the town of Aucun, which was a priority target ... The actual plant was sited on top of a mine which produced the raw materials, and which was worked round the clock by Frenchmen who might be trapped underground. The night shift, however, came up at 2 a.m. and the next crew did not start until two hours later ... Shortly after two o'clock, fire was opened using smoke bombs to bed in the baseplate [of the mortar] and give a visual sighting correction. Then a mixture of incendiary and H[igh]E[xplosive] were stuffed down the tube in quick succession. Even before the last round had been fired, the plant was ablaze from end to end, and it was clear that the enemy had no idea where the attack had come from, as they fired into the air with an anti-aircraft gun. As stealthily as the raiders had arrived, they left, removing all traces of their presence.[120]

Although special operations have considerable utility and enhance military effectiveness, those qualities alone do not guarantee improved strategic performance. No amount of skill or unorthodoxy can offset poor strategic choices, such as a mismatch between desired ends and specified means, political intransigence, poor timing, and inadequate military preparation or action. As the history of special operations demonstrates, there is an unfortunate tendency to look to special operations to stave off decisive defeat in times of desperation, when previously successful military options have failed, in the hope that "handfuls of heroes" can restore the lost fortunes of war.[121]

Although special operations are not independent war-winners, they have significant value strategically by combining material attrition with considerable moral, or psychological, erosion of an adversary's resolve. What separates special operations from conventional forces is the psychological attrition, or tremendous moral return for limited material investment, either through the actions of SOF alone or by enhancing the effects and effectiveness of conventional forces. Special operations combine the effects of striking or threatening what an adversary fears or values the most, or using force in unexpected ways, at the operational or strategic level. Targets can include individuals, national symbols, and/or important infrastructure that can be destroyed, seized temporarily, rendered ineffective, or removed. Conversely, an adversary's extended and vulnerable supply line in an austere country, or seething internal ethnic and religious unrest, can be exploited to moral effect by special operations. Special operations can also play on an adversary's preconceptions to inflict moral dislocation by using force in unanticipated ways or enabling conventional forces to perform much better.

When used effectively, with their primary strategic value in mind, special operations can have a considerable strategic and operational impact on an adversary. In disrupting an adversary's combat "rhythm" or pattern of operations, special operations are useful in forcing the adversary into making mistakes that can be subsequently exploited. More importantly, special operations can have a disproportionate effect on the morale of the enemy leadership by denying them use or leverage of their strategic or operational advantages, which can range from missiles equipped with weapons of mass destruction to core elements of terrorist or insurgent organizations. Special operations are useful as an instrument of policy by shaping an adversary's behavior and perceptions in ways that make one's style of warfare more effective.

Understanding the primary enabling value of special operations strategically, namely non-linear attrition, is an important element in overcoming the historical misuse of special operations. Synchronizing special operations with conventional operations into a focused but flexible course of action designed to achieve the policy goals of the conflict, however, can be a daunting prospect for a variety of reasons. Clausewitz alluded to this problem when he discussed the role of units engaged in flanking operations:

> Concerning the execution of these operations against lines of communication ... Their conduct must be in the hands of skillful raiders who must move daringly in small detachments and attack boldly, assaulting the enemy's weaker garrisons, convoys and minor units on the march. They must encourage the local home guards and occasionally join them in operations. The number of these units matters more than their individual strength, and they should be so organized that several can link up for a major operation without being too much hampered by the vanity and caprice of individual leaders.[122]

As the next chapter demonstrates, vanity and caprice of leaders continued to play a significant role in the ineffective use of special operations in support of the Allied breakout from the Normandy hedgerows more than a century later. Special operations, however, have been misapplied for other reasons as well, including commitment too early or too late in a conflict.[123] In both circumstances, SOF have been subsequently misused in a number of ways: relegation to reserve, training, and rear-area duties; haphazard deployment to address operational crises, including plugging gaps in conventional battle lines; unimaginative use against tactically difficult targets on the basis of prior success; and, as mentioned previously, as the final gamble to stave off defeat.

A strategy sufficiently flexible to orchestrate the various instruments of power, including special operations, reflects the "art" of strategy as opposed to the science. As the vision of strategy gets translated into the planning process, however, there is often a problem deviating from the established sequence of military actions as the strategic context changes. Planners immersed in the details of applying military resources to a strategic problem are in danger of subverting the strategy by focusing on exquisite, but often excessively complicated, military solutions at the operational, or campaign level. In other words, in attempting to bind the problem and match resources against requirements, there is a tendency for military planning to assume a life of its own.[124] The end result is a military approach decoupled from political, economic, and social realities that focuses on the goal of flawless performance and an unequivocal demonstration of military and technical superiority. In other words, the military means become severed from the ends that their application was intended to achieve

82 *Special operations, attrition, and the nature of warfare*

and serve. The elegant campaign seeks to master the grammar of strategy, and resolve a problem exclusively by military means, without reference to the logic of strategy. In certain historical cases such willful ignorance has proved disastrous strategically despite tactical and operational superiority, as the defeats of Napoleonic France, Imperial Japan, and Wilhelmine and later Nazi Germany suggest. As the next chapter demonstrates, special operations were used ineffectively in the Normandy campaign for many of these reasons.

5 "Looting a burning house"[1]
The SAS in the campaign of attrition in Normandy, 1944

"A lot of excitement," skirmishes, a total of two tanks, and a few vehicles? This certainly wasn't going to delay the enemy's retreat ... Slyunin began to get angry; it seemed that the first plan had not considered the possibility of operating with coordinated groups ... [he] couldn't understand why [his intelligence advisors] had insisted, since the distances between the group operating areas were large, and no thought had been given to concentrating them.

(I.G. Starinov, *Over the Abyss*[2])

The Allies eventually annihilated the German Army of the West, or *Westheer*, in a lengthy campaign of attrition within a larger strategy of attrition. The role played by special operations in that victory, even though difficult to quantify, was certainly negligible. Although great expectations were placed on what special operations could achieve, including the widespread uprising of the populations of Occupied Europe, the reality was that such operations diminished in scale, frequency, and importance as Allied forces moved closer towards the heart of the Third Reich. Instead of being used to inflict grievous moral and material damage on the *Westheer*'s crucial vulnerability, its logistical lines of communication back to Germany, special operations were largely used for haphazard attacks to prevent German reinforcements from reaching the initial Allied landing areas and in tactical support of advancing forces.

This chapter argues that understanding the relationship between special operations and dimensions of attrition at the level of strategy discussed previously is only part of the problem in improving the military performance of conventional forces. When used to improve strategic performance, those planning special operations campaigns must balance material attrition with the intended moral effects that special operations and conventional forces seek to achieve, as well as account for the specific political considerations that guide the application of force. As this chapter demonstrates, using special operations to inflict moral and material attrition can be difficult even in a campaign of attrition, given the difficulties associated with strategy in practice. Imperfect knowledge, competing viewpoints on how best to conduct military operations, political considerations, and bureaucratic rivalries can derail even the most effective plans through friction even before the first shots are fired against the enemy.

Special operations were not used in an aggressive, coordinated manner in Normandy. Special operations misuse or failure has often been explained in terms of conventional minds being unable to grasp "unorthodox" solutions to problems. This chapter argues that the timorous use of the Special Air Service (SAS) Brigade in Normandy stemmed from a number of factors, of which friction between personalities is one, that make strategy in practice difficult. Yet most of the senior Allied leaders involved in the Normandy campaign, including Dwight Eisenhower and Bernard Law Montgomery, were already familiar with or had used SOF to effect in previous theater commands.

The operational reasons why the SAS were under-utilized in Normandy can be explained in terms of the strategic concept of friction. Friction existed at all levels of the Allied command, comprised as it was of a coalition of forces representing a variety of political and military agendas and interests. In the lead up to the amphibious landings, significant disagreements existed over how best and when to apply force, including special operations. These disagreements extended to the special operations community itself, as the British Special Operations Executive (SOE) sought to deflect or control potential competitors to its hard-won authority over special operations in occupied Europe from the SAS and the American Office of Strategic Services (OSS). The SAS Brigade itself could not surmount friction in the form of: split responsibilities between 21 Army Group, its "tactical" authority, and the Supreme Headquarters Allied Expeditionary Forces (SHAEF) that oversaw its "strategic" use; rapid unit expansion and rigid organization along national command lines (English, Belgian, and French); competition for resources and missions with the SOE and the OSS; and a concept of operations that had proved well suited to the North African desert but was difficult to apply to more densely populated Western European rural areas. Delays in committing the SAS to Normandy, imposed by SHAEF, were just as damaging as the piecemeal deployment of forces.

The SAS had improved Allied strategic performance in the Western Desert by focusing on the key vulnerabilities of Axis forces in North Africa including the German theater army, the *Deutsches Afrika-Korps*. SAS activities were designed to weaken the combat effectiveness of the *Deutsches Afrika-Korps* by targeting its logistics and air support, as well as improving the military performance of the Allied armies. During the Normandy campaign, however, the SAS was constrained politically and militarily in its activities by SHAEF, 21 Army Group, and Special Forces Headquarters (SFHQ). Those constraints limited SAS freedom of operations and turned the advice offered by T.E. Lawrence, outlined in the preceding chapter, on its head. Rather than striking deeply and boldly in enemy territory to constrict German supply lines and routes, and target specific vulnerabilities, SAS teams were distributed unevenly throughout France to bolster resistance and conduct attacks on local German forces. In a variation of an old proverb, the SAS fell victim to the tactical attrition "sword" it attempted to wield in Normandy.

Had the SAS been used in a more coherent manner designed to tighten and cut off supply arteries, the moral and material effects on such activities in conjunction with conventional blows from the front might have significantly weakened the *Westheer*. Although special operations were no guarantee that such a plan could succeed, the coordinated use of SAS, in conjunction with SOE, OSS, resistance forces, and airpower, could have improved Allied strategic performance by shaping the battlefield for the conventional forces, thereby winning the campaign of attrition against the *Westheer* more quickly and economically.[3] The inability of the Allies to conduct a campaign of unconventional attrition prior to and during the Normandy campaign was one of the greatest lost opportunities of the war: a severely weakened *Wehrmacht* might have been overwhelmed by the Allied and Soviet armies on both fronts as early as the autumn of 1944.

In order to understand how the SAS was used in Normandy, it is necessary to review the establishment and successes of the unit in North Africa and the Mediterranean. From this evaluation, a number of problems that have plagued and continue to plague special operations activities will be discussed in detail, including focusing on individual "great raids" to the exclusion of more methodical actions aimed at eroding enemy resources. Special operations in the Normandy campaign are then placed in the context of the Allied concept of operations for the campaign as a whole. Utilizing a number of sources, including SHAEF and SFHQ documents unused in previous studies, the remainder of the chapter explores the planning and conduct of special operations in the Normandy campaign. This includes issues such as the placement of the SAS under 21 Army Group headquarters and its command and control implications in the invasion of Europe, the concept of operations for SAS use in support of the landings in the Cotentin Peninsula, and the reasons why the SAS played a diminished role during the campaign. The chapter concludes with a counterfactual assessment of how the SAS could have contributed to a more effective strategy of attrition in the Normandy campaign based on the resources and information available at the time. The failure to use the SAS in a coherent fashion in Normandy, however, has its roots in the establishment and use of the SAS by Middle East Headquarters in 1941.

The Special Air Service, 1941–4: genesis, success, growth

Contrary to popular opinion, the SAS did not begin as the brainchild of Major David Stirling.[4] Rather, the "Special Air Service Brigade" began its life as a phantom unit, created by Lieutenant Colonel Dudley Clarke, as part of a deception plan designed to convince their Italian opponents that the British had a force deliverable by air that could threaten Italian rear areas.[5] The deception plan, authorized by General Sir Archibald Wavell in November 1940, bore similarities to the "Fortitude" plan created in support of Operation Overlord four years later. The credibility of the sham airborne force was enhanced by "rumours, leakages, bogus radio traffic and displays of dummy gliders."[6] While Clarke and his colleagues of "A" Force were busy keeping the Italians, and later the Germans, occupied with their ruse, David Stirling (then a lieutenant) was becoming increasingly frustrated by his inability to make a meaningful contribution to the war.

As a member of 8 Commando, Stirling's dissatisfaction stemmed from the difficulties inherent in launching large seaborne raids against inland targets. Commando raids were part of a three-pronged British effort to strike back at Nazi Germany after the fall of France in 1940.[7] There was no shortage of volunteers for individuals looking to exchange the tedium of barracks life and maneuvers for dangerous action in the commandos. By the autumn of 1941, however, commando raids were conducted with decreasing frequency in this theater of operations due to inordinately lengthy planning times, interservice coordination demands, larger raiding force packages, limited mobility of light infantry forces from the beachhead, and improved German seaward defenses.[8] As a result, highly motivated personnel such as Stirling did more training and preparing than actual fighting.[9] Commando raids were also unable to strike inland in sufficient depth against one of the key enablers of German military success in North Africa: tactical airpower. While recuperating from injuries sustained in a parachute jump, Stirling formulated a rough plan to strike enemy airfields with small airborne forces from the vulnerable desert flank.[10]

Stirling managed to sell his raiding concept, in characteristically unorthodox fashion, to Generals Neil Ritchie and Claude Auchinleck.[11] The idea was appealing to both generals for a number of reasons. The timing of Stirling's pitch could not have been more fortuitous. Ritchie and Auchinleck were deeply involved at the time in the planning of a major British counteroffensive against German and Italian forces in North Africa, code-named "Crusader." However, operational security for the offensive had been problematic and the potential surprise value of the plan had been undermined. Both generals, therefore, were receptive to any method by which to tip the balance in the Eighth Army's favor.[12] Most importantly, Stirling's proposal was appealing to the generals on the basis of its economy. As Stirling phrased it:

> I further concluded that 200 properly selected, trained and equipped men, organized into sub-units of five should be able to attack at least thirty different objectives at the same time on the same night as compared to only one objective using the Commando technique; and that only 25% success in the former was equivalent to many times the maximum possible result in the latter.[13]

With little imposition on British Army manpower and resources, and potentially high payoff for little operational risk, Stirling's raiders could help level the qualitative imbalance that existed between the Commonwealth forces and those of the *Deutsches Afrika-Korps*.[14]

After a disastrous series of initial raids at Gazala and Timimi in November 1941, in which more than half of "L" Detachment SAS were killed, captured, or never returned from missions, Stirling modified his approach to the problem.[15] Instead of airdropping to objectives, then conducting the actions on foot and returning to base courtesy of the vehicles of the Long Range Desert Group, the SAS would acquire their own mobility in the form of Willys jeeps.[16] The jeeps would be heavily modified, to give them considerable range and firepower, and units would disperse and make their way to the objective. Most raids were conducted at night, with the jeeps entering the target area from multiple axes of approach. The moral dimension of the raids, based on the psychological frame of mind of Axis soldiers in rear areas, contributed to the overall attrition of the *Deutsches Afrika-Korps*. In the words of one "L" Detachment officer, the SAS took advantage of the feeling of "security" of enemy forces behind the front:

> For in these camps one was conscious only of the fact that the enemy were fifty or a hundred miles away as the case may be and accordingly one felt completely safe from any hostile land interference ... Presumably each man possessed a rifle; but I doubt if many of them could have laid their hands on a weapon in less than a minute, and if it was dark they would not know what to shoot at ... Exactly the same applied to the aerodromes. The pilots flew their planes and fought in the air; once they set their feet on solid ground they had finished with the war for the time being.[17]

By the time that the defenders could react to the initial shock of the attack, SAS vehicles would already be retiring as quickly as possible to predetermined rallying points.[18] To gain the maximum results from their brief assaults, SAS operators would strike specific targets designed to strain the German logistics system: bulk supplies required to sustain mechanized armies in the desert, such as fuel and ammunition dumps, and the wing roots or engines of German and Italian aircraft.[19] SAS patrols also raided Axis supply columns and collected intelligence but their forte remained airfield attacks. During the North African campaign, the SAS conducted hundreds of raids and patrols, the most important material effect of which was the destruction of between 250 and 400 enemy aircraft on the ground.[20] Deprived of both air and logistics support, the combat efficiency and strength of the *Deutsches Afrika-Korps* relented under the repeated moral and material blows dealt by the Allies from front and rear. In later campaigns in Italy and Normandy, improving strategic performance became equated with directly enhancing the tactical military performance of Allied armies, rather than focusing on the operational or strategic vulnerabilities of the *Westheer*.

The early days of the SAS during the Western Desert campaign consisted of training and raiding. In addition to combat, the SAS fought an equally bitter battle for organizational survival. Competition for resources, especially between SOF in the theater, was fierce; the number of redundant "private armies" being established, including the Special Boat Section (SBS)[21] and "Popski's Private Army (PPA)" (1st Demolition Squadron),[22] was staggering. Stirling was convinced of the virtue of his raiding concept yet the rivalry between SOF units for personnel, not to mention the casualties that the SAS had suffered during missions, meant that his force was steadily dwindling away. As a result, Stirling requested manpower from almost any available source, including idle "Layforce" commandos, as well as members of the Special Interrogation Group and recently arrived Indian battalions.[23] To ensure the survival of his force, Stirling made a

Faustian bargain with Middle East Headquarters: he would receive replacements in exchange for SAS participation in the ill-conceived Operation Agreement. Agreement consisted of an integrated commando and SOF raid, supported by conventional forces, against the ports of Tobruk and Benghazi (12 September 1942).

The conduct and results of Operation Agreement epitomize the problem of conducting great independent raids undertaken to inflict catastrophic moral and material damage, versus more numerous and modest special operations designed to inflict attrition by striking at adversary weaknesses over time and in conjunction with conventional offensives elsewhere. The purpose of Agreement was "to deal the enemy a damaging blow, one which might virtually knock him out of the African continent altogether" by destroying port, petroleum storage, and tank repair facilities.[24] The operation was characterized by substantial "mission creep." In order to minimize risk and "guarantee" success, a progressively larger raiding force was assembled for the task. The raiding force conducting the special operation grew to include two tanks, a naval task force of 11 ships, 40 jeeps, 40 supply trucks, and more than 1,500 personnel.[25] Lobbying by individual SOF and commando leaders, as well as conventional service component commanders such as the Royal Air Force (RAF), ensured that their units or branches would have a role in the impending raid.[26] Conventional force planners traded the element of surprise for mass by insisting on diversionary attacks and ancillary special operations. Special operations in the Western Desert had succeeded up to this point because the individual actions had been kept small, embodied flexibility in execution by self-contained units, and were simple in design and execution. Operational security within Middle East Headquarters continued to be poor, with staff officers openly discussing the details of the impending raid in public.[27] By substantially increasing the complexity of the action, and tying it to a rigid diversion and landing schedule possibly known to the enemy, the likelihood of success of the Tobruk and Benghazi raids was severely diminished. In addition, British special operations planning assumptions for Agreement had more to do with seemingly boundless faith and optimism than reality. The SAS's portions of Agreement were ambitious to say the least. Bolstered by armored vehicles and additional SOF, the SAS were to

> get past the perimeter defenses [of Benghazi] and then attack any shipping that he found in the harbor. Thereafter, [Stirling's] Force X was to free the 16,000 or so British soldiers reportedly held in Benghazi's large POW compound. Once sprung, these POWs would be armed with captured weapons and become part of the raiding force. So armed, they were to hold out long enough for a landing force, brought in by the Navy, to arrive and rescue them.[28]

For a number of reasons identified above, as well as the effects of friction when the plan was executed, Operation Agreement was an undisputed failure. The effects of that failure, however, lived long after the badly mauled British forces returned from the raid.²⁹ The perception in Montgomery's mind that special operations had not lived up to their promise, when put to the test at Tobruk in September 1942, had significant repercussions later in planning for the attrition of the *Westheer* in 1944.

Failure at Benghazi and Tobruk did not prevent David Stirling from lobbying for additional resources to do what the SAS did best—striking airfields and static supply bases. As a result of his lobbying, and in anticipation of even greater effects that the unit could achieve in the most senior positions in Middle East Headquarters, the SAS was expanded. On 28 September 1942, the SAS was established as a regiment of the British Army. Consisting of four squadrons and various support elements, including a Free French squadron, the new regiment contained just over 600 personnel.³⁰ As early as autumn 1942, however, Stirling was already considering the role that the SAS should play in the upcoming liberation of occupied Europe. In order to achieve maximum results, Stirling believed that the SAS needed to almost quintuple in size from its current size as a regiment to a full brigade (3,000 personnel).³¹ Although Stirling's vision for the size of the SAS became a reality in 1943, four issues limited the potential effectiveness of the SAS in future campaigns, including Normandy: the capture of David Stirling by the Germans and an ensuing leadership vacuum in the SAS for the duration of the war; rapid growth in the size of the SAS at the expense of the quality of its operators; the promotion of Bernard Law Montgomery as the senior Allied operational commander; and the placement of the SAS organizationally under command of airborne forces and without defining adequately the relationship between military (SAS) and paramilitary (SOE/OSS) SOF.

David Stirling's capture by the Germans in January 1943 was arguably the single most damaging blow to the SAS during the war. Although the death of SAS founding member John "Jock" Lewes at the end of December 1941 robbed the unit of its most capable trainer and equipper,³² the capture of Stirling removed the one individual with the strategic vision and bureaucratic skills responsible for the SAS's organizational survival and success to date. As operational conditions changed in the theater, Stirling was sufficiently flexible to anticipate new roles and missions for the SAS. In addition, Stirling used his extensive social and military connections to obtain resources and refine his special operations approach, as well as challenge the orders of his superiors when necessary.³³ Field commanders, drawn from "L" Detachment's founding group of "Originals," commanded the two regiments but sorely lacked Stirling's ability to manipulate the bureaucratic system to the SAS's advantage.³⁴ To make matters worse, when the SAS was expanded to brigade size in January 1944, an officer with suitable rank was chosen for the command. Although Brigadier Roderick McLeod eventually grew into his command responsibilities overseeing the deployment of SAS forces to occupied Europe, he had neither the special operations experience nor the political savoir-faire to fight the bureaucratic battles as the details of Operation Neptune, the landings themselves, were being finalized in the Supreme Headquarters, Allied Expeditionary Forces (SHAEF) between March and June 1944.

During May 1943 and January 1944, or the time between the attrition of the *Deutsches Afrika-Korps* and the formation of the SAS Brigade, the two regiments of the SAS had been involved in a number of special operations in the Mediterranean.[35] These operations are noteworthy for three reasons: the lack of imagination in their planning; the duplication of effort between military and paramilitary SOF; and, most importantly, the gradual reduction in strength of SAS personnel due to casualties sustained in operations or through disease.[36] The 1st Regiment SAS, for example, was reduced to fewer than 200 officers and enlisted men by December 1943.[37] With the establishment of the SAS Brigade the following month, both SAS regiments had to be brought up to an operational strength of close to 2,000 personnel as quickly as possible.[38] The requirement to quintuple the size of the SAS within six months invariably led to the relaxation of selection criteria despite inventive training and recruiting techniques.[39] The addition of two French parachute battalions and a Belgian parachute company also bolstered the Brigade.[40] Most importantly, many members of the SAS Brigade were lacking in two crucial areas on the eve of the invasion: special operations experience, which no amount of training could instill; and, aside from the French and Belgian contingents, adequate linguistic skills necessary to communicate effectively with the both the *maquis* and the local population in order to conduct an unconventional warfare campaign.[41] As the SAS Brigade consisted of uniformed military personnel that would be delivered by air into occupied France, they were placed under the control of airborne forces of 21 Army Group.[42] The commander of 21 Army Group, who exercised operational control over all Allied forces participating in the invasion, was Field Marshal Montgomery.

Based on the recommendation of his Chief of the Imperial General Staff, Winston Churchill appointed Montgomery as the commander of the Eighth Army in North Africa on 7 August 1942.[43] As soon as he arrived in theater, Montgomery improved morale immediately within the Eighth Army; he exuded confidence in both his own generalship and the fighting quality of the British soldier. Montgomery, however, also exhibited personality traits antithetical to the conduct of special operations. For example, he was fastidious and a rigid stickler for discipline and proper behavior. He also was intolerant of failure as well as the waste of precious resources. In particular, Montgomery believed that the commandos and most SOF not only drew away promising material from the conventional forces, but the investment in a special operations capability was not worth the return: "You want only my best men; my most experienced and dependable men ... What, Colonel Stirling, makes you assume that you can handle these men to greater advantage than myself?"[44] Montgomery may have been more accommodating had SOF accomplished great things with the resources under their control. Like many conventional officers, however, he based his opinion almost exclusively on the results of a few great raids that had largely been failures. Montgomery, for example, reminded Stirling during the course of their conversation of the highly visible failure at Tobruk.[45] Montgomery did see the relative value of special operations in serving pressing tactical requirements. These requirements included providing him with crucial operational intelligence to conduct operations, as was the case during the battle of the Mareth Line in March 1943.[46] For the most part, however, Montgomery envisioned the impending battle in Normandy in methodical, linear terms of Allied quantitative superiority on the front line, driven by his superior generalship, with little consideration that actions in the enemy rear area could ease his situation.

The politics and planning of Operation Overlord

In order to understand why the SAS was not used to greater effect during the Normandy campaign, namely to inflict crippling moral and material vulnerabilities of the *Westheer*, it is necessary to sketch briefly the projected plans for the invasion of Europe. With the proposed campaign "rhythm" and goals outlined, the Allied plan to disrupt the German rear area can be discussed in context. During the planning for the campaign in Normandy, which was ostensibly designed to weaken the *Westheer* through attrition, the competing political interests of coalition partners and bureaucracies responsible for the armed uprisings in Europe heavily shaped the subsequent deployment of the SAS Brigade. Even in a campaign with attrition as its designated goal, the successful use of special operations for the purposes of attrition is not guaranteed.

Political considerations, personalities, and friction would inhibit any Allied attempt to destroy the *Westheer* in an operationally elegant battle of annihilation. The campaign in the West, therefore, was planned as a series of attrition-based operations designed to liberate occupied Europe and remove Adolf Hitler from power. Within the campaign of attrition, however, special operations played only a limited role in winning victory more economically and expeditiously by severely weakening the *Westheer*. Political infighting and an approach to special operations that assumed inherent strategic effect would hamstring the SAS in the campaign of attrition long before the launch of Operation TITANIC 4 on the night of 5 June 1944.[47]

That the Allies successfully mounted an amphibious invasion of Europe, despite the problems inherent in any coalition campaign, is a testament to the quality of the political and military leaders, staff officers, and individual fighting soldiers who overcame German operational and tactical superiority. The Allies were hobbled at times by internecine squabbles over bureaucratic domains and the specific methods of achieving final victory. For his faults as a commander that are outlined in detail below, Dwight D. Eisenhower rightly deserves recognition as a military diplomat. Williamson Murray and Allan R. Millett conclude: "If Ike deserves the accolade of 'great,' it rests on his performance in managing the generals under his command, as fractious and dysfunctional a group of egomaniacs as any war had ever seen."[48] Under Eisenhower's leadership, the Allied forces from the United States, Britain and its Commonwealth, and governments-in-exile such as France and Poland never lost focus on the goal of final victory. As laid down in the Casablanca Conference, the Axis powers including Nazi Germany were required to surrender unconditionally to the Allies.[49]

The shortest path to that surrender, involving special operations, would have been a series of decisive, unrelenting battles that fixed, surrounded, and annihilated the units of Army Group West and collapsed German will. A grand culminating campaign of annihilation was impossible initially in Normandy for a number of reasons. The first was the uncertainty surrounding the invasion of France. Allied planners were conservative in their estimates of what the landings in Normandy would achieve based on the mixed record of their previous assaults.[50] Even if successful, the Allies would be numerically inferior to the Germans until sufficient forces could be built up in the beachhead, giving the Germans time to establish defenses in depth. The Allied plan was to resist German counterattacks and protect their tenuous beachhead until they had sufficient combat strength ashore to go on the offensive. Also, despite having fought the Germans for as long as five years, the Allied armies were still struggling to overcome deficiencies in training, doctrine, equipment, and experience.[51] Demonstrations of elegance and puissance at the operational level of war would have to wait until these deficiencies could be overcome. Finally, the political considerations associated with coalition invasion of Europe, including rancorous disagreements between allies, prevented the unity of effort necessary to conduct a seamless campaign of annihilation.

Expanding the beachhead would involve methodical offensives designed to weaken the defenders until the breakout could be launched. The best that the Allies could hope for was that a decimated *Westheer* could be pushed back, outmaneuvered, and surrounded in an annihilating *coup de grâce*. If the obliteration of the German armies could not be achieved immediately after the invading Allied armies had established themselves on the continent, there was little doubt in the Supreme Commander's mind that it would happen later: "You see, we had finally got sixty-three American divisions into Europe, and we wanted to hit a sledgehammer blow."[52] Prior to the landings, Eisenhower left the details of the upcoming grand battle to his land commander, General Montgomery.[53]

Eisenhower's staff planners, predominantly Americans, developed a concept of operations for Overlord whose only stipulation was where the invasion was to take place.[54] The majority of their energy, however, was directed towards efforts to support the battle: logistics and supply, including the acquisition of adequate numbers of landing craft; psychological operations; negotiations with coalition partners including governments-in-exile for use of forces and military governance after liberation; and broad policy guidance for resistance activities.[55] As an example of the logistical considerations, Allied planners were confronted with the dilemma of how to sustain landed forces, and flow follow-on forces to break out of the beachhead, without the benefit of port facilities to assist in the offloading. The Allied response was to construct, ship, and sink in place the elements of artificial harbors, called "Mulberries," to ease the offloading of supplies in both the American and British sectors.[56]

Montgomery and his staff at 21 Army Group, whose staff were primarily British and whose recommendations largely reflected recent combat experience in the Mediterranean, refined the location of the invasion, allocated forces to tasks, and developed a forecast of Allied advance from the beachhead.[57] According to the forecast developed on 26 February 1944, Montgomery's staff anticipated capture of their first port, Cherbourg, some seventeen days after invasion. While British forces continued to "hold the shoulder," or left flank of the beachhead close to Caen, the American forces would pivot around the town of Vire and sweep in directions west, south, and east. Two months from the invasion date (D+60) the Allies would be in possession of the Brittany port of Brest; one month after that (D+90) Paris would be within reach.[58] Subsequent actions and statements by Allied operational commanders, including Montgomery[59] and General George S. Patton, Jr.,[60] among others, suggested their desire to demonstrate their superior generalship by destroying the German fielded forces through maneuver and annihilation. On every attempt, save the offensive that surrounded the pitiable remnants of German Army Group B in the Ruhr Pocket in March–April 1945,[61] Montgomery, General Omar Bradley, and Patton were thwarted by friction in various forms including: superior German tactical use of available forces and terrain (the German defenses of Caen, Metz, and the Rhine); the Allies reaching the culminating point of their supply lines and the shifting of effort between armies (U.S. Third Army to the U.S. First Army in September 1944);[62] German counterstrokes (the Avranches/Mortain counterattack in August 1944 and the Ardennes offensive of December 1944, which forced the Allies to cede the operational initiative and react);[63] and the inability of Allied officers to read and react to the changing situation on the ground (the failure of 2 Canadian Corps, under the command of General Guy Simonds, to close the Falaise/Argentan Gap in August 1944).[64]

Behind the conventional battle, SHAEF could rely on an additional asset awaiting the order to begin a campaign of attrition against the Germans: the French resistance. SHAEF provided minimal policy guidance on resistance issues, beyond the political requirement to work with the representatives of governments-in-exile, as SOE was considered the hub of all resistance planning and operations.[65] Since the establishment of the SOE in July 1940, Great Britain had been maintaining contact with and providing support to resistance groups operating within various countries in occupied Europe, such as Denmark, the Netherlands, and France.

Although results in other countries such as Norway had been dramatic, by the summer of 1944 the resistance forces in France and the Low Countries had experienced mixed success.[66] Passive resistance, in the form of subversion and clandestine sabotage, had affected production in the occupied countries but nevertheless had little overall impact on the German war effort.[67] In another form of passive resistance, namely intelligence gathering, resistance forces were more successful, providing information that was timely and/or precise. An example of the precision of this information includes that collected on Adolf Hitler and his daily routine. By June 1944 "Section X" of the SOE had compiled the details of Hitler's routine at his retreat at Berghof down to the time of his breakfast and the path of his morning constitutional.[68]

Active resistance, such as overt attacks on German equipment and personnel, demonstrated the existence, reach, and capabilities of resistance forces, as well as tangible proof to fellow citizens that occupying German forces and their collaborators were unable to stop them. Stated German policy to forms of active resistance, however, was brutal and reprisals and collective punishment far exceeded the casualties that their forces suffered. SOE continued to ferry agents and supplies into occupied France but counter-espionage forces, including the German *Gestapo* and *Sicherheitsdienst* (Security Service, or SD) as well as the French *Milice*, had penetrated or intercepted a number of agent networks.[69] In addition, although French resistance was ostensibly united under the *Comité Français de la Libération Nationale* (CFLN), its overall efficacy was diminished due to regional tensions, political differences, personality clashes, and post-war aspirations to positions of power and influence.[70] As a result, the *maquis* and its major elements—the de Gaullist *Armée Secrète*, the Communist *Franc Tireurs et Partisans*, and the Giraudist *Groupe de l'Armée*—did not have the cohesion of other resistance movements, such as the partisans under local commissar leadership and overall Soviet STAVKA direction in Eastern Europe or the *Comitato di Liberazione Nazionale Alta Italia* in Italy.[71] Despite the setbacks, both the SOE and later the OSS were making preparations to insert large numbers of agents to link up with resistance groups to arm and train them; this included "arms for about half a million men, and a fair quantity of explosives as well."[72]

During the uprisings in support of the Allied landings, *maquis* forces would destroy rail and communication lines at night, as part of a plan to isolate the battlefield, as well as delay German reinforcements from reaching the beachhead.[73] The specific effect that the Resistance had in the success of the invasion, however, remains difficult to quantify:

> It is impossible to appraise the contribution of the Resistance toward softening the enemy in France before the invasion. Not only was there no systematic recording of the facts of their operations, but there was, in any case, no satisfactory yardstick by which to measure the effectiveness of an irregular force, whose role was strategic rather than tactical. Certainly the Resistance impaired the German military power both materially and morally. A fighter with a bee in his breeches is evidently not at his best. But just how much the bee contributes to his defeat is a question to which statistical method can hardly apply.[74]

The work done by resistance agents, many of whom operated covertly under civilian "cover," dictated that the SOE be placed initially under the control of a non-military agency: the Ministry of Economic Warfare. Nominally under control of the military Chiefs of Staff Committee, the civilian special operations leadership of the Ministry of Economic Warfare gained access to the Defence Committee and the War Cabinet.[75] By 1944, however, that situation had changed drastically. Due to the workings of the "old boy network" through the social status and connections between many of its senior officials, including a number of military officers now in its ranks, SOE continued to have access to British civilian and military leaders to ensure their primacy over matters dealing with resistance in occupied Europe. Although SOE/SO had its own headquarters for planning operations, the SFHQ, paramilitary special operations in occupied France were placed under the control of SHAEF, to coordinate with the French Provisional government led by Charles de Gaulle, by January 1944.

This organizational shift impacted special operations in Europe in three ways: it established SOE/SO as the source of expertise on special operations to the Supreme Commander early in the planning process of Operation Overlord, influencing future decisions on how and what special operations would be conducted;[76] it placed SOE/SO higher within the chain of command than the SAS Brigade, which had to report through a rigid bureaucratic process through the headquarters staff of 1 Airborne Corps and 21 Army Group;[77] and it gave the Gaullist government-in-exile increasing authority over proposed Allied special operations in occupied France.[78] The authority of the French government was expanded in June 1944 through the creation of an additional layer of control, further complicating the command arrangement and structure and compounding the friction that already existed between the various offices responsible for special operations. SHAEF authorized the creation of the office of the *Etat-major des Forces Français de l'Intérieur* (EMFFI) on 2 June 1944, under the command of Major-General Pierre Joseph Koenig, although it is noteworthy that the directive for Koenig to assume command was not issued until almost two weeks after the invasion on 17 June.[79] The establishment of new headquarters and offices, each with varying degrees of command and operational control, inevitably caused conflicts over authority. For example, Eisenhower dictated that EMFFI "would gradually relieve the Special Force Headquarters of its responsibilities in connection with French resistance, and that SHAEF and Special Force Headquarters would aid [Koenig] in working out a program for taking over these responsibilities," although control was not passed until late August.[80] Even before those responsibilities were transferred, tensions existed between SHAEF G-3 Operations and EMFFI as to who retained operational control of the SAS: "It appears that EMFFI have already issued orders direct to SAS Brigade for the BOURGES-ORLEANS and DOUBS operations to be carried out. I have told SAS not to take any action until further orders are issued by this Headquarters, and informed EMFFI accordingly."[81] Most importantly, command problems robbed the SAS Brigade of the commodity it could least afford to lose: time, which was required to train partisan forces, identify German logistical vulnerabilities, and prepare to strike them.

Confronted with Scylla and Charybdis: the planning for and use of the SAS Brigade in support of Overlord[82]

To an outside observer, the SAS Brigade in February 1944 appeared to be in the same state of organizational limbo as the commandos were when David Stirling expressed his frustration in 1941. There were too few apparent applications, in increasingly crowded theaters of operation, for another unit of trained and motivated special operations personnel. Senior SOE staff members were apprehensive of a potential competitor for special operations resources and control in occupied Europe, much less a "conventional" military one prepared to drop behind enemy lines in uniform, and they voiced their opinion to the Supreme Commander.[83] The suspicions were mutual, as senior SAS leaders believed that the SOE-dominated SFHQ was attempting to acquire control of the brigade.[84] During the early months of 1944 neither McLeod nor members of his staff could gain access to the Supreme Commander to lobby their case, as Stirling had done with Ritchie and Auchinleck.

The American command structure within SHAEF was more rigid and formal than the British theater commands. General Walter Beddell Smith "directed the flow of correspondence into his office and cut down the number of direct contacts between the Supreme Commander and the SHAEF deputies and staff members."[85] Given the ferocity of the policy debates in which Eisenhower was embroiled between February and April 1944, including those between the Allies and related to the invasion of southern France, Operation Anvil, it is doubtful that McLeod or even Stirling himself could have convinced Eisenhower to consider the application of the SAS for strategic effect in the upcoming campaign.

Access to Eisenhower would have been a moot point for the SAS Brigade for two additional reasons. First, the SAS Brigade headquarters staff, along with their commander and the officers overseeing special operations planning in SHAEF's G-3 Operations section, had little or no experience in the planning and conduct of special operations. All matters related to special operations were handled and coordinated by SOE representatives attached to the section. To support the integration of resistance activities with SHAEF plans, SOE detailed 26 personnel to SHAEF G-3. However of those 26, only three personnel were detached to work on plans beyond the exploitation phase of Operation Neptune. Only in late September, after Operation DINGSON in Brittany wound down, would the majority of the G-3 staff officers and senior SHAEF leaders gain an initial appreciation of the potential "strategic" role that special operations could play. A second reason which made matters worse was that all offices under the control of or working in coordination with SHAEF were eking out their separate and distinct areas of control. Unfortunately for the upcoming special operations campaign in France, most controversies were resolved months after the invasion had already occurred.

During the process of delineating specific responsibilities for the impending campaign, the leadership of both the SAS Brigade and G-3 Operations, Special Operations, clashed with their bureaucratic counterparts in the SOE-dominated SFHQ. In theory, all parties agreed that paramilitary and military special operations were intended to have strategic effects: "It must be remembered that the primary mission of Resistance Groups is strategic rather than tactical."[89] Precisely how those effects would be achieved, however, was unclear to them. Certainly in the minds of some planners the sheer estimated size of the resistance would achieve some meaningful strategic effect (see Figure 5.1).[90] By the time that the bureaucratic and political disagreements over operating areas, allocation of resources, and specific missions were resolved, special operations would be

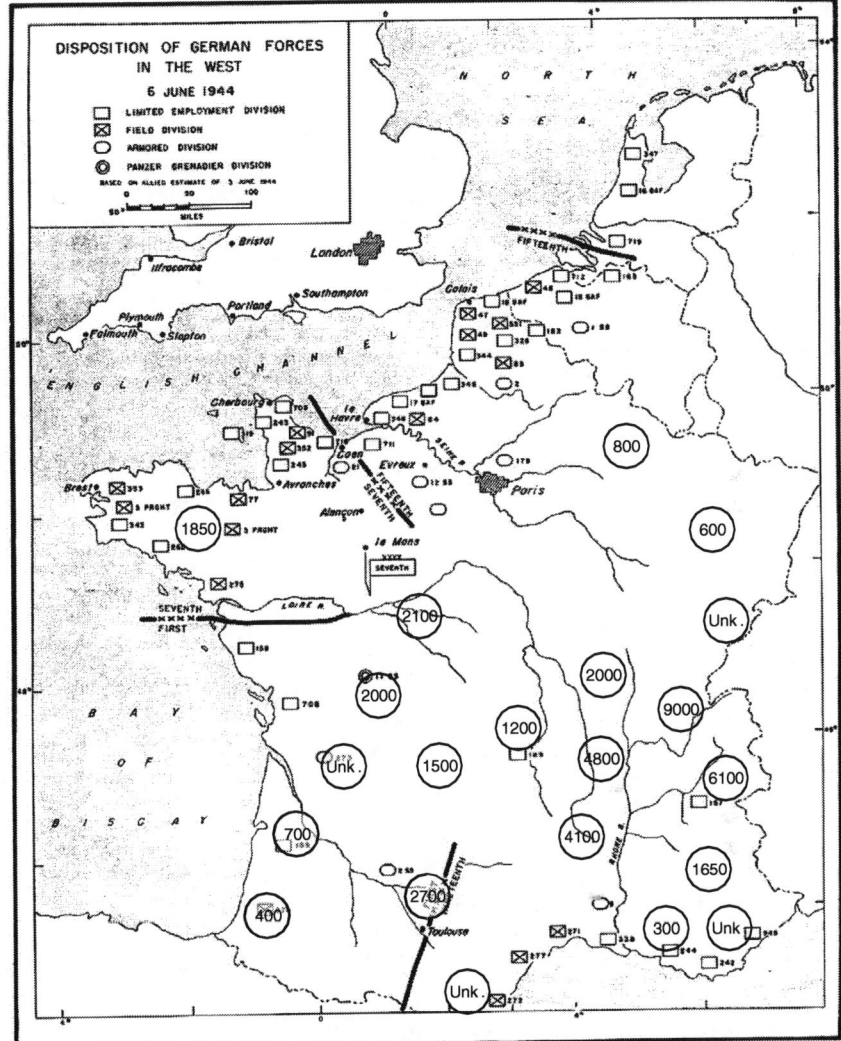

Figure 5.1 Pre-D-Day German force disposition and *maquis* strength estimates

relegated to tactical support of immediate battlefield requirements although ostensibly "strategic" in purpose and effect:

> Resistance is a strategic weapon. It is only very rarely that it can be used tactically. *The cumulative effects of numerous acts of resistance over a wide area can, if adroitly handled, pay a tactical dividend in a required area.* For this reason, control of resistance, through Special Forces Headquarters, will remain vested in the Supreme Commander [emphasis added].[91]

Rather than utilizing special operations in a fluid and cumulative plan designed to further weaken the *Westheer*, by identifying and striking shifting and increasingly crucial vulnerabilities as it adapted, the activities of the SAS were bifurcated between the tactical requirements of 21 Army Group, and unspecified strategic requirements to be identified by SHAEF. Initially, special operations authorized by SHAEF, including those conducted by the SAS, were focused exclusively on deception and tactical interdiction of German reinforcements and supplies that could tip the balance on the initial days of the invasion.

For example, one of the key concerns within SHAEF was the ability of Germans to transport and concentrate reinforcements, specifically panzer divisions, from across France to the Normandy region (see Figure 5.1). In particular, *Waffen-SS* panzer and panzer grenadier divisions posed a significant threat as they comprised the most formidable mobile land combat power of the *Wehrmacht*.[92] On the eve of Operation Neptune, Allied intelligence received from Ultra decrypts, resistance forces, and aerial reconnaissance had identified four such divisions that could respond to an invasion: the *1st SS Panzer Division* (Leibstandarte Adolf Hitler) in Belgium; the *2nd SS Panzer Division* (Das Reich) refitting around Toulouse in the south of France; the *12th SS Panzer Division* (Hitlerjugend) based in Evreux; and the *17th SS Panzer Grenadier Division* (Götz von Berlichingen) based in Tours.[93] Of these divisions, resistance forces had the best chance of delaying the arrival of two: the *1st* and *2nd SS*. Both divisions were substantial distances from the front; they could make the journey by road and rail in less than a week and perhaps provide the critical counterattacking mass necessary to collapse the defenses of the Allied lodgment. The resistance did little to prevent the arrival of the *1st SS* and its associated support units over the next month.[94] Indeed, one of its units, the heavily armored *schwere Panzer Abteilung (sPzAbt) 101* with their Tiger I tanks, was crucial in containing a British breakout attempt from the beachhead on 13 June.[95]

The delay in the movement of the *2nd SS*, however, succeeded in accomplishing the tactical dividends from resistance that were hoped for by SHAEF planners. Operators working in the SOE "circuit" WHEELRIGHT struck at two key vulnerabilities of the *2nd SS*: petroleum stocks to deny refueling, and railcar transportation to move tracked vehicles northward. Members of other circuits, such as DIGGER, FIREMAN, SHIPWRIGHT, and WRESTLER, conducted ambushes on *2nd SS* units around Tulle and Limoges and destroyed sections of rail, delaying the march by up to two days at a time.[96] Farther north, SAS team members from BULBASKET, acting on a tip from a local resistance member, identified a sizeable petroleum supply carried by rail at Châtellerault. After an SAS patrol visually confirmed the intelligence, and decided that the target was too heavily guarded for ground assault, it radioed the information back to Brigade headquarters. In an example of SOF and precision airpower working together almost 60 years before Operation Enduring Freedom in Afghanistan, RAF Mosquito FB VIs of 487 Squadron (RNZAF), some of whose pilots had participated in the famous Amiens prison raid, reacted quickly and struck the railyard, setting a number of cars alight.[97] This forced *2nd SS* to halt temporarily and attempt to obtain petrol supplies from further south.[98] Finally, SOE circuits HEADMASTER and SCIENTIST continued to harry the *2nd SS* as they approached their final destination of Torigni-sur-Vire.[99]

The direct and indirect attacks by resistance and SAS on the units and transport of the *2nd SS* achieved the following: delay to the the arrival of the unit to *Seventh Army* reserve of between 10 and 14 days; disruption of unit cohesion through numerous ambushes and German counter-guerrilla sweeps;[100] isolation of the combat units of the *2nd SS* from most of its spare parts in Toulouse and infliction of heavy losses on motorized transport;[101] and enabling of the RAF to strike at petroleum supplies and attack *2nd SS* units pinned down by ambushes.[102] Resistance and SAS attacks, however, had some anticipated and other unintended consequences. Members of *Das Reich* committed a number of atrocities on civilians in reprisal for sabotage and guerrilla acts, far in excess of the worst anxieties of senior SHAEF and SOE leaders, including the destruction of an entire town.[103]

Although the effects generated serendipitously by SAS and resistance forces against the *2nd SS* were the kind anticipated back in London, and there were a number of other successes, they occurred in isolation. Episodic tactical attrition in the form of uncoordinated delaying and degrading reinforcements, designed to improve Allied military performance, assisted in securing the beachhead but did not demonstrate the strategic effects anticipated for either the resistance or special operations once the beachhead was contained by local and reinforcing German forces. Special operations units assisted in the sporadic tactical attrition of the *Westheer* during the Normandy campaign but their impact was limited. At first glance, the statistics compiled by SAS teams in two of the four main operating areas appear impressive: Operation BULBASKET tallied 150 enemy casualties, and made 23 road and rail cuts in 18 days at a cost of 35 SAS dead,[104] while Operation HOUNDSWORTH posted 352 enemy killed, captured, or wounded, made 22 rail cuts, and attacked five industrial facilities in 92 days, at a cost of 26 SAS dead and missing (see Figure 5.2).[105] SAS attrition of German forces, however, had limited impact on German moral and material resources above the tactical level for a number of organizational and operational reasons.

The impact of the SAS in Normandy after the landings was limited due to inadequate preparation to conduct a focused unconventional warfare campaign and an overreliance on hope and serendipity by SHAEF and SFHQ planners instead. The maladies suffered by the fielded elements of the SAS Brigade included: counterattack and decimation by local security forces; betrayal by Gestapo and *Milice* agents embedded within *maquis* forces;[106] combat stress and nervous strain among operators, suggesting that judicious selection criteria were not applied when the unit was expanded;[107] and use for tactical support tasks that could have been accomplished easily by conventional units. These tasks included immediate support to advancing armies in a variety of ways, such as providing local intelligence and reconnoitering ahead of Allied columns and providing flank security to Patton's Third Army as it swept southward and eastward away from the lodgment.[108]

The planning behind the stillborn Operation NELSON, scheduled in July 1944 but subsequently cancelled, demonstrates some of the systemic problems

100 *The SAS in the campaign of attrition in Normandy, 1944*

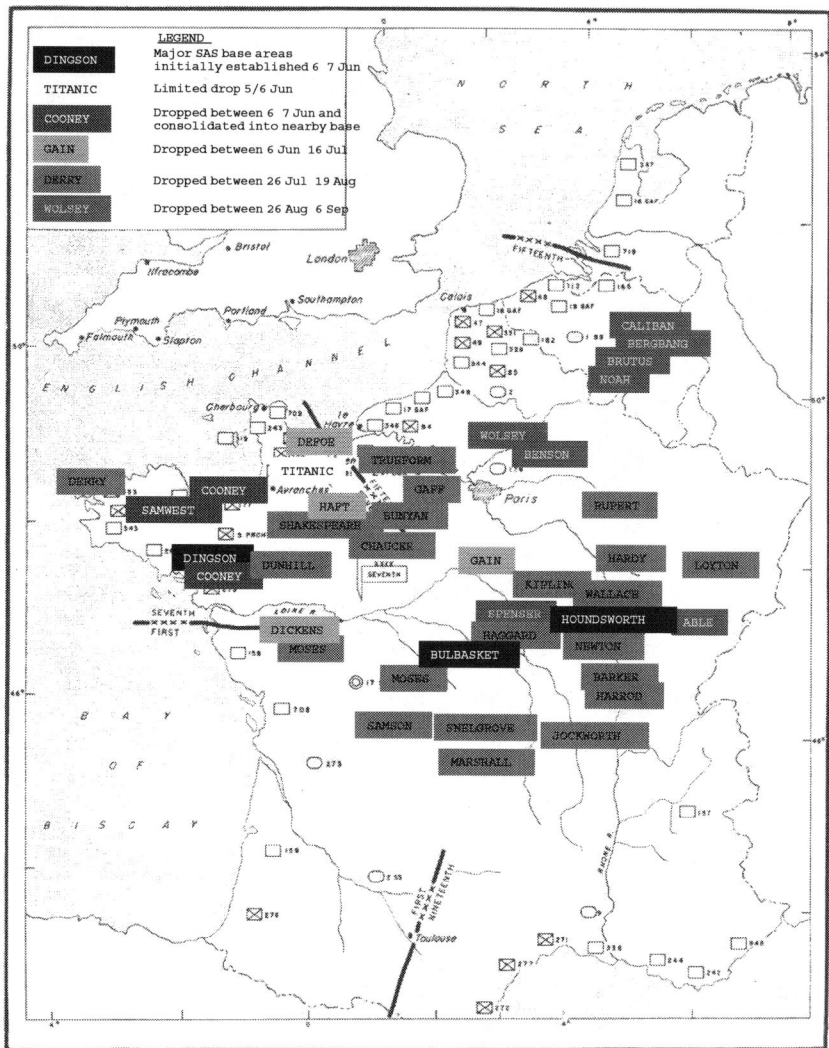

Figure 5.2 SAS operations: code names, locations, and drop dates

associated with anticipating special operations requirements after the fact and when the combat situation on the ground is fluid. In particular, NELSON implies that Allied planners wanted to demonstrate the utility of the SAS by committing forces to disrupt the German tactical logistics flow close to the front lines and have an immediate impact on battlefield events. For the operation, the entirety of "A" squadron, previously held in reserve and containing approximately 120 men, was to be airdropped along the enemy L[ines] of C[ommunication] and on proposed lines of advance of US armoured forces ... to harass enemy L of C; in the first phase to harass supplies going forward to front line, and later to attack enemy during his retreat. SAS parties would join up with Armoured Forces as they advanced.[109]

Rather than foreseeing requirements in the next phase of the offensive, being used in conjunction with other special operations units, moving deeper into enemy lines accordingly, SOF would be limited in how far they could venture from their supply base to sustain a squadron-sized element.[110]

Robbing SOF of their mobility during sustained operations behind enemy lines ensured that German security forces could confine and bring superior numbers to bear against the isolated SOF camps as was the case with BULBASKET on 2/3 July. Operators and resistance forces in BULBASKET were compromised by a local *Milice* informant, surrounded in the their forest base by SS forces, and fewer than half escaped the trap.[111] One of the reasons that doubtless contributed to the cancellation of NELSON was that A Squadron would have little time to organize itself into a coherent fighting force after its elements were airdropped, much less earn the trust of local resistance forces or be prepared to gather and transmit intelligence. Although conventional units invariably benefited from the intelligence and support obtained from the SAS, paramilitary SOF, and resistance groups in dealing with localized German threats, such tactical benefits were offset by opportunities lost in not using special operations to conduct operations deep in the enemy rear area to identify, isolate, and disrupt German supplies.

Friction and competition between special operations organizations, and the relative inexperience of staff in fomenting, focusing, and sustaining large-scale uprisings, played a factor but do not explain sufficiently why the SAS and paramilitary SOF were used for tactical purposes. In fact, a number of the points of contention over resources between the SAS, SOE, and OSS during the planning prior to Overlord, including crucial shortages of airlift and command relationships with 21 Army Group,[112] were resolved by the third week in June as all three organizations began working more closely together.[113] Some residual tensions remained. For example, SFHQ denied a number of proposed SAS operations, leading to a frank letter from McLeod to General Roy Browning, commander 1 Airborne Corps, suggesting that the SAS either be used in force or disbanded.[114] From the perspective of the field operatives from the SAS, SOE, and OSS, they began to realize the value that other organizations brought to the force mix. More specifically, each organization had its own unique qualities and key differences, but they all had a baseline understanding of the type of unconventional war they were waging and they grasped that a certain redundancy of capability could only allow the war to be waged behind enemy lines more effectively. For example, OSS Operational Groups and Jedburgh teams could train and forge resistance groups into effective combat units independently of or in conjunction with the SAS.[115] The SAS, however, had the added qualities of providing to the resistance added mass,[116] reach,[117] firepower[118] and crucial assets, such as radios, for coordinating resistance activities.[119]

Greater cooperation between paramilitary and military SOF improved effectiveness in the field but special operations did not achieve more dramatic moral and material attrition of the *Westheer* for two reasons: disagreement between SHAEF and 21 Army Group continued over the control and direction of military special operations even as SAS troops were engaged in operations in occupied France; and, SHAEF and 21 Army Group wanted to maintain operational security for the invasion and as a consequence requests to insert SOF in meaningful numbers prior to D-Day were denied. Both reasons suggest that the senior leadership of SHAEF knew neither how to employ special operations tactically or operationally nor what special operations were intended to achieve after the lodgment was secure.

One reason for the marginal use of special operations in the Normandy campaign lay in the command relationship that existed between SHAEF and the SAS Brigade through 21 Army Group. As special operations were intended to have strategic effects, it was only natural that the Supreme Commander should ultimately decide how those forces should be used.[120] The problem for the special operations and resistance forces was the command style of the Supreme Commander. Dominick Graham and Shelford Bidwell suggest that "Eisenhower's weakness was, in a word, his refusal to take command. Temperamentally, he was incapable of initiative."[121] Instead, Eisenhower deferred much of the initial planning to Montgomery and his generals, who had used SOF in North Africa and Italy, to authorize plans for the use of SAS Brigade in Normandy. Montgomery and his staff developed plans to use the SAS in "a tactical operation in BRITTANY to harass enemy movement" as well as "[o]ther small operations in connection with dummy airborne attacks."[122] Neither the Supreme Commander nor his senior SHAEF officers understood the conditions for success, or limitations inherent in strategic weapons such as resistance or special operations.[123] As a result, decisions that should have led to the establishment of effective special operations activities were deferred:

> The policy regarding the command of the SAS Reserve is being considered. SHAEF may wish for this reserve to be placed under their command. Until a decision has been given, detailed planning is impossible, but it was agreed that a Planning Committee would be necessary to coordinate the use of Resistance Groups, SAS, Jedburghs and [Operational Groups].[124]

Even after the invasion, and despite having demonstrated tactical value in Brittany and in support of Operation Anvil,[125] by the end of August 1944 the G-2 staff had concluded that "the only major dividend to the OVERLORD operation from SAS and Resistance will be obtained from the FRENCH and BELGIAN ARDENNES. No other SAS or Resistance activities are likely to have any strategic effect on the battle."[126] By the time SHAEF and 21 Army Group planners grasped how special operations could improve the strategic performance and effectiveness of the Allied armies, as opposed to improving tactical military performance, the window of opportunity to exploit resistance groups smoldering under the harsh occupation policies of the Nazis had passed, ironically just as special operations organizations were resolving their differences.[127]

Others defects hobbled planning to use the SAS Brigade to attrit German forces. SHAEF and 21 Army Group ensured that special operations would have a marginal impact on the campaign by dogmatically insisting that operational security concerns overrode the requirement to prepare SOF and the resistance for a sustained, focused unconventional warfare campaign.[128] Capable resistance forces cannot be created quickly nor can special operations campaigns be mounted overnight; they both take time to develop and plan in order to foster an effective resistance movement. Senior SHAEF leaders may not have been aware of the paradox inherent in their declaration that "it is not the policy meanwhile to organize big groups of Resistance as, until supplies and some measure of safety for the groups can be guaranteed, this might only prejudice the future possibilities of Resistance."[129]

The inherent contradiction in this statement is that by the time that large resistance groups could be organized, from anywhere from several months to a year, the Allied Army could already be closing on Berlin if the planning estimates were correct. Equally perplexing is the optimism in the dexterity of Allied special operations planning and approval from SHAEF that is apparent in the order released by the Chief of Plans and Operations Section, G-3:

> When the pattern of resistance takes such a form that offensive strategic action by resistance is possible, Brigadier Myers will submit an outline plan of action ... When the detailed plan is complete it will be passed to Headquarters, Airborne Forces, and to the appropriate branches of Special Forces Headquarters for execution ... Although the above procedures may seem cumbersome at first sight, it is considered that it will be quick in practice, since Brigadier Myers will be in such close touch with the Joint Planning Room and the Special Force War Room at BAKER STREET that the above stages will overlap.[130]

Although a cynic might suggest that Eisenhower and his G-3 were completely out of touch with the realities of the Allied planning, coordinating, and approval process, there is at least one other potential explanation aside from ones outlined previously that may account for the reticence of SHAEF to build the required unconventional warfare infrastructure sooner and unleash the forces once established. Eisenhower may have considered the implications for civil affairs, or the military governance of rear areas, as France was being liberated.[131] Although this explanation is conjectural, it is possible that Eisenhower or his deputy, Beddell Smith, did not want to provoke a mass uprising. Such an insurrection, comprised of heavily armed and well-trained French men and women of various political stripes armed and equipped by the SAS and their paramilitary counterparts, could lead to civil war, with the Allied military government responsible for quelling it afterwards.[132] Little else, with the exception of fears that the French population was suffering unduly from German and

Milice reprisals, can explain why Eisenhower made the incomprehensible decision on 10 June to halt major offensive actions by the resistance a mere five days after they had started.[133] The watchword from 10 June onwards was sabotage and subversion, not active resistance.

In any event, Eisenhower only authorized two initial advance party drops on 29 May 1944 as "part of overall plan coordinating resistance and strategic SAS action in FRANCE under our direction" to "establish safe base areas from which enemy communications can be attacked."[134] Subsequent assessments of civilian and military special operations in support of Overlord, bolstered by comments made by returning operators in after-action reports, suggest that SOF such as the SAS were dropped much too late in the campaign to be effective.[135] Although the drop dates on Figure 5.2 suggest that SAS operations were conducted as the breakout from Normandy continued apace, these were the initial drop dates of the meetings parties that would clear the way for larger drops of more substantial reinforcements. The larger operations, such as BULBASKET, HOUNDSWORTH, LOYTON, and WALLACE, took from two to four weeks after the initial drop before sizeable operations could be mounted with local resistance forces. In other examples, the isolated distraction and deception missions succeeded only too well, as "many parties were overrun after only a few days in the field."[136] In another case, Operation DUNHILL, "Four of the five sticks dropped were actually inside Allied-held territory before they had spent twenty-four hours in France."[137] By the time many missions were approved, or the airlift to insert them was made available, activity by special operations elements in support of the invasion had lost their potential value. As late as 29 July (D+51), McLeod and his staff were still urging SHAEF to commit the remaining two-thirds of the SAS to the continent "to operate in such a way as to hasten the enemy's crack."[138] But few avenues existed short of completely circumventing the existing chain of command. The SAS were part of the Airborne Corps that was "under 21 Army Group and employed tactically and did not, except through SAS representation, have any direct permanent contact with sufficiently senior formations to be in the picture regarding strategical plans."[139]

For the remainder of the war, SAS operations in Western Europe were limited to direct reconnaissance support of advancing armies and tactical blocking actions against retreating German front line forces, both of which resulted in heavy SAS losses.[140] McLeod and his staff had fought for a larger special operations contribution to victory in Europe. The final irony was that as late as 25 January 1945, potential SAS activities were still viewed by their counterparts in terms of tactical exploitation and not strategic effect:

> there may be a role for SAS parties operating in jeeps in conjunction with an offensive by ground forces. These troops would be used in the event of a break through (sic) to push ahead of the main forces and carry out attacks on communications and other suitable targets.[141]

Neptune and beyond: the SAS throttles German logistics

Counterfactual cases as to how special operations could have won victory faster or more economically in Normandy appear at first glance to be irrelevant or unnecessary.[142] Deterministically speaking, and with the benefit of hindsight, Allied victory was inevitable once the lodgments on the Cotentin peninsula were secure.[143] Whether or not the Allies would have been willing to pay the price for costly prolonged victory that occurred later than 1945 is open to debate. Although counterfactual arguments are interesting excursions into the realm of the possible, they are fraught with inherent hazards. These hazards include, but are not limited to, combinations of the following: overstating the impact of an individual link in the chain; oversimplifying the argument to link specific actions to effects;[144] introducing elements that did not exist or were in development (the "decisive weapon" argument);[145] and/or substantially reordering and moving elements without reference to their context.[146] Carefully constructed counterfactual arguments have considerable utility to strategic analysis, as they potentially offer insights into how minor changes in different variables potentially affect outcomes. Counterfactual arguments provide the greatest insights into both the "art" and complexity of strategy when they rigorously account for both the tangible, material aspects of a campaign (weather, geography, available resources), as well as the non-material components (including time) reflecting human individual and group behavior and interaction.

The reasons why the SAS did not realize their potential during the Normandy campaign are clear from the preceding section. The rationale for examining how the SAS could have been used more effectively, however, is not initially obvious. The Allies, after all, overcame tremendous obstacles in conducting landings on occupied beaches, defending and expanding their beachheads into a defensible lodgment, and breaking out of the lodgment area and encircling and destroying a considerable portion of the *Westheer's Seventh Army* during the battle for the Falaise pocket. Although the Normandy campaign exhibited all the features of an archetypal campaign of attrition, Allied success was accomplished at casualty levels that severely eroded British morale and threatened future offensive operations.[147]

Special operations could have significantly degraded German combat effectiveness and improved Allied strategic performance as part of an integrated plan designed to erode German moral and material strength in two primary ways: first, by augmenting existing Allied interdiction plans and continually harassing the tenuous, but shifting, German supply lines; and second, by shifting effort in advance of the breakout operations to supply lines, depots, and critical logistical chokepoints in the Netherlands, Belgium, and close to the German border.

The Achilles Heel of the *Westheer* was the supply system that grew increasingly tenuous as the Allies expanded and attempted to break out of the lodgment area. In terms of material support to the defense, the German logistics system moved reinforcements, equipment, ammunition, fuel, and sundries towards the front lines. Curtailing these supplies would have diminished the combat staying power and effectiveness of the forces confronting the Allies. On the moral plane, however, the logistics network was a psychological lifeline to Germany. The fighting retreat of the *Westheer* could have turned into a lengthy, disorganized rout given extended reduction of supplies, reliance of individual units upon vulnerable, organic motorized transport to provide for their own logistics lifeline from increasingly distant depots, and harassment of retreating units of the sort that eventually turned Napoleon's *Grande Armée* of 1812 into a disorganized rabble.

The SAS should have been used in an interconnected scheme that targeted the *Westheer*'s key vulnerability: the road and rail transportation of logistical supplies, including fuel, spare parts, and ammunition. Although Allied aircraft and resistance cells disrupted rail transportation and harried supply columns, the Germans adapted their frail logistical system supplying *OB West* to the circumstances. For example, the Germans constructed docks and ferries to move supplies from Paris along the Seine River.[148] The German flow of men and material continued to contain the Allied lodgment in the Cotentin peninsula for almost two months, utilizing repaired rail lines, bridges, canals, and dwindling motorized transport stocks, including reserves shifted from the Eastern Front and military districts in Germany.[149] German logistical adaptation prolonged the breakout from the beachhead for a number of reasons related to the specific elements of interdiction: airpower and intelligence.

Despite overall superiority in theater, Allied airpower had its limitations. Although there were some exceptions, by 1944 bombers could strike with reasonable accuracy against relatively immobile area targets even at night, due to advances in nighttime bombing target marking and munitions delivery procedures. Weather conditions, such as high winds and variable cloud ceilings, could severely impact high-altitude bombing effectiveness, as could human error.[150] Allied high-altitude bombing was effective against railheads and bridges but could do little to interdict supplies already on the move or able to disperse quickly. The burden of interdicting German road-bound supplies fell to Allied fighter-bombers that were available in overwhelming numbers but had limitations of their own. The munitions used by fighter-bombers, especially armor-piercing rockets, produced dramatic gun-camera footage but were notoriously inaccurate.[151] Most importantly, Allied fighter-bombers limited their activities to daylight hours, giving the Germans breathing room to move supplies from depots to the front lines. Although their initial psychological effect on the Germans was considerable, Allied tactical air forces were unable to prevent the movement of reinforcements to the front despite flying thousands of sorties per week.[152]

Allied operational intelligence gathering and processing capabilities were far superior to those of the Axis, due in large part to Ultra and Magic signals intelligence interception and decryption. The breaking of the German Enigma cipher gave the Allies an enviable window on German military movements, unit operating areas, as well as morale and supply problems. In addition, Allied photoreconnaissance capabilities and analysis skills increased as the war progressed. In the field of human intelligence sources, German occupation policies served to motivate a number of French and other Europeans to become agents and risk their lives gathering information needed by the Allies.[153] The net result was that on the eve of the invasion, the Allies had a remarkable overview of static German unit locations and defensive preparations from the Pas de Calais to Cherbourg. Once the decision was made to invade in Normandy, Allied planners had four months to refine their intelligence picture of the German defenses. In contrast, the Allies knew comparatively little about how the Germans would respond to the invasion, including moving and sustaining their forces once Overlord commenced. The intelligence picture grew less clear during the weeks after the invasion as signals intelligence and photoreconnaissance proved useful but unable to keep pace with the fluid situation on the ground, as the Germans adapted to Allied airpower through dispersal and movement by night.

To overcome these limitations, the SAS could have "shaped" the battlefield by undertaking a coordinated special operations campaign intended to disrupt further the already tenuous umbilical connections supporting the *Westheer*. Molding or shaping the battlefield using special operations requires activities focused against specific vulnerabilities, such as communications or logistics, in distributed yet loosely coordinated series of operations designed to establish the conditions for and broaden the scale of future success. In his evaluation of the only SAS operation that specifically targeted a senior German military leader during the Normandy campaign, Anthony Kemp provides a glimpse at the character of SAS shaping activities:

> [Operation] Gaff was a classic example of the application of basic SAS principles. A determinedly led small group without vast technical back-up but speaking the local language fluently managed to operate with impunity behind enemy lines for the best part of a month. They succeeded in destroying material vastly in excess of the resources employed to put them there and all returned safely. Had a hundred or so parties been spread all over France instead of concentration on troop- and squadron-sized fixed bases, it is tempting to suppose that the mayhem caused by the SAS would have been far greater.[154]

Special operations molding of the battlefield could have substantially widened the moral and material attrition "cracks" in the *Westheer* caused by the sustained pressure of the combined weight of Allied air, sea, land, and resistance forces. Although disrupted a number of times, the various units of the *Westheer* were able to conduct a fighting retreat from Normandy on the basis of pauses in combat fighting and retreat along interior lines of communication. SAS activities, combined with sustained pressure from Allied conventional air and ground attacks, could have indirectly eroded German fighting cohesion to the point of collapse.[155]

Identification of supply nodes, destruction of supply columns, and occasional ambushes and mobile raids by SAS units, in conjunction with local resistance forces, would have inflicted a significant physical and psychological toll on German forces attempting to conduct as orderly a retreat as the circumstances permitted. SAS teams and squadrons could have provided a critical bridge between the numerous and poorly armed French guerrillas fighting the battle in the rear, conventional pressure on the front lines, and the aerial methods of interdicting supplies deep behind enemy lines.[156] Working with local resistance forces could be beneficial to SAS teams but should not have been an absolute requirement, especially in the case of teams conducting road watches and other forms of special reconnaissance.[157] In the case of larger teams with their relatively heavy firepower, mobility, and ability to link resistance groups and other SOF units together, the SAS could have squeezed the German logistical pipeline even further and deeper, eventually cordoning off the retreating *Westheer* from the sanctuary of the German frontier.

During the first phase of operations, several dozen advance SAS parties, comprised of a few individuals, would parachute into France on the night before D-Day and immediately establish road and rail watches leading to and from crucial chokepoints near crossings on the Loire and Seine rivers.[158] SAS teams requiring contact with the resistance or the local population would consist of a mix of personnel, at least half of whom would be fluent French speakers and requiring a restructuring of the SAS regiments along functional as opposed to operational lines, in order to obtain information and support more easily. French resistance forces, trained and supplied by OSS and SOE operatives, at least one but preferably three to six months prior to D-Day, would conduct harassing attacks on German reinforcements closer to the beachhead and deeper into the interior of France.[159] SAS reconnaissance teams would ascertain the lay of the land, contact local resistance elements if necessary, and refine the ground intelligence picture of the German logistical network and report this information to 21 Army Group and SHAEF headquarters.[160] SAS activities would be characterized by stealth, patience, and movement to avoid location by the Germans. Where such activities would not reveal their locations, reconnaissance parties would set demolitions covertly and attack high-value targets such as command vehicles, higher headquarters, and bulk logistics carriers. SAS reconnaissance teams could be augmented by reinforcements and resupply as required by air or local resistance forces. The goal during this initial phase of operations, based on success of the landing and lasting three weeks,[161] would be to disrupt further German resupply efforts, either by locating and providing coordinates on targets for aerial attack or conducing sabotage independently or in conjunction with resistance forces.[162]

The second phase of SAS shaping operations in Normandy would have been characterized by expanding initial efforts and operating areas. Fielded teams would be bolstered by SAS "heavy" teams comprised of mobile jeep teams and armed with heavier weapons.[163] These heavy teams would increase the pressure on the German truck and rail supplies passing towards and from identified bottlenecks, forcing the Germans to commit forces to either protect their supply lines or permit unreasonable losses of subsistence supplies. SAS heavy teams would take advantage of the limited period of darkness to conduct their attacks as the Germans adapted to Allied tactical airpower and moved the bulk of their road-bound supplies.[164] Meanwhile, additional SAS reconnaissance parties would be dropped east of Paris and to the German frontier, to establish hide sites and conduct road and rail watches along arteries supplying the *Westheer*. Although this was outside of the proscribed geographical limits established for nighttime aerial insertion and resupply, based on short summer periods of darkness, this was more of a safety factor stressed by the Air Staff than it was an operational impediment. According to McLeod:

> I would like to stress the limitation on operations East of longitude 4° East. This was most unfortunate and I am convinced that if only we had been able to establish bases in Eastern France on the line of the Meuse during June or July the operations of 2. S.A.S. Regt. in Aug., Sept., and October would have been far more effective and less costly.[165]

Depending on the specific geographic location, teams would mix English-, French- or Flemish-speaking SAS operatives to contact local resistance and sympathizers and gain, compile, and transmit information on German supply routes.[166]

In the third and final SAS shaping phase for the battle of Normandy, corresponding to the Allied breakout from Normandy and drive towards Paris, the remainder of the SAS reserves would be committed to drops, in support of fielded teams, to cover gaps in the previously established logistics interdiction lines. The goal of this phase would be to isolate German fielded forces from their supplies and push an already weakened supply system to its breaking point. SAS teams, working with the resistance, would identify remaining German logistics rallying and concentration points, truck parks, and fuel depots, and pass along this information to enable air strikes, including those by other special operations units such as 617 Squadron.[167] Other SAS forces, leveraging and stiffening groups of *maquisards*, would conduct more overt attacks on supply lines and confront the Germans with sedition around every corner.[168] In addition, these forces could sustain the pressure on isolated groups of retreating Germans, harassing them much and "[keeping] them in a constant state of alert, both by night and day, depriving them of rest and leaving them exhausted" and "instill[ing] a general fear among the enemy of becoming separated from the main body of troops while seeking food and shelter."[169]

Once the Allied forces began the mobile phase of their campaign, the cumulative effect on the German forces of sustained combat, prolonged supply reduction, and incessant harassment by Allied air, sea, and ground forces would stress the very cohesive structure of the *Westheer*. Such stress was at the theoretical heart of Montgomery's "Colossal Cracks" concept of operations to break the *Westheer*.[170] Attrition through firepower, however, would be a slow, methodical process that would not guarantee success against a tactically and operationally competent adversary. The other crucial elements enabling a successful campaign against the *Westheer* would be pursuing and encircling retreating forces in addition to isolating and disrupting supplies and units seeking to stabilize the eroding situation at the front.

110 The SAS in the campaign of attrition in Normandy, 1944

The SAS, in conjunction with paramilitary SOF and resistance elements, could have played a much more focused role in the attrition of the *Westheer*. The collective weight of such moral and material weakening and stress would eventually have caused component elements of the *Westheer* to succumb to the pressure and either capitulate or collapse. As with most military campaigns, it is almost impossible to predict how quickly, or on what scale, the capitulation would have occurred. Still, had the Allies planned their offensives closer together in terms of timing, it is interesting to consider what effects the dissipation of Army Group Center,[171] the bulk of *Seventh Army,* and *Panzer Group West*, as well as the plot to assassinate Hitler, might have had on Nazi Germany in the summer of 1944.

The SAS Brigade was committed in piecemeal fashion to conduct the wrong missions too late during the Normandy campaign. Instead of striking at the crucial vulnerabilities of the *Westheer*, to improve Allied strategic performance and effectiveness, the Brigade was used instead for tactical applications. Although such applications undoubtedly improved the tactical military performance of the Allied armies by providing intelligence, tying down rear area units, and securing swaths of territory including the Brittany peninsula, they did so in a haphazard manner. By the time that the bulk of the Brigade was committed in late July or early August, planning for operations could not keep up with or anticipate quickly enough developments on the battlefield.

It is tempting to answer the question of why special operations were not used in a more effective manner by assigning the blame for perceived failure to a specific individual or organization. In the final analysis, however, a number of disparate elements combined to inhibit a more innovative application of the SAS in combat relating to its command structure and tasking. In his assessment of the role that SOF played in the North Africa campaign, John Gordon notes that "The chief flaw of the desert special-operations (sic) venture was not so much the proliferation of force but the failure to devise a controlling apparatus to keep pace with that proliferation. The structure was workable but loose."[172] In contrast, the controlling apparatus for the SAS Brigade prior to the Normandy invasion was "cumbersome" at best and not suited to assess and react to rapidly changing circumstances in the field.[173] Such command arrangements could have easily been worked out well in advance of D-Day.

Much more damaging for the SAS, and its ability to erode the *Westheer*'s moral and material vulnerabilities, was the artificial division of its responsibilities between 21 Army Group and SHAEF. SOF had been used as an enabler of attrition during the North African campaign largely because "[a] succession of British theater commanders in the Middle East grasped and exploited the situation to advantage, achieving in the process a conceptual synthesis regarding the employment of [special] forces."[174] The combined effects of merging different types of special operations, including intelligence gathering and guerrilla raids designed to weaken the *Deutsches Afrika-Korps* throughout the breadth of the theater of operations with conventional offensives to achieve maximum effect, were absent in Normandy. Instead of assisting the resistance and identifying logistical vulnerabilities of the *Westheer*, the SAS Brigade found itself on the horns of a bureaucratic dilemma instead. Its ostensible counterparts responsible for paramilitary special operations, the SOE-dominated SFHQ, saw the Brigade as a potential usurper and a drain on scarce resources. In addition, the SAS Brigade was split organizationally between Montgomery, who assigned it tasks to increase the tactical military attrition of the *Westheer*, and Eisenhower, who had no idea how to employ it to improve strategic performance but who overestimated the political risks of committing SOF early.

SHAEF staff under Eisenhower dealt with the problems of the strategic use of the resistance, including the SAS, by deferring a decision on their use in force until such time as a clearer picture of partisan activities emerged. By the time that picture came into focus, the opportunity to conduct widespread resistance operations had largely passed. SAS activities in Brittany, and other individual missions, hinted at the potential that special operations could contribute if used in a coherent, focused manner. With few politically palatable ideas to guide them, senior SHAEF staff instead decided to reinforce tactical success in Brittany to the exclusion of more widespread SAS activities elsewhere.

Controlling and liberating swaths of territory, unless it involved liberating a port intact, could not have the same strategic utility to SHAEF as depriving the *Westheer* its source of combat sustenance. In the end a bloodied *Westheer* staggered away from the trap set at Falaise to reconstitute and fight again at locations that cost the Allies dearly in casualties over the next seven months, at places including Arnhem, Metz, and the Hurtgen Forest. Had the SAS been used to sever some of the tendons of the *Westheer* and been part of an integrated team to run it to ground instead of attempting to demonstrate its own "strategic" value and prepare for subsequent operations that never materialized, the war might very well have ended earlier, with fewer Allied casualties and a potentially different map of post-war Europe.

6 Conclusion
Special operations and the nature of strategy

"The American way of war"... has come to refer to a grinding strategy of attrition ... Its time is now past, however. Spurred by dramatic advances in information technology, the U.S. military has adopted a new style of warfare that eschews the bloody slogging matches of old. It seeks a quick victory with minimal casualties on both sides. Its hallmarks are speed, maneuver, flexibility, and surprise. It is heavily reliant upon precision firepower, special forces, and psychological operations. And it strives to integrate naval, air, and land power into a seamless whole.

(Max Boot, "The New American Way of War")[1]

This work has demonstrated that understanding how special operations contribute to improving strategic performance is the cognitive lynchpin in preventing their misuse. Previous explanations of special operations misuse have centered on the divide that exists between conventional and unorthodox military minds. Conventional military thinkers, according to these accounts, are bound by dogma and doctrine and therefore do not account for the strengths and limitations of SOF. This means that SOF are committed to tasks that result in needless casualties for little apparent gain. While there is an element of truth in such assertions, they do not explain how or why some leaders have enthusiastically embraced special operations, much less why some leaders of SOF have lobbied for their forces to be used in ways that have subsequently proven disastrous. The central argument of this work is that understanding how SOF perform in extended campaigns, by inflicting moral and material attrition in conjunction with conventional forces, is crucial in order for special operations to be effective strategically.

Two themes pervade this work: one related to the nature of strategy and the other to the nature of special operations. Strategy possesses an immutable nature that technology or tactics cannot change given that it involves a competition between two or more cognizant, adaptive adversaries. The purpose of strategy is to impose one's will on the other(s) by force. That purpose, however, can only be realized through the application of organized violence to achieve political goals. The application of organized violence, however, is not without moral and material cost. Unlike business, to which it is often compared, strategy in warfare has a bill that is paid for in both treasure and blood, to paraphrase Clausewitz. Struggles between adversaries are often prolonged and last until one side decides that the goals no longer justify the continued struggle and loss. Adversaries adapt to setbacks and attempt to adjust their operational goals and tactics with varying degrees of success in order to prevent their foe from imposing their will upon them. In the end, however, the decision to abandon the conflict is based on a cumulative erosion, or attrition, of an adversary's material and non-material resources. Technology dramatically alters how destruction is inflicted but not the nature of the competition itself.

The nature of special operations is derived from their conduct and character as they are unorthodox tactical actions for strategic effect that rely on exploiting an adversary's vulnerabilities to compensate for one's own small numbers. These vulnerabilities are not exclusively material, such as insufficient force-to-space ratios or inept defensive preparations. Successful special operations also exploit moral factors, including accomplishing what was thought to be previously impossible and utilizing an adversary's doctrinaire approaches to military operations against them. Discussion of the strategic aspects of special operations, however, has been limited to overall utility or the effects achieved by individual raids or direct action missions against specific high-value targets. Strategic effect, however, is not the same as strategic performance. The cumulative effect of numerous disparate special operations, working towards a common goal in conjunction with conventional forces, is the attrition of an adversary's key moral and material resources. This psychological and physical erosion, combined with improving the strategic performance of one's own conventional forces, is how special operations contribute towards improving strategic performance. The challenge in special operations is to do the impossible not once but repeatedly, to throw and keep an adversary off balance and continue to inflict moral and material damage out of proportion to the scale of their actions.

Some theorists have suggested that strategic performance can be enhanced, and the "horrifying spectacle" avoided, through material means alone. A common theme in the theories of J.F.C. Fuller, John Warden, and John Boyd, explored in Chapter 2, is that nascent technologies, units, or processes can have wide-ranging strategic effects. Adversaries will be debilitated by speed, knowledge, precision, or by superior military means. Tanks, chemical weapons, and airpower, as well as special operations, can be used to avoid direct competition and strike directly at the decision-making apparatus, or war-making potential, that controls and supports armies and states. These military means, including special operations, appear unconstrained by the difficulties related to strategy in practice. Friction, the fog of war, logistical constraints, and the principle of continuity no longer appear to apply, or apply only to the side not in possession of the superior military means.

The basis for the conclusions of strategic paralysis theory is extrapolating observed phenomena from the tactical level to the strategic. However, the authors mistake effect for effectiveness and omit additional layers of complexity and dynamics that accompany interaction at the strategic level. Military effectiveness does not equal strategic effectiveness as the experience of the Germans in both world wars demonstrates. At the strategic level, additional factors such as social, political, cultural, and economic elements shape military responses. For example, these factors contributed to the development of British strategic bombing theory prior to the Second World War. For a variety of reasons, successive British leaders imposed constraints on military budgets that affected the development of aircraft, bombs, training, education, and doctrine. Senior leaders of the Royal Air Force (RAF) were fighting for bureaucratic and organizational survival during this period and made claims about the deterrent and economy of force value that strategic bombing could provide. Among the claims advanced by the RAF was the ability to inflict paralyzing damage on key segments of the economy, using its limited assets, which would swell into the collapse of German will itself.

Strategy is complex precisely because internal and external competition between human beings, whose behavior under stress varies individually, makes the outcome largely unpredictable. One aspect of the human condition that impinges upon strategy in practice is the idea that doctrine and application of force can be directly linked to predictable effects. Even though mounting evidence suggested that the German war industry was more resilient than initially projected, core believers within the RAF refused to accept that strategic paralysis could not work. The culture that shaped British bombing doctrine proved as durable as the German will to resist. These elements have played a role in how special operations are planned and conducted. A result of these disparate, yet interconnected, elements was the development of Barnes Wallis's bouncing bomb and the costly Dambusters special operation on 17 May 1943. Although the strategic effects of the operation remain the subject of continuing debate, the raid had little, if any, lasting influence or contribution to British strategic performance during the war.

This work has demonstrated that attrition as a strategic concept has been misinterpreted as well. Distaste for the concept of attrition has its roots in the conduct of the First World War, whose survivors sought to ensure that the "art" of warfare and dominance of the offensive could be restored. Their intellectual heirs, the advocates of operational art, paint attrition in unimaginative, dogmatic terms. It is nothing more than the tactical and operational whittling away of an enemy's force in order to seize and hold ground. This material attrition is measurable and the struggle between adversaries persists until one side grinds the other down into impotence. Attrition, so the argument goes, may be uninspired but its effects at the strategic level are predictable in nature and linear in character.

Strategies of annihilation, from which paralysis and operational art theories are drawn, suggest that wars can be won through a series of maneuvers at the operational level of war against a brittle, inept adversary. In other words, war can consist of a single, decisive engagement or an interlinked series of engagements. An adversary can do little but be overwhelmed by the "shock and awe" imposed upon them. Strategic theorists including Clausewitz, Delbrück, Mao, Lawrence, and others have understood that strategic attrition is more than just warfare by accounting or maneuver. They have taken into consideration both the moral and material dimensions of attrition at the strategic level. Quantifying intangibles such as the moral dimension of strategy is difficult if not impossible. As a result, theorists who have explored the relationship between attrition and annihilation have eschewed strategic annihilation, or the seamless, decisive offensive campaign, on the basis of political or military infeasibility or the increased scale, complexity, and lethality of modern war. In order to be a strategically effective approach to conflict, attrition must account for a number of factors. These factors include political and military practicability, the culminating point of the offensive, friction, the fog of war, and chance. More importantly, although there is a direct trajectory between the means at hand and the goals of policy, moral and material attrition occurs in a non-linear, cumulative way.

This work has demonstrated that although intuitively dissonant, special operations and attrition are intimately linked at the strategic level. Special operations have been portrayed only as individual direct action missions, or great raids, whose very nobility and audacity transcends the tactical realm and aspires toward the strategic. As subjects of investigation, individual raids are relatively easy to examine. They have defined start and end points and success or failure is immediate and obvious. Yet direct action is only one form of special operations. Scholarly investigations of the subject should account for all forms of special operations including the raising and leading of indigenous resistance forces, countering guerrillas and terrorists, and gathering timely and sensitive information covertly, among others.

As this work has shown, special operations have not been well understood theoretically. Practically, most authors have identified the sensitivity of SOF to material attrition, and the inability of conventional commanders to grasp this knowledge, as the sole reason for the misuse of special operations. SOF conduct missions of strategic importance, yet exist in finite quantities, and must therefore be used wisely. As evidence of strategic importance, authors are prone to mistake mission effects of individual direct action special operations for strategic effectiveness. At the strategic level, however, special operations are less about an epic Homeric raid than they are about the combined effects of disparate unorthodox activities in the ebb and flow of a campaign or series of campaigns. Special operations consist of numerous small-scale activities that appear individually insignificant but improve strategic performance by eroding the material resources and moral resolve of an adversary cumulatively, in conjunction with or while supporting conventional forces. In other words, special operations are not decisive, independent acts of war devoid of context. Yet special operations should not be just about whittling away enemy forces through interminable ambushes or enabling conventional forces to perform better tactically. The unique training, skills, and equipment of special operators should be used in unanticipated ways to inflict damage on key physical and psychological vulnerabilities to weaken enemy resolve and capabilities and further enhance strategic performance. Special operations combine the effects of striking or threatening what an adversary fears or values the most, or using force in unexpected ways, by shaping an adversary's behavior and perceptions in ways that make one's style of warfare more effective.

Conclusion

The misuse of special operations, a common element in their history, has occurred for a number of reasons. Yet it is more than just conventional minds unable to grasp the unique qualities of special operations. In the case of the Dambusters, the persistence of an idealistic concept of strategic bombing among senior RAF planners and staff, as well as the technical means of delivery available, led to the expenditure of a number of highly trained and equipped crews for secondary strategic effect. The use of the Special Air Service (SAS) in Normandy, however, demonstrates the difficulties of integrating special operations in a campaign of attrition. Instead of being used in conjunction with conventional and other SOF, the leaders of the SAS Brigade found themselves stuck between the proverbial rock and a hard place. Seen by their paramilitary SOF counterparts as a potential competitor for resources and missions, the SAS were also split between performing tactical tasks in support of the beach landings. Robbed of their political and military access, through the capture of David Stirling, the SAS grew to brigade size prior to the invasion of Normandy and were caught between their "tactical" and "strategic" masters. The tactical masters, 21 Army Group, wanted the SAS to be used in roles immediately behind the lines, to delay German reinforcements from reaching the beachhead and refine the tactical intelligence picture. The masters at SHAEF, including Eisenhower, viewed the SAS as a "strategic" resource. In light of the political sensitivities associated with harnessing resistance forces in an occupied country, and the risks associated with the landing itself, SHAEF adopted a "wait and see" policy towards the commitment of the SAS. In the end, the SAS was used to commit random acts of attrition against German reinforcements and rear area security detachments. Rather than harnessing these actions in a comprehensive scheme to erode the vulnerable pillar of the *Westheer*, its increasingly tenuous logistics system, the SAS was used instead to tactical effect in Brittany and in isolated locations throughout France. Special operations were not employed more coherently in Normandy and as a result, the Allied ground forces took ever-mounting losses against a *Westheer* that time and again found the reinforcements and breathing space to reconstitute itself. If the SAS was used instead to apply pressure in a rolling interdiction campaign against the German logistics system, the combined weight of material shortfalls and sustained psychological pressure from the front and in the rear might have inflicted grievous damage on the cohesion of the *Westheer* much sooner.

This work is an important step in understanding special operations as a field of study. It broadens the concept of special operations beyond individual direct action missions and defining the relationship of those operations to strategy. Understanding how special operations improve strategic performance, and degrade the effectiveness of an adversary, is crucial to preventing future misuse. In light of developments in recent conflicts, is such an understanding necessary? Events in Afghanistan and Iraq in the war on terrorism might be interpreted as evidence that special operations misuse is a thing of the past. On the surface, special operations appear to be well understood and integrated into the "seamless" set of capabilities to which Max Boot alludes.

The United States and its coalition partners, relying heavily on special operations, engaged and defeated the conventional armed forces of the Taliban and the Baathist regime of Saddam Hussein. In both cases, however, lasting victory has proven more elusive, reflecting the themes related to strategy and special operations discussed in this work. In Afghanistan, SOF, airpower, and Northern Alliance partisans caused the collapse of the Taliban regime. The initial entry forces for Operation Enduring Freedom were confronted by adversaries waiting behind prepared positions in the open who were expecting to inflict sufficient casualties to drive the Americans away. By doing the unanticipated, SOF turned what was supposed to be harassment strikes in advance of the arrival of US conventional ground units into a complete rout of Taliban and Al Qaeda forces. In Iraq, the combination of US and coalition land, air, and sea forces, including the largest use of SOF since the Second World War in the north and west of Iraq, led to the capture of Baghdad and the end of major combat operations in 21 days. Indeed, the first shot of Operation Iraqi Freedom was an attempt to inflict strategic paralysis, allegedly enabled by intelligence gathered from special sources, by decapitating the Iraqi regime. Special operations undoubtedly improved the tactical and operational performance of forces involved, especially in the northern and western sections of Iraq, including Kurdish *peshmurga* partisans and conventional mechanized units.

There is little doubt that SOF dramatically improved the tactical performance of foreign partisans and Allied conventional forces. Tactical excellence does not necessarily equate to strategic performance, especially if the goals of strategy are ill defined or the means applied are insufficient for the ends desired. Strategic performance is influenced by elements endemic to strategy, reflecting the dynamics of struggle between competing groups, including internal competition and misguided assumptions about how conflicts will evolve and end. The apparent initial military decisiveness of victories in Afghanistan and Iraq, however, is moot as organized resistance forces continue to conduct attacks against US and coalition forces. Added to this is the commitment of SOF in a variety of continuing and expanding missions in support of the global war on terrorism. Unless judicious choices are made strategically, SOF may find themselves caught in a different type of dilemma from the one that faced the SAS in Normandy. In a potentially interminable war against a network of violent Islamic extremists, SOF will undoubtedly continue to perform admirably at the tactical and operational level. SOF success could be for naught over time if they are not used in an integrated and coherent strategy that deprives global *jihadis* of not only their leaders and key logistical elements, but also the moral hub that fuels recruitment and sustains their will to continue: their ideology. As this work has made clear, there is a danger that SOF might succumb to attrition, or otherwise be grossly expanded to the point that their unique qualities are diluted.

Notes

Special operations and great raids

1. In Ralph D. Sawyer, trans., *Seven Military Classics of Ancient China* (Boulder, CO: Westview Press, 1993), p. 142.
2. Thomas Gallagher, *Assault in Norway* (London: MacDonald and Jane's, 1975), p. 132.
3. Dan Kurzman, *Blood and Water: Sabotaging Hitler's Bomb* (New York: Henry Holt, 1997), pp. 237–8.
4. The majority of works devoted to raids rely heavily on secondary sources. See for example William Breuer, *The Great Raid on Cabanatuan: Rescuing the Doomed Ghosts of Bataan and Corregidor* (New York: John Wiley, 1994); John Laffin, *Raiders: Great Exploits of the Second World War* (London: Sutton, 1999); C.E. Lucas Philips, *The Greatest Raid of All* (Boston: Little, Brown and Co., 1958); Samuel Southworth, *Great Raids in History: From Drake to Desert One* (New York: Sarpedon, 1997). Depending on how one parses Western heroic tradition, "the great raid" has its roots in either biblical parables (the Walls of Jericho) or Greek literature (such as the Trojan Horse) but nevertheless is an adjunct to individual bravery in "conventional" hand-to-hand combat. Eastern warfare places a higher emphasis on raiding according to Victor Hanson in *The Western Way of War: Infantry Battle in Classical Greece* (London: Hodder & Stoughton, 1989).
5. Historians of espionage are also prone to making similar claims. See for example Mark Seaman's assertions regarding the effect of the intelligence provided to the Germans by double agent Juan Maria Pujol in *Garbo: The Spy Who Saved D-Day* (Kew: The National Archives, 2000).
6. Lt. Col. Collins, GS0.1 (SAS), "Notes on Future of S.A.S.," McLeod 2/2/3, 7 May 1945.
7. A point made by Colin S. Gray in *Explorations in Strategy* (Westport, CT: Praeger, 1996), p. 155.
8. David Charters and Maurice Tugwell do so with precision in "Special Operations and the Threats to United States Interests in the 1980s," in Frank R. Barnett, B. Hugh Tovar, and Richard H. Schultz, eds, *Special Operations in US Strategy* (Washington: National Defense University [NDU] Press, 1984), pp. 30–3. Colin Gray builds upon this definition and discusses the problems associated with the terms "irregular warfare" and "unconventional warfare" in *Explorations in Strategy*, p. 144.
9. "Secondary or supporting operations which may be adjunct to various other operations and for which no one service is assigned primary responsibility." Department of National Defence, *Supplement 3 — Army Glossary*, B-GL-303–002 (Ottawa: Department of National Defence, undated).
10. John Arquilla, ed., *From Troy to Entebbe: Special Operations in Ancient and Modern Times* (Lanham, NY: University Press of America, 1996), pp. xv–xvi.

11 The *Sonderkommando* were unique in character and task; *SS-Sonderkommando Dirlewanger*, arguably the most infamous of the breed, consisted of poachers and other petty criminals and was used in ruthless anti-partisan operations in German occupied areas of the Soviet Union and Poland (especially during the Warsaw Uprising in 1944). The activities of this unit are outlined in French MacLean, *The Cruel Hunters: SS-Sonderkommando Dirlewanger, Hitler's Most Notorious Anti-Partisan Unit* (Atglen, PA: Schiffer, 1998). The most scholarly treatment of how the Sonderkommando and units engaged in anti-partisan and rear security duties were organized and indoctrinated is contained in Edward Westermann, *Hitler's Police Battalions: Enforcing Racial War in the East* (Lawrence, KS: University Press of Kansas, 2005), especially pp. 92–162.
12 William H. McRaven, *Spec Ops, Case Studies in Special Operations Warfare: Theory and Practice* (Novato, CA: Presidio Press, 1995), p. 2.
13 In addition to the works cited previously, see also the following works on "great raids" that equate tactical performance with strategic success: George Brock *et al.*, *Siege: Six Days at the Iranian Embassy* (London: Macmillan, 1980); Alfred Carpenter, *The Blocking of Zeebrugge* (London: Herbert Jenkins, 1922); David Eshel, *Daring to Win: Special Forces at War* (London: Cassell, 1993); Edward M. Flanagan, *The Los Banos Raid: The 11th Airborne Jumps At Dawn* (Novato, CA: Presidio, 1986); Thomas Gallagher, *The X-Craft Raid: A True Story of a Secret World War II Mission Unparalleled in the Annals of the Sea* (New York: Harcourt, Brace and Jovanovich, 1971); Kenneth Macksey, *Commando: Hit-and-Run Combat in World War II* (Chelsea, MI: Scarborough House, 1990); Hampton Sides, *Ghost Soldiers: The Forgotten Epic Story of World War II's Most Dramatic Mission* (New York: Doubleday, 2001); William Stevenson, *90 Minutes at Entebbe* (New York: Bantam, 1976); and Tony Williamson, *Counter Strike Entebbe* (London: William Collins, 1976).
14 Lucien Vandenbroucke, *Perilous Options: Special Operations as an Instrument of US Foreign Policy* (New York: Oxford University Press, 1993), p. 4.
15 With the definitional floodgate open, the author attempts to differentiate between the "military" Bay of Pigs operation and the "non-military" (i.e. psychological, in his estimation) CIA-engineered 1954 Arbenz coup in Guatemala, although both involved the use of military force and CIA assets. Ultimately, a strategic special operation rests on the author's subjective interpretation of whether or not a "military strike" was involved. Ibid., p. viii.
16 Having defined "strategic special operations," Vandenbroucke proceeds to qualify his definition as only one congregation in the broader church of special operations. Like Gray, he defers to Charters and Tugwell's definition:

> Small-scale, clandestine, covert or overt operations of an unorthodox and frequently high-risk nature, undertaken to achieve significant political or military objectives in support of foreign policy. Special operations are characterized by either simplicity or complexity, by subtlety and imagination, by the discriminate use of violence, and by oversight at the highest level. Military and non-military resources, including intelligence assets, may be used in concert.

(Ibid., p. 184; Gray, *Explorations in Strategy*, p. 145.)

17 SOF offer policymakers a low-cost, low-visibility (compared with deploying conventional forces) and potentially deniable force option. The use of the SAS in "Claret" operations during the *Konfrontasi* with Indonesia is an excellent example. For details see Peter Dickens, *SAS, The Jungle Frontier: 22 Special Air Service Regiment in the Borneo Campaign, 1963–1966* (Glasgow: Fontana, 1984), pp. 194–202.
18 Hostage rescues in peacetime, such as the Israeli raid on Entebbe (1976) and the SAS siege of the Iranian Embassy (1980), typify such self-contained acts. Edward N. Luttwak, Steven L. Canby, and David L. Thomas, "A Systematic Review of 'Commando' (Special) Operations, 1939–1980," Unpublished Report Submitted to

120 Notes

the Office of the Deputy Undersecretary of Defense for Policy Review (C & L Associates, 24 May 1982), p. I-1.
19 Commander-in-Chief, USSOCOM, *United States Special Operations Forces Posture Statement, 2003–2004* (Tampa, FL: USSOCOM, 2003), pp. 36–7.
20 Great Britain reconstituted its special operations capability in response to irregular wars within its colonial possessions. The fortunes of the special operations community in the United States were mixed until the Nunn-Cohen Amendment established the unified command for special operations in 1986. For details see Tim Jones, *Postwar Counterinsurgency and the SAS, 1945–1952: A Special Type of Warfare* (London: Frank Cass, 2001), pp. 35–7, 45–7 and J. Paul de B. Taillon, *The Evolution of Special Forces in Counter-Terrorism: The British and American Experiences* (Westport, CT: Praeger, 2001).
21 See for example the variations outlined by Mark Lloyd as well as the categorizations by Robin Neillands. Mark Lloyd, *Special Forces: The Changing Face of Warfare* (London: Arms & Armour Press, 1995), p. 11 and Robin Neillands, *In the Combat Zone: Special Forces Since 1945* (London: Weidenfeld & Nicolson, 1997), p. 3.
22 The exception being units whose primary function is ceremonial in nature (e.g. the Papal Swiss Guard). The quintessential work on the subject of elite forces is Roger Beaumont, *Military Elites* (New York: Bobbs-Merrill, 1974). John Gordon further classifies military elites into the following categories: designated (i.e., ceremonial units), functional (those that achieve elite status through action), and proto-technical (differentiated by equipment and skill-set) elites. John Gordon, *The Other Desert War: British Special Forces in North Africa, 1940–1943* (Westport, CT: Greenwood Press, 1987), pp. xviii–xix.
23 A typical mission for which British reserve SOF trained during the Cold War was intelligence gathering and reporting behind enemy lines. SOF teams were expected to remain undetected, for several weeks, after tactical nuclear strikes had been conducted. A useful, albeit brief comparative exploration of national SOF selection programs is included in Terry White, *Swords of Lightning: Special Forces and the Changing Face of Warfare* (London: Brassey's, 1992), pp. 28–62. Exceptional personal accounts of selection training, detailing the unique skills required by special operators, are Adam Ballinger, *The Quiet Soldier: On Selection With 21 SAS* (London: Chapmans, 1992) and James Rennie, *The Operators: Inside 14 Intelligence Company — The Army's Top Secret Elite* (London: Century, 1996).
24 In addition to the use of gliders, the assault troops used for the first time hollow charge warheads to penetrate the formidable armor of the fort's turrets. James Mrazek, *The Fall of Eben Emael* (Novato, CA: Presidio, 1991), pp. 47–60.
25 Much like guerrillas, SOF teams must rely only on their personal weapons and training drills to disengage from superior forces or risk being pinned and destroyed. SOF have historically taken heavy losses when used to stiffen defensive positions or spearhead conventional assaults. See for example the experience of the joint US-Canadian First Special Service Force in Italy detailed in the popular account by Robert Adelman and George Walton, *The Devil's Brigade* (New York: Bantam, 1966). US Navy Sea, Air and Land (SEALs) special operators were used for an airfield seizure mission in Panama in 1989 that was better suited to the capabilities of the US Army Ranger Regiment. During an ensuing struggle with Panamanian Defense Forces, SEAL Team Four lost four dead and nine wounded. Orr Kelly, *Brave Men, Dark Waters: The Untold Story of the Navy SEALs* (Novato, CA: Presidio, 1992), pp. 220–3, 226–30.
26 An average conventional army unit, such as an infantry brigade or division, will have attached combat service support such as signals, artillery, logistics, and air defense units. Although US Army Special Forces do have their own support and signals battalions (the 528th and 112th respectively), these units act as a bridge for supply flows from larger conventional logistics components. Conventional forces also have

attached to them crew-served weapons and units, such as mortars, grenade launchers, and heavy machine guns, to provide additional firepower.

27 Roger Beaumont has termed the misuse of *corps d'elite* in this manner as the "selection-destruction cycle." *Military Elites*, pp. 171–84.
28 Colin S. Gray, *Modern Strategy* (Oxford: Oxford University Press, 1999), p. 17.
29 Edward N. Luttwak, *Strategy: The Logic of War and Peace* (Cambridge, MA: Harvard University Press, 1987), pp. 4–5.
30 Carl von Clausewitz likens the competition between adversaries to a duel, whereas André Beaufre suggests the struggle is dialectical in nature. See Clausewitz, *On War*, Michael Howard and Peter Paret, trans. (Princeton, NJ: Princeton University Press, 1976), p. 75 and Beaufre, *Introduction to Strategy*, R.H. Barry, trans. (New York: Frederick A. Praeger, 1965), p. 22.
31 Clausewitz mentions chance and unpredictability at the end of Book One, Chapter One; friction is the subject of the terse Book One, Chapter Seven. *On War*, pp. 89; 119–21.
32 Theorists have suggested that there are as few as four and as many as seventeen dimensions of strategy. Michael Howard offers social, logistical, operational, and technological dimensions; Colin Gray perhaps splits the hair too finely when he expands this to seventeen dimensions divided into three categories: People and Politics (people, society, culture, politics, ethics); Preparation for War (economics and logistics, organization, military administration, information and intelligence, strategic theory and doctrine, and technology); and War Proper (military operations, command, geography, friction, the adversary, and time). Howard, "The Forgotten Dimensions of Strategy," *Foreign Affairs* (Vol. 57, No. 5: Summer 1979): 976–8 and Gray, *Modern Strategy*, p. 24.
33 Beaufre, *Introduction to Strategy*, p. 13. This point illustrates another problem of strategy associated with guidelines known as "the principles of war." The principles have utility as tools for understanding how to apply military force but are not inflexible "laws" per se. When the principles are used rigidly, the inherent contradictions lead to confusion. When applied timidly, for fear of breaking one or more principles, the result will be failure unless faced by a particularly unimaginative foe. The genius of a commander, or *coup d'oeil*, is in gauging how best to use his resources to achieve his goal while denying the same to his adversary. This includes knowing when to ignore certain principles of war as the circumstances warrant. It is also worthwhile to point out that a strategy that Beaufre terms "the most effective" is relative to the circumstances; sometimes the theoretical best option may be impractical or unfeasible politically or culturally. For an exhaustive guide to the Western development of the principles of war, see John Alger, *The Quest for Victory: The History of the Principles of War* (Westport, CT: Greenwood Press, 1982). Examples of misapplication of the principles of war are apparent in Charles Fair, *From the Jaws of Victory: A History of the Character, Causes and Consequences of Military Stupidity, from Crassus to Johnson and Westmoreland* (New York: Simon & Schuster, 1971). Clausewitz discusses *coup d'oeil* at length in *On War*, "On Military Genius," Book One, Chapter Three, pp. 100–12.
34 This point was well understood by Soviet theorist Aleksandr A. Svechin: "A strategist will be successful if he correctly evaluates the nature of a war, which depends on different economic, social, geographic, administrative and technical factors." *Strategy*, Kent Lee, trans. (Minneapolis, MN: East View Publications, 1992), p. 69.
35 Even if all factors are taken into account, including understanding of the adversary's capabilities and intentions, as Beaufre suggests, "There will be a special strategy to fit each situation; any given strategy may be the best possible in certain situations and the worst conceivable in others." *Introduction to Strategy*, p. 13.
36 Gray earlier equates strategic effect with political change. *Modern Strategy*, pp. 8, 19.
37 The deployment of forces for battle to achieve local objectives is the realm of tactics; coordinated deployments to achieve objectives of a campaign in a theater of war are

the realm of operations. Tactical and operational success cannot compensate for poor strategy. Ibid., p. 25.

38 See for example the comments contained in Charles Burdick and Hans-Adolf Jacobsen, eds, *The Halder War Diary, 1939–1942* (Novato, CA: Presidio Press, 1988), pp. 275–6, 333, 385. A more functional assessment of German logistical weaknesses and improvisations is found in Rainer Kriebel, *Inside the Afrika Korps: The Crusader Battles, 1941–1942,* Bruce Gudmundson, ed. (London: Greenhill, 1999), pp. 148–51, 217–22.

39 The state of the German economy has been the subject of much scholarly debate, including the question of precisely when Germany went on a wartime economic footing. As Rolf-Dieter Müller discusses at length, the true wartime economy was being planned for after the successful conclusion of Barbarossa, when Soviet resources would be plundered in preparation for the final conflict against the United States and Great Britain. Horst Boog *et al.*, eds, *Germany and the Second World War, Volume IV: The Attack on the Soviet Union,* Ewald Osers *et al.*, trans. (Oxford: Oxford University Press, 1998), pp. 1081–2.

40 Scholars continue to debate the extent to which *Unternehmen Marita*, the invasion of Yugoslavia and Greece, influenced the attack against the Soviet Union. Martin van Creveld, Brian Fugate, Gabriel Gorodetsky, and R.H.S. Stolfi minimize Marita's impact upon Barbarossa's failure; Heinz Magenheimer suggests that the delay was decisive. Creveld, *The Balkan Clue: Hitler's Strategy, 1940–1941* (London: International Studies, 1973), pp. 149–150; Fugate, *Operation Barbarossa: Strategy and Tactics on the Eastern Front, 1941* (Novato, CA: Presidio, 1984), p. 89; Gorodetsky, *Grand Delusion: Stalin and the German Invasion of Russia* (New Haven, CT: Yale University Press, 1999), p. 177; Stolfi, *Hitler's Panzers East: World War II Reinterpreted* (Norman, OK: University of Oklahoma Press, 1991), pp. 34–8; and Magenheimer, *Hitler's War: Germany's Key Strategic Decisions, 1940–1945* (London: Arms and Armour, 1998), pp. 82–3.

41 This conclusion rests on some very tentative assumptions, including a concentration of effort towards either Leningrad or Moscow. The panzer divisions of the German Army of the East, or *Ostheer*, were badly in need of rest, resupply and replenishment three weeks into the offensive; had the *Afrika-Korps* merely kept the remaining British forces in check as was intended, the panzer divisions and other reserves thrown in support of Rommel's actions might well have made the difference on the Eastern Front by sustaining the tempo of operations towards either Leningrad or Moscow. Whether or not Adolf Hitler would have made decisions differently is difficult to say; the possibility cannot be dismissed deterministically. Stolfi, *Hitler's Panzers East*, pp. 49–55; 90–6; Boog, *Germany and the Second World War, Vol. IV*, pp. 571–4.

42 For example, many of the details of the Military Assistance Command, Vietnam, Studies and Observation Group (MACVSOG), which operated in North Vietnam, Laos, and Cambodia, were only declassified a quarter-century later. An annex of the unit's command history was publicly released in 1990. A unit history based on interviews was published in 1997 and further documentation was made available to Richard Shultz through numerous Freedom of Information Act requests. See Charles F. Reske, *MAC-V-SOG Command History Annex B: The Last Secret of the Vietnam War, Volumes I and II* (Sharon Center, OH: Alpha Publications, 1990); John L. Plaster, *SOG: The Secret Wars of America's Commandos in Vietnam* (New York: Simon and Schuster, 1997); Shultz, Jr., *The Secret War Against Hanoi: Kennedy and Johnson's Use of Spies, Saboteurs, and Covert Warriors in North Vietnam* (New York: HarperCollins, 1999). A cautionary tale of the perils inherent in publishing on such topics can be found in the tumultuous publishing and distribution history of Steven Emerson's *Secret Warriors: Inside the Covert Military Operations of the Reagan Era* (New York: Putnam's, 1988).

Notes 123

43 Representative works include Vandenbroucke, *Perilous Options*; General Accounting Office, *Special Operations Forces: Opportunities to Preclude Overuse and Misuse*, GAO/NSIAD-97–85 (Washington: GAO, 1997); and E.G. Winters and Kia Paro, "Misuse of Special Operations Forces," unpublished thesis, Naval Postgraduate School (1994).
44 Books that summarize the results of the inquiries into the two separate events include Paul Ryan, *The Iranian Hostage Rescue Mission: Why It Failed* (Annapolis, MD: Naval Institute Press, 1985) and Maxine Williams, *Death on the Rock: How the British Government Got Away With Murder* (London: Larkin, 1989).
45 The trials, tribulations, and sacrifices made by the group of civilian and military personnel who convinced members of the US Congress to create USSOCOM are detailed in Susan Marquis, *Unconventional Warfare: Rebuilding US Special Operations Forces* (Washington: Brookings Institution Press, 1997) and James R. Locher III, *Victory on the Potomac: The Goldwater-Nichols Act Unifies the Pentagon* (College Station, TX: Texas A&M Press, 2002). Alfred Paddock surveys the difficulties in institutionalizing an unconventional warfare capability in the post-Second World War US Army in *US Army Special Warfare, Its Origins: Psychological and Unconventional Warfare, 1941–1952* (Washington: NDU Press, 1982).
46 In addition to the works cited previously, and in the interests of brevity, only a few representative works from each category will be cited. A more comprehensive listing of research materials reviewed during the preparation of this book is contained in the bibliography. Popular SOF battle histories include such works as Mark Bowden, *Blackhawk Down: A Story of Modern War* (New York: Atlantic Monthly Press, 1999) and William Fowler, *Operation Barras: The SAS Rescue Mission, Sierra Leone, 2000* (London: Weidenfeld & Nicolson, 2004). Unit histories can cover the range of individual campaigns or wars, or survey the history of the unit until the time of publication. Representative works are: Tony Geraghty, *Who Dares Wins: The Story of the Special Air Service, 1950–1980* (London: Arms and Armour, 1980); Shelby Stanton, *Green Berets at War: US Army Special Forces in Southeast Asia, 1956–1975* (Novato, CA: Presidio, 1985); and, Linda Robinson, *Masters of Chaos: The Secret History of the Special Forces* (New York: PublicAffairs, 2004). Biographies and autobiographies comprise the lion's share of popular SOF works and include Richard Marcinko, *Rogue Warrior* (New York: Pocket Books, 1992); Peter de la Billiere, *Looking for Trouble: SAS to Gulf Command, The Autobiography* (London: HarperCollins, 1994); and Roy Farran, *Winged Dagger: Adventures on Special Service* (London: Arms and Armour, 1986).
47 Andy McNab, *Bravo Two Zero* (London: Corgi Books, 1995), p. 16.
48 The SAS maintained colonial influence by providing training and occasionally assisting in quelling the occasional rebellion or *coup d'état*. Connor claims for example that by 1980 "The SAS was already a substantial indirect contributor to Britain's balance of payments through its role in securing allies and influence" and by looking at the political events that made it possible one can "appreciate the true importance of the Regiment's contribution to the maintenance of Britain's power, influence—and affluence—in the modern world" without describing in any detail how that was achieved. Connor, *Ghost Force: The Secret History of the SAS* (London: Weidenfeld & Nicolson, 1998), pp. xii, 235.
49 Peter Dickens is particularly guilty of gross overstatement: in his Hobbesian assessment, the SAS is the bulwark of civilization against savage Third World hordes. *SAS: The Jungle Frontier* (London: Arms and Armour Press, 1983), p. 231. See also Richard Garrett, *The Raiders: The Elite Strike Forces That Altered History* (New York: Von Nostrand Reinhold, 1980) and John Drummond, *But For These Men: How Eleven Commandos Saved Western Civilisation* (London: W.H. Allen, 1962).
50 Statements by General William Westmoreland, Commander of the US Military Assistance Command, Vietnam, indicate how general officers trained to fight conventional battles have difficulty grasping the essence or value of irregular warfare:

"[Special operations were] a kind of sideshow as far as the military was concerned ... The contribution was kind of a pinprick" and "in the final analysis [Studies and Observation Group, the US military special operations forces used in North Vietnam, Laos and Cambodia] didn't amount to a damn. The impact of it was totally incidental." Quoted in Shultz, *The Secret War Against Hanoi*, p. 277. For an assessment of Westmoreland's shortcomings and the strategic options available to the United States to win the war in Vietnam, including the use of irregular forces, see C. Dale Walton, *The Myth of Inevitable US Defeat in Vietnam* (London: Frank Cass, 2002).

51 Lincoln Bloomfield and Amelia Liess, *Controlling Small Wars: A Strategy for the 1980s* (New York: Knopf, 1970).

52 A noteworthy, but selectively quoted discussion of the negative effects of SOF on conventional force quality is contained in William Slim, *Defeat Into Victory* (London: Cassell, 1956), pp. 546–9. Other variations on the theme include J.P.O. Twohig, "Are Commandos Really Necessary," *Army Quarterly* (Vol. 57, No. 1: October 1948): 86–8; Zeb Bradford and Frederic Brown, *The US Army in Transition* (Beverley Hills, CA: Sage, 1973).

53 Steve Ryan asserts confidently, and with little explanation, that "[m]any of the tasks performed by these special operations [sic] probably could have been as competently, and at far less cost and with much less fanfare, by picked light infantry units." "Special Operations: Is Light Right?" *Asian Defence Journal* (No. 108: May 1995): 44–7.

54 Eliot Cohen relates how military elites can overthrow governments in *Commandos and Politicians: Elite Military Units in Modern Democracies*, Harvard Studies in International Affairs No. 40 (Boston, MA: Center for International Affairs, 1978). A contrasting approach, based on a Marxist-Leninist perspective that democracies other than socialist ones are illegitimate, suggests that British SOF are pillars of "democratic" regimes by being agents of state repression and terror. See John Newsinger, *Dangerous Men: The SAS and Popular Culture* (London: Pluto Press, 1997), especially pp. 5–38. A more recent example related to proposed expanded authorities for SOF in the war on terrorism is Jennifer Kibbe, "The Rise of the Shadow Warriors," *Foreign Affairs* (Vol. 83, No. 2: March/April 2004): 102–15.

55 McRaven, *Spec Ops*, p. 55.

56 Mrazek, *The Fall of Eben Emael*, p. 170.

57 As with any military "first" there are competing claims for the title. The 1929 Soviet airborne response to Afghan attacks in Tajikistan is a notable rival. Chris Bellamy, "Red Star in the West: Marshal Tukhachevsky and East–West Exchanges on the Art of War," *Royal United Service Institute Journal* (Vol. 132, No. 4: December 1987): 66.

58 In the strategic and political sense, the fall of Fort Eben Emael has substantially greater importance and meaning .Fort Eben Emael was the prelude not only to Dunkirk but also to four bitter years of war that might have been avoided had the fort held for as little as several days. It would have slowed General von Reichnau's blitzkrieg through Belgium. Only a few days would have allowed the Belgians, French and British time to take counter measures.

(Mrazek, *The Fall of Eben Emael*, pp. 167–8)

59 "Had the bridges fallen and Eben Emael survived the glidermen's attack, the Belgians could have delayed the German advance long enough for the Anglo-French forces in the north to be redeployed to the south." McRaven, *Spec Ops*, pp. 55–6.

60 Basil Liddell Hart comments that the

tiny detachment, however, made all the difference to the issue .and once the German army crossed the frontier the Belgian frontier guards on the Albert Canal would have had ample warning to blow the bridges .Airborne troops dropping silently out of the night sky offered a new way, and the only way, of securing the key bridges intact.

(*Strategy: The Indirect Approach* (New York: Praeger, 1968), p. 244)

Notes 125

61 Mrazek, *The Fall of Eben Emael*, p. 168.
62 Or, as Henri le Mire suggests evocatively, the action would "open the door whose hinge Manstein would break" in *Les Commandos Strategiques* (Paris: Jacques Grancher, 1980), p. 17.
63 Klaus Maier *et al.*, eds, *Germany and the Second World War, Volume II: Germany's Initial Conquests in Europe*, Dean McMurry *et al.*, trans. (Oxford: Oxford University Press, 1991), p. 281.
64 Strategic performance does not remain constant; it changes over time. With the benefit of hindsight, overall assessments of performance are possible. German strategic performance during the war *as a whole* was poor; in 1939–40, however, it was excellent.
65 Gregg Jones, "A Historical Perspective of Special Operations Forces as an Instrument of Strategy," unpublished thesis, Army Command and General Staff College (1991), p. 2.
66 Ibid, p. 110.
67 Gray, *Explorations in Strategy*, pp. 141–2; James Dorrian interprets Churchill's minute to the Chiefs of Staff Committee as suggesting that the Tirpitz be "neutralized." *Storming St. Nazaire* (London: Leo Cooper, 1998), p. 12.
68 McRaven, *Spec Ops*, p. 1.
69 Gray comments that "tactical success has a way of dominating serious debate over strategic utility" in discussions of special operations. Gray, *Explorations in Strategy*, p. 168. The principles outlined by McRaven are: simplicity; security; repetition; surprise; speed; and purpose. *Spec Ops*, p. 8.
70 Ibid, p. 25.
71 "[O]nce conditions become difficult, as they must when much is at stake, things no longer run like a well-oiled machine. The machine itself begins to resist, and the commander needs tremendous willpower to overcome this resistance." *On War*, Book One, Chapter Three, p. 104.
72 Examples include Colin S. Gray, 'Handful of Heroes on Desperate Ventures: When Do Special Operations Succeed?' *Parameters* (Vol. 29, No. 1: Spring 1999): 2–24; idem, "Special Operations: What Succeeds and Why? Lessons of Experience, Phase I," unpublished report (Fairfax, VA: National Institute for Public Policy, 1992); James D. Kiras, "The Strategic Utility of Special Operations in the Conflict in Afghanistan," *Defence Review* (December 2001): 45–7; Steven J. Lambakis, "'Forty Selected Men Can Shake the World': The Contributions of Special Operations to Victory," *Comparative Strategy* (Vol. 13, No. 2: Summer 1994): 211–21; Luttwak, Canby and Thomas, "A Systematic Review of 'Commando' (Special) Operations, 1939–1980"; and, Sergio Miller, "Special Forces—A Future?" *RUSI Journal* (Vol. 138, No. 4: August 1993): 70–4.
73 Gray, *Explorations in Strategy*, p. 150.
74 Ibid. Gray continues this theme in *Modern Strategy*, pp. 288–9.
75 Ibid, p. 164. Gray dismisses the need to examine strategic effect early in *Modern Strategy*: "Strategic effect is the currency that produces political change, it matters little to the strategic theorist how that effect is generated." *Modern Strategy*, p. 8. This work argues that understanding of how strategic effect is realized is crucial; past expectations and performance of special operations indicates that this aspect of strategic theory is not particularly well understood by theorists, let alone planners and policy makers.
76 Gray frames his discussion with the Tugwell and Charters definition and therefore could argue that both operations are small-scale relative to a major offensive such as Operation Overlord. For the purposes of the discussion here and to maintain the clarity of the argument, large-scale single raids-in-force like Dieppe and the activities of fielded brigade-sized light infantry formations such as the Chindits are not considered as special operations, their effect (intended or otherwise) notwithstanding. *Explorations in Strategy*, pp. 142, 157 (note 1), 175, 176–8.

2 "Seeing 'black lights' before sinking into oblivion"

1 Schneider, "A New Form of Warfare," *Military Review* (Vol. 80, No. 1: January–February 2000): 60.
2 Scales, *Certain Victory: The US Army in the Gulf War* (Washington: Brassey's, 1994), p. 112.
3 For details see Williamson Murray and Robert H. Scales, Jr, *The Iraq War: A Military History* (Cambridge, MA: Harvard University Press, 2003); Anthony H. Cordesman, *The Iraq War: Strategy, Tactics, and Military Lessons* (Westport, CT: Praeger, 2003), pp. 362–5.
4 Charles Foley, *Commando Extraordinary* (London: Longmans, Green and Co., 1954), p. 35.
5 Victor Suvorov, pseud., *Spetsnaz: The Story Behind the Soviet SAS* (London: Hamilton Hamish, 1987), pp. 6–7.
6 For an assessment of the Soviet use of special operations in both Czechoslovakia (1968) and Afghanistan (1979) to affect regime change, see John H. Merritt, "Prague to Kabul," in William H. Burgess, ed., *Inside Spetsnaz: Soviet Special Operations, A Critical Analysis* (Novato, CA: Presidio, 1990), pp. 181–201.
7 Brian Holden Reid, for example, explores Fuller's conceptualization of strategic paralysis only as it appears in Fuller's last work on armored warfare theory. "Fuller's Theory of Mechanized Warfare," in *Studies In British Military Thought: Debates With Fuller and Liddell Hart* (Lincoln, NB: University of Nebraska Press, 1998), pp. 13–32. Similarly, David Fadok discusses the theories of John Boyd and John Warden with little discussion of how their ideas evolved. *John Boyd and John Warden: Air Power's Quest for Strategic Paralysis* (Maxwell AFB, AL: Air University Press, 1995).
8 Sun Tzu, *The Art of War*, Ralph D. Sawyer, trans. (New York: Barnes and Noble, 1994), p. 177. In earlier translations, the better-known phrase "the acme of skill" was used instead of "the pinnacle of excellence." See for example Sun Tzu, *The Art of War*, Samuel B. Griffith, trans. (Oxford: Oxford University Press, 1963), p. 77.
9 For examples see Murray and Scales, *The Iraq War*, pp. 155 and Michael Smith, "Faulty phone wrecked MI6 bid to kill Chemical Ali," *Daily Telegraph* (8 January 2004).
10 First articulated publicly in J.F.C. Fuller, "Strategical Paralysis as the Object of Decisive Attack," in *On Future Warfare* (London: Sifton Praed, 1928), pp. 83–105. This chapter originally appeared as articles in *Weekly Tank Notes* (31 May and 7 June 1919).
11 A derivative of John Warden's original "five-ring" theory is called "decapitation." The term, used by Fuller, later described the "countercontrol" aspects of American nuclear strategy in the 1980s. For an excellent summary, see Timothy Lindemann, "Decapitation: Contemporary Air Power Countercontrol Strategies," unpublished thesis. School of Advanced Airpower Studies (1998), pp. 5–23. Mixing theoretical metaphors, Sue Carter refers to Fuller's "brain versus body warfare" in terms established by his friend, colleague and professional rival Liddell Hart: an "indirect approach [that] is the best alternative." "A Shot to the Space Brain: The Vulnerability of Command and Control of Non-Military Space Systems," unpublished thesis, Air Command and Staff College (1997), pp. 31–2.
12 Although he does not develop a theory of his own, David Fadok mentions Fuller's contribution in *John Boyd and John Warden*, pp. 5, 8–9. Fadok neatly surveys the theories of Boyd and Warden, although his thesis that technology has created instantaneous "maneuver-battle warfare" against control functions is unconvincing. Ibid, pp. v–vi, 9–10. Frans Osinga is another exception; he surveys the theoretical concepts that Boyd borrowed from Fuller in *Science, Strategy, and War: The Strategic Theory of John Boyd* (Delft: Eburon, 2005), pp. 50–1.
13 The degree to which Fuller and Liddell Hart influenced the development of German interwar armored doctrine is the subject of historiographic debate. On one side,

Kenneth Macksey and John Mearsheimer attacked Liddell Hart's claim as the theoretic "spark" behind officers such as Heinz Guderian and Erwin Rommel. Macksey fired the initial salvo by suggesting that Fuller, and not Liddell Hart, was the real influence on the thought of Heinz Guderian. Mearsheimer asserts that Liddell Hart knowingly padded his reputation by unethically acquiring testimonials in exchange for publishing and other personal favors. On the other side of the debate, Azar Gat defends Liddell Hart's ideas by attacking Mearsheimer's methodology, providing a chain of circumstantial evidence to support his claim and elaborating on how Liddell Hart's articles for the *Daily Telegraph* contained the germ for what became known as "blitzkrieg" warfare. Interestingly enough, Gat does not question Fuller's influence on the Germans but suggests that by the 1930s it had waned substantially. See Macksey, *Guderian: Creator of the Blitzkrieg* (New York: Stein and Day, 1976), p. 62; Mearsheimer, *Liddell Hart and the Weight of History* (Ithaca: Cornell University Press, 1988), pp. 36–48, 160–7 and 179–201; Gat, "British Influence and the Evolution of the Panzer Arm: Myth or Reality? Part I," *War in History* (Vol. 4, No. 2: Spring 1997): 150–73; and idem, "British Influence and the Evolution of the Panzer Arm: Myth or Reality? Part II," *War in History* (Vol. 4, No. 3: Summer 1997): 316–38.

14   A separate debate has been waged regarding Fuller's influence, or lack thereof, on the thought of Soviet "deep battle" architect Mikhail Tukhachevsky. Maneuver warfare proponents, the majority of whom are Soviet military specialists, suggest that Fuller's influence was limited. They point to Tukhachevsky's criticisms in the foreword of the Russian translation of *The Reformation of War* as evidence that Fuller was dismissed. At stake is the restoration of Tukhachevsky's reputation: the father of Soviet "deep battle" doctrine (PU-36) was purged by Stalin in 1937, a blow from which the Soviet armored forces did not recover until 1943. A translated copy of Tukhachevsky's foreword to *Reformation* is available in Richard Simpkin, *Deep Battle: The Brainchild of Marshal Tukhachevskii* (London: Brassey's, 1987), pp. 125–34. For works skeptical of Fuller's influence, see P.H. Vigor, "The Soviet View of Fuller and Liddell Hart," *Journal of the Royal United Services Institution* (Vol. 123, No. 1: March 1978): 77 and Chris Bellamy, "Red Star in the West: Marshal Tukhachevskiy and East-West Exchanges on the Art of War," *Journal of the Royal United Services Institution* (Vol. 132, No. 4: December 1987): 65. Authors who argue that Fuller had a significant influence on Soviet armored warfare theory are Bryan Fugate, *Operation Barbarossa: Strategy and Tactics on the Eastern Front* (Novato, CA: Presidio, 1984), p. 21 and Alaric Searle, "J.F.C. Fuller, Tukhachevsky and the Red Army, 1923–1941: The Question of the Reception of Fuller's Military Writings in the Soviet Union," *The Journal of Slavic Military Studies* (Vol. 9, No. 4: December 1996): 848–84.

15   Fuller influenced Liddell Hart heavily in the decade following the First World War; Fuller convinced Liddell Hart of the future primacy of tanks and introduced him to the concept of strategical paralysis. Liddell Hart's *Paris*, for example, is in essence an abridged version of Fuller's *Reformation of War*. Liddell Hart, *Paris, or the Future of War* (New York: E.P. Dutton, 1925) and Fuller, *The Reformation of War* (London: Hutchinson & Co., 1923).

16   See J.F.C. Fuller, *Memoirs of an Unconventional Soldier* (London: Ivor Nicholson and Watson, 1936) and Anthony J. Trythall, *"Boney" Fuller: Soldier, Strategist, and Writer, 1878–1966* (London: Cassell, 1977), pp. 4–6.

17   Brian Holden Reid surveys the various works that influenced Fuller's thought during the latter's intellectually formative years, including Oswald Spengler's *The Decline of the West. J.F.C. Fuller: Military Thinker* (London: Macmillan, 1987), pp. 9–12.

18   Fuller was roundly criticized for his resignation from the British Army's Experimental Mechanized Force just weeks after his appointment. He believed that the Army was not sufficiently committed to meaningful experimentation on the potential of mechanized forces. Ultimately, it was an article by Liddell Hart in the *Daily Telegraph*, and

not Fuller's remonstration, that compelled the British Army to take mechanization seriously. For the comments of some of Fuller's peers regarding his resignation, see Holden Reid, *J.F.C. Fuller*, pp. 150–1. An excellent account of "The Tidworth Affair" is contained in Trythall, *"Boney" Fuller*, pp. 134–44.

19 Fuller's ideas were often obscured by obtuse geometric representations, sweeping and nonsensical assertions and condescending and bombastic prose. See for example the diagrams on the principles of war contained in *The Foundations of the Science of War* (London: Hutchinson & Co., 1926), pp. 208–29; the awkward lyricism and gross overstatements in the conclusion of *The Reformation of War*, pp. 256–78; and prose such as

> A virile nation demands leadership and not grandmothership. Therefore, we are tired of the Valour of Ignorance, therefore we want the Sword of Truth. Our needs are deeds and not screeds. We are sick to death of the hire-purchase system of buying our loyalty in monthly instalments. We ask for marching orders.

in *Machine Warfare: An Enquiry into the Influences of Mechanics on the Art of War* (London: Hutchinson & Co., 1942), p. 181.

20 When Fuller pursued such interests, he did so with vigor only to regret it later; during his mystical phase he was a follower of the notorious black magician Aleister Crowley, whereas in his fascist period he collaborated with the leader of the British Blackshirts, Oswald Mosley. The splenetic preface to *Machine Warfare* did little to win him followers, especially when he openly praised the concepts underpinning the Hitler Youth and the Organization Todt as "highly democratic" ("minus their politics"). Attending Adolf Hitler's birthday celebration in 1939 also cemented the "Fuller as Fascist" view, despite his protests of doing so in the best interests of Britain. *Machine Warfare*, pp. 7, 9, 13.

21 The view that military technology would be "humanitarian" and "life-saving" in the early twentieth century was driven by idealist views of the Industrial Revolution, as well as limited experience with technology in quelling colonial unrest. This view is captured by Hudson Maxim:

> it is very strange that it should not be perfectly plain to everyone that what is true of labor-saving machinery in peace is likewise true in war. labor-saving machinery in war is life-saving machinery. The quick-firing gun is the greatest life-saving instrument ever invented. As a matter of stern fact, war is, and always has been, the biggest and most vital industry of mankind.
>
> (*Defenseless America,* New York: Hearst's International Library Co., 1915, pp. 82–3)

Humanizing warfare served another purpose for Fuller: limiting the amount of destruction and conducting warfare quickly would not disrupt commerce (*The Reformation of War*, pp. 186–8).

22 The pinnacle of his argument on waging war bloodlessly occurs in his chapter "The Elimination of War" published in 1932. Fuller suggests that the ultimate way to fight humanely is to do so without humans—namely, through the use of robots. Through the prose, however, one can also discern foreshadows of cruise and ballistic missiles, as well as unmanned aerial vehicles. J.F.C. Fuller, *The Dragon's Teeth: A Study of War and Peace* (London: Constable, 1932), pp. 296–9.

23 A source of Fuller's bitterness was the professional exclusion he experienced immediately before, during, and after the Second World War. Part of this exclusion resulted from his increasingly fascist views, which subsided after the horrors of Germany's variant of fascism were revealed. Fuller did little to challenge this perception; he continued to publish a stream of military histories and biographies. Self-promotion, however, was not beneath Fuller; he discusses the reception of his works overseas in the preface to *Machine Warfare*, even if his self-stated aim was to warn his fellow compatriots against the perils of complacency and conceit. *Machine Warfare*, pp. 16–17.

24 Liddell Hart's post-war pressure on German commanders Gunter Blumentritt, Heinz Guderian, and the family of Erwin Rommel to support his claim of influence is well documented in Mearsheimer, *Liddell Hart and the Weight of History*. Liddell Hart recalled providing the ideas and inspiration to a number of the more unorthodox Second World War commanders who were deceased. In the introduction to the reprint of William Sherman's memoirs, for example, Liddell Hart immodestly suggests that he was the source of inspiration for General George S. Patton's breakout from the Normandy beachhead. William T. Sherman, *From Atlanta to the Sea* (London: Folio Society, 1961), p. 16. Orde Wingate, the eccentric irregular warfare leader and creator of the "deep penetration" concept, allegedly learned much from Liddell Hart as well: "Wingate, then only a captain in Palestine, came to see me shortly before [the war] started, and was obviously filled with the idea of giving [Liddell Hart's "theory" of guerrilla warfare] a fresh and wider application." Liddell Hart, "Were We Wise to Foster 'Resistance Movements'?" LH10/1947/2a, January 1947, p. 2.

25 Bond, *J.F.C. Fuller*, pp. 159–60. As Bond notes, Liddell Hart made this point in his memoir published in 1965, the year before Fuller's death.

26 Liddell Hart's earliest works focused on tactical issues as well; only later did he focus on strategic ones. See Basil Liddell Hart, "The 'Man-in-the-Dark' Theory of Infantry Tactics and the 'Expanding Torrent' System of Attack," *The Journal of the Royal United Services Institution* (Vol. 66, No. 461: February 1921): 1–22.

27 The breakthrough and exploitation phases contained in Plan 1919 are part of what Stephen Biddle classifies as the "modern system" of force employment. *Military Power: Explaining Victory and Defeat in Modern Battle* (Princeton, NJ: Princeton University Press, 2004), p. 42.

28 Fuller understood the tactical aspects of broad and narrow front offensives on manpower. Plan 1919 was written with the British need to defeat the Germans as expeditiously as possible in mind. By 1918 Britain's manpower base would be less than it was during the previous year. For an offensive along a frontage of 75,000 yards, the net penetration would be less than 1.5 miles. Only when the offensive frontage was limited to 20,000 yards could gains of 6 miles be made. J.F.C. Fuller, "Tank Operations Decisive and Preparatory, 1918–1919," FP I/TS/1/1/40, December 1917, p. 6.

29 Ibid.
30 Fuller, "The Tactics of the Attack," p. 4.
31 Ibid, p. 7.
32 Ibid, p. 4.
33 Corelli Barnett, *Britain and Her Army, 1509–1970: A Military, Political and Social Survey* (London: Penguin, 1970), p. 404.
34 Fuller, "Tank Operations," p. 6.
35 Mechanization would also yield tremendous benefits for imperial defense. Discussing a hypothetical scenario taking place on the Northwest Frontier, in which specialized tanks roll towards Kabul, Fuller concludes:

> the whole operation is really too simple to be considered as partaking of warfare. Is it feasible? No, not as yet, but it can be made so within a few years. Is it worth instituting? Yes, if lives, man-power, money and time are worth economizing.
> (*The Reformation of War*, p. 195)

36 Fuller went through technology "phases" but the tank always remained predominant in his works. In 1920, he emphasized the tank exclusively; by 1926, he was discussing the value of aircraft, submarines, and chemical weapons. Looking further ahead into the future, warfare would reach an ideal mechanized state through the perfection of robotic combatants. Fuller returned to his focus on the tank in *Machine Warfare* and *Lectures on FSR III: Operations Between Mechanized Forces* (London: Sifton Praed, 1932).

37 Fuller cited frequently the pre-war work by Ivan S. Bloch. Bloch, a banker, predicted that warfare would be made impossible by the dominance of defense technologies; mankind would be better served by avoiding slaughter beforehand. See for example Fuller, *The Reformation of War,* pp. 77–8; *The Foundations of the Science of War,* pp. 26–8.

38 Colmar von der Goltz used the phrase "the nation in arms," made during a Prussian throne speech in 1860, as the title of a best-selling book. The book, on military operations, was published in the wake of Prussia's successes in the Austro-Prussian (1866) and Franco-Prussian (1870–1) wars. *The Nation in Arms: A Treatise on Modern Military Systems and the Conduct of War,* 2nd edn, Philip Ashworth, trans. (London: Hugh Rees, 1913), p. v.

39 "The Tactics of the Attack as Affected by the Speed & Circuit of the Medium 'D' Tank," FP I/TS/1/1/50, 24 May 1918, p. 3.

40 Fuller was prone to extreme flights of fancy on the one hand and sober assessments on the other. For evidence of the latter, consider the discussion of the nature of offense and defense dating from 1925:

> Bearing in mind that there is no hard and fast dividing line between the offensive and defensive in warfare, we find that the object is the same. Shielding does not consist solely in preserving our own existence, but in preserving it in order that we may more economically destroy the enemy, consequently, a defensive battle should be based on an offensive plan, which through force of circumstances cannot at once be put into operation.
>
> ("Principles of Defensive Warfare," *The Royal Engineers Journal,* Vol. 39, No. 2: June 1925: 226)

41 J.F.C. Fuller, *The Reformation of War,* pp. 26–7.

42 "The Tactics of the Attack," p. 1. Ernst Junger's description of the lethal conditions on First World War battlefields as the "storm of steel" has stuck as a defining metaphor. Less well known is Hudson Maxim's phrase penned during the war. Maxim, *Defenseless America,* p. 91 and Junger, *Storm of Steel: From the Diary of a German Storm-Troop Officer on the Western Front* (London: Chatto & Windus, 1930). Fuller succinctly describes technological developments in the decades prior to the First World War in *The Conduct of War, 1789–1961: A Study of the Impact of the French, Industrial, and Russian Revolutions on War and its Conduct* (Westport, CT: Greenwood, 1981), pp. 134–8; 175.

43 Fuller's earliest writings equating different types of "landships" to equivalent warships owed much to pioneering work by Gifford Q. Le Martel and Ernest Swinton. At one point, however, Fuller considered infantry as little more than bullet fodder. Placing infantry under armor for protection, with a gun for support, was no different than putting men in tanks. If tanks could achieve more dramatic results, namely paralysis, why bother investing in infantry carriers that would only slow down the tanks once the infantry debarked? This line of reasoning illustrates the peril inherent in broad historical extrapolation. For Fuller, tanks were analogous to armored knights during medieval times; they possessed both mobility and shock functions. A closer reading of the conduct of the battles of Agincourt and Crécy, much less the overall performance of the Crusaders against the Saracens, might have led to a reconsideration of the analogy. Martel, "A Tank Army," Fuller FP 1/TS/1/1/9, November 1916 or March 1917, especially pp. 2–5; Swinton, "Notes on the Employment of 'Tanks'," Fuller FP 1/TS/1/1/2, 27 January 1917; Fuller, "The Application of Recent Developments in Mechanics and Other Scientific Knowledge to Preparation and Training for Future War on Land," *Journal of the Royal United Services Institution* (Vol. 65, No. 458: May 1920): 227–74; idem, "Correspondence: Scientific Soldiership," *The Royal Engineers Journal* (Vol. 42, No. 4: December 1928): 743; and, Charles Oman, *The Art of War in the Middle Ages, A.D. 378–1515,* rev. edn

Notes 131

(Ithaca, NY: Cornell University Press, 1953), pp. 58–9, 126–36. As Brian Holden Reid points out, Liddell Hart's early views on infantry were just as restrictive as Fuller's. *Studies In British Military Thought*, pp. 27–9.

44 The charge that Fuller exclusively advocated a "tank-only" army stems from a misreading of his earliest writings. The phrase "Tanks, therefore, can replace infantry" is preceded by "Tanks, by reducing the resistance offered to infantry in battle, *enable a smaller body of unarmored men to accomplish a given operation more quickly* and less dangerously than would be possible for a larger body of men unaccompanied by these machines" (emphasis added). "The Application of Recent Developments in Mechanics," p. 261. In his later enthusiasm to promote the "civilizing" of war through technology, Fuller grossly overstated to make his point; the argument about capturing fleets intact through the use of aircraft, submarines, and chemical weapons is a mechanized flight-of-fantasy taken to its extreme. *The Reformation of War*, pp. 146–7. As an aside, Fuller did not see the much-quoted *Reformation* as a "serious" work. In his correspondence with Liddell Hart he wrote: "My 'Reformation of War' is simply a pot-boiler or rather a means of advertisement so that I can in future get [*The Foundations of the Science of War*] accepted. It was written in about a dozen hotel [sic] each with a jazz band!" Fuller to Liddell Hart, LH 1/302/37, 27 March 1923, p. 2.

45 "Tactics of the Attack," p. 6.

46 Fuller did speculate that airpower could become the dominant instrument of warfare, replacing land and sea power, especially if chemical weapons were used. Despite the rhetoric, Fuller maintained clear separation between the character and the nature of war. The character of war was ever changing, based on new scientific developments. The nature of war does not: "the true object, as I have frequently stated, is not to kill soldiers and sink ships, but to change a policy which these soldiers and ships are protecting." *The Reformation of War*, p. 148.

47 There were eight principles of war according to Fuller: objective; offensive; security; concentration; economy of force; movement; surprise; and cooperation. His initial articulation of the principles is located in Anonymous (J.F.C. Fuller), "The Principles of War with Reference to the Campaigns of 1914–15," *Journal of the Royal United Services Institution* (Vol. 61: February 1916): 3 and is developed further in *The Reformation of War*, p. 28.

48 Wilkinson was an advocate of defense preparation and reform in Britain at the close of the nineteenth century. As Jay Luvaas notes in his chapter on Wilkinson, *The Brain of an Army* was published at almost the same time as a government report regarding army reform (the Harrington Committee Report) but before the humiliations suffered by the British Army in South Africa during "Black Week." Wilkinson examined the composition and role of the German General Staff, which was much admired elsewhere in Europe but about which little was known. Count Helmut von Moltke praised the book and he allowed some correspondence with Wilkinson to be published in the preface to the second edition. Spenser Wilkinson, *The Brain of an Army: A Popular Account of the German General Staff*, 2nd edn (London: Constable, 1895), pp. 5–17; Jay Luvaas, *The Education of an Army: British Military Thought, 1815–1940* (London: Cassell, 1964), pp. 259–64.

49 Fuller was conscious not to extend the metaphor too far. In an acerbic side comment to Liddell Hart's expansion of the "army as body" analogy, in which Liddell Hart subdivides economy of force into generic principles, accentuating principles, elementary principles, fundamental elements, and six constituent body sections, Fuller merely comments "What about bones, testicles etc., This is playing at war." Transcript copy, Liddell Hart to Fuller, LH1/302/34, 5 March 1923, p. 4.

50 Wilkinson, *The Brain of an Army*, pp. 193–4. There are striking similarities in the language used by both Wilkinson and Fuller. Compare the above quote with the following: "When a boxer fights another he tries to get a left or right on the side of his opponent's jaw. Why? Not to break the jaw, but to *derange* the brain; because, more

than any other organ the brain controls the body [emphasis in original]." Fuller, "Strategical Paralysis as the Object of Decisive Attack," p. 88.
51 Liddell Hart outlined these terms in a letter to Fuller. Liddell Hart to Fuller, LH1/302/134, 16 April 1928.
52 Fuller, "The Tactics of the Attack," p. 3.
53 If an enemy force did not immediately surrender, or perhaps just for good measure, Fuller thought it prudent to "fire a second shot through the stomach, that is dislocate the enemy's supply system behind his protective front, [so that] his men will starve to death." Ibid.
54 Fuller, "Strategical Paralysis as the Object of the Decisive Attack," pp. 93–4.
55 Mechanized war would not only be economical, it might even be decisive and profitable: "With the Medium D Tank and Aeroplane there is no reason why we should not receive 100% interest on our investment. This represents the winning of the war in a single battle." Fuller, "Tactics of the Attack," p. 5.
56 Anticipating the next scientific developments, Fuller suggested that even tanks and aeroplanes would one day be obsolete as scientific progress marched on inexorably. The result was an attempt in the 1920s to explain the phenomenon of electromagnetic pulse (EMP): "The victorious side, all unknown to the enemy, has discovered how to derange, by means of etheric waves, the mechanism of the hostile tanks and aeroplanes .for in twenty seconds [the enemy's] entire army will be immobilized by perhaps *one man!* [emphasis in original]" *The Reformation of War*, pp. 168–9.
57 Fuller discusses his reasoning, along with the need for professionals to understand "area warfare" (non-linear land combat), in "Scientific Soldiership," *The Royal Engineers Journal* (Vol. 42, No. 2: June 1928): 198–204.
58 The normal necessary sequence, or basic formula, of a battle or campaign is "find, fix and finish (or decide)" .But in the hands of an artist of War (sic), or the mind of a scientist of war, the second phase assumes a subtler and deeper form. For by deception (mental), demoralisation and manoeuvre (physical and logistical), he produces a paralysis *followed by dislocation of the enemy's balance*. And thereby the "finish," instead of being merely a dislodging, becomes a disruption of the enemy's army—a decisive, instead of a merely deciding, blow [underlining in original].
("Original Page 5 of J.F.C. Fuller's Tactics," LH1/302/137, 23 April 1928.)
59 "[A] physical attack delivered by tanks transported by submarines against a military or naval objective should only be regarded as a stepping-stone to a moral attack on the nerves and will of the hostile nation." *The Reformation of War*, p. 181.
60 As mentioned in a previous note, Liddell Hart and his supporters perpetuated the view that Fuller wanted to dispense with all infantry. This quote suggests that infantry play the crucial role of the "axe," fixing the adversary's army to enable the "javelins" to "shiver past its flanks." Ibid., p. 172.
61 [O]ver four years were required wherein to undermine German moral; in the days of Napoleon it took twenty-two years to undermine that of the French .the muscle-moving armies took four weeks to cover the 150 miles which separates Liége from the outskirts of Paris. To-day, the aeroplane can cover this distance in one hour, and, in a few years to come, a tank will be able to accomplish this journey in one day.
(Ibid.)
62 Ibid.
63 The fascism espoused by Fuller rejected democratic degeneracy and advocated instead the development of technology, and an elite class of mechanical specialists, as the vehicle for progress. Azar Gat, *Fascist and Liberation Interpretations of War: Fuller, Liddell Hart, Douhet and Other Modernists* (Oxford: Oxford University Press, 1998), pp. 3–6.
64 *Machine Warfare*, p. 7. Fuller was a man of his era and this view, articulated by Nietzsche in *Beyond Good and Evil*, was popular among military officers of his generation. It found expression in the popular book by William Trotter, *Instinct of the Herd in Peace and War* (New York: Macmillan, 1919).

65 As David Omissi points out, tribesmen at the outermost reaches of the British Empire learned to adapt to aerial bombardment in the interwar period. Civil defense preparations in Western countries were almost non-existent as political elites clung to the belief that all signatories would uphold the "spirit" of the treaties such as the one negotiated at Locarno. On the RAF's policy of "air policing" and colonial responses to it, see *Air Power and Colonial Control*, pp. 107–33.

66 On the practical problems associated with using chemical weapons, see the details of the Italian campaign in Abyssinia in 1936 contained in Edward Spiers, *Chemical Weaponry: A Continuing Challenge* (London: Macmillan, 1989), pp. 84–8.

67 The German conduct of the war on the Eastern Front demonstrated how even the most adroit armored forces could be defeated by a combination of these elements. In particular, the German failure to destroy the Kursk salient in 1943 demonstrated the superiority of defense in depth against armored forces. For the Soviet perspective on the defense preparations prior to and conduct of the battle, see David Glantz and Harold Orenstein, eds, *The Battle for Kursk, 1943: The Soviet General Staff Study* (London: Frank Cass, 1999).

68 German generals were mystified during the invasion of Russia in 1941 when pockets of Russian forces continued to resist despite being encircled. By Fuller's reasoning, Japanese garrisons on the outermost islands in the Pacific theater should have capitulated quickly once isolated; this presumption was not matched by subsequent events, as thousands of US Army, Navy, Marine Corps, and Coast Guard personnel were to discover. Examples of Russian stubbornness when surrounded are contained in R.H.S. Stolfi, *Hitler's Panzers East: World War II Reinterpreted* (Norman, OK: University of Oklahoma Press, 1991), pp. 94–6. On the character of land combat in the Pacific theater is Eric Bergerud, *Touched With Fire: The Land War in the South Pacific* (New York: Viking, 1996).

69 Fuller later answered questions on strategic paralysis for author John Wheldon. Trythall, *"Boney" Fuller*, p. 257; Wheldon, *Machine Age Armies* (London: Abelard-Schuman, 1968), p. ix. In addition, Fuller recalled the evolution of the title "Plan 1919" in correspondence with Liddell Hart. He clarified that "Why I did not write 'tactical' was that the primary aim of the attack was to paralyse the enemy's command and not his fighting forces; that is, his strategical brain and not his tactical body." Fuller to Liddell Hart, LH 1/302/609, 19 February 1964. In his later work, Fuller steered clear of theories of warfare and grand strategic tracts and he focused instead on writing several noteworthy military histories and biographies including: *Armament and History* (London: Eyre and Spottiswoode, 1946); *The Second World War* (London: Eyre and Spottiswoode, 1948); *The Decisive Battles of the Western World and Their Influence Upon History*, 3 vols. (London: Eyre and Spottiswoode, 1954–1956); *The Generalship of Alexander the Great* (London: Eyre and Spottiswoode, 1958); *The Conduct of War; Julius Caesar: Man, Soldier and Tyrant* (London: Eyre and Spottiswoode, 1965).

70 David R. Mets, *The Air Campaign: John Warden and the Classical Airpower Theorists* (Maxwell AFB, AL: Air University Press, 1998), pp. 64–5. On Warden's influence on the planning of "Instant Thunder," see Edward Mann III, *Thunder and Lightning: Desert Storm and Airpower Debates* (Maxwell AFB, AL: Air University Press, 1995), pp. 27–47.

71 US Air Force doctrine espouses both parallel attack and paralysis:

> These facts are: (1) aerospace power is decisive, and (2) military thought has evolved away from the need to mass forces on one or two targets at a time to massing the effects of those forces simultaneously at the strategic, operational, and tactical levels of war to paralyze opponents and make them ineffective, rather than necessarily having to destroy them.
>
> (Secretary of the Air Force, *Strategic Attack*, Air Force Doctrine Document 2–1.2, Maxwell AFB, AL: Air Force Doctrine Center, 1998, pp. 14–15)

Parallel operations involve simultaneous attack of varied target sets to overwhelm and incapacitate an enemy, often resulting in decisive effects." Secretary of the Air Force, *Organization and Employment of Aerospace Power*, Air Force Doctrine Document 2 (Maxwell AFB, AL: Air Force Doctrine Center, 2000), p. 7.

72 See David A. Deptula, *Firing for Effect: Change in the Nature of Warfare* (Arlington, VA: Aerospace Education Foundation, 1995).

73 One author reaches the staggering conclusion that Air Force planning for the 1995 campaign against Serbia incorporated parallel attack, effects-based planning, and a strategy of denial simultaneously. Robert Pollock, "Roads Not Taken: Theoretical Approaches to Operation Deliberate Force," in Robert Owen, ed., *Deliberate Force: A Case Study in Effective Air Campaigning* (Maxwell AFB, AL: Air University Press, 2000), pp. 435–40, 450. Warden's ideas are also influential overseas: parallel attack has filtered into Royal Australian Air Force publications and decapitation into those of the Royal New Zealand Air Force. See for example Alan Stephens, "Kosovo, Or the Future of War," in Gary Brown, Michael Evans and Alan Stephens, eds, *The Use of Military Force in Kosovo*, Working Paper No. 54 (Canberra: Australian Defence Studies Center, 1999), available online at http://idun.itsc.adfa.edu.au/ADSC/astephens.html; Shaun Clarke, *Strategy, Air Strike, and Small Nations* (RAAF Base Fairburn: Air Power Studies Center, 1999), pp. 124–6.

74 Warden flew several hundred missions as a forward air controller spotting targets for air strikes. The planning of the Gulf War air campaign reflected the Vietnam "years that were also costly for American aircrew and aircraft and left many in the Air Force bitterly determined to avoid such a repetition." *The Air Campaign: Planning for Combat* (Washington: Pergamon-Brassey's, 1989), p. 160; Eliot Cohen, *The Gulf War Air Power Survey* (hereafter referred to as GWAPS), *Volume One: Planning and Command and Control* (Washington: Government Printing Office, 1993), p. 112.

75 For an organizational assessment of the gradual use of airpower in Vietnam, see James Thompson, *Rolling Thunder: Understanding Policy and Program Failure* (Chapel Hill, NC: University of North Carolina Press, 1980).

76 One of the most outspoken advocates against targeting restrictions after the war was the Commander-in-Chief, Pacific (CINCPAC), Admiral Ulysses S. Grant Sharp. See his bitter assessments of the bombing restrictions and overall lack of political will to do what Sharp considered necessary in *Strategy for Defeat: Vietnam in Retrospect* (Novato, CA: Presidio, 1978), pp. 99–102; 267–71. A more recent assessment on how the United States should have used airpower is contained in C. Dale Walton, *The Myth of Inevitable US Defeat in Vietnam* (London: Frank Cass, 2002), pp. 108–31.

77 A concise survey of the military and political context of Linebacker I and II, as well as the aerial mining of North Vietnamese harbors, is found in Spencer Tucker, *Vietnam* (Lexington: KY: University of Kentucky Press, 1999), pp.169–74.

78 Surveys of US Air Force missions in South Vietnam are available in John Schlight, *The War in South Vietnam: The Years of the Offensive, 1965–1968* (Washington: Government Printing Office, 1988); Robert Derr, *Air War South Vietnam* (London, Arms and Armour Press, 1991); James Corum and Wray Johnson, *Airpower in Small Wars: Fighting Insurgents and Terrorists* (Lawrence, KS: University Press of Kansas, 2003), especially pp. 225–74.

79 Personal correspondence with John Warden, 6 August 2001.

80 Ibid.

81 Ibid. Warden credits J.F.C. Fuller's *The Generalship of Alexander the Great* as one of the most influential works on his thought, as well as the instruction and guidance given by Fred Hartmann, a faculty member on the National War College staff.

82 *The Air Campaign*, pp. 3–4.

83 Michael Gordon and Bernard Trainor neatly summarize the view of both schools in *The General's War: The Inside Story of the Conflict in the Gulf* (New York: Little,

Brown & Company, 1995), p. 78; they characterize the "tactical" school, however, as limited thinkers. Ibid, p. 85.

84 For a survey of the literature and discussion of the relevant participants in the airpower debate, see Phillip Meilinger, "The Historiography of Airpower: Theory and Doctrine," *The Journal of Military History* (Vol. 64, No. 2: April 2000): 467–502. The debate regarding strategic airpower's efficacy remains a lively one; see for example Gian Gentile, *How Effective is Strategic Bombing: Lessons Learned from World War II to Kosovo* (New York: New York University Press, 2001); Robert Pape, *Bombing to Win: Air Power and Coercion in War* (Ithaca, NY: Cornell University Press, 1996); Daniel Byman and Matthew Waxman, "Kosovo and the Great Air Power Debate," *International Security* (Vol. 24, No. 4: Spring 2000): 5–38; Earl Tilford, Jr, "Operation Allied Force and the Role of Air Power," *Parameters* (Vol. 29, No. 4: Winter 1999–2000): 24–38.

85 *The Air Campaign*, p. 7.

86 The work is measured but does contain unsupported statements such as "no state has lost a war while it maintained air superiority, and attainment of air superiority consistently has been a prelude to military victory." This statement is baffling as Warden suggests on the same page that air superiority is both limited in time and geography, suggesting that like sea control, air superiority can be disputed throughout the conflict. Ibid., pp. 10–13.

87 The discussion of decisive, coordinated attacks on the operational center of gravity is balanced by the insight into strategy that "We must keep in mind, however, that the real center of gravity may not be reachable initially." Ibid., p. 131.

88 Ibid., pp. 4–5.

89 The net effect of these environmental conditions is that the operational commander must be sufficiently flexible and adapt to the new situations as they arise. Ibid., p. 123.

90 [T]he nature and objective of the war, and the nature of the enemy will suggest the forces needed for success. On some occasions, one arm will suffice, while at other times all three must be used in any of a wide combination of ways.

The concept of the "key force" is developed later in the section on "The Orchestrating of War." Ibid., pp. 7, 123.

91 Warden mentions the conclusions of US air planners after the end of the Second World War, when arguments were made that electricity, transportation, or petroleum were "panacea targets" of the German economic system. See for example Secretary of War, *United States Strategic Bombing Surveys [European War; Pacific War]* (Maxwell AFB, AL: Air University Press, 1987), pp. 33–4. Prior to the invasion of Europe in 1944, the debate on bombing railheads or POL (petroleum, oil and lubricants) targets involved panacea arguments. The notion of inflicting paralysis on German industry appeared in this debate; Solly Zuckerman suggested that bombing transport prior to the invasion would "paralyze movement in the whole region" and prevent German reinforcement. See W.W. Rostow, *Pre-Invasion Bombing Strategy: General Eisenhower's Decision of March 25, 1944* (Austin, TX: University of Texas Press, 1981), pp. 3–14.

92 The five "rings" of Warden's model appear in rough form as potential centers of gravity in *The Air Campaign*. They include: "equipment (numbers of planes or missiles); in logistics (the quantity and resilience of supply support); geography (location and numbers of operational and support facilities); in personnel (quality of pilots); or in command and control (importance and vulnerability)." *The Air Campaign*, p. 35.

93 In terms reminiscent of Fuller's "scientist of war," Warden suggests that

> Today, a single commander may well be the key to victory or defeat, if he is especially brilliant or stupid .in normal circumstances, the modern staff is capable of

keeping operations going along a fairly broad path. Therefore, it is not so much the commander who is the center of gravity, but the staff system which serves him.

(Ibid., pp. 44–5)

94 The transition from a single center to multiple centers of gravity allowed for "escape from single point failure modalities" and reflected Warden's view that what "struck me .was the importance of not depending on getting something exactly right"—in other words, integrating redundancy into his theory. Personal correspondence with John Warden, 6 August 2001.

95 The "five-ring model" has several names: the enemy as a system model, parallel attack, and inside-out warfare.

96 Cohen, *GWAPS, Volume I: Planning and Command and Control*, p. 111.

97 Richard Reynolds, *Heart of the Storm: The Genesis of the Air Campaign Against Iraq* (Maxwell AFB, AL: Air University Press, 1995), p. 17.

98 Richard Overy contends that Germany was not overwhelmed merely by superior Allied industrial output: "There was no other way for the Allies to dislodge the Axis states from their conquests in 1942 than to defeat them on the battlefield." Dislodging the Axis required a mix of combat effectiveness, military reform and production, political will to sustain the effort as well as luck. *Why the Allies Won* (London: Jonathan Cape, 1995), pp. 314–25.

99 Some US Air Combat Command officers thought that Warden's plan for the Gulf War air campaign was just as indiscriminate as Second World War bombing. Reynolds, *Heart of the Storm*, p. 40.

100 Gordon and Trainor, *The General's War*, p. 78.

101 We may not have to find and destroy 30,000 tanks if we can destroy their few hundred associated fuel or ammunition distribution points. We may not have to destroy the few hundred fuel distribution points if we can immobilize an entire society by destroying dozens of electrical generation systems. And we may not need to destroy dozens of electrical generation systems if we can capture, kill, or isolate the enemy leader.

("Employing Air Power in the Twenty-first Century," in Robert Shultz, Jr and Robert Pfaltzgraff, Jr, eds, *The Future of Air Power in the Aftermath of the Gulf War*, Maxwell AFB, AL: Air University Press, 1992, p. 69.)

102 Cohen, *GWAPS, Volume I: Planning and Command and Control*, pp. 108–9. A day-to-day narrative of the planning of the Gulf War air campaign, built upon personal recollections and highlighting the role that personalities, friction, and intraservice cultural differences play, is available in Reynolds, *Heart of the Storm*. Pages 25–9 discuss in detail the birth of "Instant Thunder."

103 American interests extended beyond the uninterrupted supply of oil; Iraq was a useful regional counterweight to Iran. American leaders were interested in deposing Saddam Hussein, while at the same time preserving Iraq's counterbalancing influence, and as a result there was little perceived need to devastate the country from the air only to have to rebuild it again. In a remarkable coincidence, this hearkens back to Fuller's reason why war should be humanized: the lifeblood of Britain, commerce, should not be disrupted by war. Cohen, *GWAPS, Volume I: Planning and Command and Control*, p. 95.

104 Reynolds, *Heart of the Storm*, pp. 17–8.

105 Targeting command and control centers during the course of conflict, as opposed to specific individuals, is one method of circumventing the self-imposed American constraint against assassination codified in Executive Order (EO) 12333. For an informed discussion of the legal viability of assassinating Saddam Hussein prior to the 1991 Gulf War, see Robert Turner, "Killing Saddam: Would It Be a Crime?" *Washington Post* (7 October 1990), pp. D1–D2. A key provision in the EO is that such actions

shall not be undertaken without the knowledge and consent of the President of the United States. The President has the authority to issue a "finding" to authorize such actions. Bob Woodward, "CIA Told to Do 'Whatever Necessary' to Kill Bin Laden: Agency and Military Collaborating at 'Unprecedented' Level; Cheney Says War Against Terror 'May Never End'," *Washington Post* (21 October 2001).

106 Edward Mann III, *Thunder and Lightning: Desert Storm and the Airpower Debates* (Maxwell AFB, AL: Air University Press, 1995), pp. 35–42.

107 As initially conceived, "Instant Thunder" identified 84 key targets to be struck in under a week. Cohen, *GWAPS, Volume I: Planning and Command and Control*, p. 112.

108 An assessment friendly to both Warden's theory and the predominance of airpower during Operation Desert Storm is found in Mann, *Thunder and Lightning*. A more guarded evaluation suggests that "for the first time in history, air power was the major determinant in a large-scale war between two formidable forces with field deployed armies." Bruce Watson *et al.*, *Military Lessons of the Gulf War* (London: Greenhill, 1991), p. 77. Anthony Cordesman and Abraham Wagner are less impressed: "The strategic bombing effort in the Gulf War had some significant successes, but it still operated without effective guidance in terms of policy direction and grand strategy." *The Lessons of Modern War, Volume IV: The Gulf War* (Boulder, CO: Westview Press, 1996), p. 541.

109 Other officers had difficulty understanding Warden's motivation and more than a few were hostile to his ideas and modus operandi. In particular, Warden's sharp exchanges with General Chuck Horner during a briefing on 20 August 1990 led to Warden being reassigned back to the United States. A recreation of the briefing exchanges between the two is available in Reynolds, *Heart of the Storm*, pp. 120–30.

110 "Air Theory for the Twenty-First Century," in Karl Magyar, ed., *Challenge and Response: Anticipating US Military Security Concerns* (Maxwell AFB, AL: Air University Press, 1994), pp. 315–7.

111 "[W]ithout a functioning brain .the body is no longer a human being, or a strategic entity" (emphasis added). "The Enemy As A System," *Airpower Journal* (Vol. 9, No. 1: Spring 1995): 45.

112 "Air Theory for the Twenty-First Century," p. 322. Robert Pape interprets Warden's theory as targeting leadership exclusively and he classifies it as a strategy of "decapitation." Decapitation acts as an adjunct to strategies of punishment, denial, and risk in Pape's typology of the coercive uses of airpower. Warden, however, believes that Pape "tried to fit my ideas into one of the bins he thought he understood" and did not grasp that "[o]ne of the beauties of system warfare is that it does not depend on finding frequently illusive leaders." *Bombing to Win*, pp. 79–80; Personal correspondence with John Warden, 6 August 2001.

113 In order to illustrate the applications of his model, Warden illustrates the five-rings of the human body, a notional state adversary, a drug cartel, and an electric company. Ibid, p. 314.

114 "Centers of gravity exist not only at the strategic level but also at the operational level." "The Enemy As A System," p. 53.

115 "We may have to make several more five-ring models to show successively lower ... subsystems. We can continue the process until we have sufficient understanding and information to act." "Air Theory for the Twenty-First Century," pp. 316, 318.

116 "The Enemy As A System," p. 54.

117 "Air Theory for the Twenty-First Century," p. 318.

118 [T]he phenomenon known as the culminating point in campaigns—that point at which the campaign is in near equilibrium where the right effort on either side can have significant effect. All of our thinking on war is based on serial effects, on ebb and flow. The capability to execute parallel war, however, makes that thinking obsolete.

("The Enemy As A System," p. 54)

119 "Employing Air Power in the Twenty-First Century," p. 79. "It is pointless to deal with enemy military forces if they can be bypassed by strategy or technology either in the defense or offense." Warden, "The Enemy As A System," p. 52.

> Contrary to Clausewitz, destruction of the enemy military is not the essence of war; the essence of war is convincing the enemy to accept your position, and fighting his military forces is at best a means to an end and worst a total waste of time and energy."
>
> ("Air Theory for the Twenty-First Century," p. 317)

120 Warden, "Air Theory for the Twenty-First Century," p. 322.
121 When a certain number of key things fail quickly, however, the system collapses on itself and is incapable of serious repair or learning .In other words, if you create too many problems for it in too short a period of time, it goes into a state of shock.

(Personal correspondence with John Warden, 6 August 2001)

122 "The Enemy as a System," p. 43.
123 Fadok, *John Boyd and John Warden*, pp. 26–7.
124 "Air Theory for the Twenty-First Century", p. 327. In all likelihood, a younger Fuller would have approved of developments in American military culture since 1945, in which scientific soldiers test models empirically to predict outcomes and develop metrics of performance, effectiveness, and success. Warden's theory of parallel attack has been submitted in one case to empirical analysis, by parallel computing methods, using three models: rational policy, bureaucratic decision, and organizational process. As with most attempts to find correlates of war, the author concludes that more research and data are required. Bradley Smith, "Parallel Attack and the Enemy's Decision Making Process," unpublished thesis, Air Command and Staff College (1998), especially pp. 30–3.
125 Fuller saw linear warfare as battle between opposing armies arrayed along fronts. As armor and aircraft could strike targets from the front all the way to the adversary's capital, Fuller developed another term: "area warfare." *The Reformation of War*, pp. 137–8.
126 See transcript of Warden interview with Michael Ignatieff, "Future War, Part One: The Revolution in Military Affairs," British Broadcasting Corporation, 15 April 2000.
127 As airpower can serve both deterrent and coercive functions, Warden supposes that twenty-first-century airpower may render nuclear weapons obsolete: "The United States can achieve virtually all military objectives without recourse to weapons of mass destruction." "Air Theory for the Twenty-First Century," p. 312. In an historical parallel, several British prime ministers thought the mere existence of an aerial bombing force would deter Germany from aggressive acts. Their values, which were projected on the German leadership, were not shared by Adolf Hitler. Malcolm Smith, *British Air Strategy Between the Wars* (Oxford: Oxford University Press, 1984), pp. 310–11.
128 Warden uses traditional Cold War deterrence rationale: "The enemy leadership acts on some cost/risk basis, but we can't know precisely what it might be. We can, however, make some reasonable guesses based on system and organization theory." "Air Theory for the Twenty-First Century," p. 319.
129 "Air Theory for the Twenty-First Century," p. 330. Fuller and Warden discussed non-lethal technological methods of quelling rebellions in similar terms: "Can we not put a combination of AC-130s and helicopters in the air equipped with searchlights, loudspeakers, rubber bullets, entangling nets, and other paraphernalia?" "Air Theory," p. 330;

> In city riots tanks are most useful to surmount barricades, and, if equipped with lachrymatory bomb projectors, will nearly always succeed in clearing houses and

centers of resistance, whereas electrified armored cars have already on more than one occasion proved their value in pushing back hostile mobs.

(Fuller, *Armored Warfare: An Annotated Edition of Lectures on F.S.R. III, Operations Between Mechanized Forces*, Harrisburg, PA: Military Service Publishing Company, 1943, p. 167)

130 "Air Theory for the Twenty-First Century," p. 331.
131 Fuller, *The Dragon's Teeth*, pp. 296–9 and Warden, "Employing Air Power in the Twenty-First Century," p. 82.
132 Boyd's briefing slides are available at http://www.belisaurius.com or http://www.d-n-i.net, websites devoted to the application of Boyd's theory to military and business strategy.
133 Boyd's final briefing, "A Discourse on Winning and Losing," is legendary among American staff officers for both its scope (a unifying theory of warfare) and length (four hours). As Jeffrey Cowan notes "Colonel Boyd refused to shorten the length of his lecture." Quoted from annotated bibliography in "From Air Force Fighter Pilot to Marine Corps Warfighting: Colonel John Boyd, His Theories on War, and their Unexpected Legacy," unpublished thesis, Marine Corps Command and Staff College (2000). Available online at http://www.d-n-i.net/FCS_Folder/boyd_thesis.htm.
134 Senior leaders in the US Marine Corps were heavily influenced by Boyd's theory and they lobbied successfully to have existing materials archived in Quantico, Virginia.
135 An obituary, written by Boyd's biographer Grant Hammond, is available online at http://www.belisaurius.com/modern_business_strategy/hammond/essential_boyd.htm. Boyd has numerous supporters and even more numerous interpreters; the most recent example is the curious evaluation by Chester Richards, *A Swift, Elusive Sword: What if Sun Tzu and John Boyd did a National Defense Review?* (Washington: Center for Defense Information, 2001).
136 Kill ratios between United States Army Air Force fighters and the *Luftwaffe* during the Second World War were approximately 9:1. During the Korean War, kill ratios jumped to 11 Soviet Bloc aircraft lost for every American plane. American air combat performance dropped significantly during the Vietnam War to 3.5:1. Factors responsible for the decline included the removal of air-to-air cannons, reliance on infrared or radar-guided missiles and the atrophying of close-quarter "dogfighting" skills. For details on combat loss ratios and the history of aerial combat tactics, see Robert Shaw, *Fighter Combat: Tactics and Maneuvering* (Annapolis, MD: Naval Institute Press, 1985).
137 "[T]he MiG-15 was faster, had a higher operational ceiling and could turn tighter than the F-86." Grant Hammond, *The Mind of War: John Boyd and American Security* (Washington: Smithsonian Institution Press, 2001), p. 35.
138 On the role played by Soviet and Communist Chinese pilots during the Korean War, including appendices which detail the unit designation, location, and kill claims of those forces contrasted against friendly loss reporting, see Xiaoming Zhang, *Red Wings Over the Yalu: China, the Soviet Union, and the Air War in Korea* (College Station, TX: Texas A&M Press, 2002).
139 James Stevenson, *The Pentagon Paradox: The Development of the F-18 Hornet* (Annapolis, MD: Naval Institute Press, 1993), pp. 45–7.
140 Boyd was so confident in his tactical theories and skills that he had a standing challenge: he could defeat any pilot within 40 seconds from the most disadvantageous position. Hammond, *The Mind of War*, p. 7. An accessible discussion of fighter tactics heavily influenced by Boyd, including the concepts of energy maneuverability and agility, is found in Shaw, *Fighter Combat*.
141 Biographies of Boyd include Hammond, *The Mind of War* and Robert Corum, *Boyd: The Fighter Pilot Who Changed the Art of War* (New York: Little, Brown & Company, 2002). Boyd's major works on fighter tactics span from "Aerial Attack Study" in 1960 to "New Conception for Air-to-Air Combat" in 1976.

142 Boyd was a member of the "fighter mafia" within the Pentagon during the early 1970s. The "fighter mafia" championed the YF-16, with its fly-by-wire control system, as a more versatile and agile aircraft than the heavily favored, less maneuverable and highly expensive FX. In the end lobbying by the "fighter mafia" ensured the survival of the highly successful F-16 Falcon program. Details of the "fighter mafia" struggle are available in Stevenson, *The Pentagon Paradox,* pp. 77–103 and James Burton, *The Pentagon Wars: Reformers Challenge the Old Guard* (Annapolis, MD: Naval Institute Press, 1993).

143 "New Conception for Air-to-Air Combat," unpublished briefing (4 August 1976), slide 19.

144 "War is nothing but a duel on a larger scale." Clausewitz, *On War,* Book One, Chapter One, p. 75.

145 "Destruction and Creation," unpublished article (3 September 1976), p. 15. Available online at http://www.belisarius.com/modern_business_strategy/boyd/destruction/destruction_and_creation.htm.

146 Adapted from the graphic available online at http://www.belisarius.com/modern_business_strategy/ boyd/essence/ooda_loop_sketch.htm.

147 External inputs are information received during the observation and orientation phase; internal inputs include cultural traditions and heritage, among others.

148 Although Clausewitz suggests that "war most closely resembles a game of cards" he warns against denying its nature: "It would be futile—even wrong—to try and shut one's eyes to what war really is from sheer distress at its brutality." Clausewitz, *On War,* Book One, Chapter One, p. 76.

149 "Patterns of Conflict," unpublished briefing (December 1986), slide 140.

150 Boyd also incorporated Gödel's Proof of Inconsistency and Heisenburg's Principle of Indeterminacy into his theories: "Taken together, these three notions support the idea that any inward-oriented and continued effort to improve the match-up of concept with observed reality will only increase the degree of mismatch .Put another way, we can expect unexplained and disturbing ambiguities, uncertainties, anomalies, or apparent inconsistencies to emerge more and more often. Furthermore, unless some kind of relief is available, we can expect confusion to increase until disorder approaches chaos—death." "Destruction and Creation," p. 16 and Hammond, *The Mind of War,* p. 119.

151 "Thus, the highest realization of warfare is to attack the enemy's plans." Sun Tzu, "The Art of War," in Ralph Sawyer, trans., *The Seven Military Classics of Ancient China* (Boulder, CO: Westview Press, 1993), p. 161 and Fadok, *John Boyd and John Warden,* p. 15.

152 To risk distilling the point even further, Boyd was suggesting an organizational version of the Roman maxim *divide et impera*: "The-Name-of-the-Game: Morally-mentally-physically isolate elements of adversary or adversaries from one another and overwhelm them by being able to penetrate and splinter their moral-mental-physical being at any and all levels." "Patterns of Conflict," slide 137.

153 Barry Watts, *Clausewitzian Friction and Future War,* McNair Paper No. 52 (Washington: National Defense University Press, 1996), pp. 130–2.

154 The other keys to staying inside an adversary's OODA loop are initiative, harmony, and variety. Fadok, *John Boyd and John Warden,* pp. 14–15.

155 Boyd speculated that the use of technology as a "crude club," the inability to develop tactics suited to new technologies, and de-emphasis on the human dimensions of conflict led to Allied emphasis on material attrition during the First and Second World Wars. "Patterns of Conflict," slides 49, 55.

156 See for example the British approaches to maritime Spain and continental France contained in Geoffrey Parker, *The Grand Strategy of Philip II* (New Haven, CT: Yale University Press, 1998) and Christopher Hall, *British Strategy in the Napoleonic War, 1803–15* (Manchester: Manchester University Press, 1992).

157 Boyd suggests that maneuver warfare would be attritional in character at the tactical level as each side thrust and parried. At the strategic level, however, maneuver would be the prevalent characteristic—presuming of course that the enemy did not anticipate breakthroughs and initiate counter-maneuvers that would lead to deadlock. "Patterns of Conflict," slide 154.
158 "Get inside adversary observation-orientation-decision-action loops (at all levels) by being more subtle, more indistinct, more irregular, and quicker—yet appear to be otherwise." Ibid., slide 175. Boyd's thoughts on this subject mirror those of Liddell Hart, insofar as "unorthodox mindset" equates directly with Liddell Hart's "indirect approach."
159 Ibid., slide 70.
160 Boyd suggested several hyphenated avenues to accomplish this goal: menace-uncertainty-mistrust; ambiguity-deception-novelty; and mask-distort-magnify. Ibid., slide 128.
161 The cause-effect relationship is summarized neatly: "Generate uncertainty, confusion, disorder, panic, chaos .to shatter cohesion, produce paralysis and bring about collapse." Ibid., slide 132.
162 Colin Gray, *Modern Strategy* (Oxford: Oxford University Press, 1999), p. 94.
163 An excellent summary of Clausewitz's concept of "general friction" is contained in Watts, *Clausewitzian Friction and Future War*, pp. 7–13, 27–35.
164 The battle of Antietam during the American Civil War resulted from the Union capture of General Robert E. Lee's campaign plan without his knowledge. Despite the forewarning, Union commander Major General George McClellan failed to capitalize fully on the situation and destroy the Confederate Army of Northern Virginia. For a first-hand account of the events, see George McClellan, *Report on the Organization and Campaigns of the Army of the Potomac: To Which is Added an Account of the Campaign in Western Virginia, With Plans of Battle-Fields* (New York: Sheldon and Company, 1864), pp. 353–93.
165 The weather conditions in the Ardennes forest during the German 1944 *Wacht am Rhein* offensive prevented Allied airpower from interfering with German panzer columns. Those same conditions, and the nature of the terrain, also robbed German columns of their mobility and played havoc with German elite and SOF. General details of the campaign are available in Trevor DuPuy, David Bongard and Richard Anderson, Jr, *Hitler's Last Gamble: The Battle of the Bulge, December 1944-January 1945* (Shrewsbury: Airlife Publishing Ltd, 1994). The most detailed survey of German special operations during the Ardennes campaign is Michael Schedewitz, *The Meuse First and Then Antwerp: Some Aspects of Hitler's Offensive in the Ardennes*, Wendy Bonk, trans. (Winnipeg, MB: J.J. Fedorowicz Publishing, 1999), pp. 135–72.
166 British SOF suffered considerably from mechanical failure during the Falklands War (1982), for examples, see Anthony Kemp, *SAS: The Savage Wars of Peace, 1947 to the Present* (London: John Murray, 1994), p. 171; Ken Connor, *Ghost Force: The Secret History of the SAS* (London: Weidenfield and Nicolson, 1998), pp. 236–54; Roger Perkins, *Operation Paraquat: The Battle for South Georgia* (London: Picton, 1986).
167 For example, General Wesley Clark, NATO Supreme Allied Commander in Europe during the Kosovo air campaign, predicted that Serbian resistance to NATO demands would end after 48 hours of aerial bombing. Slobodan Milosevic did not capitulate as anticipated. William Arkin and Robert Windrem, "The Other Kosovo War: Baby Steps—and Missteps—for Information Warfare," *MSNBC News* (30 August 2001). Available online at http://www.msnbc.com/news/ 607032.asp?cpl‡.
168 Jefferson Davis, President of the Confederate States of America, routinely chose the least competent individuals for high-ranking command positions in the crucial western theater of operations. The basis for his decision was friendship rather than military competence. His few capable appointments, such as Albert Sidney Johnston and

Braxton Bragg, were more than offset by the sheer ineptitude and intransigence displayed by "friends" such as Leonidas Polk, P.G.T. Beauregard, Gideon Pillow, and John Floyd. Steven Woodworth, *Jefferson Davis and His Generals: The Failure of Confederate Command in the West* (Lawrence, KS: University of Kansas Press, 1990), especially pp. 29–30, 80–5, 102–7.

169 Prussian commander Helmuth von Moltke the Elder is credited with the remark that "No plan of operations extends with certainty beyond the first contact with the enemy's main strength." Quoted in Gray, *Modern Strategy*, p. 331.
170 *On War*, Book One, Chapter Eight, p. 120.
171 Ibid., Book Eight, Chapter Four, pp. 595–6.
172 See for example Ibid., Book Six, Chapter Twenty-Seven, pp. 485–7.
173 Various points of contention include: the existence of one center or many centers of gravity; the level of war at which the concept applies (strategic, operational, tactical); and its relative value, either as a practical planning tool or a conceptual aid. One author believes he has settled the conceptual/doctrinal discontinuity, a feat akin to settling the theological differences that separates the Protestant and Catholic faiths, by linking center of gravity to systems theory. See Dale Eikmeier, "The Center of Gravity Debate Resolved," unpublished thesis, Army Command and General Staff College (1999). Works that debate various issues relating to center of gravity include: Antulio Echevarria II, *Clausewitz's Center of Gravity: Changing Our Warfighting Doctrine—Again!* (Carlisle, PA: Strategic Studies Institute, USAWC, 2002); Seow Hiang Lee, "Center of Gravity or Center of Confusion: Understanding the Mystique," unpublished thesis, Air Command and Staff College (1999); Darfus Johnson, "Center of Gravity: The Source of Operational Ambiguity and Linear Thinking in the Age of Complexity," unpublished thesis, Army Command and General Staff College (1999); Steven Metz and Frederick Downey, "Centers of Gravity and Strategic Planning," *Military Review* (Vol. 68, No. 4: April 1988): 22–33; Milan Vego, "Center of Gravity," *Military Review* (Vol. 80, No. 2: March–April 2000): 23–9; William Mendel and Lamar Tooke, "Operational Logic: Selecting the Center of Gravity," *Military Review* (Vol. 73, No. 6: June 1993): 2–11; and Kevin Giles, "Center of Gravity: Determination, Analysis, and Application," unpublished thesis, Army War College (1996).
174 Michael Handel suggests that the "inherent contradictions" of *On War* reflect the nature of the subject; Edward Luttwak classifies the contradictions of war as "paradoxical logic." Handel, *Masters of War: Classical Strategic Thought* (London: Frank Cass, 1996), pp. 31–7, 181–3; Edward Luttwak, *Strategy: The Logic of War and Peace* (Cambridge, MA: Belknap Press, 1987).
175 Lee applies the principle of Occam's razor too finely when he distinguishes between "Book Six-Clausewitzian" and "Book Eight-Clausewitzian" centers of gravity, but his treatment of the subject is nevertheless well reasoned. *Center of Gravity or Center of Confusion*, pp. 7–8.
176 These categories roughly equate to Clausewitz's list of operational centers of gravity: the army, the leader, seizure of the center of administration (the capital), public opinion, and principal ally. *On War*, Book Eight, Chapter Four, p. 596.
177 The ostensible goal of the North Vietnamese offensive, namely a "General Uprising" of the population designed to overthrow the government of South Vietnam, was not achieved. The fact that the Johnson and Nixon administrations were able to continue the war effort for another four years suggests that the result of the conflict was not a foregone conclusion after Tet. As an example of the "law of unintended consequences," however, the Tet Offensive is unparalleled. For details on the impact of Tet on the Viet Cong, see James Kiras, "Viet Cong Organization and Operations: A Critical Assessment Based On RAND Documents," unpublished thesis, University of Toronto, 14 December 1990.
178 Warden, "The Enemy as a System," p. 53.

179   Critics charge that Clausewitz placed too much emphasis on the destruction of the enemy's army as the decisive point of operational military action, yet the objectives of his "pure concept of war" are rendering the enemy forces unable to continue the fight and occupying the enemy's territory, as the conflict "cannot considered to have ended so long as the enemy's *will* has not been broken" (emphasis in original). *On War*, Book One, Chapter Two, p. 90.

3   "A dark picture of destruction"

1   German report quoted in James Leasor and Leslie Hollis, *War at the Top* (London: Companion Book Club, 1960), p. 135.
2   Biographical and autobiographical accounts of the raid, by its participants, are included in: Russell Brandon, *Cheshire VC: A Story of Peace and War* (London: Evans Brothers Ltd, 1954); Andrew Boyle, *No Passing Glory: The Full and Authentic Biography of Group Captain Cheshire, VC, DSO, DFC* (London: Collins, 1955); Guy Gibson, *Enemy Coast Ahead* (Cheshire: Goodall Publications Ltd, 1986); Susan Ottoway, *Dambuster: A Life of Guy Gibson, VC, DSO*, DFC** (London: Leo Cooper, 1996); Alan Cooper, *Born Leader: The Story of Guy Gibson VC* (London: Independent Books, 1993); idem, *The Men Who Breached the Dams* (London: William Kimber, 1982); Tom Bennett, *617 Squadron: The Dambusters at War* (Wellingborough: Patrick Stephens Ltd, 1986); and Eric Fry, *An Airman Far Away: The Story of an Australian Dambuster* (Kenthurst, Australia: Kangaroo Press, 1993). The planning, conduct, and aftermath of the raid are handled in John Sweetman, *Operation Chastise, The Dams Raid: Epic or Myth* (London: Jane's, 1982); Paul Brickhill, *The Dambusters*, rev. edn (London: Bell & Hyman, 1977).
3   As a bibliographical aside, most works on the Second World War European air war make mention of the Dambusters Raid as a footnote if at all. See for example Martin Middlebrook and Chris Everitt, *The Bomber Command War Diaries: An Operational Reference Book, 1939–1945* (Middlesex: Viking, 1985), p. 388 and John Terraine, *The Right of the Line: The Royal Air Force in the European Campaign, 1939–1945* (Hertfordshire: Wordsworth, 1997), pp. 538–9. The official assessment of the bombing campaign neglects to mention the raid entirely. British Bombing Survey Unit, *The Strategic Air War Against Germany, 1939–1945* (London: Frank Cass, 1998). A notable exception is the chapter devoted to the raid in the official British history of the air war: Charles Webster and Noble Frankland, *The Strategic Air Offensive Against Germany, 1939–1945, Volume II: Endeavour* (London: Her Majesty's Stationary Office, 1961), pp. 168–89. Monographs focusing exclusively on the raid tend to exaggerate its importance. A noteworthy exception is Sweetman's *Operation Chastise, The Dams Raid*. The author, however, is primarily concerned with setting straight the specific details of the raid. Sweetman devotes a mere twelve pages of his work to the organizational, theoretical, and planning basis of the raid.
4   *The Bomber Offensive* (London: Batsford, 1968), p. 220.
5   Other combat support missions considered "special operations," by virtue of their organizational affiliation, are area defoliation missions conducted as part of Operation Ranch Hand as well as AC-47 gunship missions during the Vietnam War. Michael Haas, *Apollo's Warriors: United States Air Force Special Operations during the Cold War* (Maxwell AFB, AL: Air University Press, 1997), pp. 246–65.
6   As noted in the previous chapter, the debate over the strategic or tactical utility of airpower continues. Malcolm Smith notes sagely that

> "Tactical" and "strategic" mark the two poles of the possible military use of air power. In effect, however, there is a large grey area between these two extremes where the categories blend and confused .A hierarchy of the three media of war (air, sea and land power) cannot be decided *in vacuo* but must be related to the

strategic configuration of the nation to be defended and of the nation likely to be hostile, and it must be related to the war aims of both.

(*British Air Strategy Between the Wars,* Oxford: Oxford University Press, 1984, p. 3)

7 For a comprehensive listing of sources in the airpower debate, see Philip S. Meilinger, *Airmen and Air Theory: A Review of the Sources* (Maxwell AFB, AL: Air University Press, 2001).

8 Missions like the suppression of enemy air defenses (SEAD), pathfinding, and pararescue fall within this category. Although the personnel that conduct such missions are highly skilled and their equipment often specialized, they are nonetheless fulfilling a *tactical*, combat support role. See for example D.C.T. Bennett, *Pathfinder* (London: Sphere Books, 1972); Jack Brehm and Pete Nelson, *That Others May Live: Inside the World's Most Daring Rescue Force* (London, Ebury Press, 2000); and, for a joint perspective on SEAD, see details of AFSOC helicopters "enabling" US Army attack helicopters in destroying Iraqi frontline radar sites during the Gulf War. James W. Bradin, *From Hot Air to Hellfire: The History of Attack Aviation* (Novato, CA: Presidio Press, 1994), pp. 1–23.

9 John Keegan suggests that the dawn of the age of airpower has already arrived:

There are certain dates in the history of warfare that mark real turning points. November 20, 1917 is one, when at Cambrai the tank showed that the traditional dominance of infantry, cavalry and artillery on the battlefield had been overthrown. November 11, 1940 is another, when the sinking of the Italian fleet at Taranto demonstrated that the aircraft carrier and its aircraft had abolished the age-old supremacy of the battleship. Now there is a new turning point to fix on the calendar: June 3, 1999, when the capitulation of President Milosevic proved that a war can be won by air power alone. "Please, Mr Blair, never take such a risk again."

(*Sunday Telegraph,* 6 June 1999)

10 The degree to which air power forces an adversary to surrender remains the subject of much debate. Robert Pape contends, for example, that "strategic bombing does not work. Strategic bombing for punishment and decapitation does not coerce, and strategic bombing is rarely the best way to achieve denial." *Bombing to Win: Air Power and Coercion in War* (Ithaca, NY: Cornell University Press, 1996), p. 314. Benjamin Lambeth makes a cautious case for the role airpower played in Serbian submission in Kosovo, exploring such additional facets as psychological operations and peer pressure. See Chapter 4, "Why Milosevic Gave Up When He Did," *NATO'S Air War For Kosovo: A Strategic and Operational Assessment,* MR-1365-AF (Santa Monica, CA: Rand, 2001), pp. 67–86.

11 For reasons outlined below, British air planners drew mistaken conclusions from "air policing" experience gained in colonial territories in the Middle East and southwest Asia.

12 The context in which the term "raid" is used can be instructive. In a comprehensive study of special operations published in 1982, the authors suggest that "there is no absolute distinction between [special operations] and raiding actions mounted by regular-type forces, and especially elite forces of various kinds. *[Special operations] are self-contained acts of war mounted by self-sufficient forces operating within hostile territory.*" Edward N. Luttwak, Steven L. Canby, and David L. Thomas, "A Systematic Review of 'Commando' (Special) Operations, 1939–1980," unpublished report for the Office of Deputy Undersecretary of Defense for Policy Review, C&L Associates, 24 May 1982, p. I-1.

13 For example, although the Second Battle of Schweinfurt was important in the evolution of American daylight bombing strategy in the Second World War, it hardly

14 Colin S. Gray, *Explorations in Strategy* (Westport, CT: Praeger, 1996), p. 173. Arguably, the Doolittle Raid was well within the capabilities of conventional forces to conduct. The unique dimension of the raid was its cross-service character, involving the launching of Army medium bombers off the deck of a Navy carrier.

deserves consideration as a special operation much less as a "great raid." See W. Raymond Wood, "Second Schweinfurt," in Samuel Southworth, ed., *Great Raids in History: From Drake to Desert One* (New York: Sarpedon, 1997), pp. 222–3.

15 For reasons described below the American raid on the Ploesti oilfields, in addition to the attempts to destroy V-2 launch sites using the remote-controlled aircraft under "Operation Aphrodite," deserve consideration as special operations. For popular accounts of Ploesti and Aphrodite, see James Dugan and Carroll Stewart, *Ploesti: The Great Ground-Air Battle of 1 August 1943* (New York: Random House, 1962) and Jack Olsen, *Aphrodite: Desperate Mission* (New York: G.P. Putnam's, 1970), especially pp. 136–50.

16 The unconventional delivery of the Upkeep bombs lends literal weight to the statement that technology drives tactics. In order for the bombs to "bounce" across the water and strike the dam without breaking up, the Lancasters had to fly at just above the surface of the water at 240 miles per hour. Gibson, *Enemy Coast Ahead*, p. 238.

17 Gibson cites this figure in his memoirs but John Sweetman challenges it in his exhaustive assessment of the mission. Sweetman contends that the reality of finding experienced volunteers overruled the operational requirement and that a small minority of pilots had flown as few as 10 missions. His argument, however, is undermined by a complete lack of source notation for his conclusions aside from a comprehensive bibliography. As a result, the question of whether or not this discrepancy in experience is related to the high casualty figures for the operation remains unanswered. Ibid., pp. 225–8; *Operation Chastise: The Dams Raid*, pp. 59–60.

18 In his study of literature on future war, I.F. Greene sets three authors apart from their peers: Albert Robida, H.G. Wells, and Sir Arthur Conan Doyle. Most authors of war and invasion-scare literature could not break out of the conceptual box of incremental technological change affecting the military situation between existing powers. Robida, Wells, and Conan Doyle were noteworthy exceptions; both Robida and Wells used literary explorations of the future of warfare as a vehicle for social commentary, whereas Conan Doyle drew an accurate portrait of the character of unrestricted submarine warfare. *Voices Prophesying War, 1763–1984* (London: Oxford University Press, 1966), pp. 90–106.

19 "And as the exhaustion of the mechanical resources of civilisation clears the heavens of airships at last altogether, Anarchy, Famine, and Pestilence are discovered triumphant below." Wells foresaw two types of flying machines: airships with which to conduct bombings of population centers; and "Butteridge" machines, one-man fighters that could carry bombs. *The History of Mr Polly and The War in the Air* (London, Odhams Press, 1936), p. 358.

20 Wells' work contains two broad themes: "new" technology always defeats "old" technology, in specific, airpower rendered surface ships obsolete; and technological development vastly exceeds social and political development. Quote cited in Clarke, *Voices Prophesying War*, pp. 100–1; Wells, *War in the Air*, pp. 223, 257, 352–4.

21 As Tim Travers points out, Wells believed that airpower had tremendous destructive potential but the payloads of airships limited the moral effect of the attack. What would follow was a series of aerial blows and counterblows lasting until industries could not produce the advanced machines and munitions of war. "Future Warfare: H.G. Wells and British Military Theory, 1895–1916," in Brian Bond and Ian Roy, eds, *War and Society: A Yearbook of Military History* (London: Croon Helm, 1975), pp. 67–87, especially pp. 74–6.

22 William "Billy" Mitchell, for example, suggested that "Air forces will attack centers of production of all kinds, means of transportation, agricultural areas, ports and shipping;

not so much the people themselves. They will destroy the means of making war because now we cannot cut a limb from a tree, pick up a stone from a hill and make it our principal weapon. Today to make war we must have great metal and chemical factories that have to stay in one place, take months to build, and, if destroyed, cannot be replaced in the usual length of a modern war." *Winged Defense* (New York: G.P. Putnam, 1925), pp. 16–17. Mitchell could not envision the relocation or distribution of production facilities, as the Germans did in response to the Allied bombing campaign (1943–5) or as the Soviets did to offset German territorial conquest (1941–2).

23 Although the panic generated by German zeppelin and bomber raids on major cities such as Edinburgh and London was much overplayed in the popular press, in at least one instance a raid at Kingston-upon-Hull led to rioting in the streets and the institution of civil patrols. A committee mandated to explore Britain's air defense in 1917, under the leadership of Jan Christian Smuts, both established the Royal Air Force as its own service and presaged airpower "as an independent means of war operations." "Committee on Air Organisation and Home Defence Against Air Raids," AIR 8/2, 17 August 1917.

24 The lift and range capabilities of aerial bombers underwent dramatic expansion during the second decade of the twentieth century. Initially aviators improvised attack means and methods; during the Italo-Turkish War of 1911, for example, hand grenades and other infantry munitions were dropped from reconnaissance aircraft. David Wragg, *The Offensive Weapon: The Strategy of Bombing* (London: Robert Hale, 1986), p. 27. The Imperial Germans used lighter-than-air ships to carry relatively heavy bomb loads (almost 8,000 pounds) at extremely slow speeds for night raids on British cities. The zeppelins, however, flew high to avoid anti-aircraft fire and often had to jettison bomb loads just to stay aloft. In addition, the airships achieved lift using highly flammable gas and they were extremely vulnerable to intercepting fighter aircraft armed with incendiary bullets. By the end of the war, the British had developed the Handley Page V/1500, or "bloody paralyser" in reference to the effect it was intended to have on the Germans, which had a payload of 3,200 pounds, defensive armament, a range of 1,100 miles and a speed almost twice that of zeppelins. Scot Robertson, *The Development of RAF Strategic Bombing Doctrine, 1919–1939* (Westport, CT: Praeger, 1995), p. 61; F.W. Lanchester, *Aircraft in Warfare: The Dawn of the Fourth Arm* (Sunnyvale, CA: Lanchester Press, 1995), pp. 9–21.

25 Carl von Clausewitz, *On War*, Michael Howard and Peter Paret, trans. (Princeton, NJ: Princeton University Press, 1976), Book One, Chapter One, p. 75. Billy Mitchell duplicated Clausewitz's logic from an airpower perspective—airpower is the decisive way to accomplish the goal: "The influence of air power on the ability of one nation to impress its will on another in an armed conflict will be decisive." *Winged Defense*, p. 214

26 British societal mistrust of "the garrison state" can be traced primarily to the excesses conducted by Oliver Cromwell's "New Model Army" in the name of religious purity. According to E.S. Turner,

> It was the fate of the New Model Army in its later, tyrannous years—the years when its troopers shut down race meetings and screwed the necks of fighting cocks—to fill the country with a lasting hatred and distrust of the military.
> (*Gallant Gentlemen: A Portrait of the British Officer, 1600–1956,* London: Michael Joseph, 1956, p. 26)

27 Prior to the First World War, Britain was unique among the great powers in relying exclusively on a professional volunteer army. Continental powers such as France and Germany developed instead systems of rapid conscription and mobilization. The financial burden imposed by training reservists and stockpiling equipment was immense; as Colonel Frederick Maurice wrote in 1889:

> If we have afoot a force of something like 70,000 men, complete in all its arms, and actually ready to take the field, that represents pretty nearly the limit of the power with which we could, under any circumstances, strike our blow. Now if we were to submit to all the strain of universal service under which the Continent is groaning; not though we spent upon our army all the milliards which Germany wrung from France, which she has employed for military service.
> (*The Balance of Military Power in Europe: An Examination of the War Resources of Great Britain and the Continental States*, Edinburgh: William Blackwood and Sons, 1889, p. 34)

In order to re-establish a fighting force after the virtual destruction of the professional army in 1914–15, Field Marshal Lord Kitchener opened wide the recruiting gates to enthusiastic volunteers. The "new" army, backed by incompetent staff work, was decimated at the Somme in 1916:

> The British command wrongly decided that its half-trained troops were only capable of a deliberate advance in rigid lines .The reserves were to go forward close behind the assaulting troops to avoid delays in exploitation experienced in earlier battles .The machine guns cut down the slow-moving British lines like grass.
> (Corelli Barnett, *Britain and Her Army, 1509–1970: A Military, Political and Social Survey*, London: Allan Lane The Penguin Press, 1970, pp. 394–5)

28 In his discussion of the current realities of "British command of the seas," Frederick Maurice notes:

> German submarines even without the support of a victorious fleet gravely endangered our supplies of food .But it very soon became apparent to the most ardent believers in the efficacy of sea power that times had changed. What Bacon had said in the sixteenth .was not true in the twentieth century, when submarines based on the French ports of the Channel coast and backed by German guns established on the French coast could have made it very difficult to feed London.
> (*British Strategy: A Study in the Applications of the Principles of War*, London: Constable, 1929, pp. 41–2)

29 The quick, and nearly bloodless resolution of these incidents stood in contrast to the bloody, and still controversial British Army actions to quell rioting mobs in Amritsar, India (1919). For details on British air policing actions see George Gagnon, *Air Control: Strategy for a Smaller United States Air Force* (Maxwell AFB, AL: Air University Press, 1993), pp. 7–9 and David Omissi, *Air Power and Colonial Control: The Royal Air Force, 1919–1939* (Manchester: Manchester University Press, 1990), pp. 10–11, 112–13. A contemporary account of British actions at Amritsar is contained in Charles Gwynn, *Imperial Policing* (London: Macmillan and Co., 1934), pp. 34–64.

30 Omissi, *Air Power and Colonial Control*, p. 166. Moral effects are described in pp. 152ff.

31 In addition to a compelling argument, Trenchard initially had a valuable politically ally—the future Prime Minister, Winston S. Churchill. Churchill's desire to preserve the independence of the RAF had less to do with his convictions regarding airpower than it did with his political aspiration to become the first Minister of Defence. David Divine, *The Broken Wing: A Study in the British Exercise of Air Power* (London: Hutchinson, 1966), pp. 153–4.

32 Omissi, *Air Power and Colonial Control*, p. 210–12. James Corum reinforces this basic point and offers five relevant lessons for those within the US Air Force who advocate a doctrine of air control. "The Myth of Air Control: Reassessing the History," *Aerospace Power Journal* (Vol. 14, No. 4: Winter 2000): 74–5.

33 In addition to the humanity of air policing the Secretary General of the Air League of the British Empire pointed out the economy of aerial punitive actions:

148   *Notes*

> In Iraq the Air Force took over control in aid of local forces because the cost of military occupation in that tractless land was too high to be borne. Defence expenditure on Imperial troops fell from an average of £8,000,000 sterling annually to an average of £2,500,000. The risks run by scattered military garrisons—very real risks as the rising of 1923 showed—were avoided and the most difficult problem of imposing peace on the hills of Kurdistan imposed.
>
> (J.M. Chamier, "Policing the Empire," in Nigel Tangye, ed., *The Air is Our Concern: A Critical Study of England's Future in Aviation,* London: Methuen and Company, Ltd, 1935), p. 178)

34   According to an author transcribing Trenchard's dicta, the guiding principles of British airpower theory relate entirely to their moral effect:

> And it is not the destruction of life or property which the bombers cause that matters; it is the destruction of *morale* [emphasis in original], the disturbance of life, the dislocation of routine. The moral effect is more important than the material. Keep on raiding: that is the right strategy in the air, according to the Trenchard school.
>
> (J.M. Spaight, *The Sky's the Limit: A Study of British Air Power,* London: Hodder and Stoughton, 1940, p. 18)

35   J.F.C. Fuller, *The Dragon's Teeth: A Study of War and Peace* (London: Constable, 1932), p. 291. Tami Davis Biddle provides a lucid assessment of Trenchard's "moral argument" theory in "British and American Approaches to Strategic Bombing: Their Origins and Implementation in the World War II Combined Bomber Offensive," *The Journal of Strategic Studies* (Vol. 18, No. 1: March 1995): 92–7.

36   Trenchard's fears were not groundless; the RAF had been pared from 185 to 28 squadrons after the First World War and some individuals called for even more drastic reductions or outright elimination to save Treasury money. Basil Liddell Hart, *The Defence of Britain* (London: Faber and Faber, 1939), p. 150.

37   An early and succinct assessment of the prevalent views in 1927 was given by an author writing under the pseudonym "Squadron Leader":

> By the majority of writers, too much stress has been laid on the horrors that this form of war is capable of inflicting on the civilian population. This has led to the conclusion that it will be possible for future wars to be brought to an end by aircraft acting alone. There are other writers who, with an exaggerated estimate of the offensive capabilities of this arm, have treated the subject wholly from the offensive aspect, ignoring the limitations of aircraft and the counter-measures of defence.
>
> (*Basic Principles of Air Warfare: The Influence of Air Power on Sea and Land Strategy,* Aldershot: Gale & Polden, Ltd, 1927, p. 115)

38   [John] Salmond suggested that reactions to bombing characteristically went through three phases. The initial attacks might produce a sudden panic, particularly if the people in question had never been bombed before. Once it was realized that bombing did not produce extensive material damage, however, panic would soon give way to indifference or even contempt for the air attacks. Finally, after a sustained bombing offensive, the continued disruption of everyday life would create intense weariness and a longing for peace.

(Omissi, *Air Power and Colonial Control*, pp. 110–11)

39   Ibid. Trenchard and Salmond continued to correspond on the subject; they agreed, for example, that airpower achieved its moral effect through the destruction of property. Salmond, however, stressed the value of using the appropriate military instrument suited to the local circumstances, such as aircraft, infantry, or armored cars. See for example correspondence quoted in Andrew Boyle, *Trenchard: Man of Vision* (London: Collins, 1962), pp. 509–11.

40 Quoted in Tami Davis Biddle, "British and American Approaches to Strategic Bombing," p. 92. Trenchard had little empirical evidence to support his claim. Instead, he expanded upon Napoleon's well-known maxim that "the material is to the moral as one is to three" and embellished it for good measure.

41 For example, Trenchard opined that

> I do not wish for a moment to imply that the air by itself can finish the war. It will materially assist, and will be one of the many means of exercising pressure on the enemy, in conjunction with sea-power and blockade and the defeat of his armies.
> (Quoted in Boyle, *Trenchard*, p. 577)

42 Air Marshal Sir Robert Saundby, one of the supporters of Operation Chastise, summarized the views of the movement in the following way:

> The system [of air control] was, however, bitterly attacked by many people who had an instinctive horror of air operations, and especially of bombing. Most of these people were honest and well-meaning, though hardly any of them had the faintest idea of how the system worked. The air control system was often publicly condemned as unworthy of a civilized people, and accusations of quelling disorders by 'indiscriminate bombing' were made by those who should, and indeed sometimes did, know better." The disarmament movement was even stronger in its condemnation of the bombing of "civilized" people.
> *(Air Bombardment: The Story of Its Development*, New York: Harper & Brothers, 1961, p. 41. See also Boyle, *Trenchard*, pp. 508–9)

43 After the First World War, the most influential theorists included: J.F.C. Fuller, F.W. Lanchester, and Basil Liddell Hart. Liddell Hart wrote in his 1925 bestseller, for example

> Imagine for a moment London, Manchester, Birmingham, and half a dozen other great centers simultaneously attacked, the business localities and Fleet Street wrecked, Whitehall a heap of ruins, the slum districts maddened into the impulse to break loose and maraud, the railways cut, factories destroyed. Would not the general will to resist vanish, and what use would be the still determined fractions of the nation, without organization and central direction?
> *(Paris, or The Future of Warfare*, New York: E.P. Dutton, 1925, pp. 41–2)

Two years before the Second World War, Liddell Hart ignored his own role in creating public anxiety regarding air attacks and commented that

> Memory, of air attacks in the last war, is as much the propellant as any knowledge of air development since. Small as was the force employed in these raids [during the First World War], it cause greater and wider nerve strain than any other agent of warfare. The effects have not disappeared with the cessation of the cause: they are traceable in the general tendency among the public, whenever they think of war, for the thought to be associated immediately with the idea of being bombed from the air. And from this apprehension springs a natural exaggeration."
> *Europe in Arms* (London: Faber and Faber, 1937), p. 12.

44 Tami Davis Biddle scathingly comments that "Instead of fostering critical thinking, the RAF Staff College taught a rather single-minded dogma that students had to internalise even before they matriculated. Too often it seemed that more attention was paid to fox-hunting than to target finding and bomb aiming." "British and American Approaches to Strategic Bombing," p. 101.

45 Although the United States Air Force only gained its service independence from the Army in 1947, its pilots received considerably more professional training and development than their British counterparts prior to the Second World War. In particular, the Air Corps Tactical School offered instruction and training while also housing facilities for the development of doctrine. As a result, the Air War Plan Division,

which initially consisted of four officers ranking no higher than Lieutenant Colonel, developed a succinct but comprehensive air offensive plan for use against Germany in under two weeks. For details see James C. Gaston, *Planning the American Air War: Four Men and Nine Days in 1941, An Inside Narrative* (Washington: National Defense University Press, 1982).
46 Boyle, *Trenchard*, pp. 580–1.
47 Smith, *British Air Strategy Between the Wars*, pp. 109–10.
48 Hugh Trenchard, "Memorandum from Royal Air Force Chief of Air Staff Hugh Trenchard to chiefs of staff sub-committee on the War Object of an Air Force, 2 May 1928," reprinted in Gérard Chaliand, ed., *The Art of War in World History: From Antiquity to the Nuclear Age* (Berkeley, CA: University of California Press, 1994), p. 906.
49 Liddell Hart, *The Defence of Britain*, p. 148.
50 Smith, *British Air Strategy Between the Wars*, p. 115.
51 Even more remarkable is the criticism mounted by Sir Thomas Inskip, the civilian Minister for Coordination, who challenged the foundation of Bomber Command's strategic theory. He argued that the RAF was first and foremost a defensive organization, designed to protect Britain from aerial attack. Any offensive actions would take place after the defensive battle was won. Inskip also suggested that the "knockout blow" theory was specious. For further details on this subject, see ibid, pp. 182–91.
52 Baldwin's remarks were designed to stimulate disarmament initiatives, not advocate the doctrine of Bomber Command; his "catch-phrase," however, may have been written by someone else. For details, see Terraine, *The Right of the Line*, p. 13; Stanley Baldwin, "The Bomber Will Always Get Through," in Eugene M. Emme, ed., *The Impact of Air Power: National Security and World Politics* (New York: D. van Nostrand Company, 1959), pp. 51–2.
53 Baldwin, "The Bomber Will Always Get Through," p. 51.
54 Historians have debated two broad claims: politically, that the fear articulated so clearly by Baldwin laid the path for Britain's policy of appeasement towards Nazi Germany; and, operationally, that the USAAF used Baldwin's claim to support their view that bombers did not require fighter escort and could rely instead upon their own defensive armament for protection.
55 John R. Carter, *Airpower and the Cult of the Offensive* (Maxwell AFB, AL: Air University Press, 1998), p. 35. Trenchard had argued deterministically that disarmament measures would fail:

> If this restriction [the use of airpower only against armed forces] were feasible, I should be the last to quarrel with it; but it is not feasible. In a vital struggle all available weapons always have been used and always will be used. All sides made a beginning in the last war, and what has been done will be done.
> (Trenchard, "Memorandum," p. 910)

56 Malcolm Smith suggests that Air Staff support for parity was

> a means to a military end which amounted to much more than a short-term policy, namely strategic parity and the primacy of the counter-offensive doctrine. The Air Staff tried to elide numerical with strategic parity in their argument for re-equipment, tending to disguise the real strategic significance of what they were after. The RAF spent three years chasing changing and often somewhat hypothetical estimates of whatever the Germans meant by 'front line strength'.
> (*British Air Strategy Between the Wars*, p. 173)

57 The 1936 Inskip Report called into question the destructive capability of the RAF and suggested that Britain should adopt a strategy of attrition against German airpower by leveraging British economic strength. The report was not well received in Air Staff

circles. Ibid., pp. 183–5; Tami Davis Biddle, "British and American Approaches to Strategic Bombing," p. 105.
58 *Men, Money, and Diplomacy: The Evolution of British Strategic Foreign Policy, 1919–1926* (Ithaca, NY: Cornell University Press, 1989), p. 180.
59 Table derived from PLANS (Op.), "Copy No. 17, Western Plans," AIR 9/96, 1 September 1939.
60 A memo dated 3 December 1938 by Deputy Director of RAF plans, Air Commodore John Slessor, is interesting for a number of reasons. Not only does he give an order of priority for W.A. campaigns, listing the plan against the Ruhr industries first, but his third option differs from that suggested by Middlebrook and Everitt (W.A. 20 vice W.A. 4; see next fn.). The choice is revealing primarily because it reflects the awe in which senior RAF officers held strategic bombing. Before unleashing the full fury of British airpower, Slessor suggests the implementation of "A 'gloves on' plan for initial action"—in other words, to escalate incrementally rather than unleashing the full fury of British airpower. "The Basis of Bomber Planning During This Winter is to be as Follows," AIR 9/96, 11 March 1938.
61 Middlebrook and Everitt, *The Bomber Command War Diaries*, p. 19.
62 According the official historians of the RAF's strategic bombing campaign,

> The 1939 force would, of course, not be able to wipe out the industry of the Ruhr. But if it concentrated attack on the nineteen power plants and twenty-six coking plants enumerated in the intelligence report sent to [Bomber Command], they could be put out of action in a fortnight by 3,000 sorties with a loss of 176 aircraft, and Germany's war-making power reduced to a standstill.
> (Charles Webster and Noble Frankland, *The Strategic Air Offensive Against Germany, 1939–1945, Volume I: Preparation,* London: HMSO, 1961, p. 97)

63 Plans 2, "Note on the Relative Merits of Oil and Power as Objectives for Air Attack," AIR 9/96, 16 October 1939.
64 The question of which target was more suitable for attack, oil or electricity, was the subject of considerable debate within the RAF. It is noteworthy that the even when proponents of bombing oil laid out their arguments, they did so within a framework of strategic paralysis:

> In view of the comparatively small effort required for a modified oil plan, it might pay us to *make certain* of Germany's collapse in a measureable time through a shortage of oil before embarking on a more difficult plan (i.e., Power in the Ruhr) which relies for rapid success largely on moral effect.
> (Ibid., underlining in original)

65 Alan Cooper, *The Men Who Breached the Dams: 617 Squadron, 'The Dambusters'* (London: William Kimber, 1982), pp. 11–12.
66 Sweetman, *Operation Chastise*, pp. 1–2.
67 Other dams in the Ruhr Catchment included the Lister (22 million m^3 volume), the Ennepe (15 million m^3 volume), and the Henne (11 million m^3 volume). In the Eder and Diemel Catchment, the Diemal dam had a water volume of 20 million m^3. "Air Attack on Dams," AIR 20/4369, 5 February 1943, p. 5.
68 D.D. Plans (Ops), "Copy of minutes from A13(b) No. 36 (Not seen by DCAS)," AIR 9/96, 25 October 1940.
69 According to British assessments, the following volume of water was required for each industry: "1 cubic metre per ton of coal raised .2.cubic metres of water per ton of coke produced .2.cubic metres of water per ton of pig-iron produced. Foundries are even larger consumers in proportion to output." "The Economic and Morale Effects of the Destruction of the Möhne Dam and the Added Effects Which Would Result From Destruction at the Same Time of the Sorpe and Eder Dams," AIR 8/1238, 28 March 1943, p. 5

70　Robertson, *The Development of RAF Strategic Bombing Doctrine*, p. 151.
71　Although the authors of the official history of the RAF strategic bombing campaign point out that it is easy for strategists and historians to criticize decisions made after the fact, with the benefit of information unavailable to decision makers at the time, one cannot excuse the lack of basic intelligence gathering on or surveys of German war industries to gain a better *informed* appreciation of its vulnerabilities. One can, however, understand the planning problems associated with not knowing the effects or results of a lengthy strategic bombing campaign given a dearth of experience. Webster and Frankland, *The Strategic Air Offensive Against Germany*, Vol. 1, p. 30.
72　Ibid., pp. 139, 212. The *Luftwaffe* also severely underestimated the ability of coordinated fighter and flak defenses to wreak havoc on escorted daylight bombing raids. Heavy losses on fighter sweeps and in actions such as *Adler Tag, Schwartze Donnerstag*, and in daylight raids over London forced the *Luftwaffe* to adopt less accurate night bombing only in October 1940. Williamson Murray, *Strategy for Defeat: The Luftwaffe, 1939–1945* (Maxwell AFB, AL: Air University Press, 1983), pp. 48–55; W.H. Tantrum, IV, and E.J. Hoffschmidt, eds, *The Rise and Fall of the German Air Force, 1939–1945* (Old Greenwich, CT: WE Inc., 1969), pp. 79–96; and Cajus Bekker, *The Luftwaffe War Diaries* (New York: Doubleday, 1968), p. 176.
73　The pre-war RAF circular error probable estimate (the radius in which 50 percent of bombs are expected to hit) of high altitude, daylight bombing in 1938 was 300 yards. The tests that supported these conclusions were conducted in almost pristine conditions, without accounting for adverse factors such as the weather or enemy action. Subsequent bombing experience demonstrated that this estimate was off by a significant order of magnitude. Night bombing proved more problematic; as "Bomber" Harris observed:

> With the equipment then available it would be extremely lucky to hit a large town by night. This did happen occasionally; for example, some 30 aircraft bombed Stettin in September, 1941, and got 80 per cent of their bombs *within 2 miles* (italics added) of the aiming point.
> (Arthur Harris, *Bomber Offensive,* London: Collins, 1947, p. 81)

74　*The Strategic Air Offensive*, p. 129. According to war projections for April 1939, the total number of bombers available to Bomber Command were 168 "heavy" bombers and 320 "medium" bombers; these medium bombers included the Fairey Battle, entire squadrons of which were destroyed during the 1940 campaign to defend France. D.D. Plans, "The Basis of Bomber Planning During this Winter is to be as Follows:-," AIR 9/96, 3 November 1938.
75　Although some models, such as the Vickers Wellington, carried a four-gun rear turret that proved disruptive to fighter attacks from astern, the choice of armament limited its effectiveness. In order to minimize both cost and potential logistical problems, existing .303 caliber infantry machine guns were adapted instead. Existing fighter armament had greater range and lethality; German fighter pilots learned to destroy the rear turret from beyond the latter's range or attack the bomber's unprotected flanks instead. Webster and Frankland, *The Strategic Air Offensive*, p. 200.
76　*The Development of RAF Strategic Bombing Doctrine*, p. 83.
77　Ibid., pp. 85–6.
78　British medium bombers attacking ships in Wilhelmshaven and Brunsbüttel from low altitude on 4 September 1939 suffered losses equivalent to one-quarter of the attacking force; losses in low-level attacks during the Battle of France in May–June 1940 were also heavy. Middlebrook and Everitt, *The Bomber Command War Diaries*, pp. 22, 41–55.
79　The destructive effect of an explosive shock wave dissipates if there is nothing to contain it. If a shock wave can be contained it will have a much greater destructive effect. Tamping explosives is the technical term used to describe this; rather than just placing

explosives on the face of a structure to be destroyed, the explosives are either placed within a cavity made in the structure or are covered with sandbags or other materials. In the case of bombs developed for the special operation, water pressure at 30 feet below the surface would provide sufficient tamping to contain the shock wave to a much narrower area.

80 Although Admiralty officials continued to press for torpedo attacks, two arguments shelved such plans: the torpedo-carrying aircraft available possessed limited range and could not reach the targets in the Ruhr Valley, even using modified bombers; and torpedoes had proven ineffective at destroying jetties, much less gravity dams. "Employment of Bomber Aircraft against Dams and Reservoirs," AIR 14/817, 3 July 1940.

81 Other proposed solutions were simply beyond the technology available at the time. For example, Dr. R.G. Harris put forward an idea resurrected by the planners of "Operation Aphrodite" in 1944—using remotely piloted drones to "fly" aircraft into the target. Sweetman, *Operation Chastise*, p. 6.

82 "Adjunct to Memorandum on Possible Uses of the Short Range High Capacity Torpedo," AIR 14/817, 2 September 1940. The eccentric Finch-Noyes would eventually be attached to Combined Operations, the organization responsible for commando raids in Occupied Europe. He gained a degree of notoriety as the inventor of the "Giant Panjandrum," yet another rocket-powered stand-off weapon. Essentially a huge spool housing an explosive charge between its wheels, the Panjandrum was designed to be launched from landing craft offshore and destroy enemy fortifications on the beach. The inability to the control the weapon, which made it almost as dangerous to its operators as to the Germans, doomed the project. For details see Gerald Pawle, *The Secret War, 1939–1945* (London: The Companion Book Club, 1958), pp. 221–8.

83 According to Finch-Noyes, the torpedo would have a 3:1 casing to explosive ratio, yet later in the document he suggests that a 3,000-pound torpedo would contain 2,000 pounds of explosive. He expected a modified Wellington to be able to carry two of these weapons. "Appendix A," AIR 14/817, 2 September 1940.

84 Finch-Noyes had personal reasons for developing weapons that could be delivered outside of the range of defensive armaments. His son, Geoffrey, was killed on 13 June 1940 leading a squadron of Fairey Swordfish biplanes from 800 Squadron against the battleship *Scharnhorst* in Trondheim, Norway. Fleet Air Arm Archive website, http://www.fleetairarmarchive.net/RollofHonour/Cos/CommandingOfficers-f.htm.

85 "Appendix A," AIR 14/817, 2 September 1940.

86 "Letter from Finch-Noyes to Air Marshal Sir Richard E.C. Peirse," AIR 14/817, 2 April 1941.

87 "The Attack of Dams," AIR 14/817, 13 July 1940.

88 "Employment of Bomber Aircraft against Dams and Reservoirs," AIR 14/817, 3 July 1940.

89 "Loose Minute, Group Captain Ops to SASC," AIR 14/817, 2 June 1941.

90 See for example Barnes Wallis, "The Man and His Bomb: The Dam-Busting Weapon," *Aerospace Historian*, Vol. 20 (1973); J.E. Morpurgo, *Barnes Wallis: A Biography* (London: Longmans, 1972); I. Hutchings, "Bouncing Bombs of the Second World War," *New Scientist* (2 March 1978): 563–7; Brickhill, *The Dam Busters*, pp. 5–34; Cooper, *The Men Who Breached the Dams*, pp. 13–23; and Sweetman, *Operation Chastise*, pp. 28–58.

91 Based on tests conducted against the Nant-y-Gro dam in Wales in August 1942, a seven-ton bomb could destroy a dam similar to the Möhne if it was no more than 50 feet away. Placing a charge directly in contact with the dam wall cut the required amount of explosive by two-thirds. "Air Attack on Dams, Part I: General Discussion of the Problem," AIR 20/4369, 5 February 1943.

92 Brickhill, *The Dam Busters*, pp. 7–13.

93 The Australian, British, and Germans may have used "skip-bombing" on an individual basis, but only the American Fifth Air Force in the Pacific developed it as a standard operating procedure. The aviators of George Kenney's Fifth Air Force experimented heavily with the optimal means and methods for low-level, masthead height attacks. The degree to which Kenney encouraged new and innovative solutions to improving bombing accuracy marks him as one of the most flexible and innovative airmen in the United States Army during the Second World War. Thomas E. Griffith, Jr., *MacArthur's Airman: General George C. Kenney and the War in the Southwest Pacific* (Lawrence, KS: University of Press of Kansas, 1998), pp. 82–3 and Timothy Gann, *Fifth Air Force Light and Medium Bomber Operations during 1942 and 1943* (Maxwell AFB, AL: Air University Press, 1993), pp. 8–10.

94 The naval version of Upkeep, a spherical device code-named "Highball," was much less successful due to control and stability problems encountered with the weapon after it was released. Highball had a tendency to shift its rotational axis in flight, leading to a phenomenon with which most amateur golfers are familiar: the "slice" left or right that increased as the weapon made additional contact with the water's surface.

95 Brickhill, *The Dam Busters*, p. 59; Sweetman, *Operation Chastise*, pp. 52–8.

96 In the course of discussion, Mr. Wallis suggested that the Eder dam (45 miles E.S.E. of the Mohne) with a capacity nearly double that of the Mohne Dam, constituted a most important target. It was agreed that the possibility of a simultaneous attack upon the two dams should be considered.

(A.C.A.S. (Ops.), "Report on a Meeting held at Air Ministry on 15th February 1943 To discuss the possibility of attacking a certain Mohne dam with a new weapon," AIR 20/996, 16 February 1943, correction in original)

97 Quoted in Sweetman, *Operation Chastise*, p. 19.

98 Quoted in Ibid.

99 Mirror-imaging occurs when knowledge about an adversary's intentions is limited. The default assumption is that adversaries think in the same ways we do: they share similar values and thresholds of pain. As one of the pillars of deterrence theory is credibly threatening what the adversary values most, such mistaken assumptions can have drastic consequences. For an explanation of how American national intelligence estimates are derived, from which strategic plans are developed, see Williard Matthias, *America's Strategic Blunders: Intelligence Analysis and National Security Policy, 1936–1991* (University Park, PA: Penn State University Press, 2001), pp. 298–301.

100 Quoted in Sweetman, *Operation Chastise*, p. 45.

101 The idea that the main object of bombing German industrial cities was to break the enemy's morale proved to be wholly unsound; when we had destroyed almost all the larger industrial cities in Germany the civil population remained apathetic, while the Gestapo saw to it that they were docile, and, in so far as there was work left for them to do, industrious. But it seemed quite a natural opinion in 1941.

(Harris, *Bomber Offensive*, p. 78)

102 Harris' discussion of "panacea" targets demonstrates his considerable enmity towards the economic analysts of the Ministry of Economic Warfare: "These were targets which were supposed by the economic experts to be such a vital bottleneck in the German war industry that when they were destroyed the enemy would have to pack up. Apart from the single instance of the synthetic oil plants—and they only constituted a real bottleneck in the last year of the war—the arguments of the economic experts invariably proved fallacious." *Bomber Offensive*, p. 220. Other panacea targets included molybdenum mines, ball-bearing factories, and Swedish iron ore.

103 Initially misinformed about the differences between Upkeep and Highball, Harris's pre-emption of Wallis's idea consisted of "What the hell do you damned inventors want? My boys' lives are too precious to be thrown away by you." Sweetman, *Operation Chastise*, p. 44.

104 Winterbotham was Chief of Air Intelligence, Secret Intelligence Service, from 1930 to 1945. Additionally, he convinced Henry Tizard and G.M. Garro-Jones, Private Secretary of the Minister of Production, of the utility of Wallis's concept. F.W. Winterbotham, *Secret and Personal* (London: William Kimber, 1969), p. 152.

105 Sir Henry Tizard is largely remembered for the role he played in applying science to the field of air defense before the Second World War, an issue that he worked in conjunction with Winston Churchill. As a result, Tizard was one of Churchill's most trusted advisors. It should be noted that given Tizard's role during the war as Chairman of the Committee for the Scientific Survey of Air Defence, he was instrumental in supporting a number of special operations during the Second World War that included the Bruneval Raid. A succinct biography of Tizard is contained in R.V. Jones, *Most Secret War: British Scientific Intelligence, 1939–1945* (London: Coronet Books, 1979), pp. 25; 40–1.

106 Harris's comment on the mission is revealing, as it speaks to the overall quality of his "boys" and the correctness of his strategy and less to the necessity for aerial special operations: "Such a disaster, brought about by only nineteen aircraft, must undoubtedly have caused great alarm and despondency in Germany. The greater number of our attacks during the Battle of the Ruhr was equally successful." *Bomber Offensive*, p. 159.

107 The moral effects of destroying the dams had propaganda value against the German public: "Exceptional opportunities would be presented for successful measures of political warfare." "The Economic and Moral Consequences of the Destruction of German Dams," AIR 8/1238, 2 April 1943.

108 AIR 8/1238, "The Economic and Morale Effects of the Destruction of the Möhne Dam and the Added Effects Which Would Result From Destruction at the Same Time of the Sorpe and Eder Dams," 28 March 1943.

109 AIR 20/4369, "Air Attack on Dams, Part II: The Effect on German Industry of the Destruction of Certain Dams," 5 February 1943.

110 Ibid.
111 Ibid.
112 Ibid.
113 "ACAS (ops) to CAS," AIR 8/1238, 5 April 1943.
114 One of the most important tools used to convince various Air Ministry officials and senior scientific advisors was test footage taken of Upkeep drops and the destruction of scale model dams. Sweetman, *Operation Chastise*, p. 44.

115 This list has been adapted from the unsurpassed categories of strategic utility of special operations contained in Colin S. Gray, *Explorations in Strategy* (Westport, CT: Greenwood, 1996), pp. 168ff.

116 The "Battle of the Ruhr" began 5 March and ended on 26 July with raids on Essen, home of the Krupps Steel Works. Harris had ample concern about husbanding his resources; during the five-month sustained "battle," the RAF lost 640 aircraft and over 3,700 personnel. Alan Cooper, *The Air Battle of the Ruhr: RAF Offensive, March to July 1943* (Shrewsbury: Airlife, 1992), p. 142.

117 Joint Planning Staff, "Operation 'Highball'," CAB 121/266, 17 March 1943.

118 Surprise is arguably the most important element in any direct action special operation. In order to preserve the element of surprise, the planning details of any special operation should be limited to as few people as possible. Air Ministry planners were so concerned that Operation Chastise would be compromised that flight crews were not briefed until the day before the raid. Cooper, *The Men Who Breached the Dams*, p. 66. Churchill, concerned that the Germans might grasp the scope of the plan and improve anti-aircraft defenses, ordered an aerial reconnaissance "exclusion zone" around the dams area. Sam Bassett, *Royal Marine* (London: Peter Davies, 1962), p. 203. On Admiralty issues related to Highball see Ad Hoc "Highball" Sub-Committee, "Annex: 'Highball' and 'Upkeep', Memorandum by the Ad Hoc Committee," CAB 121/266, 18 March 1943.

119 Sweetman, *Operation Chastise*, p. 80.
120 In his post-war history of "air bombardment," Richard Saundby mentions in passing Operation Chastise. He downplays his own role in the affair: "Their destruction, it was thought [by members of the Plans Directorate of the Air Staff], would have a serious effect on the productive capacity of the area." *Air Bombardment*, p. 151.
121 Wallis expressed concern that Upkeep might not work against a central core dam such as the Sorpe less than a week before the planned raid. The commander of 5 Group, Air Chief Marshal Ralph Cochrane, suggested delivering the bomb in parallel with the water face of the dam, at a higher altitude, without backspin. The bomb would simply enter the water and explode at depth, hopefully cracking the hardened core. Sweetman, *Operation Chastise*, p. 92.
122 It is speculation that Ministry of Economic Warfare assessments were starting to influence Portal's thinking but he nevertheless downplayed the effects of attacking the Möhne Dam in a meeting of the Chiefs of Staff on 7 April. He added, however, "that it was still an operation well worth while." "Part of C.O.S. (43) 68th Meeting (0) held on WEDNESDAY, 7th April, 1943, at 10.30 a.m.," CAB 121/266.
123 With a touch of irony, a sense of history, or just serendipity, 617 Squadron was officially established on 1 April 1943: April Fool's Day, which was also the day on which the RAF was established in 1918. Tom Bennett, *617 Squadron: The Dambusters at War* (Wellingborough: Patrick Stephens Limited, 1986), p. 8.
124 Low-level is slightly misleading in this case; 617 Squadron practiced target approaches from 50 to 200 feet. Such flying at night required considerable piloting and navigational skills. *Enemy Coast Ahead*, p. 226.
125 Gibson, *Enemy Coast Ahead*, pp. 230–1.
126 Among the list of innovations developed in support of this operation, aside from the bomb itself, were those in support of accurate delivery of the bomb. They included a spotlight system for determining true altitude above water at night and a simple bombsight based on the principles of trigonometry that calculated the point at which the weapon should be released. Gibson, *Enemy Coast Ahead*, p. 247; Cooper, *The Men Who Breached the Dams*, p. 56; Brickhill, *The Dam Busters*, pp. 56, 58–9.
127 During 9–27 April, 617 Squadron conducted 115 exercises. See mission summary statistics reproduced in Cooper, *The Men Who Breached the Dams*, pp. 50, 52 and 56.
128 The Inter-Services Topographical Department, led by Sam Bassett, compiled a range of data on the dams derived from sources as diverse as pre-war German technical treatises and vacation and reconnaissance photographs. The key to solving the problem, however, resided in a botanist at Kew Gardens "who not only visited the dam but had written a thesis on the flora surrounding it." Bassett, *Royal Marine*, pp. 201–5.
129 "The Economic and Moral Effects of the Destruction of the Möhne Dam and the Added Effects Which Will Result From the Destruction at the Same Time of the Sorpe and Eder Dam," AIR 8/1238, 28 March 1943.
130 See for example Gibson, *Enemy Coast Ahead*, pp. 267–87; Cooper, *The Men Who Breached the Dams*, pp. 91–120; and Brickhill, *The Dam Busters*, pp. 69–91. The definitive source, derived from documents and eyewitness reports, remains John Sweetman, *Operation Chastise*, pp. 105ff.
131 Stephen Flower, using British documents including the operational logs of 617 Squadron, suggests that five bombs were dropped on the Möhne Dam in *Barnes Wallis' Bombs: Tallboy, Dambuster & Grand Slam* (Briscombe Port: Tempus, 2004), pp. 61–3. J.E. Morpurgo, citing a German report from September 1943, suggests that only four bombs were used and perhaps only one caused the dam to crack, thereby validating Barnes Wallis's theory. To Morpurgo's credit, however, he suggests that some of the specific facts of the raid may never be known due to the fog and friction of war. *Barnes Wallis*, pp. 267–8, 271–2. Neither author, unfortunately, provides source citations on which their conclusions are based.

132 Details for this paragraph have been drawn from Charles Webster and Noble Frankland, *The Strategic Air Offensive Against Germany, 1939–1945, Volume II: Endeavour, Part 4* (London: HMSO, 1961), p. 173–82; Sweetman, *Operation Chastise*, pp. 105–45.
133 Sweetman, *Operation Chastise*, pp. 157–60.
134 The exception was the banal entry in the war diary of the headquarters of the Wehrmacht which mentions that the dam supplied water for personal and industrial uses, but not power. Walther Hubatsch, ed., *Kriegstagebuch des Oberkommando der Wehrmacht (Wehrmachtführungstab), Band III: 1. Januar 1943 – 31. Dezember 1943* (Frankfurt am Main: Bernard & Graefe Verlag, 1963), p. 494.
135 For Hitler, the failure of the *Luftwaffe* to prevent the attack was yet another indication of Hermann Göring's incompetence. Joseph Goebbels, true to form, found a self-justifying anti-Semitic connection that he subsequently turned into propaganda:

> The former Berlin Reuters correspondent, Bettany, claimed that the plan for the attack stemmed from a Jew who had emigrated from Berlin. I had this written up as a short news item for the papers in the Reich, especially in the areas that suffered the disaster. This shows once again how dangerous the Jews are and how right we are to put them behind bars.
> (Elke Fröhlich, ed., *Die Tagebücher von Joseph Goebbels, Teil II Diktate 1941–45, Band 8 April–Juni 1943*, München: K.G. Saur, 1993, pp. 316, 322)

136 Morpurgo, *Barnes Wallis*, pp. 275–6.
137 Albert Speer, *Inside the Third Reich* (New York: Macmillan, 1970), p. 280.
138 Ibid., p. 280; Sweetman, *Operation Chastise*, p. 161.
139 United States Strategic Bombing Survey, Report 208, *21 Rheinische-Westfalische Elektrizitaetswerk A G* (Washington: US Government Printing Office, 1947), p. 19.
140 Brickhill, *The Dam Busters*, p. 94.
141 With the exception of aircraft and naval construction, which experienced slight dips in production, all sectors of German war economy continued to increase production until many industrial areas were overrun. For detailed German production estimates, see Figures 20–30 and Table 25 contained in British Bombing Survey Unit, *The Strategic Air War Against Germany, 1939–1945* (London: Frank Cass, 1998), pp. 90–1.
142 Although 617 Squadron was ostensibly created for only one mission, it was not disbanded. After the Dam Raid, 617 was used for a variety of purposes including the bombing of the Dortmund-Ems Canal which cost the squadron dearly in men and equipment. As a result, 617 Squadron subsequently focused on high-altitude, precision bombing. For this task they were given special equipment including Barnes Wallis's 12,000- and 22,000-pound bombs nicknamed "Tallboy" and "Grand Slam." The Squadron conducted a number of pinpoint attacks on industrial and high-value military targets that were impossible for other squadrons to either hit or destroy. In other cases, Churchill wanted to avoid collateral damage to French civilians; 617 Squadron destroyed half of the Gnôme and Rhôe plant in Limoges in February 1944. Three to five of the bombs dropped were 12,000-pound "blockbuster" bombs released from 15,000 feet; they landed within 300 feet of the target marker. The only fatalities in this night action were coronary arrests among a few elderly residents of the adjacent town. As a special operations force, 617 Squadron continued to develop precision-bombing techniques and methods that improved the overall quality of Bomber Command. For details of the February 1944 attack see United States Strategic Bombing Survey, Report 145, *Gnome et Rhone Limoges, France* (Washington: US Government Printing Office, 1945).
143 Walther Hubatsch, ed., *Kriegstagebuch des Oberkommando der Wehrmacht (Wehrmachtführungstab), Band III*, p. 494.
144 The American "sleeping giant" had only been awakened by the Japanese attack on Pearl Harbor on 7 December 1941; there was a strong lobby within the United States

158 Notes

to avenge the "infamy" before dealing with Nazi Germany. Others suspected that British lobbying for a Europe-first strategy concealed ambitions to expand Her Majesty's influence at the expense of her allies.

145 During the final weeks of the Second World War, American military leaders continued to accept Josef Stalin's declarations at face value while ignoring any British discussions of the potential political ramifications of a drive towards Berlin. See Anthony Beevor, *The Fall of Berlin, 1945* (New York: Viking, 2002), pp. 139–44.
146 "British Publicity in the United States," AIR 19/304, 15 May 1942.
147 Goebbels scornfully noted in his diary that "The English and Americans are discussing practically nothing but air warfare. Their successful raid on the German dams created a great sensation both in London and in Washington. Of course they knew exactly what they have achieved by this time." Fröhlich, ed., *Die Tagebücher von Joseph Goebbels*, p. 322.
148 Robert Rhodes James, ed., *Winston S. Churchill, His Complete Speeches, 1897–1963, Vol. 8: 1943–1949* (London: Chelsea House, 1974), pp. 6777–8.
149 "A.H.M.S. to Vice C.A.S.," AIR 19/304, 30 December 1942.
150 In an interesting twist on the paradoxical logic of strategy, the British suspected (rightly) that the Germans had captured an Upkeep mine intact from a crash-landed Chastise Lancaster. Members of the Chief of Staff Committee, and various sub-committees, only realized the vulnerability of their own dams to attack after the special operation had been conducted. A number of schemes to defend the dams were suggested, including minefields, barrage balloons, countermine barriers, catenaries (suspended wires designed to interrupt the flight of the bomb), dazzle lights, and smoke were considered. "Defence of Dams and Reservoirs," AIR 8/1102, 27 August 1943, pp. 3–4.
151 German defensive preparations are discussed in detail in Sweetman, *Operation Chastise*, pp. 280–1.
152 Speer, *Inside the Third Reich*, p. 281.
153 Fröhlich, ed., *Die Tagebücher von Joseph Goebbels*, pp. 315–6.
154 Middlebrook and Everitt, *The Bomber Command War Diaries*, p. 388.
155 Brickhill, *The Dam Busters*, p. 94.
156 United States Strategic Bombing Survey, Report 64b, *The Effects of Strategic Bombing on German Morale, Vol. 1* (Washington: US Government Printing Office, 1947), p. 46.
157 See for example the evaluation contained in James S. Corum, *The Luftwaffe: Creating the Operational Air War, 1918–1940* (Lawrence, KS: University Press of Kansas, 1997), pp. 268–9.
158 Fröhlich, ed., *Die Tagebücher von Joseph Goebbels*, p. 316.
159 Speer, *Inside the Third Reich*, pp. 281–3.
160 It was Speer who brought Hitler Dornberger's concept of the A-4 [V-2] as a weapon of mass destruction and a substitute for the Luftwaffe, and convinced the Führer it was feasible. To reinforce his position, Speer brought Dornberger and von Braun with their models and film to the Führer's headquarters.
(Benjamin King and Timothy Kutta, *Impact: The History of Germany's V-Weapons in World War II,* Rockville Center, NY: Sarpedon, 1998, p. 69)
In an ironic twist, this was precisely how Barnes Wallis had convinced "Bomber" Harris and others of the feasibility of his proposal.
161 Michael Neufeld, *The Rocket and the Reich* (Cambridge, MA: Harvard University Press, 1996), pp. 139–40, 191.
162 King and Kutta, *Impact*, p. 69.
163 Quoted in Józel Garlinski, *Hitler's Last Weapons: The Underground War against the V1 and V2* (New York: New York Times Books, 1978), p. 75.
164 At the start of 1945, with Allied armies bearing down on numerous fronts, the German public "drank in Goebbel's stream of lies that the Führer would unleash new 'wonder weapons' against their enemies, as if he were about to assume the role of a

wrathful Jupiter flinging lightning bolts as a symbol of his power." Beevor, *The Fall of Berlin*, p. 4. German scientists and arms manufacturers continued to design, build and develop hundreds of new weapons prototypes, rather than producing improved versions of a few models in quantity. Most of the designs were subsequently captured and evaluated by their adversaries, including delta-wing aircraft, flying wings, submarines that could recharge their batteries while submersed, infrared weapons sights, superheavy tanks, and ballistic missile systems. In discussing the V-2's drain on specific German resources, most notably instruments and electrical components, one author summarized the weapon as "a triumph of German engineering but certainly was not a monument to good sense." Murray, *Strategy for Defeat*, p. 189.

165 The impact of Hitler's meddling on the development of the wonder weapons is still the matter of some debate. In the case of the Me-262, some historians have argued that these jet fighters could have been used exclusively to shoot down Allied bombers as early as the autumn of 1944. Hitler's order to mount bomb racks, for ground attack missions, has been portrayed as either decisive or negligible. Heinz Magenheimer, for example, suggests that a considerable number of other operational and production factors were more important in delaying the combat debut of this aircraft. *Hitler's War: Germany's Key Strategic Decisions, 1940–1945*, Helmut Bögler, trans. (London: Arms and Armour, 1998), pp. 233–4.

166 The V-1 "flying bomb" offensive began with a whimper, not the anticipated bang, on 13 June 1944. Due to technical and production delays, the V-2 offensive did not start until 11 September 1944, long after the Allies had liberated Paris. King and Kutta, *Impact*, pp. 157, 243.

4 Death by a thousand cuts

1 Professor Rosinki, trans., "The Failure of the War of Exhaustion," *Army Quarterly* (Vol. 35: October 1937 – January 1938): 118.

2 Admiral Sir Reginald Custance remains a noteworthy exception. He articulated in a single page the essence of warfare:

> Whatever be the form of government and whatever be the internal political dissensions, each side starts, consciously or unconsciously, in every war with an object, which may be called National or Political, and with an aim, which may be called Military, to use the armed force to attain the National or Political object. Hence, the idea of war as a political act includes both the National or Political object and the Military aim. By "armed force" is meant the armed sea, land, and air forces, including *both their moral and their physical attributes*.
>
> (*A Study of War*, Port Washington, NY: Kennikat Press, 1970, p. 1 (emphasis added)

3 On technological developments in war, see J.F.C. Fuller, *The Conduct of War, 1789–1961* (Westport, CT: Greenwood Press, 1981), especially pp. 86–94, 113–30; Martin van Creveld, *Technology and War: From 2000 B.C. to the Present* (New York: Free Press, 1989); and Guy Hartcup, *The Silent Revolution: Development of Conventional Weapons, 1945–1985* (London: Brassey's, 1993). The pace of changes in the character of warfare has increased dramatically over the past two centuries. Contrary to popular belief, many authors in the nineteenth century understood that technology had vastly increased the power of the defender. Defensive positions could be overcome by rapid maneuver threatening the flanks of a defender's position or through force of will. Few foresaw the tactical and operational problem posed by a continuous line of fortifications that developed during the "Race to the Sea" in late 1914. On military thought prior to the First World War, see Azar Gat, *The Development of Military Thought: The Nineteenth Century* (Oxford: Clarendon Press,

1992); Jehuda Wallach, *The Dogma of the Battle of Annihilation: The Theories of Clausewitz and Schlieffen and Their Impact on the German Conduct of Two World Wars* (Westport, CT: Greenwood Press, 1986); and Antulio J. Echevarria II, *After Clausewitz: German Military Thinkers Before the Great War* (Lawrence, KS: University Press of Kansas, 2000).

4   Another example of a strategic concept whose interpretation has changed over time is deterrence. As originally conceived, deterrence only works if one could threaten with credible force what an adversary valued most. Deterrence presumes that an adversary is well understood and the things that they value can be threatened militarily. In lieu of better understanding of Soviet values and intentions, a number of US theorists developed a dogmatic interpretation of the concept in which the mere existence of technologically superior nuclear weapons and delivery systems, rather than credible methods of using them, defined their deterrent value. See for example the discussion contained in Barry H. Steiner, *Bernard Brodie and the Foundations of American Nuclear Strategy* (Lawrence, KS: University Press of Kansas, 1991), pp. 241–6. Counterweights to such interpretations are contained in Colin S. Gray, *The Second Nuclear Age* (Boulder, CO: Lynne Rienner, 1999), pp. 88–93 and Keith B. Payne, *The Fallacies of Cold War Deterrence and a New Direction* (Lexington, KY: University Press of Kentucky, 2001), pp. 17–37.

5   I am indebted to Edward Westermann for pointing out the subtle but substantial distinction in translating this term. Clausewitz, *On War*, Book Eight, Chapter Eight (Princeton, NJ: Princeton University Press, 1976), p. 615 and idem, *Vom Kriege*, Book Eight, Chapter Eight (Leipzig: H. Schaufuss, 1935), p. 616.

6   See for example the Translator's Foreword in Hans Delbrück, *History of the Art of War, Volume IV: The Dawn of Modern Warfare*, trans. Walter J. Renfroe, Jr. (Lincoln, NB: University of Nebraska Press, 1990), p. viii. Dr. Hal Winton deserves special mention for pointing out the variations in how the translation is rendered and the significant difference between the two terms.

7   Prior to the Second World War, such theorists included J.F.C. Fuller and Basil H. Liddell Hart. In writing their separate biographies of the two senior Union generals during the American Civil War, Fuller and Liddell Hart clashed bitterly on the subject of attrition and annihilation. Liddell Hart portrayed William T. Sherman as a brilliant strategist who understood the "indirect approach" to warfare. In contrast, he cast Ulysses S. Grant as a ruthless advocate of a bloody attrition strategy against an operationally astute, maneuvering opponent: General Robert E. Lee. Fuller, on the other hand, suggested that attrition and annihilation worked hand in glove with each another. He argued that Sherman only had freedom of maneuver so long as Grant tied down the center of gravity of the Confederacy: the Army of Northern Virginia. See for example Brian Holden Reid, "British Military Intellectuals and the American Civil War: Maurice, Fuller, and Liddell Hart," in *Studies in British Military Thought: Debates with Fuller and Liddell Hart* (Lincoln, NB: University of Nebraska Press, 1998), pp. 141–5; Liddell Hart, *Sherman: The Genius of the Civil War* (London: Ernest Benn, 1930), pp. 9, 328–9; Fuller, *Grant and Lee: A Study in Personality and Generalship* (London: Eyre and Spottiswoode, 1959), pp. 229–32. More recently, advocates of restoring operational art to warfare have polarized the debate. According to Richard Simpkin, operationally "the addict of attrition seizes and holds a piece of ground .which lies between the enemy and the attainment of his strategic objective." *Race to the Swift: Thoughts on Twenty-First Century Warfare* (London: Brassey's, 1985), p. 20. Simpkin's pupil, Shimon Naveh, suggests that fixation with attrition can be attributed directly to the writings of Clausewitz:

> For Clausewitz and his followers attrition is entirely different. It is essentially an unpremeditated and random outcome endured by both belligerent sides, resulting from the linear patterns of the tactical engagement. Moreover, at the strategic

level, attrition is an inevitable consequence of the sole initiative that leads towards the positive aim. In other words, in strategic terms, attrition represents self-inflicted damage, which the aggressor suffers at his own initiative.
>> (*In Pursuit of Military Excellence: The Evolution of Operational Theory*, London: Frank Cass, 1997, p. 65, n. 56)

8   An early attempt to alter the popular perception regarding the insensitivity of British senior leaders to casualties by useless frontal assaults on German positions is contained in John Terraine, *The Smoke and the Fire: Myths and Anti-Myths of War, 1861–1945* (London: Leo Cooper, 1992), pp. 170–81. The myth, however, is persistent: see for example the book by John Laffin, *British Butchers and Bunglers of World War One* (Surrey: Bramley, 1989). An initial attempt at a corrective is Carter Malkasian, *A History of Modern Wars of Attrition* (Westport, CT: Greenwood, 2002), p. 1. The American perception of the term "attrition" is colored by that country's experience in Vietnam. Attrition is equated as much with the hollow measure of effectiveness known as the "body count," reflecting superior American firepower, as it is with a belief in North Vietnamese patience and willingness to take casualties.

9   This observation is also based on the author's participation in a series of wargames held during 2002–4 by various offices of the Office of the Secretary of Defense and the Joint Staff. Trevor DuPuy suggests that there are two kinds of attrition: personnel and material. He also identifies the causes of attrition and develops a simulation "cycle" of the process in *Attrition: Forecasting Battle Casualties and Equipment Losses in Modern War* (Falls Church, VA: NOVA Publications, 1990), pp. 2–4. A discussion of simulation-based attrition, tailored for SOF and designed to correct a shortfall in US Special Operations Command's Joint Mission Analysis process, is contained in Gregory R. Wilson, "Modeling and Evaluating US Army Special Operations Forces Combat Attrition Using Janus(A)," unpublished thesis, Naval Postgraduate School (September 1995).

10 See for example F.N. Dyer, W.P. Burke, R.A. Williams, and R.E. Hilligoss, *Relationships among Rates of Attrition in Training and Subsequent Attrition in Line Units*, ARI-RR-1377 (Alexandria, VA: Army Research Institute for the Behavior and Social Sciences, 1984); Jennifer L. Hestermann, "The Erosion of the Enlisted Force: A Study of Attrition," unpublished thesis, Air Command and Staff College (1999).

11 Although Terry White casts a wide net in his definition of SOF, to include a number of conventional elite light infantry units, his description of selection and continuation training is a useful exploration of the process. *Swords of Lightning: Special Forces and the Changing Face of Warfare* (London: Brassey's, 1992), pp. 19–62. In his book on Britain's 14 Intelligence Company, used in Northern Ireland, James Rennie suggests that special operations in dense, urban environments impose different selection and training requirements. These requirements placed a premium on observational skills and blending in with the local populous. As couples were less conspicuous than a car full of fit, brush-cut males (or men dressed to appear as women) in an urban environment, the result was that the ranks of 14 IC were opened to include female operators. *The Operators: Inside 14 Intelligence Company—the Army's Top Secret Elite* (London: Century, 1996), pp. 15, 166.

12 William McRaven, *Spec Ops, Case Studies in Special Operations Warfare: Theory and Practice* (Novato, CA: Presidio, 1995), pp. 2–3.

13 Peter de la Billière, *Looking for Trouble: SAS to Gulf Command, The Autobiography* (London: HarperCollins, 1994), p. 345.

14 Ken Connor, *Ghost Force: The Secret History of the SAS* (London: Weidenfield & Nicolson, 1998), p. 254.

15 Although it is too early for comprehensive assessments to be made of Operation Iraqi Freedom, historians will doubtless note that the regime of Saddam Hussein was effective only in creating the illusion of military power. Debilitated by wars with Iran and a

coalition of nations in 1991, as well as a decade of sanctions, the armed forces of Iraq in 2003 were better suited to crushing internal opposition than mounting serious opposition to American-led coalition forces. Attempts to decapitate the regime early failed, the intelligence picture was unclear throughout the campaign, and bold coalition operational maneuver was halted by both the weather and the requirement for the logistical "tail" to catch up with the lead elements.

16 George Gawrych, *The 1973 Arab-Israeli War: The Albatross of Decisive Victory*, Leavenworth Paper No. 21 (Leavenworth, KS: Combat Studies Institute, 1996), p. 38.

17 Richard Betts and Colin Gray provide reminders that the nature of strategy can be informed by the ideas of, but is not amenable to, analysis by chaos and complexity theory. See for example Betts, "Is Strategy an Illusion," *International Security* (Vol. 25, No. 2: Fall 2000): 5–50; Gray, "Why is Strategy Difficult," *Joint Forces Quarterly* (No. 22: Summer 1999): 6–12; idem, *Strategy for Chaos: Revolutions in Military Affairs and the Evidence of History* (London: Frank Cass, 2002).

18 For the evolution of Schlieffen's campaign plan thinking, as reflected in his various *Denkschriften*, see Zuber, "The Schlieffen Plan Reconsidered," *War in History* (Vol. 6, No. 3: July 1999): 276ff. Holger Herwig highlights the contemporary controversy surrounding Schlieffen's plan in *The First World War: Germany and Austria-Hungary, 1914–1918* (London: Arnold, 1997), pp. 46–52.

19 Regarding the German war planners on the eve of the First World War, Dennis Showalter concludes that "The essence of strategy is the calculating of relationships among ends, means, and will. Let the process of calculation obscure the values of the relationships, and the result is not bad strategy but no strategy." *Tannenberg: Clash of Empires* (Hamden, CT: Archon, 1991), p. 34.

20 These levels of war, it should be noted, are not universally accepted. Levels suggested by other authors include grand strategy, high policy, grand tactics, operational theater, etc. To keep the discussion clear and concise, only these three levels will be discussed here. Strategy is the bridge between policy and action. Operations are the employment of forces in a theater of war to achieve some or all of the goals of policy. The actual employment of forces on the battlefield comprises the realm of tactics.

21 The dangers in overly simplifying an inherently complicated subject are self-evident, especially if it conforms to the audience's predispositions. As David Jablonsky notes, Army "students weaned on the structural certitude of the five-paragraph field order and the Commander's Estimate naturally find such structure (strategy can be understood as a mixture of ways, ends, and means) comforting in dealing with the complexity of strategy." Comfort, however, can subsume comprehension for those not inclined to explore the subject further. "Why Is Strategy Difficult?" in Gary Guertner, ed., *The Search for Strategy: Politics and Strategic Vision* (Westport, CT: Greenwood Press, 1993), p. 3.

22 Hew Strachan outlines the differences between total and limited war, including the problem of differing stakes between competitors, in "Essay and Reflection: On Total War and Modern War," *International History Review* (Vol. 22, No. 2: June 2000): 341–70.

23 Clausewitz adds that "Pure defense, however, would be completely contrary to the idea of war, since it would mean that only one side was waging it." *On War*, Book Six, Chapter One, p. 357.

24 A rough indication of the quality of the soldiers in European armies during the Age of the Enlightenment is reflected in the statement by Frederick the Great:

> Many soldiers can be governed only with sternness and occasionally with severity. If discipline fails to keep them in check they are apt to commit the crudest excesses Since they greatly outnumber their superiors, they can be held in check only through fear.
>
> (Jay Luvaas, trans. and ed., *Frederick the Great on the Art of War*, New York: Free Press, 1966)

A more detailed treatment of disciplinary measures required in armies of the period is contained in Philip J. Haythornthwaite, *The Armies of Wellington* (London: Arms and Armour, 1994), pp. 64–71.

25 See the descriptions contained in Hubert Camon, *La guerre Napoléonienne—les systèmes d'operations, Théorie et technique* (Paris: Chapelot, 1907); David Chandler, *The Campaigns of Napoleon* (London: Weidenfeld & Nicolson, 1966), pp. 332–67; and Gunther E. Rotherberg, *The Art of War in the Age of Napoleon* (Stapleford: Spellmount, 1997), pp. 22–30. More recently, scholarly debate has focused on the Napoleonic period as a case study in the debate associated with the so-called "revolution in military affairs." See for example MacGregor Knox, "Mass politics and nationalism as military revolution: The French Revolution and after," in Knox and Williamson Murray, eds, *The Dynamics of Military Revolutions, 1300–2050* (Cambridge: Cambridge University Press, 2001), pp. 57–73 and Gray, *Strategy for Chaos*, pp. 138–69.

26 The primary advantages that Napoleon's army had over its rivals were flexibility and speed. Corps maneuvered independently, according to a general plan of action, yet were comprised of combined arms to handle most contingencies on their own; his army, freed from the magazine system of supply, achieved march rates his adversaries could not match. As a result, Napoleon could concentrate his forces using grand maneuvers to surprise his adversaries and encircle them. The officers of a number of European armies prior to the First World War, who were weaned on rote learning of Napoleonic battles, attempted to imitate battles such as Jena believing that morale could overcome advances in defensive firepower. G.F.R. Henderson, "Tactics of the Three Arms Combined," in *The Science of War* (London: Longmans, Green and Co., 1905), p. 72. Although Napoleon strove to achieve an "ideal" battle, he rarely achieved it. He adapted his plan to suit new developments and changing conditions as Jean Colin notes in *Les Transformations de la Guerre* (Paris: Ernest Flammarion, 1912), p. 110.

27 Clausewitz's *On War* was the incomplete product of a life's work. The dialectical construct of his arguments, as well as shifts in discussion between tactical, operational, and strategic levels of war, are enough to confuse most readers. Turgid translations have also not helped matters. Authors critical of Clausewitz are quick to dismiss his theories based on these shortcomings, or they selectively quote material to demonstrate that the Clausewitzian universe is exclusively focused on the single, decisive battle: "Destruction of the enemy forces is the overriding principle of war .battle is the one and only means that warfare can employ." Lamar Tooke, "Blending Maneuver and Attrition," *Military Review* (Vol. 80, No. 2: March–April 2000): 10. Clausewitz, however, was discussing battle from the campaign, or operational perspective. When Clausewitz discusses battle from the strategic perspective, the difference is noticeable:

> We regard a great battle as a decisive factor in the outcome of a war or campaign, but not necessarily the only one. Campaigns whose outcomes have been determined by a single battle have become fairly common only in recent times, and those cases in which they have settled an entire war are very rare exceptions.
> (*On War*, Book Four, Chapter Eleven, p. 260)

The Howard-Paret translation of *On War* contains a useful guide to reading the work for the new reader written by Bernard Brodie. The guides to Clausewitz's ideas penned by Michael Handel still remain the most useful to the subject. See the second and third revised editions of *Masters of War: Classical Strategic Thought* (London: Frank Cass, 1996; 2000) and *Who is Afraid of Carl von Clausewitz? A Guide to the Perplexed*, 8th edn (Newport, RI: Naval War College, 1999).

28 The culminating point is a useful concept but not a universal "principle" of war. Although strategic depth is often the key enabler of the culminating point, one should

not discount the value of political, social, and economic considerations. For example, small countries lack strategic depth but that does not mean that they cannot force an opponent to reach a culminating point. To overcome this weakness, their leaders could adopt irregular warfare to gain local superiority and defeat an adversary in detail as occurred in Cyprus during the resistance to British occupation. For a discussion of the relationship between time, space, and available forces in irregular conflicts, see James D. Kiras, "Terrorism and Irregular Warfare," in John Baylis, Eliot Cohen, Colin Gray, and James Wirtz, eds, *Strategy in the Contemporary World: An Introduction to Strategic Studies* (Oxford: Oxford University Press, 2002), pp. 213–15. Political considerations can erode the will of leaders to continue a struggle despite the military logic of doing so. Concern over adverse public reaction to media footage of "The Highway of Death" in Kuwait led George Bush to end hostilities against Iraqi forces in 1991, allowing substantial Republican Guard forces to escape destruction. Robert H. Scales, Jr., *Certain Victory: The US Army and the Gulf War* (Washington: Brassey's, 1994), p. 315.

29 Clausewitz suggests that "although the equation of time and space does underlie everything else and is, so to speak, the daily bread of strategy, it is neither the most difficult nor the decisive factor." *On War*, Book Three, Chapter Eight, p. 196.

30 A point made in Michael Howard, *Clausewitz* (Oxford: Oxford University Press, 1983), p. 55.

31 Raymond Aron neatly uses one of Clausewitz's analogies to explain the rationale for adopting a defensive strategy:

> The four types of resistance represent as many successive stages of the defensive, each involving a greater sacrifice for the defender but at further expense of the attacker, with this circumstance favorable to the defender which he borrows and which the enemy pays for in cash. Loss of territory will weaken the defender in the future; the advance weakens the attacker at once.
>
> *(Clausewitz: Philosopher of War*, Christine Booker and Norman Stone, trans, Englewood Cliffs, NJ: Prentice Hall, 1985, p. 156)

32 Clausewitz, *On War*, Book Six, Chapter Nine, p. 392.

33 Clausewitz, *On War*, Book Eight, Chapter Three, p. 582.

34 According to H. Rothfels, Clausewitz indicated revising *On War* four years prior to his death

> to distinguish between "*two kinds of war,*" one in which the object is "the overthrow of the enemy," another, in which the object is merely "to make some conquests on the frontiers of his country, either for the purpose of retaining them permanently, or for turning them to account as a matter of exchange in the peace process.
>
> ("Clausewitz," in Edward Mead Earle, ed., *Makers of Modern Strategy: From Machiavelli to Hitler,* Princeton, NJ: Princeton University Press, 1948, p. 108)

35 The standard treatment of Delbrück's historical method and theories remains Gordon Craig, "Delbrück: The Military Historian," in Peter Paret, ed., *Makers of Modern Strategy: From Machiavelli to the Nuclear Age* (Princeton: Princeton University Press, 1986), pp. 326–53.

36 Military historians owe an equal, if not greater debt to Delbrück. Had he not developed *Sachkritik* or insisted that ancient authors were prone to exaggeration, the "facts" as presented by Herodotus, Thucydides, Xerxes, and others might still be interpreted literally. Works by John Keegan, John Terraine, and Victor Davis Hanson demonstrate the value in challenging the assertions of accepted history. Keegan, *The Face of Battle* (New York: Knopf, 1976); Terraine, *The Smoke and the Fire: Myths and Anti-Myths of War, 1861–1945* (London: Sidgwick and Jackson, 1980); Hanson, *The Western Way of War: Infantry Battle in Classical Greece* (New York: Knopf, 1989). Delbrück's work continues to be a source of controversy. Terence Zuber, for example, suggests that

Delbrück's prejudice against decisions made by the German General Staff during the First World War greatly enhanced the myth surrounding Count Albert von Schlieffen's "Plan" to fight a two-front war. "The Schlieffen Plan Reconsidered," pp. 263–4.

37 "[T]he nature of strategy leads to a central problem, the problem of the double form of strategy, the strategy of annihilation and the strategy of attrition, a problem that necessarily dominates all strategic thought and action." Delbrück, *History of the Art of War*, Vol. IV, p. 293.
38 Ibid., p. 296.
39 Having failed to defeat decisively the Western members of the Entente in 1914–1915, the leaders of Imperial Germany settled on an operational attrition campaign at Verdun. One author goes so far as to suggest that "Verdun was essentially an application of limited means in a total war. Limited means can prove productive in limited wars but seldom do in total wars." Farrar, Jr., "Peace Through Exhaustion," p. 493.
40 Clausewitz, *On War*, Book One, Chapter One, p. 80. Delbrück agreed with Clausewitz that given sufficient space and time, an offensive would reach its culminating point: "A strategic offensive, therefore, does not automatically reach its climax in a battle but often wears itself out in a simple gain of space, the occupation of a region that can be exploited." *History of the Art of War*, Vol. IV, p. 295.
41 Delbrück, *History of the Art of War*, Vol. IV, p. 424.
42 Craig, "Delbrück," *Makers of Modern Strategy* (1948), p. 273.
43 "In all conduct of war the unexpected and chance plays a large role, and the mastering of this dark element of uncertainty through decisiveness is one of the most important qualities of a commander." Delbrück, *History of the Art of War*, Vol. IV, p. 306. Clausewitz was more explicit:

> If the mind is to emerge unscathed from this relentless struggle with the unforeseen, two qualities are indispensable: *first, an intellect that, even in the darkest hour, retains some glimmerings of the inner light which leads to truth; and second, the courage to follow this faint light wherever it may lead.* The first of the qualities is described by the French term *coup d'oeil*; the second is determination
> (*On War*, Book One, Chapter Three, p. 102, emphasis in original)

44 Craig, "Delbrück," *Makers of Modern Strategy* (1948), pp. 274–5.
45 "It was known that [the 16th century Swiss] always wished to return home again soon; it was also always difficult for the national leaders to obtain the pay for them over a long period." Delbrück, *History of the Art of War*, Vol. IV, pp. 294–5.
46 Craig, "Delbrück," *Makers of Modern Strategy* (1948), p. 274.
47 Alcibiades was the architect of the Sicilian expedition, as well as providing military advice to both the Spartans (Athens' mortal enemy) and Persia (the mortal enemy of all of the Hellenes) after having been banished from his home. Barry Strauss and Josiah Ober advance "the Alcibiades Syndrome" as an explanation for the fall of Athens during the Peloponnesian War:

> The symptoms are easy to distinguish: on the one hand, extraordinary talent—ambition, charm, persuasiveness combining both charisma and flimflam; on the other hand, extraordinary egotism. The ultimate goal in life is supreme political power, and everything—friendship, love, sex, education, sports, politics, and warfare—becomes subordinated to that goal.
> (*The Anatomy of Error: Ancient Military Disasters and Their Lessons for Modern Strategists,* New York: St. Martin's, 1990, pp. 50–1)

Alcibiades' speech to Tissaphernes is contained in Robert Strassler, *The Landmark Thucydides: A Comprehensive Guide to the Peloponnesian War* (New York: Free Press, 1996), p. 508.

48 Delbrück debated with fellow historian Otto Hintze on the strategic form pursued by Prussian monarch Frederick the Great. At stake was the reputation of the king in a

contemporary context that favored decisive battle above all else. Hintze suggested that Frederick utilized both forms simultaneously, with one form subsuming another; it was a question of scale. Delbrück responded that

> If the decisive point, therefore, is the broad scope, then the difference between the one type of strategy and the other is nothing more than a difference between significant and insignificant commanders. But this difference has been correctly understood only by that scholar who has recognized that the mission of the strategist is no less important and, as a result of its two-sidedness [the poles of maneuver and battle], is often even more difficult from a subjective viewpoint than that of a strategy of annihilation. Consequently, the difference does not lie in the larger or smaller scope of operations.
> ("Supplement: On The Contrast Between the Strategies of Attrition and Annihilation," *History of the Art of War*, Vol. IV, p. 441)

A bibliography of the academic exchange between Delbrück and Hintze is contained in Craig, "Delbrück," *Makers of Modern Strategy* (1948), fn. 60, p. 274.

49 Born in 1878, Aleksandr A. Svechin rose to the rank of Major-General after having served actively in both the Tsarist and Red armies. Svechin was a student of military history and a keen intellect whose primary contribution to military art and science is the coining of the phrase "operational art." He challenged the military *theories de jour* on the basis that they were not applicable to the Soviet Union at that time. In particular, he crossed swords intellectually with Mikhail Tukhachevskii on the extent to which the Soviets should mechanize their armed forces. Svechin was most influential in the Soviet Union during the military debates of the 1920s, especially in the field of military education and wargaming, but his star waned as Tukhachevskii's waxed during the 1930s. Accused of advocating bourgeois ideas by Tukhachevskii, Svechin contented himself with teaching courses and translating Clausewitz's *On War* into Russian. The primacy of a military strategy of attrition or annihilation mattered little to Stalin; the political annihilation of his enemies did. Both Tukhachevskii and Svechin were "purged" by Stalin for their perceived crimes in 1937–8. Jacob W. Kipp, "Major-General A.A. Svechin and Modern Warfare: Military History and Military Theory" in Aleksandr Svechin, *Strategy*, Kent Lee, ed. (Minneapolis, MN: East View Publications, 1992), pp. 23–56.

50 V.K. Triandafillov argued that conditions of modern warfare demanded a different approach to force structure and operations. Although war no longer consisted of the single decisive battle, a series of operations could be linked together to achieve the same effect:

> Deep and crushing blows may put entire state organisms out of the game quite rapidly. Where the large states are concerned, these blows may lead to the rout of their armed forces piecemeal, in large packets. These blows are a truer means of rapid attrition of enemy personnel and material resources, of creations of objectively favorable conditions for socio-political upheavals in the enemy country.
> (*The Nature of the Operations of Modern Armies*, William Burhans, trans, London: Frank Cass, 1994, p. 150)

Triandafillov presented this "ideal" representation of what "successive operations" could achieve and then counterbalanced it with the formidable logistical and materials obstacles to be overcome.

51 Tukhachevskii understood the problems facing the attacker given the size of contemporary armies, their firepower lethality, and a defender operating on interior lines. His answer was to strike throughout the defender's depth and use mechanized mobility to disrupt the defender and continue the offensive simultaneously. The goal of "deep operations" was nothing less than the annihilation of the enemy army: "Every battle, offensive and defensive alike, has as its aim the defeat of the enemy. But only

an all-out attack on the primary axis, leading to a relentless pursuit, will achieve annihilation of the enemy's forces and resources." "General Principles, PU-36, Chapter 1," in Richard Simpkin, *Deep Battle: The Brainchild of Marshal Tukhachevskii* (London: Brassey's, 1987), p. 177.
52 A point reinforced by Makhmut Gareev in *If War Comes Tomorrow? The Contours of Future Armed Conflict*, Jacob Kipp, ed., and Yakov Fomenko, trans. (London: Frank Cass, 1998), pp. 98–9.
53 Svechin, *Strategy*, p. 244.
54 Ibid., p. 246.
55 Kipp, "Major-General A.A. Svechin and Modern Warfare" in Ibid., pp. 41–2.
56 See for example George Meyers, *Strategy* (Washington, DC: Byron S. Adams, 1928), pp. 132–9. Although contemporary strategists have largely ignored Meyers' work, it remains relevant in attempting to link together what in the US are considered to be the four "elements" of strategy or instruments of national power: diplomatic, informational, military, and economic. Meyers ambitiously attempts to develop a comprehensive framework for making policy decisions using the principles of war and elements of Clausewitzian theory. Relevant to this discussion is his inclusion of two military options in his cost–benefit outline: "absolute war" and "wars of lesser magnitude." Another noteworthy work unrelated to debates on force planning or military preparations, written exclusively for the purposes of understanding various theories of war, is Hervé Coutau-Bégarie, *Traité de Stratégie* (Paris: Economica, 1999). See especially the author's discussion and framework charts on the forms of strategy on pages 348–61.
57 J.C. Wylie's discussion of forms of strategy appears to be derived from Clausewitz, although Wylie attributed the initial idea to Dr. Herbert Rosinski. Rosinski lectured extensively on Clausewitz at Oxford, Princeton, and the US Naval War College. Although Wylie characterized *On War* as having "a sophistication that has so far been unexcelled" he criticizes the work for the wrong reasons: "Clausewitz .is not sufficiently inclusive nor is he sufficiently fundamental in that he does not reach the heart of the problem—the strategic patterns of thought from which grow the actions of war itself." This suggests that Wylie's study did not include the final book of the work. J.C. Wylie, *Military Strategy: A General Theory of Power Control* (New Brunswick, NJ: Rutgers University Press, 1967), pp. 17; 23. Information on Rosinski, including a list of works and his biography, is contained in Antulio J. Echevarria II, "Borrowing from the Master: Uses of Clausewitz in German Military Literature Before the Great War," *War in History* (Vol. 3, No. 3: Summer 1996): 274–92.
58 Wylie, *Military Strategy*, p. 24.
59 Ibid., p. 24.
60 Ibid., p. 104.
61 In particular, historian Archer Jones suggests that strategy should be framed by the geographic and temporal duration of the military action. In his estimation, there are two forms of strategy: raiding and persisting. A raiding strategy seeks to cause economic and political damage and limit the exposure of military forces. A persisting strategy is distinguished from a raiding strategy by imposing military forces on enemy geography, generally to force a military decision at a favorable time and place. *The Art of War in the Western World* (New York: Barnes and Noble, 1987), pp. 54–7.
62 The technological pace at which nuclear weapons were developed stimulated discussions on possible options for nuclear weapons use. Low-yield weapons, delivered by tactical ballistic missiles, fired from artillery tubes or emplaced as mines, had the potential to offset Soviet numerical superiority in Central Europe. The debate regarding the utility of tactical nuclear weapons continued until the collapse of the Soviet Union in 1991. An early work that advocates broad discussion of battlefield weapons use is G.C. Reinhardt and W.R. Kintner, *Atomic Weapons in Land Combat* (Harrisburg, PA: Military Service Publishing, 1954). A quarter of a century after this

work was published, the authors of another work lamented that "Defining a tactical nuclear weapon is a thankless task, since to do so inevitably involves one's definition of tactical nuclear warfare; and, to date, a commonly accepted definition does not exist." William R. Van Cleave and Saul T. Cohen, *Tactical Nuclear Weapons: An Examination of the Issues* (New York: Crane Russak, 1978), p. 13. Much of the current Western thinking associated with maneuver warfare, and by extension strategic paralysis, had its roots in discussions of how to defeat a Soviet invasion of Europe by applying operational art instead of nuclear weapons. See for example F.W. Mellenthin and R.H.S. Stolfi, *NATO Under Attack: Why the Western Alliance Can Fight Outnumbered and Win in Central Europe without Nuclear Weapons* (Durham, NC: Duke University Press, 1984). What those discussions did not consider was that the Soviets were willing to use both operational art *and* tactical nuclear/chemical weapons to achieve their goals.

63 An excellent survey of the literature of limited war theory, as it applies to nuclear weapons, is contained in Lawrence Freedman, *The Evolution of Nuclear Strategy* (London: Macmillan, 1981), pp. 98–105.

64 For a survey of the theories of Lawrence and Mao, see Kiras, "Terrorism and Irregular Warfare," pp. 208–32.

65 Although little more than well-conceived strategy in practice, defense thinkers struggling with the problem of American hegemony have suggested that adversaries who do not fight against the strengths of the United States are engaging in a new type of conflict: "asymmetric warfare." See for example Steven Metz and Douglas V. Johnson II, *Asymmetry and US Military Strategy: Definitions, Background, and Strategic Concepts* (Carlisle, PA: Strategic Studies Institute, 2000). The claims that such approaches to warfare are new or unique are challenged in Steven Lambakis, James D. Kiras, and Kristen Kolet, *Understanding "Asymmetric" Threats to the United States* (Fairfax, VA: National Institute for Public Policy, 2002).

66 Lawrence provides a concise summary of the conditions for success in irregular warfare:

> In fifty words: Granted mobility, security (in the form of denying targets to the enemy), time, and doctrine (the idea to convert every subject to friendliness), victory will rest with the insurgents, for the algebraical factors are in the end decisive, and against them perfections of means and spirit struggle quite in vain.
> (T.E. Lawrence, "The Evolution of a Revolt,"
> *The Army Quarterly,* Vol. 1, No.1: 1920: 69)

67 Ernesto "Che" Guevara believed that his particular theory for revolution was applicable universally, given its unanticipated success in Cuba. Not taking account of the specific conditions in Bolivia not only proved his theory wrong but it cost him his life as well. The basis of Marxist-Leninist revolutionary theory is the uprising of the oppressed, urban proletariat that overthrows the bourgeoisie. When this model was tried in 1930 in China, a country with a rural, agrarian-based peasant society, the results were disastrous. Mao gleaned two lessons for guerrilla warfare in China from his participation in the 1930 uprising: it is a long-term proposition that cannot be rushed; and the conditions for it must take into account the rural peasantry. Kiras, "Terrorism and Irregular Warfare," pp. 212–16. A concise survey outlining how Mao adapted his theory of irregular warfare to suit conditions in China is contained in Thomas A. Marks, *Maoist Insurgency Since Vietnam* (London: Frank Cass, 1996), pp. 8–15.

68 Interesting similarities exist between the Arab Revolt (1916–18) and the various wars between Libya and Chad (1978–87). In both cases, Western advisors initially attempted to mold Arab and Chadian forces to conform to Western doctrine: each resulted in failure as the forces fled the battlefield after receiving their first exposure to war under the conditions of the day. Key individuals suggested equipping the Arab and Chadian armies to suit their cultural style of warfare instead. The results of the

Arab Revolt under Lawrence's supervision are well known. The Chadian example remains more obscure but in many cases is more remarkable. Equipped with commercial pick-up trucks, anti-tank missiles, and machine guns, and using superior mobility and tribal "swarming" tactics, the *Force Armée Nationale Tchadien* inflicted a number of humiliating defeats on the Libyans in 1986–7 that resulted in a more permanent ceasefire. For details see Kenneth M. Pollack, *Arabs at War: Military Effectiveness, 1948–1991* (Lincoln, NB: University of Nebraska Press, 2002), pp. 375–412.

69 In Lawrence's assessment,

> The value of the tribes is defensive only, and their real sphere is guerrilla warfare. They are intelligent and very lively, almost reckless, but too individualistic to endure commands, or fight in line, or help each other. It would, I think, be impossible to make an organized force out of them. Their initiative, great knowledge of the country, and mobility, make them formidable in the hills, and their penchant is all for taking booty. They would dynamite a railway, plunder a caravan, steal camels, better than anyone, while fed and paid by an Arab authority.
>
> ("Military Notes," in Malcolm Brown, ed., *Secret Despatches From Arabia and Other Writings by T.E. Lawrence,* London: Bellew Publishing, 1991, p. 66)

70 These three elements roughly correspond to correlation of forces and consideration of non-material factors, such as motivation and morale. T.E. Lawrence, *The Seven Pillars of Wisdom: A Triumph* (London: Jonathan Cape, 1935), p. 192.

71 T.E. Lawrence, *Revolt in the Desert* (London: Jonathan Cape, 1927), p. 96.

72 Ibid.

73 As much as Lawrence talked about maneuver without battle, he did not object to a biographer writing that "Even Marshal Saxe might have questioned Lawrence's extreme standard of economy, yet Marshal Foch would surely have approved his paramount aim of conserving every possible man to expend, if necessary, at Aqaba." Basil H. Liddell Hart, *T.E. Lawrence: In Arabia and After* (London: Jonathan Cape, 1934), p. 198. Correspondence between Liddell Hart and Lawrence prior to the publication of his biography was reproduced in idem and Robert Graves, *T.E. Lawrence to his Biographers* (New York: Doubleday, 1963).

74 Lawrence's goal, which was influenced by his romantic notions of the Arab peoples, became a moot point with the signing of the Sykes-Picot Treaty (1916) that divided the Arab regions between the British and French. These divisions and others were arbitrary; the European negotiators "tended to define [zones of influence] in terms of geographical boundaries rather than of more subtle influences" such as social or cultural lines. Hew Strachan, *The First World War, Volume I: To Arms* (Oxford: Oxford University Press, 2001), p. 542.

75 "When human society advances to the point where classes and states are eliminated, there will be no more wars, counter-revolutionary or revolutionary, unjust or just; there will be the era of perpetual peace for mankind." "Strategy in China's Revolutionary War," in Mao Zedong, *Selected Military Writings of Mao Tse-Tung* (Peking: Foreign Languages Press, 1966), p. 81.

76 "On Protracted War," in Ibid., pp. 210–11. Mao later discusses offsetting conditions for the enemy related to the first stage: one positive, the other negative. Displaying a keen awareness of the various dimensions of strategy, Mao characterizes negative change as

> for the worse and manifests itself in hundreds of thousands of casualties, the drain on arms and ammunition, deterioration of troop morale, popular discontent at home, shrinkage of trade, the expenditure of over ten thousand million yen, condemnation by world opinion, etc.
>
> (Ibid., p. 215)

77 *Mao Tse-Tung on Guerrilla Warfare*, Samuel Griffith, trans. (New York: Praeger, 1961), pp. 66–9.
78 "On Protracted War," pp. 212–14.
79 The complexity of Mao's theory becomes evident when one understands the difficulties associated with shifting between phases of guerrilla warfare. Knowing when the conditions are right for advancing the revolution to the next stage requires sober assessment of both the insurgent and counter-revolutionary forces and structure. The case of North Vietnamese General Vo Nguyen Giap is instructive. Considered to be a strategic genius as the architect of American defeat in Vietnam, Giap nevertheless misgauged the conditions to advance to the next stage of Maoist war on three occasions: the 1965 Ia Drang Offensive, which sought to cut South Vietnam in half through conventional invasion; the 1968 Tet Offensive, during which the expectations for a "General Uprising" of the South Vietnamese failed to materialize; and the 1972 Easter Offensive, in which the decisive conventional thrust of the insurgents was defeated by a combination of stubborn South Vietnamese resistance and American airpower. Much like the principles of war, Mao's stages of insurgency are merely signposts for success. Knowing when to violate those principles or stages is to understand the art, as opposed to the science, of war. Marks, *Maoist Insurgency Since Vietnam*, p. 7 and James Mrazek *The Art of Winning Wars* (London: Leo Cooper, 1968), pp. 11–18.
80 "On Protracted War," pp. 214–15.
81 Ibid., p. 249.
82 See for example ibid., pp. 208–31. Two authors suggest that "Mao Tse-Tung has done for war what Lenin did for imperialism and Marx for capitalism: he has given war 'scientific' schemata." Edward L. Katzenbach, Jr. and Gene Z. Hanrahan, "The Revolutionary Strategy of Mao Tse-Tung" in Franklin Mark Osanka, ed., *Modern Guerrilla Warfare: Fighting Communist Guerrilla Movements, 1941–1961* (New York: Free Press, 1962), p. 132.
83
> In war as a whole, too, quick decision is sought at all times and in all countries, and a long drawn-out war is considered harmful. China's war, however, must be handled with the greatest patience and treated as a protracted war .But   *if their criticism* [of protracted war] *had been applied not to strategy but to campaigns and battles, they would have been right.*
>
> (Mao Zedong, "Strategy in China's Revolutionary War," p. 143, emphasis added)

84 As Samuel Griffith notes,

> It is interesting to examine Mao's strategical and tactical theories in light of his principles of "unity of opposites." This seems to be an adaptation to military action of the ancient Chinese philosophical concept of *Yin-Yang*. Briefly, the *Yin* and the *Yang* are elemental and pervasive. Of opposite polarities, they represent female and male, dark and light, cold and heat, recession and aggression. Their reciprocal interaction is endless. In terms of the dialectic, they may be likened to the thesis and antithesis from which the synthesis is derived.
>
> *(Mao Tse-Tung on Guerrilla Warfare*, p. 25)

85 Mao's works are rife with discussions related to harmony, or balance. See for example his discussion on the reasons for the temporary imbalance that exists between Chinese and Japanese forces in "On Protracted War," p. 209. More pointedly, Mao suggests that "Hence campaigns of annihilation are the means of attaining the objective of strategic attrition. In this sense war of annihilation *is* war of attrition [emphasis in original]." Ibid., p. 249.
86 For details see Robert Accinelli, *Crisis and Commitment: United States Foreign Policy Towards Taiwan, 1950–1955* (Chapel Hill, NC: University of North Carolina Press, 1996).
87 John Cann concludes that the Portuguese, in defense of their colonies in Africa such as Guinea-Bissau,

focused on a subdued, low-tempo style of fighting that was a function of its constrained resources and low technology. Portugal knew from the beginning that it was going to have to fight a long war, and thus it would have to fight well and cheaply to sustain the conflict.

(*Counterinsurgency in Africa: The Portuguese Way of War, 1961–1974*, Westport, CT: Greenwood Press, 1997, p. 187)

As the French learned in Algeria, military success was not enough to guarantee victory. The victory had to be won politically as well, domestically and in the colony.

88 *White Tigers: My Secret War in North Korea* (Washington: Brassey's, 1996), p. 192. The study from which Malcom quotes his statistics, conducted by the Operations Research Office of Johns Hopkins University for the Headquarters, Army Forces Far East, cites three quantifiable metrics to evaluate partisan success: "casualties were inflicted, material was captured, and the enemy was caused to employ troops in counterpartisan security activities." Frederick Cleaver *et al.*, *UN Partisan Warfare in Korea, 1951–1954*, ORO-T-64 (AFFE), (Chevy Chase, MD: Johns Hopkins University, 1956), p. 16.

89 The report by the officer in charge of Korean partisans in 1952, Jay Vanderpool, severely understated the psychological effects he intended to achieve using special operations: "Communist or North Korea Labor Party leaders who will not render partisan assistance to our forces will be assassinated .If succeeding Communist leaders are assassinated, the ambitions of minor leaders will be dampened." Headquarters, Far East Command Liaison Detachment (Korea), "Subject: Guerrilla Operations Outline, 1952," 11 April 1952, p. 3.

90 Don Blackburn began his special operations career working with indigenous forces against the Japanese in the Philippines during the Second World War. He later helped solidify the tenuous foundation created for US Army Special Forces in the wake of the Korean War. During the war in Vietnam, Blackburn coordinated military "special activities" for the Joint Staff, including the Military Assistance Command Vietnam Studies and Observation Group (MACV-SOG). Leroy Manor, with combat flight experience in two previous wars, oversaw the US Air Force's nascent foreign internal defense aviation training in Southeast Asia. Benjamin Schemmer, *The Raid* (London: Book Club Associates, 1977), pp. 80–1 and Susan Marquis, *Unconventional Warfare: Rebuilding US Special Operations Forces* (Washington: Brookings Institution Press, 1997), p. 82.

91 Schemmer, *The Raid*, p. 259.

92 One of the few weak points of Williamson Murray and Allan Millett's single volume history of the Second World War is the dismissal by the authors of the contribution of resistance activities, and by extension special operations, to Allied victory. Although acknowledging the bravery of specific individuals and the resistance movement as a whole, the authors nevertheless conclude that partisan and sabotage activities did not draw German attention on either the Western or Eastern fronts. *A War to be Won: Fighting the Second World War* (Cambridge, MA: Harvard University Press, 2000), pp. 406–7.

93 Quoted in Andrew Mack, "Why Big Nations Lose Small Wars: The Politics of Asymmetric Conflict," *World Politics* (Vol. 27, No. 2: January 1975): 184–5.

94 *On War*, Book Three, Chapter One, p. 178. Clausewitz was showing his contempt for contemporary authors to draw elaborate geometric figures depicting formations and troop movements.

95 This point highlights the danger of interpreting "classics" of strategy literally. A narrow reading of Sun Tzu conveys the impression that an adversary can be defeated psychologically with clever stratagems and little need for battle. In contrast, Clausewitz has been interpreted as the justification for seeking decisive battle regardless of casualties. Such narrow interpretations do a disservice to both works. A tonic for such an interpretation is contained in Handel, *Masters of War*, pp. 1–4.

96 The raid on St. Nazaire, code-named "Operation Chariot," was designed to render unusable the dry dock capable of repairing the damaged German battleship Tirpitz. For further details see James G. Dorrian, *Storming St. Nazaire* (London: Leo Cooper, 1998) and C.E. Lucas Phillips, *The Greatest Raid of All* (London: Heinemann, 1958).

97 Israeli naval commandos and engineers assaulted, seized, and dismantled the Soviet-manufactured Egyptian radar station located on Green Island. The raid allowed the development of countermeasures to jam this specific type of radar. Arieh Avneri, *War of Attrition* (Tel Aviv: Olive Books, 1972), pp. 189–92; Steven Hartov, "The Israelis at Green Island" in Samuel A. Southworth, ed., *Great Raids in History: From Drake to Desert One* (New York: Sarpedon, 1997), pp. 265–77.

98 Operation Eagle Claw was mounted to rescue 53 Americans taken prisoner and held hostage in revolutionary Iran. The rescue plan called for fixed and rotary wing aircraft to refuel at a remote improvised airstrip, code named "Desert One," prior to flying on to their staging area closer to Tehran ("Desert Two"). Inter-service rivalries, interoperability problems, an ad hoc rescue force, poor security tactics, equipment failure, and environmental conditions all played a role in the final scrubbing of the mission after two aircraft collided and were destroyed. The resulting enquiry into the failure to rescue American hostages held in Tehran, as well as Congressional pressure to ensure that such a disaster never occurred again, led to the creation of the US Special Operations Command in 1987. For further details, see James H. Kyle, *The Guts to Try* (New York: Orion, 1990); Paul B. Ryan, *The Iranian Desert Rescue: Why It Failed* (Annapolis, MD: Naval Institute Press, 1985); and Lucien S. Vandenbroucke, *Perilous Options: Special Operations as an Instrument of US Foreign Policy* (Oxford: Oxford University Press, 1993), pp. 114–51.

99 The discussion of the strategic utility of special operations contained in Colin S. Gray, *Explorations in Strategy* (Westport, CT: Praeger, 1996), pp. 168–80 remains unmatched.

100 For an excellent overview of the mission, see McRaven, *Spec Ops*, pp. 333–80. A useful firsthand account of the raid is contained in Muki Betser, *Secret Soldier: The True Life Story of Israel's Greatest Commando* (New York: Atlantic Monthly Press, 1996), pp. 234–69. The raid is also known under the code name "Operation Thunderball."

101 Fritz Heinzen overstates the importance of Operation Jonathan when he suggests that "As was true at Entebbe, the stakes may well be the survival of a nation's morale, or 'soul'." "The Future of Raids", in Southworth, ed., *Great Raids in History*, p. 316. As with claims associated with strategic bombing and the so-called "body bag" phenomenon that limits U.S activities, SOF advocates are prone to overstating the moral effect of an individual action.

102 Robert Jervis, "Complexity and the Analysis of Political and Social Life," *Political Science Quarterly* (Vol. 112, No. 4: Winter 1997–8): 570.

103 According to the US Army's vision for future combat operations, networked sensors, lighter vehicles, and improved strategic lift capability permit the following:

> Early entry Army forces arrive at multiple and possibly austere points of entry as a coherent, integrated combined arms team capable of rapidly concentrating combat power and fighting upon arrival—achieving a new paradigm where deploy equals employ. Another way of stating that is [Port of Embarkation, POE] equals Line of Departure (LD).
>
> (Objective Force Task Force, *The Objective Force in 2015* Arlington, VA: Department of the Army, 2002, p. 32)

104 See for example the conclusions reached by Richard Betts, "Compromised Command," *Foreign Affairs* (Vol. 80, No. 4: July/August 2001): 129; Christopher J. Bowie, Robert P. Haffa, Jr., and Robert Mullins, *Future War: What Trends in America's Post-Cold War Military Conflicts Tell Us About Early 21st Century Warfare*

(Washington, DC: Northrup Grumman Analysis Center, 2003), pp. 34–5. German author and military officer Rudolf von Caemmerer speculated that the widespread adoption of the telegraph for military use would have similar implications. *The Development of Strategical Science During the 19th Century*, Karl von Donat, trans. (London: Hugh Rees, 1905), pp. 171–2.
105 See for example MacGregor Knox's remarks on the limitations of predictive theory derived from history in "Continuity and Revolution in Strategy" in Williamson Murray, MacGregor Knox and Alvin Bernstein, eds, *The Making of Strategy: Rulers, States and War* (Cambridge, MA: Cambridge University Press, 1994), p. 645. Colin Gray suggests that the strategist has no alternative but to rely on history as the basis for developing strategy even though such efforts are bound to be disappointed when the first shots are fired. *Strategy for Chaos*, p. 131.
106 Chaos theory suggests that there are patterns to the randomness that can be interpreted and exploited by the keen observer. I am grateful to my colleague G. Scott Gorman for his insightful comments and discussions on the subject.
107 Wylie, *Military Strategy*, p. 24.
108 During the Vietnam War, special operations were used in four uncoordinated ways: the training and dropping of Vietnamese agents into North Vietnam to establish agent networks and conduct sabotage; reconnaissance and strike missions along the sections of the Ho Chi Minh Trail in neighboring Laos and Cambodia; patrols and raids in riverine areas; and countering infiltration into South Vietnam from a series of static bases close to the border with Laos and Cambodia. Fears over potential Chinese intervention prevented the US from invading North Vietnam using conventional forces. Special operations were limited in effectiveness due to North Vietnamese counterintelligence efforts, aggressive patrolling and spotters near the Ho Chi Minh Trail, and senior American military leadership hostile to its own irregular warriors. For details on the poorly executed missions of OPLAN-34A which led to the imprisonment or execution of almost all Vietnamese agents involved, see Sedgwick Tourison, *Secret Army, Secret War: Washington's Tragic Spy Operation in North Vietnam* (Annapolis, MD: Naval Institute Press, 1995), pp. 110–28. Works relating to the Military Assistance Command, Vietnam, Studies and Observation Group (MACV-SOG) are discussed in detail in a preceding chapter. US Navy Sea, Air and Land (SEAL) missions in Viet Cong-controlled territory such as the Rung Sat Special Zone are summarized in T.L. Bosiljevac, *SEALs: UDT/SEAL Operations in Vietnam* (London: Greenhill, 1990). An assessment of the role played by Green Berets against the Viet Cong is available in Francis J. Kelly, *US Army Special Forces, 1961–1971* (Washington, DC: Department of the Army, 1985), pp. 160–75.
109 A useful summary and assessment is contained in W. Andrew Terrill, "The Nature and Value of Commando Operations during the Egyptian–Israeli War of Attrition," *Small Wars & Insurgencies* (Vol. 8, No. 2: Autumn 1997): 16–34. The dangers associated with using special operations repeatedly and unimaginatively, in a campaign of tactical attrition and reprisals, are evident in Israel's prolonged struggle against Hezbollah in which a number of operations have been unsuccessful. For an example of one such special operation that was ambushed, see Samuel J. Katz, "Incident at Ansariya," *Jane's Intelligence Review* (Vol. 10, No. 1: January 1998): 24–8. For a broader perspective on Israeli special operations against Hezbollah, see Clive Jones, "Israeli Counter-Insurgency Strategy and the War in South Lebanon, 1985–1997," *Small Wars & Insurgencies* (Vol. 8, No. 3: Winter 1997): 82–108.
110 Mark Urban suggests that "Even though secrecy was vital to the type of operation the SAS wanted to conduct, various political figures and members were keen to exploit the propaganda value of the Regiment." *Big Boys' Rules: The SAS and The Secret Struggle Against The IRA* (London: Faber & Faber, 1993), p. 7.
111 Tony Geraghty, *Who Dares Wins: The Story of the Special Air Service, 1950–1980* (London: Arms and Armour Press, 1980), p. 138.

112 In the military realm, other contributing factors that led to the breaking of the stalemate on the Western Front included tactical and doctrinal adaptation, the fielding of new offensive technologies, and the development of the kernels of twentieth-century combined arms mechanized warfare. Tim Travers suggests otherwise. He argues that there was little innovation in the British Army during the final year of war. In other words, the German Army exhausted itself, British plans for mechanized warfare embodied in "Plan 1919" remained untested, and the experience of the war hobbled the thinking of a future generation of military leaders. *How the War Was Won: Command and Technology in the British Army on the Western Front, 1917–1918* (London: Routledge, 1992), pp. 175–82. J.P. Harris suggests that the British Army under Haig and Rawlinson utilized new technologies and tactics to inflict considerable casualties on the already weakened Germans, achieving the objectives of the war at reasonable cost. *Amiens to the Armistice: The BEF in the Hundred Days' Campaign, 8 August-11 November 1918* (London: Brassey's, 1998), pp. 294–300. One technology developed and fielded to break the "stalemate of the trenches" was gas warfare. Especially relevant is the discussion on the rationale for development and the effectiveness of British chemical warfare contained in Albert Palazzo, *Seeking Victory on the Western Front: The British Army & Chemical Warfare in World War I* (Lincoln, NB: University of Nebraska Press, 2000).

113 Competent adversaries learn to adapt, or offset, the advantages of their opponents. The current "style" of warfare practiced by the United States is heavily dependent on air superiority, precision-guided munitions, and the systems which enable it to project power over long distances. Any adversary seeking to challenge the United States would have to offset these characteristics. An early discussion of the realities of American power projection is contained in Bruce Bennett, Sam Gardiner, and Daniel B. Fox, "Not Merely Planning for the Last War," in Paul K. Davies, ed., *New Challenges for Defense Planning: Rethinking How Much is Enough* (Santa Monica, CA: RAND, 1994), pp. 477–514. A more recent summary is found in Sam J. Tangredi, *All Possible Wars? Toward a Consensus View of the Future Security Environment, 2001–2025*, McNair Paper No. 63 (Washington, DC: Institute for National Strategic Studies, 2000), pp. 63–85.

114 Annihilating an adversary requires tremendous will, a degree of amorality, the ability to synchronize all elements to achieve the purpose, and a supportive population. Ancient history contains several examples, including the fate of the Melians and the Carthaginians, where the populous was destroyed or sold into slavery. For details see Paul B. Kern, *Ancient Siege Warfare* (Bloomington, IN: Indiana University Press, 1999), especially pp. 62–85, 135–62 and 323–51. More recently, however, even the most willing dictators have found this task difficult to accomplish given inadequate resources, time, or fear of retaliation.

115 Dennis M. Drew and Donald M. Snow, *Making Strategy: An Introduction to National Security Processes and Problems* (Maxwell AFB, AL: Air University Press, 1988), p. 1.

116 "Strategic effect for strategic performance should be treated as composite measures, albeit not usually lending themselves to exact computation, that can provide net assessment." Colin S. Gray, *Modern Strategy* (Oxford: Oxford University Press, 1999), p. 20.

117 These conditions for victory include disrupting or denying the adversary's ability to control his forces. The contribution of special operations made decisive victory appear achievable in the early phases of German invasion of the Soviet Union in June 1941:

> Organization and command differentiate armies from mobs, and, for the Red Army, both organization and command dissolved rapidly. Even before the first air strikes, Brandenburger special operations troops in Red Army uniforms had parachuted or infiltrated into Soviet rear areas. There they set about cutting telephone

Notes 175

lines, seizing key bridges, and spreading alarm and confusion. In the area of the main German effort, north of the Pripiat' Marshes, the headquarters of Lieutenant General A.A. Korobkov's 4th Army was never able to establish communications with headquarters above or below it.
> (David M. Glantz and Jonathan M. House, *When Titans Clashed: How the Red Army Stopped Hitler,* Lawrence, KS: University Press of Kansas, 1995, p. 49)

118 Mark Bowden suggests that the Task Force Ranger commander

> had also been very careful to vary their tactics. They usually came in on helicopter and left by vehicles, but sometimes they came in on vehicles and left by helicopters. Sometimes they came and left on choppers, or on vehicles. So the template changed.
> (*Blackhawk Down: A Story of Modern War,* New York: Atlantic Monthly Press, 1999, p. 22)

In a comparison of numbers of casualties inflicted, Task Force Ranger "won" the tactical engagement in Somalia.

119 Quoted in Jonathon Stevenson, *Losing Mogadishu: Testing US Policy in Somalia* (Annapolis, MD: Naval Institute Press, 1995), p. 94.

120 Anthony Kemp, *The SAS at War: The Special Air Service Regiment, 1941–1945* (London: John Murray, 1991), p. 159. Ian Wellsted, a participant in the 11 August attack on the refinery charged with destroying the wheelhouse of the mineshaft during the assault, is less sanguine about the attack's effects:

> In the end it transpired that we had not done nearly as much damage as we had hoped. Although highly spectacular, it was not in fact very useful. But as a model of a nice little operation going according to plan, it was delightful.

A half-century after the attack, Wellsted suggested that the damage caused was limited to "clouds of steam rising from a broken pipe" and a severed electrical power line. *SAS: With the Maquis* (London: Greenhill, 1994), p. 175.

121 Colin S. Gray, "Handfuls of Heroes on Desperate Ventures: When Do Special Operations Succeed?" *Parameters* (Vol. 29, No. 1: Spring 1999): 2–24. In the case of Nazi Germany, special operations were fallow territory from the end of the first phase of Operation Barbarossa in the summer of 1941 until late 1943. Nazi interest in special operations was reinvigorated after the German defeat at Stalingrad, and the Soviet recapture of territory, as well as the internal shifting of power towards Heinrich Himmler's *Schutzstaffeln* (SS) in 1943. Aside from the rescue of Benito Mussolini, German special operations after 1941 failed in almost every instance they were used due to faulty intelligence, insufficient equipment, and excessively difficult tasks (such as the attempts to destroy the Allied bridges over the Rhine and Oder rivers in 1945. James Lucas, *Kommando: German Special Forces of World War Two* (London: Guild Publishing, 1985), p. 165. Poor coordination, in the form of occasional strikes against and harassment of airfields and shipping, limited the effectiveness of Japanese guerrilla operations and raids by graduates from its commando school from 1944 onwards. Culture played a significant role in shaping the employment of Japanese special operators; self-sacrifice in the name of the Emperor became an end in and of itself with the hope that significant effects could be generated by isolated actions. For details see Stephen C. Mercado, *The Shadow Warriors of Nakano: A History of the Imperial Japanese Army's Elite Intelligence School* (Washington, DC: Brassey's, 2002).

122 Clausewitz, *On War*, Book Six, Chapter Twenty-Four, p. 465.

123 In an ironic example of success that came too late, special operations against the Viet Cong infrastructure began to bear fruit as part of a coordinated interagency effort designed to deal with the insurgency after the North Vietnamese had already decided to shift efforts toward a conventional invasion of the south. For an assessment of the effectiveness of SOF in *Phung Hoang*, or the Phoenix project, see Dale Andradé,

176 *Notes*

Ashes to Ashes: The Phoenix Program and the Vietnam War (Lexington, MA: Lexington Books, 1990), pp. 171–2, 195–9. Mark Moyar dismisses the role of SOF in the CIA-led program in *Phoenix and the Birds of Prey: The CIA's Secret Campaign to Destroy the Viet Cong* (Annapolis, MD: Naval Institute Press, 1997), p. 158.

124 The corollary to this statement is that political objectives must be attainable with the military and economic resources at hand. The British campaign in the Falklands in 1982, for example, was conducted beyond the limits of the United Kingdom's military capabilities. For example, Vulcan bombers had to be retrofitted with in-air refueling probes removed from museum aircraft in order to carry out "Black Buck" missions against an airfield.

5 Case study

1 The phrase has been adapted from a Chinese "strategem," identified by Sinologist Harro von Senger, that allegedly advises "exploiting another's troubles or crisis for your own advantage; attack the enemy when he is in a state of chaos." *The Book of Strategems: Tactics for Triumph and Survival*, Myron B. Gubitz, trans. and ed. (New York: Viking, 1991), p. 67.
2 Starinov, *Over the Abyss: My Life in Soviet Special Operations*, Robert Suggs, trans. (New York: Ivy Books, 1995), pp. 305–6.
3 Strategy is value neutral; it is neither "good" nor "bad." The perils of judging strategic decisions in hindsight is discussed in Richard Betts, "Is Strategy an Illusion?" *International Security* (Vol. 25, No. 2: Fall 2000): 8–14. Critical analysis, however, can be done on strategic performance or the way in which strategy is executed. While it is true that what really matters is merely performing better than your adversary throughout the duration of the conflict, undertaking a strategy of attrition merely to achieve victory, without attempting to do so in the most favorable manner possible, can lead to imposed costs that render victory hollow. The social, economic, and psychological cost of the First World War to both Great Britain and France is a case in point.
4 See for example Virginia Cowles, *The Phantom Major* (London: Odham's Press, 1958), p. 10 and John Strawson, *A History of the S.A.S. Regiment* (London: Guild Publishing, 1985), p. 17.
5 Michael Howard, *British Intelligence in the Second World War, Volume 5: Strategic Deception* (London: HMSO, 1990), p. 33. Howard suggests that the idea to establish the SAS came from a captured Italian officer's diary in the early phases of Anglo-Italian conflict in North Africa; John Gordon, citing correspondence with General Sir Neil Ritchie and an interview with Brigadier Guy Prendergast, opines that the ruse was established and maintained for the benefit of the Germans. John Gordon, *The Other Desert War: British Special Forces in North Africa, 1940–1943* (Westport, CT: Greenwood Press, 1987), p. 80.
6 Howard, *British Intelligence, Vol. 5*, p. 34.
7 The other two prongs were the bombing offensive and support to resistance movements in Occupied Europe.
8 H.W. Wynter "The History of Commandos and Special Service Troops in the Middle East and North Africa (January 1941 to April 1943)," in *Special Forces in the Desert War, 1940–1943* (Kew: Public Records Office, 2001), pp. 244–75 and Julian Thompson, *The Imperial War Museum Book of War Behind Enemy Lines* (London: Sidgwick & Jackson, 1998), p. 50.
9 Alan Hoe reconstructs a conversation that Stirling had with fellow commando Jock Lewes

> There is no sensible operation being planned for us. In fact, it looks as though we're all going to be farmed out to other units as reinforcements to sit in trenches

and twiddle our thumbs while some bloody Hun pilot gets us in our sights ... There are a lot of damned good soldiers getting cheesed off with inactivity out there.

(*David Stirling: The Authorised Biography of the Creator of the SAS*, London: Warner Books, 1994, pp. 60–1)

10 Thompson, *The Imperial War Museum Book of War Behind Enemy Lines*, p. 50.
11 Stirling, still using crutches, bypassed his chain of command, snuck into the regional headquarters of the British Army, and proceeded to bluff his way into an audience with first Ritchie and later Auchinleck. Gordon, *The Other Desert War*, p. 80.
12 In support of Operation Crusader, and in addition to the actions of "L" Detachment SAS, two special operations were planned to assist Ritchie and Auchinleck in achieving the goals of their offensive. The first was the reorganization of the Long Range Desert Group, changing it from a semi-autonomous intelligence gathering and raiding force into the "eyes and ears" of the Eighth Army. This reorganization would pay significant dividends in Operation Crusader, although not enough to offset the poor British conduct of operations. The other special operation in support of Crusader is more significant. Acting on intelligence from a variety of sources, Ritchie and Auchinleck attempted to decapitate the leadership of the *Deutsches Afrika-Korps* by going directly after its brains: the German HQ at Beda Littoria, thought to house General Erwin Rommel; Italian HQ at Cyrene; and the Italian intelligence center at Apollonia. The so-called "Keyes raid" was the epitome of British daring and courage but ultimately failed due to faulty intelligence. Rommel was not in the compound as anticipated and most of the raiders were killed or captured. Wynter, "The History of Commandos and Special Service Troops in the Middle East and North Africa (January 1941 to April 1943)," pp. 276–87 and Elizabeth Keyes, *Geoffrey Keyes of the Rommel Raid* (London: George Newnes Ltd., 1956), pp. 218–55.
13 "Memorandum by Col. David Stirling, DSO, OBE, on the Origins of the Special Air Service Regt.," McLeod 1/10/2, 8 November 1948.
14 Commonwealth forces possessed undeniable quantitative superiority on the eve of Operation Crusader. The bulk of the Axis forces were comprised of light tanks and older aircraft; for example, of the 430 Axis aircraft available in theater, only 35 were the most recent German fighter variant, the Me-109F4. Numerical superiority, however, could not overcome significant British shortcomings in armored warfare doctrine, combined arms experience, and tactical acumen. Gerhard Schreiber *et al.*, eds, *Germany and the Second World War, Volume III: The Mediterranean, South-East Europe, and North Africa, 1939–1941*, Dean S. Murray *et al.*, trans. (Oxford: Oxford University Press, 1995), pp. 726–8.
15 The SAS were designed initially as a subunit of their illusory parent to maintain the deception effort. During the Gazala and Timimi attacks, SAS operators were airdropped in high winds and scattered. Of the initial 53 members of "L" Detachment prior to the raid, fewer than 22 remained for operations conducted the following month. "Memorandum by Col. David Stirling, DSO, OBE, on the Origins of the Special Air Service Regt.," McLeod 1/10/5 and Anthony Kemp, *The SAS at War: The Special Air Service Regiment, 1941–1945* (London: John Murray, 1991), p. 16–18.
16 Originally designed to meet US Army Quartermaster specifications for a four-wheel drive vehicle with an empty weight of 1,300 pounds, the jeep offered unprecedented mobility, speed, and range. Modified to suit individual crew preferences but containing a condenser (to recover water vapor), numerous machine guns, and extra cans of fuel, the jeep allowed two-man SAS teams to strike Axis targets almost 150 miles behind enemy lines. Cowles, *The Phantom Major*, p. 164 and Ken Connor, *An Illustrated History of the SAS* (London: Cassell, 2000), p. 21. According to one evaluation,

> Not only was the cross-country performance of these four-wheel-drive vehicles [Jeeps] far superior to that of the 30-cwt Chevrolets, but they were less conspicuous

and a great deal easier to conceal; and despite their small size, they had a range of some 300 miles.

("Notes from Theaters of War, No. 22: Long Range Desert Group," 26/GS Publications, Chief of the Imperial General Staff, December 1945, WO 231/28, p. 33)

17 Malcolm James, *Born of the Desert,* London: Collins, 1945, p. 14.
18 Both approaches used by the SAS to attack targets on airfields had merits. Opening fire on aircraft while driving through airfields limited the exposure time of the operators but also limited the time available to attack. Infiltrating on foot, in contrast, allowed operators to destroy a number of aircraft provided they were not detected. When the explosive charges detonated, Axis airfield defenders assumed initially that they were under attack from aircraft of the Royal Air Force and focused their efforts against airborne threats while the defenders snuck away. However, if the operators were discovered during their act of sabotage, they had only small arms and foot mobility with which to attempt to affect their escape. For a harrowing account of an ultimately unsuccessful example of the latter, see J.V. Byrne, *The General Salutes A Soldier: With The SAS and Commandos in World War Two* (London: Hale, 1986), pp. 14–17; 35–43.
19 To complicate the *Wehrmacht*'s already formidable logistical burden in North Africa, SAS operators chose wing roots on the same side of aircraft attacked, so that spares could not be cannibalized from other aircraft.
20 One problem with the body of literature devoted to SOF is the acceptance and reproduction of statistics without further scholarly inquiry. Setting the statistical record straight in North Africa is outside the scope of this dissertation. An example from the campaign in the Western Desert relates to the number of aircraft the SAS destroyed. Malcolm James, an SAS medic whose memoir appeared months after the surrender of Nazi Germany in May 1945, stated that "We destroyed a total of *approximately* four hundred aircraft in the desert" (emphasis added). *Born of the Desert,* p. 318. Two authors of regimental histories of the SAS quote James verbatim; see Philip Warner, *The Special Air Service* (London: William Kimber, 1971), p. 79 and Strawson, *A History of the SAS Regiment*, p. 84. Other authors have cited without question the figure of 400 aircraft destroyed. See for example Hoe, *David Stirling,* p. 226 and Kemp, *The SAS at War*, p. 234. Virginia Cowles, in contrast, suggests that the SAS only destroyed 250 aircraft although she might have only accounted for combat as opposed to transport aircraft. *The Phantom Major*, p. 9. RAND analyst Alan Vick has arrived at a different figure, 367 aircraft destroyed summarized by month and place of attack, although he appears to rely on data synthesized from a handful of published memoirs and secondary sources. *Snakes in the Eagle's Nest: A History of Ground Attacks on Air Bases* (Santa Monica, CA: RAND, 1995), pp. 56–7.
21 The SBS was the brainchild of Roger "Jumbo" Courtney, who was convinced of the military utility of small teams of specially selected and trained operators using a form of kayak called "Folbots." From its modest roots, the SBS proved its value in conducting beach reconnaissance and raids in the Mediterranean and Aegean Seas from 1942 to 1945. The Special Boat Squadron was formed after a split in the *1st SAS Regiment* led to the division of forces between this unit and the "Special Raiding Squadron" at the end of the North Africa campaign. The SBS was only one of two British SOF units disbanded and subsequently re-established during the early years of the Cold War. I am indebted to Lieutenant Colonel (retd) Keith Edlin, Secretary of the SAS Regimental Association, for offering invaluable advice in this section. On the formation of the SBS, see James D. Ladd, *SBS, Invisible Raiders: The History of the Special Boat Squadron from World War Two to the Present* (London: Arms and Armour, 1983), pp. 15–28. Details of the reconstitution of the SBS, primarily due to the efforts of H.G. "Blondie" Hasler, are found in John Parker, *SBS: The Inside Story of the Special Boat Service* (London: Headline, 1997), pp. 103–29.

22 Aside from memoirs by the commander and senior officers, the PPA is all but forgotten now. See for example Vladimir Peniakoff, *Popski's Private Army* (London: Reprint Society, 1953); Bob "Park" Yunnie, *Warriors on Wheels* (London: Hutchinson, 1959); and Ben Owen, *With Popski's Private Army* (London: Janus, 2000). The author of a history of British SOF in the Second World War concludes that aside from the SAS, LRDG, and SBS "[t]here are others, including PPA, which one finds hard to see how they contributed to Allied victory in any quantifiable way." Thompson, *The Imperial War Museum Book of War Behind Enemy Lines*, p. 420.

23 The Long Range Desert Group had already absorbed as replacements numbers of Commonwealth troops from New Zealand and Rhodesia. W.B. Kennedy Shaw describes the context for recruiting special operators during 1940 in *Long Range Desert Group: The Story of its Work in Libya, 1940–1943* (Bath: Cedric Chivers, 1970), pp. 18–22. David Lloyd Owen assesses the qualities of the New Zealanders and Rhodesians in *The Desert My Dwelling Place: With the Long Range Desert Group in North Africa* (London: Arms and Armour, 1986), pp. 58–9. Robbed of this potential recruiting pool, Stirling was forced to look for replacements elsewhere. The Special Interrogation Group (SIG) had skills suitable for the role: originally conceived as an independent unit, SIG was comprised of German-speaking Jewish émigrés from across Europe as well as those who fled Nazi Germany. In order to complete the deception, SIG members often utilized captured German uniforms and equipment. Gordon, *The Other Desert War*, p. 105.

24 Gordon Landsborough, *Tobruk Commando: The Raid to Destroy Rommel's Base* (London: Greenhill, 1989), p. 37.

25 Gordon, *The Other Desert War*, p. 120.

26 Landsborough, *Tobruk Commando*, p. 36.

27 Ibid., pp. 71–2.

28 Gordon, *The Other Desert War*, p. 120.

29 The Germans were quick to implement changes once the raid was over. According to one author, Agreement

> led to a general overhaul of the defensive arrangements on the enemy line of communications, and to a decision to reinforce Siwa, Jarabub and Jalo. Three German replacement battalions were posted to Sollum, and for a short time the Pavia Division was kept at Mersa Matruh instead of moving forward.
> (Saul Kelly, *The Lost Oasis: The Desert War and the Hunt for Zerzura,* Boulder, CO: Westview, 2002, p. 235)

30 Kemp, *The SAS at War*, pp. 73–4. Establishment of the SAS as a regiment came at the price of organizational freedom; Stirling's command was placed under the Director of Military Operations, with explicit instructions to obey his chain of command (i.e. not take his complaints directly to General Headquarters).

31 Hoe, *David Stirling*, pp. 219–20.

32 Among his other talents, Lewes developed makeshift "sticky" bombs to attach to aircraft that subsequently bore his name. Gordon, *The Other Desert War*, pp. 80–1.

33 Eric Morris, *Guerrillas in Uniform: Churchill's Private Armies in the Middle East and the War Against Japan, 1940–1945* (London: Hutchinson, 1989), p. 163.

34 The legendary special operator, Blair "Paddy" Mayne, commanded the *Special Raiding Squadron* and the *1st Regiment SAS*. Mayne was courageous, strong, and determined; legend has it that when not on operations, however, he was as dangerous to the British Army as he was the Germans. Mayne possessed some organizational skills but brigade command may have exceeded his talents. William Stirling, David's brother, was a consummate organizer; his command of 2nd Regiment SAS is noteworthy for its efficient management. Although the specific details of William Stirling's resignation from command are unknown, the timing coincides with the release of the plan to use special operations in support of Operation Overlord. Kemp,

The SAS at War, pp. 129–30 and Hamish Ross, *Paddy Mayne* (Stroud: Sutton Publishing, 2003), pp. 160–1.

35 For a survey of these operations, which includes the ill-fated raid on Termoli, see Thompson, *War Behind Enemy Lines*, pp. 257–82 and Bradford and Dillon, *Rogue Warrior of the SAS*, pp. 70–90.

36 SAS personnel were used in direct support of immediate battlefield objectives, not as rear area raiders. As with many other SOF, the SAS make poor light infantry in conventional fights, whether on the offensive or the defensive. See the assessment of the problems associated with the misuse of light infantry in Scott R. McMichael, *A Historical Perspective on Light Infantry*, Research Survey No. 6 (Fort Leavenworth, KS: Combat Studies Institute, 1987), pp. 232–6. In particular, the SAS were squandered in Sicily and Italy in a number of costly reconnaissance missions and raids and that had negligible operational or strategic value. Roy Farran commented that "Hitherto our operations since Taranto had been no more our proper role than the original sea-landing had been the normal task of the Airborne Division." *Winged Dagger: Adventures on Special Service* (London: Arms and Armour, 1986), p. 199. The net result was the loss of a number of experienced SAS personnel, including leaders such as Major John Geoffrey Appleyard. For details see J.E. Appleyard, *Geoffrey: Being the Story of "Apple" of the Commandos and Special Air Service Regiment* (London: Blandford Press, 1946), pp. 158–74.

37 Kemp, *The SAS at War*, p. 120.

38 Ibid, p. 141. The authorized strength of a standard British infantry brigade in 1943 was closer to 3,000 personnel. Chris Ellis and Peter Chamberlain, eds, *Handbook of the British Army, 1943* (London: Purnell Book Services, 1975), p. 24.

39 According to Roger Ford, members of Auxiliary Units, formed as part of the Home Guard in 1940, may have "perhaps accounted for as much as fifty per cent of new recruits to the two British (SAS) regiments after the Brigade was formed." *Fire from the Forest: The SAS Brigade in France 1944* (London: Cassell, 2003), p. 12.

40 Gordon Harrison, *The United States Army in World War II: Cross-Channel Attack* (Washington, DC: Center for Military History, 1989), p. 207 and Paul McCue, *SAS Operation Bulbasket: Behind the Lines in Occupied France, 1944* (London: Leo Cooper, 1996), p. 3.

41 Ian Wellsted notes that a premium was placed on physical conditioning, sabotage, escape and evasion, and association with the regiment during his training period. Language training was half-heartedly attempted with little success. *SAS: With the Maquis* (London: Greenhill, 1994), pp. 25–7. To offset the language deficiency SAS parties were often dropped with Jedburgh, Operational Group, or SOE team members.

42 The wisdom of this policy was questioned in an assessment written at the end of the European campaign: "especially if the enemy are not going to discriminate with captured personnel whether they are in uniform or not." Lt. Col. Collins, GS0.1 (SAS), "Notes on Future of S.A.S.," McLeod 2/2/5, 7 May 1945.

43 Winston S. Churchill, *The Second World War, Volume IV: The Hinge of Fate* (London: The Reprint Society, 1953), p. 377–81.

44 Cowles, *The Phantom Major*, p. 239 and Hoe, *David Stirling*, p. 211. Reconstructed conversations are suspect in any memoir but the author suggests that an observer in the room, Sir John Hackett, independently verified its theme and content. Montgomery approved of SOF so long as they did not impose requirements on the conventional resources under his control.

45 Ibid., p. 240.

46 Special operations, or more accurately the information obtained by SOF, provided Montgomery with an alternative to battering straight through prepared German defensive positions. He intended to circumvent the German positions by

an outflanking movement to the west of the Matmata hills: to be synchronised with a limited frontal attack. The problem then was: could a route through the sand sea be found? It will be remembered that I had launched reconnaissances into this area from the Agheila area before Christmas. A passable route was found by the Long Range Desert Group and the plan then took shape.

(Bernard Law Montgomery, *The Memoirs of Field-Marshal Montgomery,* London: Fontana, 1960, p. 163)

See also the recollection of the events by the Intelligence officer of the Long Range Desert Group, contained in Kennedy Shaw, *Long Range Desert Group*, pp. 234–8.

47 Operational TITANIC 4 was one of a handful of pre-D-Day missions approved by Eisenhower. Six SAS operators, in addition to numerous fake parachutists, were dropped to sow doubt among the Germans that an invasion was taking place and buy time for the landing forces. All six operators were killed or captured by the Germans shortly after landing. The effect of this specific deception mission on the Germans remains doubtful. To Commander, SAS Troops from Headquarters Airborne Troops (Main), "SAS Troops Operational Instruction No. 1," HQ AirTps/TS/2500/40/G(L), 28 May 1944, SHAEF 370–30/27A.

48 Murray and Millett, *A War To Be Won: Fighting the Second World War* (Cambridge, MA: Harvard, 2000), p. 416.

49 The demand for the unconditional surrender of Germany and Japan has been framed as the greatest policy failure of the Anglo-American alliance during the Second World War. Winston Churchill provided an eloquent defense for the policy in *The Second World War, Volume IV*, pp. 548–3.

50 The Allies had varying degrees of success in opposed amphibious landings in Europe, North Africa, and the Mediterranean prior to Neptune. The first large-scale landing, undertaken at Dieppe in France, suffered significant losses. Attempts to offset German land defensive lines in Italy with maritime flanking operations at Salerno and Anzio resulted in little more than narrow lodgments established along the coast due to quick German reaction in containing the landings. Samuel Eliot Morison provides a lucid accounting of the factors that governed the decision to invade in 1944, as opposed to earlier or later, in *Strategy and Compromise* (Boston, MA: Little, Brown and Co., 1958), pp. 45–7.

51 One of the points of failure in the British and Commonwealth forces during the Second World War was the inability of British industry to design and produce an adequate main battle tank until late in the struggle. Part of the problem was an inability to shake the dogma that tank design should follow the naval model: slow, well-armored "battleship" tanks would punch through defensive lines, in support of infantry advances, and fast, poorly armored "cruisers" would engage the enemy tank force alone and use their speed to exploit the breakthrough. The interim solution was acceptance and upgunning of the US-designed Sherman medium tank. The design of the Sherman reflected US armored warfare doctrine that stressed a battle fought between enemy armor caught between the defensive firepower of US tank destroyers and the offensive maneuver of medium tanks. British and US forces received a rude awakening when they captured examples of the well-armed and armored *Panzerkampfwagen VI*, or Tiger I tank, in May 1943. The inability of the US Army to overcome the inertia of doctrine, largely because a few senior Army officers were wedded to it, and field a tank capable of tackling the Tiger and its successors until February 1945 contributed to the high attrition of experienced tank crews and sorely taxed the resources of a first-rate US armored recovery vehicle force. Allied tank development and production is discussed in detail in A.J. Smithers, *Rude Mechanicals: An Account of Tank Maturity During the Second World War* (London: Leo Cooper, 1987). The flaws inherent to US armored warfare doctrine during the Second World War are examined in Christopher R. Gabel, *Seek, Strike, and Destroy: US Army Tank Destroyer Doctrine in*

World War II, Leavenworth Paper No. 12 (Fort Leavenworth, KS: Combat Studies Institute, 1985) and Roman Jarymowycz, *Tank Tactics: From Normandy to Lorraine* (Boulder, CO: Lynne Rienner, 2001), pp. 203–17. For first-hand accounts of the shortcomings of American tanks and the high attrition rates of crews in Normandy, see William B. Folkestad, *The View from the Turret: The 743rd Tank Battalion During World War II* (Shippensburg, PA: Burd Street Press, 2000), pp. 37–53 and Belton Y. Cooper, *Death Traps: The Survival of an American Armored Division in World War II* (Novato, CA: Presidio, 1998), pp. 14–43.

52   Eisenhower was speaking specifically about the controversy surrounding the invasion of southern France, Operation Anvil/Dragoon, and Churchill's preference for a thrust through the Balkans. James Nelson, ed., *General Eisenhower on the Military Churchill* (New York: Norton, 1970), p. 43.

53   General Montgomery did not receive the rank with which his name is usually associated, Field Marshal, until 1 September 1944.

54   The COSSAC staff developed a number of plans related to the invasion of Europe. Some plans were developed exclusively for deception purposes, including STARKEY, TINDALL, and WADHAM, which sought to convince the Germans that the Allies were going to invade at the Pas-de-Calais, Norway, and Brest peninsula respectively. Other COSSAC plans, under the codename RANKIN, were developed to cover contingencies should Germany's fortunes and military dispositions change radically in Europe as a result of the conflict with the Soviet Union. Forrest C. Pogue, *The United States Army in World War II: The Supreme Command* (Washington, DC: Center for Military History, 1954), pp. 105–6 and Samuel Eliot Morison, *History of the United States Naval Operations in World War II, Vol. XI: The Invasion of France and Germany, 1944–1945* (Edison, NJ: Castle Books, 2001), pp. 18–21. The initial plan for Operation Neptune, the actual assault at Normandy, was not issued until 1 February 1944. Both plans have been reproduced online by Encyclopedia Britannica; the COSSAC Plan, or "Digest of Operation 'Overlord'" at http://search.eb.com/normandy/pri/ Q00294.html and "'Neptune' Initial Joint Plan" at http://search.eb.com/normandy/pri/ Q00295.html.

55   See for example Pogue, *The Supreme Command*, pp. 66–71 and Harry Coles and Albert Weinberg, *The United States Army in World War II: Civil Affairs: Soldiers Become Governors* (Washington, DC: Center for Military History, 1986), pp. 672–3.

56   A storm wrecked the American Mulberry, "A," on 19–21 June, creating supply difficulties. The British Mulberry, "B," remained in use until December 1944. For details on how the Mulberries were constructed, see F.A. Osmanski, "Mulberry 'B,' D+4 (10 June)–D+147 (31 October), 1944," G-4 Division, SHAEF, 5 November 1944, available online at http://carlisle-www.army.mil/cgi-bin/usamhi/DL/showdoc.pl?docnum#16. The effect of the destruction of Mulberry "A" on Allied logistical and force flow is covered in Clifford L. Jones, "The Administrative and Logistical History of the ETO, Part IV: Neptune: Training, Mounting, the Artificial Ports," 8–3.1 AA Vol. 6, Historical Division, United States Army Forces, European Theater, March 1946, pp. 110–34.

57   Montgomery detailed his initial reaction to the COSSAC plan for Overlord in *Normandy to the Baltic* (London: Hutchinson, 1945), pp. 4–11. According to Montgomery's post-war recollection, he "explain[ed] to [Eisenhower] the tactical faults of the COSSAC plan. On having these faults pointed out, Eisenhower asked Montgomery to examine the whole plan in England, and gave him the authority to do so." Quoted in Nigel Hamilton, *Master of the Battlefield: Monty's War Years, 1942–1944* (New York: McGraw-Hill, 1983), p. 489.

58   Harrison, *Cross-Channel Attack*, pp. 187–8.

59   Substantial controversy surrounds Operation Goodwood and the Montgomery's intent. Montgomery suggested that the ill-fated Operation Goodwood would "muck up and write off as many enemy troops as possible" prior to a potential British

maneuver that would surround the most formidable German divisions in his sector. Richard Lamb, *Montgomery in Europe, 1943–1945: Success or Failure?* (New York: Franklin Watts, 1984), pp. 125. John Keegan disagrees. He suggests instead that all Montgomery intended was to whittle down German forces in his sector in support of an American breakout. *Six Armies in Normandy: From D-Day to the Liberation of Paris* (Middlesex: Penguin, 1983), pp. 191–2. A summary of the debate, starting with Montgomery's press conference on the success of Goodwood on 18 July 1944, is contained in Carlo D'Este, *Decision in Normandy* (New York: Dutton, 1983), pp. 202–11; 391–9.

60 Once Allied forces had broken out of the Normandy lodgment, Patton sought to keep the Germans off-balance by incessant pursuit and battle. The end result would be weakening of German forces along the line with little defensive depth, so that the Allies could attack, encircle, and destroy them at will. *War As I Knew It* (New York: Bantam, 1980), pp. 129–30, 330.

61 According to the Supreme Commander's calculations, 325,000 Germans were trapped in the Ruhr pocket and 21 divisions destroyed. Dwight D. Eisenhower, *Crusade in Europe* (New York: Doubleday, 1948), pp. 404–6.

62 Patton was given command of US Third Army on 28 July. During the following month, divisions under his command swept into Brittany and eastward as far as Verdun. Patton claimed that if his army had received supplies instead of General Omar Bradley's First Army, he could have penetrated through "unmanned" German defensive works and into the Reich itself. Just how the supplies would have reached Patton remains unclear; supply convoys of trucks from the Normandy beaches were already operating at maximum capacity. *War As I Knew It*, pp. 113–21.

63 The role played by Ultra, or the decryption of German signals, in informing the Allies of German intentions prior to the Mortain offensive which began on 7 August is overstated in Ralph Bennett, *Ultra in the West: The Normandy Campaign of 1944–45* (New York: Scribner's, 1980), pp. 111–9. For a corrective on the limitations of Ultra, see Peter Tompkins, "Are Human Spies Superfluous," in George C. Chalou, ed., *The Secrets War: The Office of Strategic Services in World War II* (Washington, DC: National Archives and Records Administration, 1992), pp. 129–39. Bennett also contends that there was ample, albeit unclear, decrypted German radio traffic indicating movement of forces prior to the Ardennes offensive; it is also clear that senior Allied leaders believed the German Army defeated by December 1944 and incapable of major offensive action. Ibid., pp. 191–2.

64 Author and noted tactician John English is particularly critical of Simonds in *The Canadian Army and the Normandy Campaign: A Study of Failure in High Command* (Westport, CT: Praeger, 1991), pp. 305–14. Terry Copp does not dispute the shortcomings of 2 Canadian Corps and its commander in this battle but also points out the less than stellar performance of British and American units involved in the closing the Falaise Gap. *Fields of Fire: The Canadians in Normandy* (Toronto: University of Toronto Press, 2003), p. 265.

65 Resistance plans developed by SOE, and later OSS, had to be vetted and approved by the representative leadership of government-in-exile in which the activities were to take place. For operations in Normandy, for example, SOE had to liaise with the CFLN, which was later folded into the EMFFI. To complicate matters further, activities in southern France fell under a different headquarters in Algiers, the Special Projects Operation Center. E.K. Cookridge, *Set Europe Ablaze* (New York: Thomas Crowell, 1966), p. 99.

66 In Norway, for example, the resistance provided intelligence and support on the German "fleet in being" threatening convoys to the Soviet Union and embodied in the battleship Tirpitz. The Germans kept moving the battleship to different fiords to thwart British attempts to locate and sink her. Norwegian SOE operatives provided continuous reports on the movement of the Tirpitz, as well as damage inflicted during

raids, until her final destruction in Tromso fiord on 12 November 1944. The details of the Vemork raid, conducted to deprive Germany of heavy water with which to conduct atomic bomb research, are outlined in the introductory chapter. Jak. P. Mallmann Showell, *The German Navy in World War II: A Reference Guide to the Kriegsmarine, 1935–1945* (Annapolis, MD: Naval Institute Press, 1979), pp. 102–4.

67 Despite posting impressive statistics, such as numbers of rail stock destroyed and rail cuts made in the months prior to D-Day, operational sabotage methods often betrayed the identity of the perpetrators. German suspicions of active participation and/or collusion by French industrial and railway workers led to their wholesale replacement, removing the ability to sabotage when it was required most, namely during and after the invasion had taken place. Cookridge, *Set Europe Ablaze*, p. 198.

68 Section X had been gathering information on Hitler's routines at different locations as part of Operation Foxley. Foxley was the code name given by SOE to plans to assassinate Hitler that had been originally authorized by Cabinet in June 1941. In autumn 1944, the time that SOE had compiled sufficient intelligence to devise an assassination plan that stood a reasonable chance of success, senior allied leaders believed that killing *der Führer* would be counterproductive. They based this conclusion on Hitler's increasingly irrational behavior and the desire not to make a martyr out of him. For details see Denis Rigden, *Kill the Führer: Section X and Operation Foxley* (Stroud: Sutton, 1999), especially pp. 1–9, 20–38. That the moral aspects of strategy are more elusive than material ones to understand is demonstrated in the schemes to influence Hitler psychologically. In one particularly harebrained plan, "OSS psychologists had suggested that it might be possible to induce a nervous breakdown in Hitler if he could be exposed to vast quantities of hard-core pornography." Russell Miller, *Behind the Lines: An Oral History of Special Operations in World War II* (New York: St Martin's, 2002), p. 206.

69 The historian and former SAS operator M.R.D. Foot recounts how careless actions by SOE operatives led to the rolling up of agent networks and the manipulation of British wireless codes in France in *SOE: An Outline History of the Special Operations Executive, 1940–46* (London: British Broadcasting Corporation, 1984), pp. 136–41; 219–22. Jay Jakub adds that "[t]he Gestapo's intensive countersubversive campaign in 1943, meanwhile, resulted in the loss of 'virtually all of SOE's principal agents (and) sub-agents around Paris together with many tons of hidden weapons'." *Spies and Saboteurs: Anglo-American Collaboration and Rivalry in Human Intelligence Collection and Special Operations, 1940–45* (London: Macmillan, 1999), p. 157.

70 The Resistance was also crippled as a result of poor operational security by MI6 operatives fleeing France in May 1940, who left behind ledgers detailing names and payment amounts to agents on the British payroll in Europe. One of the major obstacles to unified resistance was the inability to agree on who would lead the movement. It was not until May 1943 that a single body met to consider the future plans for resistance in France: "a *Conseil National de la Résistance* which fused politicians, trade unionists, churchmen, soldiers, and anti-politicians into a single national body, pledged to evict both Hitler and Pétain and to bring in [Charles] de Gaulle." M.R.D. Foot, *Resistance: An Analysis of European Resistance to Nazism, 1940–45* (London: Eyre Methuen, 1976), pp. 136, 240.

71 Joint Intelligence Sub-Committee, "Report: French Resistance," CAB 121/311/49. There is little debate regarding the effectiveness with which Soviet partisan forces were controlled by STAVKA; on their military effectiveness against the Germans, however, opinions remain divided. As noted previously, Williamson Murray and Allan Millett are dismissive of the partisan's contributions to victory; David Glantz, Otto Heilbrunn, and Edgar Howell suggest it was crucial in tying up scarce German assets and disrupting interior lines of communications at crucial junctures. Murray and Millett, *A War To Be Won*, p. 407; Glantz, *Soviet Operational Military Art: In Pursuit of Deep Battle* (London: Frank Cass, 1991), p. 127; Heilbrunn, *Partisan Warfare*

(London: Allen & Unwin, 1962), pp. 181–4; and Howell, *The Soviet Partisan Movement, 1941–1944*, DA-PAM 20–244 (Washington, DC: Department of the Army, 1956), pp. 161–71. A concise assessment of the Italian partisan movement, including its cohesion and the relations between various groups, is contained in Laurence Lewis, *Echoes of Resistance: British Involvement with the Italian Partisans* (Tunbridge Wells: Costello, 1985), pp. 21–9.

72 Foot, *SOE*, p. 223.
73 Despite internal rivalries and the crippling of a number of agent networks, M.R.D. Foot states that the French Resistance nevertheless were responsible for "950 rail cuts on the night of 5/6 June 1944, the night of 'Neptune'" as well as "the dislocation of long-distance telephones." *Resistance*, p. 252.
74 Harrison, *Cross-Channel Attack*, p. 207.
75 The War Cabinet also served to settle disputes and develop compromise solutions, such as the one that arose over the course of resistance in France in 1943. M.R.D. Foot, *SOE in France: An Account of the Work of the British Special Operations Executive in France, 1940–1944* (London: HMSO, 1966), p. 232.
76 Jakub, *Spies and Saboteurs*, p. 161.
77 See the organizational charts contained in "Resistance in Southern France: Operational Control & Communications," Appendix "A" to SHAEF/17240/13/Ops, 10 May 1944, SHAEF 370–30/1D; Foot, *SOE in France*, p. 38; Pogue, *Supreme Command*, p. 159.
78 This authority extended to policy and some aspects of planning but could prove illusory in initial practice, as was the case just prior to D-Day. SOE presented EMFFI with a fait accompli, namely planning and conducting operations without EMFFI approval, on the grounds of preserving the operational security of invasion plan. Jakub, *Spies and Saboteurs*, p. 169.
79 Pogue, *Supreme Command*, p. 236.
80 Ibid., p. 237.
81 From Major C.V. Wintour, Ops C Sub-Section to Chief, Operations Section, Subject: SAS Operations, SHAEF/17240/19/Ops C(Fwd)/61A, 26 August 1944, SHAEF 370–30/61A.
82 In the mythical quest for the Golden Fleece, Jason and the Argonauts passed through a strait guarded by the six-headed monster Scylla and the whirlpool Charybdis. Leaders and military planners of the SAS Brigade were confronted by the perils inherent to the bureaucratic maze of SHAEF, the political challenges of coordinating activities with EMFFI, and the reticence of the "established" paramilitary special operations community of the SOE/OSS.
83 SOE objections to SHAEF were made on the basis of potential German reprisals against French civilians. Ford, *Fire From the Forest*, p. 22.
84 The rumor prompted Brigadier E.E. Mockler Ferryman to write to the Assistant Chief of Staff, G-3 Operations, that "it may be thought that Special Forces Headquarters are trying to obtain command [of the SAS]. This is by no means so; in fact such a command would be an embarrassment to us." Brigadier E.E. Mockler-Ferryman to Major-General H.R. Bull, EEMF/506, 19 May 1944, SHAEF 370–30/10A.
85 Forrest Pogue highlights a difference between the more informal British staff system and the one instituted by Beddell Smith for SHAEF that would prove problematic for the SAS: "all staff studies originating in the SHAEF divisions came to the chief of staff before being passed on to the Supreme Commander. In this way papers that did not need General Eisenhower's approval were handled by Smith." *Supreme Command*, pp. 62–3.
86 In a trend that continues in a modified form today, American military organization distinguishes different functions within the general staff by letter and number. During the Second World War there were five general staff functions: G-1was responsible for personnel issues; G-2 provided intelligence assessments; G-3 handled all operational

186 *Notes*

issues; G-4 controlled supply; and G-5 provided civil affairs support. In Pogue's assessment "The nerve center of SHAEF was the G-3 Division. Here planning and operations were combined." Ibid., p. 68.

87 "Special Operation/Special Operations Executive Plan," Annex 25, First US Army: Operations Plan "Neptune," available online at http://search.eb.com/normandy/pri/Q00340.html.

88 Although the French 4th Parachute Battalion had taken 44 percent casualties during its operations in Brittany as part of DINGSON from June until September 1944, the battalion had spearheaded the liberation of the peninsula at little cost to the US Third Army. Colonel J.H. Alms, Chief Ops C Subsection to the Chief, Operations Section, "Subject: SAS Operations," SHAEF/17240/4/Ops(C), 23 August 1944, SHAEF 370–30/59X and "Operational State of SAS Troops at 22 Aug. 44," HQ AirTps/TS/2500/40/G(L), SHAEF 370–30/59XA.

89 "Special Operation/Special Operations Executive Plan," Annex 25.

90 Map reproduced from Harrison, *Cross-Channel Attack*, p. 5; estimates on *maquis* strength derived from "Map: Maquis," CAB 122/780, undated. According to the former head of the SOE, Major-General Colin Gubbins, the French resistance movement comprised some 100,000 individuals. "SOE and Regular and Irregular Warfare," in Michael Elliott-Bateman, ed., *The Fourth Dimension of Warfare, Volume I: Intelligence/ Subversion/Resistance* (New York: Praeger, 1970), p. 105.

91 "Directive on Joint Operations by Resistance Forces and SAS Troops" [Draft], SHAEF/17240/8/Ops, May 1944, SHAEF 370–30/7B.

92 As representatives of the ideals of the Third Reich, the soldiers of the panzer and panzer grenadier divisions of the *Waffen-SS* received preferential allotment of training, reinforcements, and the latest equipment, including heavy tanks, from 1942 onwards. The only other comparable ground forces within the German Armed Forces included the *Luftwaffe* namesake of its patron, the *Hermann Göring Division*, as well as the regular *Heer*'s *Großdeutschland Division*. Not surprisingly, the *Luftwaffe* panzer division was named in honor of its patron. Allied intelligence had also identified and located the regular army *Panzer Lehr Division* southeast of Paris but severely underestimated its combat effectiveness. From early monitoring the Allies knew that the *Lehr Division* taught new recruits the basics of panzer tactics; what they did not know was that the division was not only comprised of new recruits, but also the instructors and combat veterans themselves. For an assessment of the relative combat capabilities of German panzer divisions available to respond to the beachhead, see David C. Isby, ed., *Fighting the Invasion: The German Army at D-Day* (London: Greenhill, 2000), pp. 95–7.

93 Hans Stöber, *Die Sturmflut und das Ende: Geschichte der 17. SS-Panzergrenadieredivision "Götz von Berlichingen," Band I: Die Invasion* (Osnabrück: Munin Verlag, 1976), p. 28 and Hubert Meyer, *Kriegsgeschichte der 12. SS-Panzerdivision "Hitlerjugend," Band I* (Osnabrück: Munin Verlag, 1982), pp. 19, 42. In addition to providing approximate strength and locations, Ultra decrypts also tracked the movement of the two SS panzer divisions comprising the *2nd SS Panzer Corps* from refitting in Normandy back to the Eastern Front in March 1944. Bennett, *Ultra in the West*, p. 48.

94 Niklas Zetterling, *Normandy 1944: German Military Organization, Combat Power and Organizational Effectiveness* (Winnipeg, MB: J.J. Fedorowicz, 2000), p. 306.

95 A week after Allied forces landed in Europe there were exploitable gaps within the German line. Operation Perch was a British action designed to work around the left flank of the overextended *Panzer Lehr Division* and seize the town of Villers-Bocage, threatening the rear of both *Panzer Lehr* and the *12th SS Division*. The subsequent tactical action in the town has been covered exhaustively in a number of works, although authors disagree on some of the specific details; the result was that the offensive was repulsed after the British 22 Armored Brigade was mauled in a

counterattack by a single platoon of Tiger tanks from the *sPzAbt 101*. Michael Reynolds, *Steel Inferno: 1 SS Panzer Corps in Normandy* (Staplehurst: Spellmount, 1997), pp. 102–12.
96 Kenneth Macksey, *The Partisans of Europe in World War II* (London: Hart-Davis, MacGibbon, 1975), p. 191 and Foot, *SOE in France*, p. 398.
97 The advance team achieved this early success for BULBASKET. The main body of the team had not arrived in occupied France as the pilots of transport aircraft had difficulty in locating the drop zone. McCue, *SAS Operation Bulbasket*, pp. 28–37, 207 and Max Hastings, *On the Offensive: Das Reich* (London: Pan, 1995), pp. 218–9.
98 Bennett, *Ultra in the West*, p. 68.
99 Foot, *SOE in France*, p. 398 and Harrison, *Cross-Channel Attack*, p. 442.
100 *2nd SS* Headquarters suggested that "some operations against guerrillas cannot be avoided." Quoted in Bennett, *Ultra in the West*, p. 68. A translation of the *2nd SS* instructions to combat resistance groups, which includes reprisal ratios for every German killed or wounded, is available as Appendix A, "French Resistance," 7 September 1944, HS8/423.
101 According to documents quoted by Max Hastings, *2nd SS* was desperately short of spare parts and the means to transport them. *On the Offensive: Das Reich*, pp. 164–5. Niklas Zetterling agrees that transportation and spares were in short supplies but objects to ascribing their scarcity to resistance or RAF attacks. In his estimation "Quite simply, a large part of the division did not move at all from its original area in southern France." *Normandy 1944*, p. 321.
102 Foot, *SOE in France*, p. 398.
103 Members of *3rd Company, 1st Battalion, Der Fuhrer Regiment* surrounded the town of Oradour-sur-Glane on 10 June 1944. Throughout the day they destroyed the town and massacred 642 of its inhabitants in retaliation for the disappearance of the commander of *3rd Battalion*. The town has been preserved as it was destroyed as a war memorial. Hastings, *On the Offensive: Das Reich*, p. 181–3 and the official Oradour website, http://oradoursurglane.free.fr.
104 McCue, *SAS Operation Bulbasket*, pp. 179, 218–20.
105 Wellsted, *SAS: With the Maquis*, pp. 216–7. Map derived from "Typescript Map," McLeod 4/3.
106 BULBASKET and GAIN were two such operations compromised. McCue, *Operation Bulbasket*, p. 174 and Ford, *Fire From the Forest*, pp. 107–8
107 "Report on visit to SOUTHERN MORBIHAN by Comd SAS Troops," 19 August 1944, SHAEF G-3-Div Ops "C," SHAEF 370–30/56XB. Conditions were no doubt exacerbated by the issuance to and use by SAS troops of Benzedrine tablets to stay awake. For a description of the effects, including hallucinations brought on by adrenaline rushes and a lack of sleep, see Wellsted, *SAS: With the Maquis*, pp. 34–6.
108 Resistance forces were invaluable to the US Army in freeing conventional forces from mopping-up operations in the Brittany peninsula, as well as securing the Loire River flank of Patton's Third Army. Patton, however, does not single out the resistance for praise in his memoir. Employing ipso facto logic, Patton suggests that his decision to leave his flank unguarded was made on his

> belief that the Germans, while they had ample force, did not have sufficient mobility to strike fast, and that the ever-efficient XIX Tactical Air Command would spot any force large enough to hurt us and be able to hold it down long enough to permit the greatly superior mobility of the American troops to intervene. The soundness of the decision was indicated by the result.
>
> (*War As I Knew It*, p. 361)

Given US skepticism over the timeliness and value of intelligence derived from Ultra decrypts, reinforced by its failure to provide adequate advance warning of the German counterattack at Mortain, Patton and other US commanders utilized French

188   *Notes*

109 Resistance forces to secure rear areas and provide immediate warning of German counterattacks. S.J. Lewis, *Jedburgh Team Operations in Support of the 12th Army Group, August 1944* (Leavenworth, KS: Combat Studies Institute, 1991), pp. 61–2.
109 "Operation NELSON: Outline Plan," HQ AirTps/TS/2270/12/1/G.(L)., 19 July 1944, SHAEF 370–30/50B. NELSON was never mounted as Allied planners were thwarted by the speed of forces heading towards Paris. Kemp, *The SAS at War*, p. 173.
110 S.J. Lewis suggests that the failure of the Jedburghs in Normandy was due, in part, to "new organizations attempting to conduct special operations with the new means of radio and aircraft." *Jedburgh Team Operations in Support of 12th Army Group, August 1944*, p. 60. Evidence from the China-Burma-India theater during the early part of 1944, however, suggests that technology was developed sufficiently to sustain special operations. General Orde Wingate's Chindits conducted long-range penetration missions behind Japanese lines in Burma. The Chindits deployed a brigade's worth of light infantry raiding columns supported by significant air assets. In support of deep penetration columns operating behind Japanese lines, the Chindits "called for air resupply approximately every four to five days" and achieved success in resupply through: "good, reliable communications; expert liaison [between ground and air elements]; fast responses to Chindit requests; well-executed [Standard Operating Procedures]; fighter protection; and bold, skilled pilots." McMichael, *A Historical Perspective on Light Infantry*, p. 30.
111 McCue, *Operation Bulbasket*, p. 174.
112 In addition to debate on the use of 38 Group airlift assets, other crucial resource shortages included Eureka beacons to guide airdrops and "S" phones to communicate with aircraft flying overhead. The acquisition by the SAS of specialized equipment had to come from existing SFHQ stocks. "Minutes of Meeting Held on 30th May, 1944, on Special Operations," SHAEF/17240/19/Ops(A), 1 June 1944, SHAEF 370–30/29XA. For other examples of debate regarding air resources and operating, see "Second Outline Plan for Employment of SAS Troops," HQ AirTps/TS/2500/40/G, 20 May 1944, SHAEF 370–30/10A; "Operation 'Overlord' SF/SAS Operations," MUS/761/1/1/951, 24 May 1944, SHAEF 370–30/16A; and "Co-ordination of S.O.E./S.I.S. Air Operations with Commands concerned," 326/44/D. of I. (R), 24 May 1944, SHAEF 370–30/19A.
113 One of the crucial agreements between 21 Army Group, Headquarters Airborne Forces and SFHQ was signed two days before the invasion. "Planning for SAS Operations," HQ AirTrps/TS/2500/40/G, 4 June 1944, SHAEF 370–30/31XA.
114 Ford, *Fire From the Forest*, p. 31.
115 The primary differences between the Operational Groups and the Jedburghs were their size and mission. Operational Groups were platoon-sized elements charged with attacking targets; Jedburgh teams rarely exceeded six men and their mission was to train elements of the resistance. Both units operated in uniform, although as the SAS was to discover, this formality meant little to the Germans. Following Hitler's *Kommandobefehl* issued in October 1942, anyone captured behind German lines was "to be slaughtered to the last man." McCue, *SAS Operation Bulbasket*, p. 205. For particulars on the composition of and differences between the Operational Groups and Jedburghs, see Jakub, *Spies and Saboteurs*, pp. 180–1.
116 The largest operational SAS group sent to the field was the French 4th Parachute Battalion of 475 men operating in Brittany; most other SAS units in operational areas averaged over 50 personnel. "Operational State of SAS Troops at 22 Aug. 1944," HQ AirTps/TS/2500/40/G.(Liaison), 22 August 1944, SHAEF 370–30/59XA.
117 The reach of resistance groups could be extended by conducting motorized operations using jeeps or locally acquired transportation.
118 In addition to anti-tank weapons such as mines, bazookas, and Projector, Infantry, Anti-Tank (PIATs) provided to the resistance, Operation HOUNDSWORTH was also supplied with airdropped 6-pounder anti-tank guns and 3-inch mortars. Kemp, *The SAS at War*, p. 156 and Wellsted, *SAS: With the Maquis*, pp. 65, 159.

119 Competition for resources between the SAS, SOE, and the Special Intelligence Service resulted in too few "Eureka" radio beacons being fielded in support of special operations behind German lines. In addition, supplies dropped by air could be scattered far from intended drop zones, or worse still, "roman candle" straight into the ground due to parachute failure. Ian Wellsted recounts that of the three wireless sets dropped with his advance reconnaissance party on 7 June, one receiver and one transmitter were destroyed during the landing and the other transmitter was not recovered. Wellsted, *SAS: With the Maquis*, pp. 33, 59. Supply problems and time constraints associated with the fluidity of the battlefield forced SFHQ to consider shipping 40 jeeps by glider or by sea through Cherbourg in support of Operation WALLACE. From Airborne Troops to 38 Group, "Operation WALLACE," Ref. No. SAS-203. SHAEF 272/18, 18 August 1944, SHAEF 370–30/55B.

120 Brigadier Ferryman, head of SFHQ, pointed this out to the head of G-3 Operations on 18 May 1944:

> As SHAEF is the controller of strategy in FRANCE and, in the main, controls Resistance activity and the use of SAS Troops, it is felt that SAS, while remaining administratively under 21 Army Group, should pass under the command of SHAEF." "Joint Operations by Resistance Forces and SAS Troops,
> (MUS/761/1/1/904, 18 May 1944, SHAEF 370–30/8A)

121 *Coalitions, Politicians and Generals: Some Aspects of Command in Two World Wars* (London: Brassey's, 2003), p. 216.

122 "Strategic planning for Resistance and SAS operations," SHAEF/17240/19/Ops, May 1944, HS6/604/115–6.

123 Eisenhower eventually grasped how special operations could improve German military performance and erode the moral and material vulnerabilities of the Allies. In his memoirs, he suggests that "a few determined men could have inflicted almost decisive damage upon our lines of communication" during the North African campaign, forcing the deployment of French troops to guard them. *Crusade in Europe*, p. 122.

124 "Minutes of Conference, 4 May 44, on SOE/SO – SAS Co-operation," MUS/761/1/743, 5 May 1944, HS6/604/136.

125 On the role played by the French 4th Parachute Battalion, SAS Brigade in supporting the Third Army in Brittany, see Eisenhower's assessment in *Report by the Supreme Commander to the Combined Chiefs of Staff on the Operations in Europe of the Allied Expeditionary Force, 6 June 1944 to 8 May 1945* (Washington, DC: Government Printing Office, 1946), p. 41. In an example of tactical actions assuming strategic importance after the fact, and in the absence of SHAEF's "strategic" planning for the SAS, it should be recalled that the operations in Brittany were considered to be tactical in scope, providing direct support to 21 Army Group operations. "Control of SAS Troops and Resistance," SHAEF/17240/8/Ops, May 1944, HS6/604/114. Arthur Layton Funk evaluates the contributions of the resistance, backed by the SAS and others, to the campaign in southern France in support of the US Seventh Army in *Hidden Ally*, pp. 253–60.

126 From Major C.V. Wintour, Ops C Sub-Section to Chief, Operations Section, Subject: SAS Operations, SHAEF/17240/19/Ops C (Fwd)/61A, 26 August 1944, SHAEF 370–30/61A.

127 Forrest Pogue suggests that Montgomery toyed with the idea in late July 1944 of air-dropping small units behind German lines in southern France to work with resistance forces. He adds that according to Sir Alan Brooke, however, Montgomery had in mind units patterned on Wingate's Chindits. Their success in that theater resulted from freedom of maneuver granted by low population densities in their operating area. In any event, such units would have duplicated the efforts of the already ample Resistance forces available in the area chosen for Operation Anvil. *George C. Marshall: Organizer of Victory, 1943–1945* (New York: Viking, 1973), p. 393.

128 Thompson, *War Behind Enemy Lines*, p. 306.
129 "HQ Airborne Troops – SAS Tps Operation Instruction N0.1, Amendment No. 1," HQ AirTps/TS/2500/40/G(L), 1 June 1944, SHAEF 370–30/28A.
130 "Strategic planning for Resistance and SAS operations," SHAEF/17240/19/Ops, May 1944, HS6/604/115.
131 Eisenhower scaled back the contribution to the invasion made by individuals or organizations that he thought had undermined his authority as Supreme Commander. For example, Eisenhower reacted swiftly when he discovered that the French Committee of National Liberation had already issued invasion currency to British and American troops although no agreement had been reached with the French government in exile. In response, Eisenhower "forbid the 180 French liaison officers trained for civil affairs duties to sail with the assault units on D-Day" but later allowed some to sail with the fleet. Pogue, *Supreme Command*, p. 232.
132 In one message referring to the control of resistance elements using French military personnel, Smith wrote:

> This is most satisfactory. We also have plans for use of SAS Troops further north in the same role. We foresee, however, both an operational and administrative pitfall in these projects and we intend to introduce troops with caution and in a manner which will not establish a continuing commitment for aircraft and supplies.
>
> (To Freedom for Gammell From Smith Signed Eisenhower, SHAEF/ 17240/19/Ops(A)/S-52650, 27 May 1944, SHAEF 370–30/27A)

133 Arthur Funk concludes that Eisenhower ordered the scaling back of resistance activities because the Supreme Commander was convinced that the Germans were fooled by Fortitude. *Hidden Ally*, p. 45.
134 Bigot Priority, From SHAEF to Headquarters Airborne Troops, SHAEF/17240/8/Ops(A)/S-52972, 1 June 1944, SHAEF 370–30/27AA.
135 Lewis, *Jedburgh Team Operations in Support of 12th Army Group*, p. 62; Thompson, *War Behind Enemy Lines*, p. 330.
136 Kemp, *The SAS at War*, p. 137.
137 Ford, *Fire From the Forest*, p. 153.
138 "Employment of SAS Troops," SHAEF 370–30/50Z.
139 Lt. Col. Collins, "Notes on Future of S.A.S.," McLeod 2/2/2.
140 Ford, *Fire From the Forest*, pp. 279–81.
141 What is all the more remarkable is that this was the conclusion of Tom Stoneborough, "Head of the OSS Section and is responsible for coordinating the employment of all special troops with both G-2 and G-3 Divisions." Major D.J. Cliffe to Chief, Airborne Section, "Report on Visit to Sixth Army Group," 23 January 1945, SHAEF 370–30/35A.
142 A conclusion related to the "broad front, narrow front" controversy between Montgomery and Eisenhower and reached by Ronald Andidora in *Home by Christmas: The Illusion of Victory in 1944* (Westport, CT: Greenwood Press, 2001), pp. 146–54.
143 Niklas Zetterling, for example, takes issue with the way in which German archival material has been selectively quoted to sustain the impression that the Allies were fighting an uphill battle numerically. According to his calculations, the Allies could land and field in combat more forces that the Germans could move in to stop them. *Normandy 1944*, pp. 27–34. Similar arguments have been used in assessments of why Germany lost the maritime war in the Atlantic. For example, conventional wisdom holds that the United States produced more Liberty ships than the Germans could sink. Other considerations, such as improved Allied tactical and operational performance, are deemed irrelevant. See for example John Ellis, *Brute Force: Allied Strategy and Tactics in the Second World War* (New York: Viking, 1990).

144 For example, Erik Durschmied overreaches when he suggests that a single photograph, showing the execution of a Viet Cong prisoner in Saigon during the Tet Offensive, was "the hinge factor in Vietnam" as the basis for his counterfactual. *The Hinge Factor: How Chance and Stupidity Have Changed History* (New York: Arcade Publishing, 2000), pp. 328–30.

145 Walter Boyne neatly summarizes and subsequently demolishes the counterfactual claims surrounding Nazi Germany's first operational jet fighter, the Messerschmitt Me 262:

> The romance of the Me 262 is enhanced by the long standing myth that but for Hitler's bumbling incompetence, it would have been in service a year earlier than its 1944 operational debut, and that it would have swept Allied bombers from the sky, possibly changing the course of the war, or at the least permitting exhausted Germany a negotiated peace. Such speculation is profitless, for the entire force of the Me 262 program was but a dust mote in the furious avalanche of Allied power.
> (*Messerschmitt Me 262: Arrow to the Future,* Washington, DC: Smithsonian Institution Press 1980, p. 5)

146 An example would be to suggest that German airpower could have defeated the Normandy landings if it was forward-deployed and concentrated in sufficient numbers in France. Such a suggestion ignores several realities: the primary role of the *Luftwaffe* by 1944, with its dwindling assets, was in combating the combined Allied bomber offensives over the Reich. In addition, *Luftwaffe* assets were dispersed in reaction to increasingly aggressive Allied fighter sweeps prior to the invasion. For discussions on the status of the *Luftwaffe* prior to the invasion, see W.H. Tantum IV and E.J. Hoffschmidt, eds, *The Rise and Fall of the Luftwaffe: History of the Luftwaffe in WW2* (Old Greenwich, CT: WE Inc., 1969), pp. 327–2; Williamson Murray, *Strategy for Defeat, 1933–1945* (Maxwell AFB, AL: Air University Press, 1983), pp. 263–77; E.R. Hooten, *Eagle in Flames: The Fall of the Luftwaffe* (London: Brockhampton Press, 1999), pp. 284–5.

147 See for example the discussion of the state of British morale contained in Stephen A. Hart, *Montgomery and "Colossal Cracks": The 21st Army Group in Northwest Europe, 1944–45* (Westport, CT: Praeger, 2000), pp. 28–35.

148 Russell A. Hart, *Clash of Arms: How the Allies Won in Normandy* (Boulder, CO: Lynne Rienner, 2001), p. 388.

149 Although Allied logistics supporting the lodgment have been discussed in considerable detail, the inadequate system backing German forces has received comparatively little scholarly attention. A crucial initial effort is Russell A. Hart, "Feeding Mars: The Role of Logistics in the German Defeat in Normandy, 1944," *War in History* (Vol. 3, No. 4: 1996): 418–35.

150 Twice during the Normandy campaign, high-altitude bombing was used in an attempt to break German defensive lines prior to ground offensives. During the most infamous example, in support of Operation Cobra, a number of bombers dropped their loads short and killed over 130 American soldiers. Murray and Millett, *A War to be Won*, pp. 426–9.

151 The effectiveness of Allied fighter-bombers against German ground vehicles throughout the Western European campaign, and in the breakout from Normandy in particular, remains a controversial subject. Post-war interviews with German military leaders suggested that tactical airpower was a decisive element in their defeat, especially against armor. Commonwealth military operations researchers, however, arrived at drastically different conclusions after post-battle analysis. Few of the vehicles they examined showed signs of damage from tactical air strikes. German assessments of Allied airpower are contained in Isby, *Fighting the Invasion*, p. 240; idem, ed., *Fighting in Normandy: The German Army from D-Day to Villers-Bocage* (London: Greenhill, 2001), pp. 114–5, 205; 224–5; F.W. von Mellenthin, *Panzer Battles: A Study of the*

Employment of Armor in the Second World War (Norman, OK: University of Oklahoma Press, 1956), pp. 316–23; and Heinz Guderian, *Panzer Leader*, Constantine Fitzgibbons, trans. (New York: E.P. Dutton, 1952), pp. 328–9. Tactical airpower advocates were prone to overstating its effectiveness; see for example the claims made by IX Tactical Air Command contained in Thomas Hughes, *Over Lord: General Pete Qaesada and the Triumph of Tactical Air Power in World War II* (New York: Free Press, 1995), p. 224. The conclusions of contemporary operations research scientists that challenge the claims of tactical airpower advocates are contained in Robert Vogel, "Tactical Air Power in Normandy: Some Thoughts on the Interdiction Plan," *Canadian Military History* (Vol. 3, No. 1: Spring 1994): 37–47 and Terry Copp, "Scientists and the Art of War: Operations Research in 21 Army Group," *Journal of the Royal United Services Institute for Defence Studies* (Vol. 136, No. 4: April 1991): 65–70.

152 According to a senior German logistics officer, rail traffic was significantly halted. The Germans nevertheless were able to move forward 1,900 tons of supplies to forces attempting to contain the Allied breakout. Eduard Mark, *Aerial Interdiction: Air Power and the Land Battle in Three American Wars* (Washington, DC: Center for Air Force History, 1994), p. 252, n. 105.

153 M.R.D. Foot provides a lucid exploration of both the motivations and qualities of those who resisted the Nazis in *Resistance*, pp. 11–21.

154 Kemp, *The SAS at War*, p. 173. Roger Ford suggests that Kemp is wrong in his assessment, agreeing with SOE conclusions that distributed SAS parties could not be supplied, lacked sufficient linguistic skills and would not be able to communicate with SFHQ. *Fire From the Forest*, pp. 151–2.

155 According to several authors, German fighting cohesion was maintained by a combination of *kampfgemeinschaft*, or "strong comradely ties." See for example Martin van Creveld, *Fighting Power: German and US Army Performance, 1939–1945* (Westport, CT: Greenwood, 1982), p. 94. The motivational root of those ties, in terms of culture, social norms, or ideology, remains contentious. In addition, pauses in the fighting allowed units to reform, reequip, and integrate reinforcements. See the discussion of German losses and measures taken to restore order and reequip the *Heer* in Hugh M. Cole, *The United States Army in World War II: The Lorraine Campaign* (Washington, DC: Center for Military History, 1950), pp. 29–35.

156 The two-part summary of French resistance accomplishments in Western Europe written by SOE discusses delay of German line units to the front and sabotage to rail lines but offers little insight on the disruption of German logistics. "French Resistance, Part I," 7 September 1944, HS8/423/1–18.

157 Lt. Col. L.E.O.T. Hart stresses "concealment, mobility, surprise, and small numbers" for such intelligence-gathering work in "The Special Air Service," McLeod 2/5/2.

158 Such bottlenecks included the Orleans Gap, the two weakened but functioning bridges over the Loire and the Seine ferry crossing at Elbeuf, among others. Hart, *Clash of Arms*, pp. 387–9.

159 Although SOE planners made the point that dropping uniformed SAS personnel might raise false hopes and spark premature uprisings, they offered the SAS Brigade little organizational room for maneuver. In initial planning documents, SOE staff were adamant in "maintain[ing] the position that SAS troops are not being sent to organize resistance" and "that SAS should be used for the benefit of resistance and not resistance for the benefit of SAS." "SAS and its Relation to SOE/SO," MUS/761/1/685, 1 May 1944, HS6/604/146, 150. The success or failure of SAS activities, by extension, would depend entirely on SOE-established, fostered, and/or supplied resistance groups in France.

160 Communications are the lynchpin of the shaping plan, as many of the proposed activities of SAS teams are predicated on transmitting acquired information and arranging for resupply. In addition to Jedburgh teams working with fielded SAS personnel, the Brigade could also draw upon the members of the attached communications unit

known as "Phantom" to provide additional signals support. One of the reasons that SAS drops were organized around static bases was to limit the number of two-way radios dropped into occupied France. The sets were bulky, delicate, and prone to breakdowns and the SAS had too few sets. Although Eureka beacons were distributed in quantity just prior to the invasion, the SAS was limited by "the shortage of trained operators" and not radios. "Notes on Liaison with SAS Brigade," 24 May 1944, HS6/604/78. Prior to the invasion, SOE calculated that no more than 50 percent of the Jedburgh sets dropped would "come up on the air." "SAS and its Relation to SOE/SO," HS6/604/147.

161 Should the landing fail, SAS teams would be extracted using the escape and evasion network established and run by MI9. Using MI9 to recover SAS personnel was suggested in ibid.

162 In addition to the example of the SAS providing information that led to the destruction of oil tankers in Châtellerault mentioned previously, other units were able to provide the following information: "On 8 Jul a signal was received giving pin-points of a GERMAN Command Post, at LENNON, for the NORTH Coast defences of FINISTRETTE. The target was successfully bombed by the R.A.F." "French Resistance, Part II," 24 March 1945, HS8/423/45.

163 Brigadier McLeod distinguished "advance recce parties" from "main recce parties" along similar lines. The primary difference between the approach outlined here, and that used by the SAS during the Normandy campaign, is direct nighttime resupply of fielded teams versus the establishment of sizeable, relatively static base camps that resembled oasis bases utilized by the SAS in North Africa. Oasis bases were perfectly suitable to large, unoccupied swathes of desert but not for sustaining operations in rural, populated Western Europe. "SAS Brigade Operation Instruction No. 15: Operation Overlord, 1 SAS Regt," 2 June 1944, HS6/604/54–6.

164 By July, roughly two-thirds of all German supplies were transported by truck to the front. Mark, *Aerial Interdiction*, p. 252, n. 105.

165 "Notes on paper by Lt. Col. Collins," McLeod 2/3/1, May 1945.

166 According to an SOE report written in September 1944, "By D-day some 198 independent [wireless telegraph] links with LONDON were distributed and operating throughout FRANCE" whose "volume .averaged upwards of 11 signals a day for the period June-September 1944." It is reasonable to assume that the SAS could have trained and integrated enough operators in the months prior to D-Day for use in distributed multinational reconnaissance teams. "French Resistance, Part II," 24 March 1945, HS8/423/45.

167 After the events described in Chapter 3, 617 Squadron was recast to drop 12,000-pound "Tallboy" bombs developed by Barnes Wallis with high levels of accuracy. The bombs, released from altitude and reaching speeds close to that of sound, had reinforced noses and delayed action fuses. The subsequent underground detonation created effects similar to those that occur naturally in earthquakes. On 8 June 617 Squadron attacked and collapsed a German logistics chokepoint, the Saumer railroad tunnel. Rather than attacking other logistical arteries, however, 617 Squadron spent the remainder of the summer of 1944 switching targets between bombing German motor torpedo boat and submarine pens, as well as various V-weapon sites and facilities. For details see Alan Cooper, *Beyond the Dams to the Tirpitz: The Later Operations of 617 Squadron* (London: William Kimber, 1983), pp. 75–102.

168 Paraphrased from T.E. Lawrence, who used the expression "sedition putting up her head" to describe how the Arab Revolt would appear to the Turks. *The Seven Pillars of Wisdom: A Triumph* (London: Jonathan Cape, 1935), p. 192.

169 The quotes are taken from Denis Davidov, one of the most formidable Russian partisan leaders of the Napoleonic Wars. *In the Service of the Tsar Against Napoleon: The Memoirs of Denis Davidov, 1806–1814*, Gregory Troubetzkoy, trans. and ed. (London: Greenhill, 1999), p. 185.

194 *Notes*

170 "Colossal Cracks" refers to Montgomery's plan to preserve critical British manpower resources by applying heavy, methodical firepower to fix and pulverize. Stephen Hart offers that it is "an attritional method based on *matériel* that eschewed operational maneuver" but fully in line with British political requirements at the time. *Montgomery and "Colossal Cracks"*, p. 10.
171 The Soviet operation, codenamed "Bagration," consisted of five offensives beginning in June and lasting until October that cost the Germans almost 500,000 casualties and eliminated the German Army Group Center as a command. David M. Glantz and Jonathan House, *When Titans Clashed: How the Red Army Stopped Hitler* (Lawrence, KS: University Press of Kansas, 1995), pp. 195–215.
172 Gordon, *The Other Desert War*, p. 186.
173 "Notes on Liaison with SAS Brigade," HS6/604/82.
174 Gordon, *The Other Desert War*, p. 187.

6 Conclusion

1 Boot, "The New American Way of War," *Foreign Affairs* (Vol. 82, No. 4: July/August 2003): 41–2.

Bibliography

Primary sources (unpublished)

Public Records Office

AIR 8/2, Separate Air Force.
AIR 8/1238, Destruction of German Dams: Economic Effect.
AIR 8/1102, Protection of Dams & Reservoirs in U.K.
AIR 9/96, War Plans: Policy and Assumptions.
AIR 14/817, Attacks on German Reservoirs and Dams.
AIR 19/304, Publicity in U.S.A.
AIR 20/996, Operations "Highball" and "Upkeep": Minutes of Meetings.
CAB 121/266, Operation "Highball" (development of weapons for use against enemy ships and dams).
CAB 121/311, French Resistance Groups.
CAB 122/780, Resistance Groups in France.
HS 6/604, SAS Operations under SHAEF control.
HS 8/423, French Resistance Parts I and II; Delays to German Build-Up in Northern Battle Area from 6 June 1944.
WO 231/28, Notes on the Operations of the Long Range Desert Group.

National Archives

SHAEF 370/30, Strategic Planning for Resistance and SAS Operations.

Liddell Hart Center for Military Archives

FP I/TS/1, Tank Training, Tactics, Operations, 1916–1918.
LH 1/302, Correspondence between Maj Gen John Frederick Charles Fuller and Liddell Hart, 1920–1966, and between Mrs. J F C Fuller and Liddell Hart, and Kathleen Liddell Hart 1966–1968.
LH 10/1947, Published articles by Liddell Hart, including book reviews, with related papers, 1946–1950.
McLeod 1, Papers relating to operations of the Special Air Service (SAS) during World War Two, and to its formation, 1944–1948.

McLeod 2, Papers relating to the SAS following operations in Northern Europe, World War Two, 1945–1958.
McLeod 4, Maps and diagram relating to SAS operations in France, 1944.

Center for Military History

Osmanski, F.A. "Mulberry 'B,' D+4 (10 June) – D+147 (31 October), 1944." G-4 Division, SHAEF, 5 November 1944.
Jones, Clifford L. "The Administrative and Logistical History of the ETO, Part IV: Neptune: Training, Mounting, the Artificial Ports." 8–3.1 AA Vol. 6. Historical Division, United States Army Forces, European Theater, March 1946.

Primary sources (including SOF memoirs)

Asher, Michael. *Shoot to Kill: A Soldier's Journey Through Violence*. London: Guild Publishing, 1990.
Ballinger, Adam. *The Quiet Soldier: On Selection With 21 SAS*. London: Chapmans, 1992.
Bassett, Sam. *Royal Marine*. London: Peter Davies, 1962.
Beckwith, Charlie. *Delta Force*. London: Arms and Armour Press, 1984.
Betser, Muki and Robert Rosenberg. *Secret Soldier: The True Life Story of Israel's Greatest Commando*. New York: Atlantic Monthly Press, 1996.
Boog, Horst *et al.*, eds *Germany and the Second World War, Volume IV: The Attack on the Soviet Union*, Translated by Ewald Osers *et al.* Oxford: Oxford University Press, 1998.
Borghese, J. Valerio. *Sea Devils: Italian Navy Commandos in World War II*. Translated by James Cleugh. Annapolis, MD: Naval Institute Press, 1995.
British Bombing Survey Unit. *The Strategic Air War Against Germany, 1939–1945*. London: Frank Cass, 1998.
Burdick, Charles and Hans-Adolf Jacobsen, eds. *The Halder War Diary, 1939–1942*. Novato, CA: Presidio Press, 1988.
Byrne, J.V. *The General Salutes A Soldier: With The SAS and Commandos in World War Two*. London: Hale, 1986.
Calvert, Mike. *Fighting Mad: One Man's Guerrilla War*. London: Airlife, 1996.
Carney, John T. and Benjamin Schemmer. *No Room for Error: The Story Behind the USAF Special Tactics Unit*. New York: Ballantine, 2003.
Churchill, Winston S. *The Second World War*, 6 vols. London: The Reprint Society, 1953.
Cohen, Eliot *et al. The Gulf War Air Power Survey*, 5 vols. Washington: Government Printing Office, 1993.
Cole, Hugh M. *The United States Army in World War II: The Lorraine Campaign*. Washington, DC: Center for Military History, 1950.
Coles, Harry and Albert Weinberg. *The United States Army in World War II: Civil Affairs: Soldiers Become Governors*. Washington, DC: Center for Military History, 1986.
Commander-in-Chief, United States Special Operations Command. *United States Special Operations Forces Posture Statement, 2003–2004*. Tampa, FL: USSOCOM, 2003.
———. *SOF Vision 2020*. Tampa, FL: US Special Operations Command, 1998.

Cooper, Johnny. *One of the Originals: The Story of a Founder Member of the SAS*. London: Pan Books, 1991.
Cowles, Virginia. *The Phantom Major: The Story of David Stirling and the SAS Regiment*. London: The Companion Book Club, 1958.
Crichton-Stuart, Michael. *G Patrol: The Guards Patrol of the Long Range Desert Patrol*. London: Tandem, 1958.
Crossland, Peter. *Victor Two*. London: Book Club Associates, 1996.
Curtis, Mike. *CQB: Close Quarter Battle*. London: Transworld, 1997.
Davidov, Denis. *In the Service of the Tsar Against Napoleon: The Memoirs of Denis Davidov, 1806–1814*. Translated and edited by Gregory Troubetzkoy. London: Greenhill, 1999.
Davies, Barry. *Shadow of the Dove*. London: Bloomsbury, 1996.
———. *Fire Magic: Hijack at Mogadishu*. London: Bloomsbury, 1994.
de la Billière, Peter. *Looking for Trouble: SAS to Gulf Command, The Autobiography* London: HarperCollins, 1994.
———. *Storm Command: A Personal Account of the Gulf War*. London: HarperCollins, 1992.
Department of National Defence. *Supplement 3 — Army Glossary*, B-GL-303–002. Ottawa: Department of National Defence, n.d.
Devereux, Steve. *Terminal Velocity*. London: Smith Gryphon, 1997.
Donahue, James. *Mobile Guerrilla Force: With the Special Forces in War Zone D*. Annapolis, MD: Naval Institute Press, 1996.
Eisenhower, Dwight D. *Crusade in Europe*. New York: Doubleday, 1948.
Ewald, Johann. *Diary of the American War: A Hessian Journal*. Translated by Joseph H. Tustin. New Haven, CT: Yale University Press, 1979.
Falconer, Duncan. *First Into Action*. London: Little, Brown and Company, 1998.
Farran, Roy. *Operation Tombola*. London: Arms and Armour Press, 1986.
———. *Winged Dagger: Adventures on Special Service*. London: Arms and Armour, 1986.
———. *Winged Dagger*. London: Fontana Books, 1956.
Fiennes, Ranulph. *Where Soldiers Fear to Tread*. London: Hodder and Stoughton, 1975.
Foley, Charles. *Commando Extraordinary*. London: Longmans, Green and Co., 1954.
Foot, M.R.D. *SOE in France: An Account of the Work of the British Special Operations Executive in France, 1940–1944*. London: HMSO, 1966.
Franks, Tommy R. "Operation Iraqi Freedom–Lessons Learned." Statement Before The Senate Armed Services Committee (9 July 2003).
Fröhlich, Elke, ed. *Die Tagebücher von Joseph Goebbels, Teil II Diktate 1941–45, Band 8 April-Juni 1943*. München: K.G. Saur, 1993.
Garner, Joe. *Code Name: Copperhead, My True Life Exploits as a Special Forces Soldier*. London: Simon & Schuster, 1994.
General Accounting Office. *Special Operations Forces: Opportunities to Preclude Overuse and Misuse*, GAO/NSIAD-97–85. Washington: GAO, 1997.
Gibson, Guy. *Enemy Coast Ahead*. Cheshire: Goodall Publications Ltd, 1986.
Gormly, Robert. *Combat Swimmer: Memoirs of a Navy SEAL*. New York: Dutton, 1998.
Guderian, Heinz. *Panzer Leader*. Translated by Constantine Fitzgibbons. New York: E.P. Dutton, 1952.

Bibliography

Hany, Eric L. *Inside Delta Force: The Story of America's Elite Counterterrorist Unit.* New York: Delacorte Press, 2002.

Harris, Arthur. *Bomber Offensive.* London: Collins, 1947.

Harrison, Gordon. *The United States Army in World War II: Cross-Channel Attack.* Washington, DC: Center for Military History, 1989.

Hart, Russell, A. *Clash of Arms: How the Allies Won in Normandy.* Boulder, Co: Lynne Rienner, 2001.

Hoe, Alan. *David Stirling: The Authorised Biography of the Creator of the SAS.* London: Warner Books, 1994.

Howard, Michael. *British Intelligence in the Second World War, Volume 5: Strategic Deception.* London: HMSO, 1990.

Hubatsch, Walther, ed. *Kriegstagebuch des Oberkommando der Wehrmacht (Wehrmachtführungstab), Band III: 1. Januar 1943–31. Dezember 1943.* Frankfurt am Main: Bernard & Graefe Verlag, 1963.

Hunter, Gaz. *The Shooting Gallery.* New York: Cassell, 1998.

James, Malcolm. *Born of the Desert.* London: Collins, 1945.

James, Robert Rhodes, ed. *Winston S. Churchill, His Complete Speeches, 1897–1963, Vol. 8: 1943–1949.* London: Chelsea House, 1974.

Jeapes, Tony. *SAS Secret War.* London: Harper Collins, 1996.

Jones, R.V. *Most Secret War: British Scientific Intelligence, 1939–1945.* London: Coronet Books, 1979.

Junger, Ernst. *Storm of Steel: From the Diary of a German Storm-Troop Officer on the Western Front.* London: Chatto & Windus, 1930.

Kelly, Francis. *The U.S. Army Special Forces, Vietnam Studies.* Washington: Department of the Army, 1985.

Kennedy, Michael. *Soldier "I" SAS.* London: Bloomsbury, 1989.

Kennedy Shaw, W.B. *Long Range Desert Group: The Story of its Work in Libya, 1940–1943.* Bath: Cedric Chivers Ltd., 1970.

Kriebel, Rainer. *Inside the Afrika Korps: The Crusader Battles, 1941–1942.* Edited by Bruce Gudmundson. London: Greenhill, 1999.

Kyle, James. *The Guts to Try.* New York: Orion, 1990.

Leonov, Viktor. *Blood on the Shores: Soviet Naval Commandos in World War II.* Annapolis, MD: Naval Institute Press, 1993.

Lewis, Rob. *Fishers of Men.* London: Hodder & Stoughton, 1999.

Lloyd Owen, David. *The Desert My Dwelling Place: With the Long Range Desert Group in North Africa.* London: Arms and Armour Press, 1986.

Locher III, James R. *Victory on the Potomac: The Goldwater-Nichols Act Unifies the Pentagon.* College Station, TX: Texas A&M Press, 2002.

McAleese, Peter. *No Mean Soldier: The Story of the Ultimate Professional Soldier in the SAS and Other Forces.* London: Orion Books, 1993.

McCallion, Harry. *Killing Zone.* London: Bloomsbury, 1995.

McClellan, George. *Report on the Organization and Campaigns of the Army of the Potomac: To Which is Added an Account of the Campaign in Western Virginia, With Plans of Battle-Fields.* New York: Sheldon and Company, 1864.

Maclean, Fitzroy. *Eastern Approaches.* London: The Reprint Society, 1951.

McNab, Andy. Pseudonym. *Bravo Two Zero*. London: Corgi Books, 1995.
Maier, Klaus *et al.*, eds. *Germany and the Second World War, Volume II: Germany's Initial Conquests in Europe*. Translated by Dean McMurry *et al.* Oxford: Oxford University Press, 1991.
Malcom, Ben. *White Tigers: My Secret War in North Korea*. Washington: Brassey's, 1996.
Marcinko, Richard. *Rogue Warrior*. New York: Pocket Books, 1992.
Masters, Peter. *Striking Back: A Jewish Commando's War Against the Nazis*. Novato, CA: Presidio, 1997.
Meyer, Hubert. *Kriegsgeschichte der 12. SS-Panzerdivision "Hitlerjugend,"* 2 vols. Osnabrück: Munin Verlag, 1982.
Montgomery, Bernard Law. *The Memoirs of Field-Marshal Montgomery*. London: Fontana, 1960.
———. *Normandy to the Baltic*. London: Hutchinson, 1945.
Morison, Samuel Eliot. *History of the United States Naval Operations in World War II, Vol. XI: The Invasion of France and Germany, 1944–1945*. Edison, NJ: Castle Books, 2001.
Objective Force Task Force. *The Objective Force in 2015*. Arlington, VA: Department of the Army, 2002.
Patton Jr., George S. *War As I Knew It*. New York: Bantam, 1980.
Peniakoff, Vladimir. *Popski's Private Army*. London: Reprint Society, 1953.
Pogue, Forrest C. *The United States Army in World War II: The Supreme Command*. Washington, DC: Center for Military History, 1954.
Reid-Daly, Ron, and Peter Stiff. *Selous Scouts: Top Secret War*. Alberton, South Africa: Galago, 1982.
Rennie, James. *The Operators: Inside 14 Intelligence Company—The Army's Top Secret Elite*. London: Century, 1996.
Reske, Charles F. *MAC-V-SOG Command History Annex B: The Last Secret of the Vietnam War*, 2 vols. Sharon Center, OH: Alpha Publications, 1990.
Richards, Brooks. *Secret Flotillas, Volume II: Clandestine Sea Operations in the Mediterranean, North Africa and the Adriatic, 1940–1944*. London: Frank Cass, 2004.
———. *Secret Flotillas, Volume I: Clandestine Sea Operations to Brittany, 1940–1944*. London: Frank Cass, 2004.
Ryan, Chris. *The One That Got Away*. London: Book Club Associates, 1995.
Schlight, John. *The War in South Vietnam: The Years of the Offensive, 1965–1968*. Washington: Government Printing Office, 1988.
Schreiber, Gerhard *et al.*, eds. *Germany and the Second World War, Volume III: The Mediterranean, South-East Europe, and North Africa, 1939–1941*. Translated by Dean S. Murray *et al.* Oxford: Oxford University Press, 1995.
Scully, Will. *Once a Pilgrim*. London: Headline, 1998.
Secretary of the Air Force. *Organization and Employment of Aerospace Power*. Air Force Doctrine Document 2. Maxwell AFB, AL: Air Force Doctrine Center, 2000.
———. *Strategic Attack*. Air Force Doctrine Document 2–1.2. Maxwell AFB, AL: Air Force Doctrine Center, 1998.
Secretary of War. *United States Strategic Bombing Surveys [European War; Pacific War]*. Maxwell AFB, AL: Air University Press, 1987.
Sherman, William T. *From Atlanta to the Sea*. London: Folio Society, 1961.

200   Bibliography

Skorzeny, Otto. *Skorzeny's Special Missions*. London: Greenhill, 1997.
Speer, Albert. *Inside the Third Reich*. New York: Macmillan, 1970.
Spence, Cameron. *All Necessary Measures*. London: Michael Joseph, 1998.
———. *Sabre Squadron*. London: Michael Joseph, 1997.
Spencer Chapman, F. *The Jungle is Neutral*. London: The Reprint Society, 1950.
Stahl, Bob. *You're No Good to Me Dead: Behind Japanese Lines in the Philippines*. Annapolis, MD: Naval Institute Press, 1995.
Starinov, I.G. *Over the Abyss: My Life in Soviet Special Operations*. Translated by Robert Suggs. New York: Ivy Books, 1995.
Stöber, Hans. *Die Sturmflut und das Ende: Geschichte der 17. SS-Panzergrenadieredivision "Götz von Berlichingen,"* 2 vols. Osnabrück: Munin Verlag, 1976.
Strekhnin, Yuriy. *Commandos from the Sea: Soviet Naval Spetsnaz in World War II*. Annapolis, MD: Naval Institute Press, 1996.
Supreme Headquarters Allied Expeditionary Force. *Report by the Supreme Commander to the Combined Chiefs of Staff on the Operations in Europe of the Allied Expeditionary Force, 6 June 1944 to 8 May 1945*. Washington, DC: Government Printing Office, 1946.
Sutherland, David. *He Who Dares: Recollections of Service in the SAS, SBS and MI5*. Annapolis, MD: Naval Institute Press, 1999.
United States Strategic Bombing Survey. Report 64b. *The Effects of Strategic Bombing on German Morale, Vol. 1*. Washington: US Government Printing Office, 1947.
———. Report 208. *21 Rheinische-Westfalische Elektrizitaetswerk A G*. Washington: US Government Printing Office, 1947.
———. Report 145. *Gnome et Rhone Limoges, France*. Washington: US Government Printing Office, 1945.
von Mellenthin, F.W. *Panzer Battles: A Study of the Employment of Armor in the Second World War*. Norman, OK: University of Oklahoma Press, 1956.
Walsh, Michael. *SEAL! From Vietnam's PHOENIX Program to Central America's Drug Wars: Twenty-six Years with a Special Operations Warrior*. New York: Pocket Books, 1994.
Watson, James. *Point Man*. New York: William Morrow and Co., 1993.
Webster, Charles and Noble Frankland. *The Strategic Air Offensive Against Germany, 1939–1945,* 4 vols. London: Her Majesty's Stationery Office, 1961.
Wellsted, Ian. *SAS: With the Maquis: In Action with the French Resistance, June-September 1944*. London: Greenhill, 1994.
Yunnie, Bob. *Warriors on Wheels*. London: Hutchinson, 1959.

Manufactured memoirs, hoaxes, or questionable sources

Bruce, Paul (pseud., Paul Inman). *The Nemesis File: The True Story of an SAS Execution Squad*. London: Blake, 1995.
Fiennes, Ranulph. *The Feather Men*. London: Bloomsbury, 1991.
King, Bob. *Spooky 8: The Final Mission*. New York: St. Martin's, 1999.
Smith, Warner. *Covert Warrior: Fighting the CIA's Secret War in Southeast Asia and China, 1965–1967*. Novato, CA: Presidio, 1996.

Secondary sources

Books and monographs

Accinelli, Robert. *Crisis and Commitment: United States Foreign Policy Towards Taiwan, 1950–1955*. Chapel Hill, NC: University of North Carolina Press, 1996.

Adams, James. *Secret Armies: The Full Story of the SAS, Delta Force and Spetsnaz*. London: Pan Books Ltd., 1989.

Adelman, Robert and George Walton. *The Devil's Brigade*. New York: Bantam, 1966.

Adkin, Mark. *Urgent Fury: The Battle for Grenada*. Lexington, MA: Lexington Books, 1989.

Alger, John. *The Quest for Victory: The History of the Principles of War*. Westport, CT: Greenwood Press, 1982.

Andidora, Ronald. *Home by Christmas: The Illusion of Victory in 1944*. Westport, CT: Greenwood Press, 2001.

Andradé, Dale. *Ashes to Ashes: The Phoenix Program and the Vietnam War*. Lexington, MA: Lexington Books, 1990.

Appleyard, J.E. *Geoffrey: Being the Story of "Apple" of the Commandos and Special Air Service Regiment*. London: Blandford Press, 1946.

Aron, Raymond. *Clausewitz: Philosopher of War*. Translated by Christine Booker and Norman Stone. Englewood Cliffs, NJ: Prentice Hall, 1985.

Arostegui, Martin. *Twilight Warriors: Inside the World's Special Forces*. London: Bloomsbury, 1995.

Arquilla, John, ed. *From Troy to Entebbe: Special Operations in Ancient and Modern Times*. Lanham, NY: University Press of America, 1996.

Asher, Michael. *The Real Bravo Two Zero*. London: Cassell, 2002.

Avneri, Arieh. *War of Attrition*. Tel Aviv: Olive Books, 1972.

Barnett, Corelli. *Britain and Her Army, 1509–1970: A Military, Political and Social Survey*. London: Penguin, 1970.

Barnett, Frank R., Richard H. Schultz, Jr., and B. Hugh Tovar, eds. *Special Operations in US Strategy*. Washington: National Defense University Press, 1984.

Baylis, John *et al.*, eds. *Strategy in the Contemporary World: An Introduction to Strategic Studies*. Oxford: Oxford University Press, 2002.

Beaufre, André. *Introduction to Strategy*. Translated by R.H. Barry. New York: Frederick A. Praeger, 1965.

Beaumont, Roger. *War, Chaos, and History*. Westport, CT: Greenwood Press, 1994.

———. *Special Operations and Elite Units, 1939–1988: A Research Guide*. Westport, CT: Greenwood Press, 1988.

———. *Military Elites*. New York: Bobbs-Merrill, 1974.

Beevor, Anthony. *The Fall of Berlin, 1945*. New York: Viking, 2002.

Bekker, Cajus. *The Luftwaffe War Diaries*. New York: Doubleday, 1968.

Bennett, D.C.T. *Pathfinder*. London: Sphere Books, 1972.

Bennett, Ralph. *Ultra in the West: The Normandy Campaign of 1944–45*. New York: Scribner's, 1980.

Bennett, Tom. *617 Squadron: The Dambusters at War*. Wellingborough: Patrick Stephens Ltd, 1986.

Bibliography

Bergerud, Eric. *Touched With Fire: The Land War in the South Pacific.* New York: Viking, 1996.

Bermudez Jr., Joseph. *North Korean Special Forces,* 2nd edn. Annapolis, MD: Naval Institute Press, 1998.

Biddle, Stephen. *Military Power: Explaining Victory and Defeat in Modern Battle.* Princeton, NJ: Princeton University Press, 2004.

Bloomfield, Lincoln and Amelia Liess. *Controlling Small Wars: A Strategy for the 1980s.* New York: Knopf, 1970.

Bond, Brian and Ian Roy, eds. *War and Society: A Yearbook of Military History.* London: Croon Helm, 1975.

Bosiljevac, T.L. *SEALs: UDT/SEAL Operations in Vietnam.* London: Greenhill Books, 1990.

Bowden, Mark. *Blackhawk Down: A Story of Modern War.* New York: Atlantic Monthly Press, 1999.

Bowie, Christopher J., Robert P. Haffa, Jr., and Robert Mullins. *Future War: What Trends in America's Post-Cold War Military Conflicts Tell Us About Early 21st Century Warfare.* Washington, DC: Northrup Grumman Analysis Center, 2003.

Boyle, Andrew. *Trenchard: Man of Vision.* London: Collins, 1962.

———. *No Passing Glory: The Full and Authentic Biography of Group Captain Cheshire, VC, DSO, DFC.* London: Collins, 1955.

Boyne, Walter. *Messerschmidt Me 262: Arrow to the Future.* Washington, DC: Smithsonian Institution Press 1980.

Bradford, Ray, and Martin Dillon. *Rogue Warrior of the SAS.* London: John Murray, 1987.

Bradford, Zeb, and Frederic Brown. *The U.S. Army in Transition.* Beverley Hills, CA: Sage, 1973.

Bradin, James W. *From Hot Air to Hellfire: The History of Attack Aviation.* Novato, CA: Presidio Press, 1994.

Brandon, Russell. *Cheshire VC: A Story of Peace and War.* London: Evans Brothers Ltd, 1954.

Brehm, Jack and Pete Nelson. *That Others May Live: Inside the World's Most Daring Rescue Force.* London, Ebury Press, 2000.

Breuer, William. *The Great Raid on Cabanatuan: Rescuing the Doomed Ghosts of Bataan and Corregidor.* New York: John Wiley, 1994.

Breytenbach, Jan. *They Live By the Sword.* Alberton, South Africa: Lemur, 1990.

Brickhill, Paul. *The Dam Busters.* London: Bell & Hyman Ltd, 1984.

Briscoe, Charles et al. *Weapon of Choice: U.S. Army Special Operations Forces in Afghanistan.* Fort Leavenworth, KS: Combat Studies Institute Press, 2003.

Brock, George et al. *Siege: Six Days at the Iranian Embassy.* London: Macmillan, 1980.

Brown, Gary, Michael Evans, and Alan Stephens, eds. *The Use of Military Force in Kosovo,* Working Paper No. 54. Canberra: Australian Defence Studies Center, 1999.

Brown, Malcolm, ed. *Secret Despatches From Arabia and Other Writings by T.E. Lawrence.* London: Bellew Publishing, 1991.

Burgess, William, ed. *Inside Spetsnaz: Soviet Special Operations, A Critical Analysis.* Novato, CA: Presidio Press, 1990.

Burton, James. *The Pentagon Wars: Reformers Challenge the Old Guard.* Annapolis, MD: Naval Institute Press, 1993.

Camon, Hubert. *La guerre Napoléonienne—les systèmes d'operations, Théorie et technique*. Paris: Chapelot, 1907.
Cann, John. *Counterinsurgency in Africa: The Portuguese Way of War, 1961–1974*. Westport, CT: Greenwood Press, 1997.
Carpenter, Alfred. *The Blocking of Zeebrugge*. London: Herbert Jenkins, 1922.
Carter, John R. *Airpower and the Cult of the Offensive*. Maxwell AFB, AL: Air University Press, 1998.
Chaliand, Gérard, ed. *The Art of War in World History: From Antiquity to the Nuclear Age*. Berkeley, CA: University of California Press, 1994.
Chalou, George C., ed. *The Secrets War: The Office of Strategic Services in World War II*. Washington, DC: National Archives and Records Administration, 1992.
Chandler, David. *The Campaigns of Napoleon*. London: Weidenfeld & Nicolson, 1966.
Chinnery, Philip. *Any Time, Any Place: A History of USAF Air Commando and Special Operations Forces*. Shrewsbury: Airlife Publishing Ltd., 1994.
Clancy, Tom and Carl Stiner. *Shadow Warriors: Inside the Special Forces*. New York: Putnam's, 2002.
———. *Special Forces: A Guided Tour of U.S. Army Special Forces*. New York: Berkeley, 2001.
Clarke, Shaun. *Strategy, Air Strike, and Small Nations*. RAAF Base Fairburn: Air Power Studies Center, 1999.
Clausewitz, Carl von. *On War*. Translated by Michael Howard and Peter Paret. Princeton, NJ: Princeton University Press, 1976.
Cleaver, Frederick *et al*. *UN Partisan Warfare in Korea, 1951–1954*, ORO-T-64 (AFFE). Chevy Chase, MD: Johns Hopkins University, 1956.
Cohen, Eliot. *Commandos and Politicians: Elite Military Units in Modern Democracies*, Harvard Studies in International Affairs No. 40. Boston, MA: Center for International Affairs, 1978.
Cole, Barbara. *The Elite: The Story of the Rhodesian Special Air Service*. Transkei, South Africa: The Three Knights, 1984.
Colin, Jean. *Les Transformations de la Guerre*. Paris: Ernest Flammarion, 1912.
Collins, John. *Special Operations Forces: An Assessment*. Washington: NDU Press, 1994.
Conboy, Kenneth, and Dale Andradé. *Spies and Commandos: How America Lost the Secret War in North Vietnam*. Lawrence, KS: University Press of Kansas, 2000.
Connor, Ken. *An Illustrated History of the SAS*. London: Cassell, 2000.
———. *Ghost Force: The Secret History of the SAS*. London: Weidenfield & Nicolson, 1998.
Cookridge, E.K. *Set Europe Ablaze*. New York: Thomas Crowell, 1966.
Cooper, Alan. *Born Leader: The Story of Guy Gibson VC*. London: Independent Books, 1993.
———. *The Air Battle of the Ruhr: RAF Offensive, March to July 1943*. Shrewsbury: Airlife, 1992.
———. *Beyond the Dams to the Tirpitz: The Later Operations of 617 Squadron*. London: William Kimber, 1983.
———. *The Men Who Breached the Dams: 617 Squadron, "The Dambusters"*. London: William Kimber, 1982.

Cooper, Belton Y. *Death Traps: The Survival of an American Armored Division in World War II*. Novato, CA: Presidio, 1998.

Copp, Terry. *Fields of Fire: The Canadians in Normandy*. Toronto: University of Toronto Press, 2003.

Cordesman, Anthony and Abraham Wagner. *The Lessons of Modern War, Volume IV: The Gulf War*. Boulder, CO: Westview Press, 1996.

Corum, James S. and Wray Johnson. *Airpower in Small Wars: Fighting Insurgents and Terrorists*. Lawrence, KS: University Press of Kansas, 2003.

———. *The Luftwaffe: Creating the Operational Air War, 1918–1940*. Lawrence, KS: University Press of Kansas, 1997.

Corum, Robert. *Boyd: The Fighter Pilot Who Changed the Art of War*. New York: Little, Brown & Company, 2002.

Coutau-Bégarie, Hervé. *Traité de Stratégie*. Paris: Economica, 1999.

Cowles, Virginia. *The Phantom Major*. London: Odham's Press, 1958.

Cummings, Dennis. *The Men Behind the Trident: SEAL Team One in Vietnam*. Annapolis, MD: Naval Institute Press, 1997.

Custance, Reginald. *A Study of War*. Port Washington, NY: Kennikat Press, 1970.

Davies, Paul K., ed. *New Challenges for Defense Planning: Rethinking How Much is Enough*. Santa Monica, CA: RAND, 1994.

Delbrück, Hans. *History of the Art of War*. 4 vols. Translated by Walter Renfroe, Jr. Lincoln, NB: University of Nebraska Press, 1990.

Deptula, David A. *Firing for Effect: Change in the Nature of Warfare*. Arlington, VA: Aerospace Education Foundation, 1995.

Derr, Robert. *Air War South Vietnam*. London, Arms and Armour Press, 1991.

D'Este, Carlo. *Decision in Normandy*. New York: Dutton, 1983.

Dickens, Peter. *SAS, The Jungle Frontier: 22 Special Air Service Regiment in the Borneo Campaign, 1963–1966*. Glasgow: Fontana, 1984.

———. *SAS: The Jungle Frontier*. London: Arms and Armour Press, 1983.

Divine, David. *The Broken Wing: A Study in the British Exercise of Air Power*. London: Hutchinson, 1966.

Dodge, Theodore Ayrault. *Great Captains – A Course of Six Lectures: Alexander, Hannibal, Caesar, Gustavus Adolphus, Frederick and Napoleon*. Boston, MA: Ticknor and Co., 1889.

Dorrian, James. *Storming St. Nazaire*. London: Leo Cooper, 1998.

Drago, Steven *et al.*, eds. *Air and Space Power: Theory and Doctrine, MAS 330*. New York: Forbes Custom Publishing, 1998.

Drew, Dennis M. and Donald M. Snow. *Making Strategy: An Introduction to National Security Processes and Problems*. Maxwell AFB, AL: Air University Press, 1988.

Drummond, John. *But For These Men: How Eleven Commandos Saved Western Civilisation*. London: WH Allen, 1962.

Dugan, James and Carroll Stewart. *Ploesti: The Great Ground-Air Battle of 1 August 1943*. New York: Random House, 1962.

DuPuy, Trevor *et al.* *Hitler's Last Gamble: The Battle of the Bulge, December 1944–January 1945*. Shrewsbury: Airlife Publishing Ltd, 1994.

———. *Attrition: Forecasting Battle Casualties and Equipment Losses in Modern War.* Falls Church, VA: NOVA Publications, 1990.
Durschmied, Erik. *The Hinge Factor: How Chance and Stupidity Have Changed History.* New York: Arcade Publishing, 2000.
Dyer, F.N. et al. *Relationships among Rates of Attrition in Training and Subsequent Attrition in Line Units*, ARI-RR-1377. Alexandria, VA: Army Research Institute for the Behavior and Social Sciences, 1984.
Dyson, John. *Sink the Rainbow! An Enquiry into the "Greenpeace" Affair.* London: Victor Gollancz Ltd, 1986.
Earle, Edward Mead, ed. *Makers of Modern Strategy: From Machiavelli to Hitler.* Princeton, NJ: Princeton University Press, 1948.
Echevarria II, Antulio J. *After Clausewitz: German Military Thinkers Before the Great War.* Lawrence, KS: University Press of Kansas, 2000.
Elliott-Bateman, Michael, ed. *The Fourth Dimension of Warfare, Volume I: Intelligence/Subversion/Resistance.* New York: Praeger, 1970.
Ellis, Chris and Peter Chamberlain, eds. *Handbook of the British Army, 1943.* London: Purnell Book Services, 1975.
Ellis, John. *Brute Force: Allied Strategy and Tactics in the Second World War.* New York: Viking, 1990.
Els, Paul. *We Fear Naught but God: The Story of the South African Special Forces, "The Recces."* Johannesburg: Covos-Day Books, 2000.
Elting, John R. *The Super-Strategists: Great Captains, Theorists, and Fighting Men Who Have Shaped the History of Warfare.* New York: Charles Scribners, 1985.
Emerson, Steven. *Secret Warriors: Inside the Covert Military Operations of the Reagan Era.* New York: Putnam's, 1988.
Emme, Eugene M., ed. *The Impact of Air Power: National Security and World Politics.* New York: D. van Nostrand Company, 1959.
English, John. *The Canadian Army and the Normandy Campaign: A Study of Failure in High Command.* Westport, CT: Praeger, 1991.
Eshel, David. *Daring to Win: Special Forces at War.* London: Cassell, 1993.
Evanhoe, Ed. *Darkmoon: Eighth Army Special Operations in the Korean War.* Annapolis, MD: Naval Institute Press, 1995.
Ewald, Johann. *Treatise on Partisan Warfare.* Translated by Robert A. Selig and David Curtis Skaggs. Westport, CT: Greenwood Press, 1991.
Fadok, David. *John Boyd and John Warden: Air Power's Quest for Strategic Paralysis.* Maxwell AFB, AL: Air University Press, 1995.
Fair, Charles. *From the Jaws of Victory: A History of the Character, Causes and Consequences of Military Stupidity, from Crassus to Johnson and Westmoreland.* New York: Simon & Schuster, 1971.
Fane, Douglas and Don Moore. *The Naked Warriors.* Annapolis, MD: Naval Institute Press, 1995.
Ferris, John. *Men, Money, and Diplomacy: The Evolution of British Strategic Foreign Policy, 1919–1926.* Ithaca, NY: Cornell University Press, 1989.
Fishman, Jack. *And The Walls Came Tumbling Down.* London: Souvenir Press, 1982.

Bibliography

Flanagan, Edward M. *The Los Banos Raid: The 11th Airborne Jumps At Dawn*. Novato, CA: Presidio, 1986.

Flower, Stephen. *Barnes Wallis' Bombs: Tallboy, Dambuster & Grand Slam*. Briscombe Port: Tempus, 2004.

Foley, Charles. *Commando Extraordinary*. London: Longmans, Green and Company, 1954.

Folkestad, William B. *The View from the Turret: The 743rd Tank Battalion During World War II*. Shippensburg, PA: Burd Street Press, 2000.

Foot, M.R.D. *SOE: An Outline History of the Special Operations Executive, 1940–46*. London: British Broadcasting Corporation, 1984.

———. *Resistance: An Analysis of European Resistance to Nazism, 1940–45*. London: Eyre Methuen, 1976.

Ford, Roger. *Fire from the Forest: The SAS Brigade in France 1944*. London: Cassell, 2003.

Fowler, William. *Operation Barras, The SAS Rescue Mission: Sierra Leone 2000*. London: Weidenfeld & Nicolson, 2004.

———. *SAS, Behind Enemy Lines: Covert Operations 1941 to the Present Day*. London: HarperCollins, 1997.

Freedman, Lawrence. *The Evolution of Nuclear Strategy*. London: Macmillan, 1981.

Fry, Eric. *An Airman Far Away: The Story of an Australian Dambuster*. Kenthurst, Australia: Kangaroo Press, 1993.

Fugate, Bryan. *Operation Barbarossa: Strategy and Tactics on the Eastern Front, 1941*. Novato, CA: Presidio, 1984.

Fuller, J.F.C. *The Conduct of War, 1789–1961: A Study of the Impact of the French, Industrial, and Russian Revolutions on War and its Conduct*. Westport, CT: Greenwood, 1981.

———. *Julius Caesar: Man, Soldier and Tyrant*. London: Eyre and Spottiswoode, 1965.

———. *Grant and Lee: A Study in Personality and Generalship*. London: Eyre and Spottiswoode, 1959.

———. *The Generalship of Alexander the Great*. Eyre and Spottiswoode, London, 1958.

———. *The Decisive Battles of the Western World and Their Influence Upon History*, 3 vols. Eyre and Spottiswoode, London, 1954–6.

———. *The Second World War*. London: Eyre and Spottiswoode, 1948.

———. *Armament and History*. London: Eyre and Spottiswoode, 1946.

———. *Armored Warfare: An Annotated Edition of Lectures on F.S.R. III, Operations Between Mechanized Forces*. Harrisburg, PA: Military Service Publishing Company, 1943.

———. *Machine Warfare: An Enquiry into the Influences of Mechanics on the Art of War*. London: Hutchinson & Co., 1942.

———. *Memoirs of an Unconventional Soldier*. London: Ivor Nicholson and Watson, 1936.

———. *The Dragon's Teeth: A Study of War and Peace*. London: Constable, 1932.

———. *Lectures on FSR III: Operations Between Mechanized Forces*. London: Sifton Praed, 1932.

———. *On Future Warfare*. London: Sifton Praed, 1928.

———. *The Foundations of the Science of War*. London: Hutchinson & Co., 1926.

———. *The Reformation of War*. London: Hutchinson & Co., 1923.

Gabel, Christopher R. *Seek, Strike, and Destroy: U.S. Army Tank Destroyer Doctrine in World War II*, Leavenworth Paper No. 12. Fort Leavenworth, KS: Combat Studies Institute, 1985.

Gagnon, George. *Air Control: Strategy for a Smaller United States Air Force*. Maxwell AFB, AL: Air University Press, 1993.

Gallagher, Thomas. *Assault in Norway: The True Story of the Telemark Raid*. London: MacDonald and Jane's, 1975.

———. *The X-Craft Raid: A True Story of a Secret World War II Mission Unparalleled in the Annals of the Sea*. New York: Harcourt, Brace and Jovanovich, 1971.

Gann, Timothy. *Fifth Air Force Light and Medium Bomber Operations during 1942 and 1943*. Maxwell AFB, AL: Air University Press, 1993.

Gareev, Makhmut. *If War Comes Tomorrow? The Contours of Future Armed Conflict*. Edited by Jacob Kipp and translated by Yakov Fomenko. London: Frank Cass, 1998.

Garlinski, Józef. *Hitler's Last Weapons: The Underground War against the V1 and V2*. New York: New York Times Books, 1978.

Garrett, Richard. *The Raiders: The Elite Strike Forces That Altered History*. New York: Von Nostrand Reinhold, 1980.

Gaston, James C. *Planning the American Air War: Four Men and Nine Days in 1941, An Inside Narrative*. Washington: National Defense University Press, 1982.

Gat, Azar. *Fascist and Liberation Interpretations of War: Fuller, Liddell Hart, Douhet and Other Modernists*. Oxford: Oxford University Press, 1998.

———. *The Development of Military Thought: The Nineteenth Century*. Oxford: Clarendon Press, 1992.

Gawrych, George. *The 1973 Arab-Israeli War: The Albatross of Decisive Victory*, Leavenworth Paper No. 21. Leavenworth, KS: Combat Studies Institute, 1996.

Geraghty, Tony. *Beyond the Front Line: The Untold Exploits of Britain's Most Daring Cold War Spy Mission*. London: HarperCollins, 1996.

———. *Who Dares Wins: The Story of the Special Air Service, 1950–1980*. London: Arms and Armour Press, 1980.

Glantz, David M., and Harold Orenstein, eds. *The Battle for Kursk, 1943: The Soviet General Staff Study*. London: Frank Cass, 1999.

——— and Jonathan M. House, *When Titans Clashed: How the Red Army Stopped Hitler*. Lawrence, KS: University Press of Kansas, 1995.

———. *Soviet Operational Military Art: In Pursuit of Deep Battle*. London: Frank Cass, 1991.

Gordon, John. *The Other Desert War: British Special Forces in North Africa, 1940–1943*. Westport, CT: Greenwood Press, 1987.

Gordon, Michael and Bernard Trainor. *The General's War: The Inside Story of the Conflict in the Gulf*. New York: Little, Brown & Company, 1995.

Gorodetsky, Gabriel. *Grand Delusion: Stalin and the German Invasion of Russia*. New Haven, CT: Yale University Press, 1999.

Graham, Dominick and Shelford Bidwell. *Coalitions, Politicians and Generals: Some Aspects of Command in Two World Wars*. London: Brassey's, 2003.

Graves, Robert. *T.E. Lawrence to his Biographers*. New York: Doubleday, 1963.

Bibliography

Gray, Colin S. *Strategy for Chaos: Revolutions in Military Affairs and the Evidence of History*. London: Frank Cass, 2002.
———. *Modern Strategy*. Oxford: Oxford University Press, 1999.
———. *The Second Nuclear Age*. Boulder, CO: Lynne Rienner, 1999.
———. *Explorations in Strategy*. Westport, CT: Praeger, 1996.
Greene, I.F. *Voices Prophesying War, 1763–1984*. London: Oxford University Press, 1966.
Griffith, Jr., Thomas E. *MacArthur's Airman: General George C. Kenney and the War in the Southwest Pacific*. Lawrence, KS: University of Press of Kansas, 1998.
Guertner, Gary, ed. *The Search for Strategy: Politics and Strategic Vision*. Westport, CT: Greenwood Press, 1993.
Gwynn, Charles. *Imperial Policing*. London: Macmillan and Co., 1934.
Haas, Michael. *Apollo's Warriors: United States Air Force Special Operations During the Cold War*. Maxwell AFB, AL: Air University Press, 1997.
———. *Air Commando! 1950–1975: Twenty-five Years at the Tip of the Spear*. Hurlburt Field, FL: AFSOC, 1994.
Hall, Christopher. *British Strategy in the Napoleonic War, 1803–15*. Manchester: Manchester University Press, 1992.
Hamilton, Nigel. *Master of the Battlefield: Monty's War Years, 1942–1944*. New York: McGraw-Hill, 1983.
Hamley, Edward Bruce. *The Operations of War, Explained and Illustrated*. Edinburgh: William Blackwood and Sons, 1909.
Hammond, Grant. *The Mind of War: John Boyd and American Security*. Washington: Smithsonian Institution Press, 2001.
Handel, Michael. *Who is Afraid of Carl von Clausewitz? A Guide to the Perplexed*, 8th edn. Newport, RI: Naval War College, 1999.
———. *Masters of War: Classical Strategic Thought*. London: Frank Cass, 1996.
Hanson, Victor. *The Western Way of War: Infantry Battle in Classical Greece*. New York: Knopf, 1989.
Harris, J.P. *Amiens to the Armistice: The BEF in the Hundred Days' Campaign, 8 August–11 November 1918*. London: Brassey's, 1998.
Hart, Stephen A. *Montgomery and "Colossal Cracks": The 21st Army Group in Northwest Europe, 1944–45*. Westport, CT: Praeger, 2000.
Hartcup, Guy. *The Silent Revolution: Development of Conventional Weapons, 1945–1985*. London: Brassey's, 1993.
Hastings, Max. *On the Offensive: Das Reich*. London: Pan, 1995.
Haythornwaite, Philip J. *The Armies of Wellington*. London: Arms and Armour, 1994.
Heilbrunn, Otto. *Warfare in the Enemy's Rear*. New York: Praeger, 1963.
———. *Partisan Warfare*. London: Allen & Unwin, 1962.
Henderson, G.F.R. *The Science of War*. London: Longmans, Green and Co., 1905.
Hoe, Alan. *David Stirling: The Authorised Biography of the Creator of the SAS*. London: Warner Books, 1994.
———. *Re-enter the SAS: The Special Air Service and the Malayan Emergency*. London: Leo Cooper, 1994.
Hogan Jr., David. *Raiders or Elite Infantry? The Changing Role of the US Army Rangers from Dieppe to Grenada*. Westport, CT: Greenwood, 1992.

Holden Reid, Brian. *Studies In British Military Thought: Debates With Fuller and Liddell Hart*. Lincoln, NB: University of Nebraska Press, 1998.

———. *J.F.C. Fuller: Military Thinker*. London: Macmillan, 1987.

Hooten, E.R. *Eagle in Flames: The Fall of the Luftwaffe*. London: Brockhampton Press, 1999.

Horn, Bernd et al. *Force of Choice: Perspectives on Special Operations*. Kingston, ON: McGill-Queen's University Press, 2004.

Horner, David. *SAS: Phantoms of the Jungle*. St. Leonards, Australia: Allen & Unwin, 1989.

Howard, Michael. *Clausewitz*. Oxford: Oxford University Press, 1983.

Howell, Edgar. *The Soviet Partisan Movement, 1941–1944*, DA-PAM 20–244. Washington, DC: Department of the Army, 1956.

Hughes, Thomas Alexander. *Over Lord: General Pete Qaesada and the Triumph of Tactical Air Power in World War II*. New York: Free Press, 1995.

Isby, David C. *Leave No Man Behind: Liberation and Capture Missions*. London: Weidenfeld & Nicholson, 2004.

———, ed. *Fighting in Normandy: The German Army from D-Day to Villers-Bocage*. London: Greenhill, 2001.

———, ed. *Fighting the Invasion: The German Army at D-Day*. London: Greenhill, 2000.

Jakub, Jay. *Spies and Saboteurs: Anglo-American Collaboration and Rivalry in Human Intelligence Collection and Special Operations, 1940–45*. London: Macmillan, 1999.

Jarymowycz, Roman. *Tank Tactics: From Normandy to Lorraine*. Boulder, CO: Lynne Rienner, 2001.

Jennings, Christian. *Midnight in Some Burning Town: British Special Forces Operations from Belgrade to Baghdad*. London: Weidenfeld & Nicolson, 2004.

Jones, Archer. *The Art of War in the Western World*. New York: Barnes and Noble, 1987.

Katz, Samuel. *Follow Me! A History of Israel's Military Elite*. London: Arms and Armour Press, 1989.

Keegan, John. *History of Warfare*. New York: Knopf, 1993.

———. *Six Armies in Normandy: From D-Day to the Liberation of Paris*. Middlesex: Penguin, 1983.

———. *The Face of Battle*. New York: Knopf, 1976.

Kelly, Orr. *From a Dark Sky: The Story of U.S. Air Force Special Operations*. Novato, CA: Presidio Press, 1996.

———. *Never Fight Fair! Navy SEALs' Stories of Combat and Adventure*. Novato, CA: Presidio, 1995.

———. *Brave Men, Dark Waters: The Untold Story of the Navy SEALs*. Novato, CA: Presidio, 1992.

Kelly, Ross. *Special Operations and National Purpose*. Lexington, MA: D.C. Heath and Co., 1984.

Kelly, Saul. *The Lost Oasis: The Desert War and the Hunt for Zerzura*. Boulder, CO: Westview, 2002.

Kemp, Anthony. *SAS: The Savage Wars of Peace, 1947 to the Present*. London: John Murray Ltd, 1994.

———. *The SAS At War: The Special Air Service Regiment*. London: John Murray Ltd, 1991.

Kemp, Paul. *Underwater Warriors*. Annapolis, MD: Naval Institute Press, 1996.
Kern, Paul B. *Ancient Siege Warfare*. Bloomington, IN: Indiana University Press, 1999.
Keyes, Elizabeth. *Geoffrey Keyes of the Rommel Raid*. London: George Newnes Ltd, 1956.
King, Benjamin, and Timothy Kutta. *Impact: The History of Germany's V-Weapons in World War II*. Rockville Center, NY: Sarpedon, 1998.
King, Michael. *Rangers: Selected Combat Operations in World War II*. Leavenworth Paper No. 11, Fort Leavenworth, KS: Combat Studies Institute, 1985.
Knox, MacGregor, and Williamson Murray, eds. *The Dynamics of Military Revolutions, 1300–2050*. Cambridge: Cambridge University Press, 2001.
Kurowski, Franz. *The Brandenburgers: Global Mission*. Winnipeg, MB: J.J. Fedorowicz, 1997.
Kurzman, Dan. *Blood and Water: Sabotaging Hitler's Bomb*. New York: Henry Holt, 1997.
Kyle, James H. *The Guts to Try*. New York: Orion, 1990.
Ladd, James. *SAS Operations*. London: Robert Hale, 1986.
———. *SBS: The Invisible Raiders, The History of the Special Boat Squadron from World War Two to the Present*. London: Arms & Armour Press, 1983.
———. *Commandos and Rangers of World War II*. London: Book Club Associates, 1978.
Laffin, John. *British Butchers and Bunglers of World War One*. Surrey: Bramley, 1989.
Lamb, Richard. *Montgomery in Europe, 1943–1945: Success or Failure?* New York: Franklin Watts, 1984.
Lambakis, Steven et al. *Understanding 'Asymmetric' Threats to the United States*. Fairfax, VA: National Institute for Public Policy, 2002.
Lambeth, Benjamin. *NATO'S Air War For Kosovo: A Strategic and Operational Assessment*, MR-1365-AF. Santa Monica, CA: Rand, 2001.
Lanchester, F.W. *Aircraft in Warfare: The Dawn of the Fourth Arm*. Sunnyvale, CA: Lanchester Press, 1995.
Landsborough, Gordon. *Tobruk Commando: The Raid to Destroy Rommel's Base*. London: Greenhill, 1989.
Last, David and Bernd Horn. *Choice of Force: Special Operations for Canada*. Kingston, ON: McGill-Queen's University Press, 2005.
Lawrence, T.E. *The Seven Pillars of Wisdom: A Triumph*. London: Jonathan Cape, 1935.
———. *Revolt in the Desert*. London: Jonathan Cape, 1927.
Leasor, James and Leslie Hollis. *War at the Top*. London: Companion Book Club, 1960.
Lee, Alex. *Force Recon Command: A Special Marine Unit in Vietnam, 1969–1970*. Annapolis, MD: Naval Institute Press, 1995.
Le Mire, Henri. *Les Commandos Strategiques*. Paris: Jacques Grancher, 1980.
Lewis, Laurence. *Echoes of Resistance: British Involvement with the Italian Partisans*. Tunbridge Wells: Costello, 1985.
Liddell Hart, Basil H. *Strategy: The Indirect Approach*. New York: Praeger, 1968.
———. *The Defence of Britain*. London: Faber and Faber, 1939.
———. *Europe in Arms*. London: Faber and Faber, 1937.
———. *T.E. Lawrence: In Arabia and After*. London: Jonathan Cape, 1934.
———. *Sherman: The Genius of the Civil War*. London: Ernest Benn, 1930.
———. *Great Captains Unveiled*. Boston, MA: Little, Brown, and Co., 1928.
———. *Paris, or the Future of War*. New York: E.P. Dutton, 1925.

Linville Jumper, Roy Davis. *Death Waits in the 'Dark': The Senoi Praaq, Malaysia's Killer Elite*. Westport, CT: Greenwood, 2001.
Lloyd, Mark. *Special Forces: The Changing Face of Warfare*. London: Arms & Armour Press, 1995.
Lucas, James. *Kommando: German Special Forces of World War Two*. London: Guild Publishing, 1985.
Lucas Phillips, C.E. *The Raiders of Arakan*. London: William Heinemann, 1971.
———. *The Greatest Raid of All*. Boston: Little, Brown and Co., 1958.
———. *Cockleshell Heroes*. London: Pan Books Ltd., 1957.
Luttwak, Edward N. *Strategy: The Logic of War and Peace*. Cambridge, MA: Belknap Press, 1987.
Luvaas, Jay, trans. and ed. *Frederick the Great on the Art of War*. New York: Free Press, 1966.
———. *The Education of an Army: British Military Thought, 1815–1940*. London: Cassell, 1964.
McAleese, Peter. *McAleese's Fighting Manual: The Definitive Soldier's Handbook*. London: Orion, 1998.
McCue, Paul. *SAS Operation Bulbasket: Behind the Lines in Occupied France, 1944*. London: Leo Cooper, 1996.
McKie, Ronald. *The Heroes*. New York: Harcourt, Brace and Company, 1960.
Macksey, Kenneth. *Commando: Hit-and-Run Combat in World War II*. Chelsea, MI: Scarborough House, 1990.
———. *Guderian: Creator of the Blitzkrieg*. New York: Stein and Day, 1976.
———. *The Partisans of Europe in World War II*. London: Hart-Davis, MacGibbon, 1975.
MacLean, French. *The Cruel Hunters: SS-Sonderkommando Dirlewanger, Hitler's Most Notorious Anti-Partisan Unit*. Atglen, PA: Schiffer, 1998.
McMichael, Scott R. *A Historical Perspective on Light Infantry*, Research Survey No. 6. Fort Leavenworth, KS: Combat Studies Institute, 1987.
McRaven, William H. *Spec Ops, Case Studies in Special Operations Warfare: Theory and Practice*. Novato, CA: Presidio Press, 1995.
Magenheimer, Heinz. *Hitler's War: Germany's Key Strategic Decisions, 1940–1945*. Translated by Helmut Bögler. London: Arms and Armour, 1998.
Malkasian, Carter. *A History of Modern Wars of Attrition*. Westport, CT: Greenwood, 2002.
Mallmann Showell, Jak. P. *The German Navy in World War II: A Reference Guide to the Kriegsmarine, 1935–1945*. Annapolis, MD: Naval Institute Press, 1979.
Mann III, Edward. *Thunder and Lightning: Desert Storm and Airpower Debates*. Maxwell AFB, AL: Air University Press, 1995.
Marcinko, Richard. *The Rogue Warrior's(r) Strategy for Success: A Commando's Principles of Winning*. New York: Pocket Books, 1997.
Mark, Eduard. *Aerial Interdiction: Air Power and the Land Battle in Three American Wars*. Washington, DC: Center for Air Force History, 1994.
Marks, Thomas A. *Maoist Insurgency Since Vietnam*. London: Frank Cass, 1996.
Marquis, Susan. *Unconventional Warfare: Rebuilding U.S. Special Operations Forces*. Washington: Brookings Institution Press, 1997.
Matthias, Williard. *America's Strategic Blunders: Intelligence Analysis and National Security Policy, 1936–1991*. University Park, PA: Penn State University Press, 2001.

Bibliography

Maurice, Frederick. *British Strategy: A Study in the Applications of the Principles of War.* London: Constable, 1929.

———. *The Balance of Military Power in Europe: An Examination of the War Resources of Great Britain and the Continental States.* Edinburgh: William Blackwood and Sons, 1889.

Maxim, Hudson. *Defenseless America.* New York: Hearst's International Library Co., 1915.

Mearscheimer, John J. *Liddell Hart and the Weight of History.* Ithaca: Cornell University Press, 1988.

Meilinger, Philip S. *Airmen and Air Theory: A Review of the Sources.* Maxwell AFB, AL: Air University Press, 2001.

Mellenthin, F.W. and R.H.S. Stolfi. *NATO Under Attack: Why the Western Alliance Can Fight Outnumbered and Win in Central Europe without Nuclear Weapons.* Durham, NC: Duke University Press, 1984.

Mercado, Stephen C. *The Shadow Warriors of Nakano: A History of the Imperial Japanese Army's Elite Intelligence School.* Washington, DC: Brassey's, 2002.

Mets, David R. *The Air Campaign: John Warden and the Classical Airpower Theorists.* Maxwell AFB, AL: Air University Press, 1998.

Metz, Steven and Douglas V. Johnson II. *Asymmetry and U.S. Military Strategy: Definitions, Background, and Strategic Concepts.* Carlisle, PA: Strategic Studies Institute, 2000.

Meyers, George. *Strategy.* Washington, DC: Byron S. Adams, 1928.

Middlebrook, Martin, and Chris Everitt. *The Bomber Command War Diaries: An Operational Reference Book, 1939–1945.* Middlesex: Viking, 1985.

Miller, Russell. *Behind the Lines: An Oral History of Special Operations in World War II.* New York: St Martin's, 2002.

Mitchell, William. *Winged Defense.* New York: G.P. Putnam, 1925.

Moore, Robin. *The Hunt for Bin Laden: Task Force Dagger, On the Ground with the Special Forces in Afghanistan.* New York: Random House, 2003.

———. *The Green Berets.* New York: Crown, 1965.

Morison, Samuel Eliot. *Strategy and Compromise.* Boston, MA: Little, Brown and Co., 1958.

Morpurgo, J.E. *Barnes Wallis: A Biography.* London: Longmans, 1972.

Morris, Eric. *Guerrillas in Uniform: Churchill's Private Armies in the Middle East and the War Against Japan, 1940–1945.* London: Hutchinson, 1989.

———. *Churchill's Private Armies: British Special Forces in Europe, 1939–1942.* London: Hutchinson, 1986.

Moyar, Mark. *Phoenix and the Birds of Prey: The CIA's Secret Campaign to Destroy the Viet Cong.* Annapolis, MD: Naval Institute Press, 1997.

Mrazek, James. *The Fall of Eben Emael.* Novato, CA: Presidio, 1991.

———. *The Art of Winning Wars.* London: Leo Cooper, 1968.

Murray, Williamson and Allan Millett. *A War to be Won: Fighting the Second World War.* Cambridge, MA: Harvard University Press, 2000.

——— et al., eds. *The Making of Strategy: Rulers, States and War.* Cambridge, MA: Cambridge University Press, 1994.

———. *Strategy for Defeat: The Luftwaffe, 1939–1945*. Maxwell AFB, AL: Air University Press, 1983.
Naveh, Shimon. *In Pursuit of Military Excellence: The Evolution of Operational Theory*. London: Frank Cass, 1997.
Neillands, Robin. *In the Combat Zone: Special Forces Since 1945*. London: Weidenfeld & Nicolson, 1997.
Nelson, James, ed. *General Eisenhower on the Military Churchill*. New York: Norton, 1970.
Neufeld, Michael. *The Rocket and the Reich*. Cambridge, MA: Harvard University Press, 1996.
Newsinger, John. *Dangerous Men: The SAS and Popular Culture*. London: Pluto Press, 1997.
Nicholson, Frances. *The SAS Sex Survival Handbook*. London, UK: Blake Publishing, 1999.
Odom, Thomas. *Dragon Operations: Hostage Rescue Operations in the Congo, 1964–1965*, Leavenworth Paper No. 14, Fort Leavenworth, KS: Combat Studies Institute, 1988.
Olsen, Jack. *Aphrodite: Desperate Mission*. New York: G.P. Putnam's, 1970.
Oman, Charles. *The Art of War in the Middle Ages, A.D. 378–1515*, rev. edn. Ithaca, NY: Cornell University Press, 1953.
Omissi, David. *Air Power and Colonial Control: The Royal Air Force, 1919–1939*. Manchester: Manchester University Press, 1990.
Osanka, Franklin Mark, ed. *Modern Guerrilla Warfare: Fighting Communist Guerrilla Movements, 1941–1961*. New York: Free Press, 1962.
Osinga, Frans. *Science, Strategy, and War: The Strategic Theory of John Boyd*. Delft: Eburon, 2005.
Ottoway, Susan. *Dambuster: A Life of Guy Gibson, VC, DSO*, DFC**. London: Leo Cooper, 1996.
Overy, Richard. *Why the Allies Won*. London: Jonathan Cape, 1995.
Owen, Ben. *With Popski's Private Army*. London: Janus, 2000.
Owen, David Lloyd. *The Desert My Dwelling Place: With the Long Range Desert Group in North Africa*. London: Arms and Armour, 1986.
Owen, Robert, ed. *Deliberate Force: A Case Study in Effective Air Campaigning*. Maxwell AFB, AL: Air University Press, 2000.
Paddock Jr., Alfred. *US Army Special Warfare, Its Origins: Psychological and Unconventional Warfare, 1941–1952*. Washington: National Defense University Press, 1982.
Palazzo, Albert. *Seeking Victory on the Western Front: The British Army & Chemical Warfare in World War I*. Lincoln, NB: University of Nebraska Press, 2000.
Pape, Robert. *Bombing to Win: Air Power and Coercion in War*. Ithaca, NY: Cornell University Press, 1996.
Paret, Peter, ed. *Makers of Modern Strategy: From Machiavelli to the Nuclear Age*. Princeton: Princeton University Press, 1986.
Parker, Geoffrey. *The Grand Strategy of Philip II*. New Haven, CT: Yale University Press, 1998.

Parker, John. *SBS: The Inside Story of the Special Boat Service.* London: Headline Book Publishing, 1997.

Paschall, Rod. *LIC 2010: Special Operations & Unconventional Warfare in the Next Century.* Washington: Brassey's, 1990.

Pawle, Gerald. *The Secret War, 1939–1945.* London: The Companion Book Club, 1958.

Payne, Keith B. *The Fallacies of Cold War Deterrence and a New Direction.* Lexington, KY: University Press of Kentucky, 2001.

———. *Deterrence in the Second Nuclear Age.* Lexington, KY: University of Kentucky Press, 1996.

Perkins, Roger. *Operation Paraquat: The Battle for South Georgia.* Somerset: Picton Publishing, 1986.

Phillips, William. *Night of Silver Stars: The Battle of Lang Vei.* Annapolis, MD: Naval Institute Press, 1997.

Plaster, John. *Secret Commandos: Behind Enemy Lines with the Elite Warriors of SOG.* New York: Simon and Schuster, 2004.

———. *SOG: The Secret Wars of America's Commandos in Vietnam.* New York: Simon & Schuster, 1997.

Pogue, Forrest C. *George C. Marshall: Organizer of Victory, 1943–1945.* New York: Viking, 1973.

Pollack, Kenneth M. *Arabs at War: Military Effectiveness, 1948–1991.* Lincoln, NB: University of Nebraska Press, 2002.

Pugliese, David. *Shadow Wars: Special Forces in the New Battle Against Terrorism.* Ottawa, ON: Esprit de Corps Books, 2003.

———. *Canada's Secret Commandos: The Unauthorized Story of Joint Task Force Two.* Ottawa, ON: Esprit de Corps Books, 2002.

Ramsay, Jack. *SAS: The Soldier's Story.* London: Macmillan, 1996.

Reinhardt, G.C. and W.R. Kintner. *Atomic Weapons in Land Combat.* Harrisburg, PA: Military Service Publishing, 1954.

Reynolds, Michael. *Steel Inferno: 1 SS Panzer Corps in Normandy.* Staplehurst: Spellmount, 1997.

Reynolds, Richard. *Heart of the Storm: The Genesis of the Air Campaign Against Iraq.* Maxwell AFB, AL: Air University Press, 1995.

Richards, Chester. *A Swift, Elusive Sword: What if Sun Tzu and John Boyd did a National Defense Review?* Washington: Center for Defense Information, 2001.

Rigden, Denis. *Kill the Führer: Section X and Operation Foxley.* Stroud: Sutton, 1999.

Robertson, Scot. *The Development of RAF Strategic Bombing Doctrine, 1919–1939.* Westport, CT: Praeger, 1995.

Robinson, Linda. *Masters of Chaos: The Secret History of the Special Forces.* New York: PublicAffairs, 2004.

Ross, Hamish. *Paddy Mayne.* Stroud: Sutton Publishing, 2003.

Rostow, W.W. *Pre-Invasion Bombing Strategy: General Eisenhower's Decision of March 25, 1944.* Austin, TX: University of Texas Press, 1981.

Rotherberg, Gunther E. *The Art of War in the Age of Napoleon.* Stapleford: Spellmount, 1997.

Ryan, Mike. *Special Operations in Iraq.* Barnsley: Pen and Sword Books, 2004.

Ryan, Paul B. *The Iranian Rescue Mission: Why It Failed*. Annapolis, MD: Naval Institute Press, 1985.

Saundby, Robert. *Air Bombardment: The Story of Its Development*. New York: Harper & Brothers, 1961.

Sawyer, Ralph D., trans. *Seven Military Classics of Ancient China*. Boulder, CO: Westview Press, 1993.

Scales, Jr., Robert H. *Certain Victory: The U.S. Army and the Gulf War*. Washington: Brassey's, 1994.

Schedewitz, Michael. *The Meuse First and Then Antwerp: Some Aspects of Hitler's Offensive in the Ardennes*. Translated by Wendy Bonk. Winnipeg, MB: J.J. Fedorowicz Publishing, 1999.

Schemmer, Benjamin. *The Raid*. London: Book Club Associates, 1977.

Seaman, Mark. *Garbo: The Spy Who Saved D-Day*. Kew: The National Archives, 2000.

Seymour, William. *British Special Forces*. London: Sidgwick & Jackson, 1985.

Sharp, Ulysses S. Grant. *Strategy for Defeat: Vietnam in Retrospect*. Novato, CA: Presidio, 1978.

Shaw, Robert. *Fighter Combat: Tactics and Maneuvering*. Annapolis, MD: Naval Institute Press, 1985.

Showalter, Dennis. *Tannenberg: Clash of Empires*. Hamden, CT: Archon, 1991.

Shultz Jr., Richard. *The Secret War Against Hanoi: Kennedy and Johnson's Use of Spies, Saboteurs, and Covert Warriors in North Vietnam*. New York: HarperCollins, 1999.

──────, and Robert Pfaltzgraff, Jr., eds. *The Future of Air Power in the Aftermath of the Gulf War*. Maxwell AFB, AL: Air University Press, 1992.

Sides, Hampton. *Ghost Soldiers: The Forgotten Epic Story of World War II's Most Dramatic Mission*. New York: Doubleday, 2001.

Simpkin, Richard. *Deep Battle: The Brainchild of Marshal Tukhachevskii*. London: Brassey's, 1987.

──────. *Race to the Swift: Thoughts on Twenty-First Century Warfare*. London: Brassey's, 1985.

Smith, Malcolm. *British Air Strategy Between the Wars*. Oxford: Oxford University Press, 1984.

Smithers, A.J. *Rude Mechanicals: An Account of Tank Maturity During the Second World War*. London: Leo Cooper, 1987.

Southworth, Samuel. *Great Raids in History: From Drake to Desert One*. New York: Sarpedon, 1997.

Spaight, J.M. *The Sky's the Limit: A Study of British Air Power*. London: Hodder and Stoughton, 1940.

Spencer, David. *From Vietnam to El Salvador: The Saga of the FMLN Sappers and Other Guerrilla Special Forces in Latin America*. Westport, CT: Praeger, 1996.

Spiers, Edward. *Chemical Weaponry: A Continuing Challenge*. London: Macmillan, 1989.

"Squadron Leader." (pseud.). *Basic Principles of Air Warfare: The Influence of Air Power on Sea and Land Strategy*. Aldershot: Gale & Polden, Ltd, 1927.

Stahl, Peter. *KG 200: The True Story*. London: Jane's Publishing Company, 1981.

Stanton, Shelby. *Green Berets at War: US Army Special Forces in Southeast Asia, 1956–1975*. Novato, CA: Presidio, 1985.

Stein, Jeff. *A Murder in Wartime.* New York: St. Martin's Press, 1992.

Steiner, Barry H. *Bernard Brodie and the Foundations of American Nuclear Strategy.* Lawrence, KS: University Press of Kansas, 1991.

Stevenson, James. *The Pentagon Paradox: The Development of the F-18 Hornet.* Annapolis, MD: Naval Institute Press, 1993.

Stevenson, Jonathon. *Losing Mogadishu: Testing U.S. Policy in Somalia.* Annapolis, MD: Naval Institute Press, 1995.

Stevenson, William. *90 Minutes at Entebbe.* New York: Bantam, 1976.

Stolfi, R.H.S. *Hitler's Panzers East: World War II Reinterpreted.* Norman, OK: University of Oklahoma Press, 1991.

Strachan, Hew. *The First World War, Volume I: To Arms.* Oxford: Oxford University Press, 2001.

Strassler, Robert. *The Landmark Thucydides: A Comprehensive Guide to the Peloponnesian War.* New York: Free Press, 1996.

Strauss, Barry and Josiah Ober. *The Anatomy of Error: Ancient Military Disasters and Their Lessons for Modern Strategists.* New York: St. Martin's, 1990.

Strawson, John. *A History of the S.A.S. Regiment.* London: Guild Publishing, 1985.

Sumida, Jon Tetsuro. *Inventing Grand Strategy and Teaching Command: the Classic Works of Alfred Thayer Mahan Reconsidered.* Baltimore, MD: Johns Hopkins University Press, 1997.

Suvorov, Victor (pseud.). *Spetsnaz: The Story Behind the Soviet SAS.* London: Hamilton Hamish, 1987.

Svechin, Aleksandr A. *Strategy.* Translated and edited by Kent Lee. Minneapolis, MN: East View Publications, 1992.

Sweetman, John. *Operation Chastise, The Dams Raid: Epic or Myth.* London: Jane's, 1982.

Swinson, Arthur. *The Raiders: Desert Strike Force.* New York: Ballantine, 1968.

Taillon, J. Paul De B. *The Evolution of Special Forces in Counter-Terrorism: The British and American Experiences.* Westport, CT: Praeger, 2001.

Tangredi, Sam J. *All Possible Wars? Toward a Consensus View of the Future Security Environment, 2001–2025*, McNair Paper No. 63. Washington, DC: Institute for National Strategic Studies, 2000.

Tangye, Nigel, ed. *The Air is Our Concern: A Critical Study of England's Future in Aviation.* London: Methuen and Company, Ltd, 1935.

Tantrum, IV, W.H. and Hoffschmidt, E.J., eds. *The Rise and Fall of the German Air Force, 1939–1945.* Old Greenwich, CT: WE Inc., 1969.

Terraine, John. *The Right of the Line: The Royal Air Force in the European Campaign, 1939–1945.* Hertfordshire: Wordsworth, 1997.

Terraine, John. *The Smoke and the Fire: Myths and Anti-Myths of War, 1861–1945.* London: Leo Cooper, 1992.

Thompson, James. *Rolling Thunder: Understanding Policy and Program Failure.* Chapel Hill, NC: University of North Carolina Press, 1980.

Thompson, Julian. *The Imperial War Museum Book of War Behind Enemy Lines.* London: Sidgwick & Jackson, 1998.

Thompson, Leroy. *The Rescuers: The World's Top Anti-Terrorist Units.* Boulder, CO: Paladin, 1986.

Tourison, Sedgwick. *Secret Army, Secret War: Washington's Tragic Spy Operation in North Vietnam*. Annapolis, MD: Naval Institute Press, 1995.
Travers, T.H.E. *How the War Was Won: Command and Technology in the British Army on the Western Front, 1917–1918*. London: Routledge, 1992.
Trenowden, Ian. *Stealthily by Night: The COPPists, Clandestine Beach Reconnaissance and Operations in World War II*. London: Crecy Books Limited, 1995.
Trest, Warren A. *Air Commando One: Heinie Aderholt and America's Secret Air Wars*. Washington: Smithsonian, 2000.
Triandafillov. V.K. *The Nature of the Operations of Modern Armies*. Translated by William Burhans. London: Frank Cass, 1994.
Trotter, William. *Instinct of the Herd in Peace and War*. New York: Macmillan, 1919.
Trythall, Anthony J. *"Boney" Fuller: Soldier, Strategist, and Writer, 1878–1966*. London: Cassell, 1977.
Tucker, Spencer. *Vietnam*. Lexington: KY: University of Kentucky Press, 1999.
Turner, E.S. *Gallant Gentlemen: A Portrait of the British Officer, 1600–1956*. London: Michael Joseph, 1956.
Tzu, Sun. *The Art of War*. Translated by Ralph D. Sawyer. New York: Barnes and Noble, 1994.
———. *The Art of War*. Translated by Samuel B. Griffith. Oxford: Oxford University Press, 1963.
Ullman, Harlan et al. *Shock & Awe: Achieving Rapid Dominance*. Washington: National Defense University Press, 1996.
Urban, Mark. *Big Boys' Rules: The SAS and The Secret Struggle Against The IRA*. London: Faber & Faber, 1993.
Van Cleave, William R. and Saul T. Cohen. *Tactical Nuclear Weapons: An Examination of the Issues*. New York: Crane Russak, 1978.
van Creveld, Martin. *Technology and War: From 2000 B.C. to the Present*. New York: Free Press, 1989.
———. *Fighting Power: German and U.S. Army Performance, 1939–1945*. Westport, CT: Greenwood, 1982.
———. *The Balkan Clue: Hitler's Strategy, 1940–1941*. London: International Studies, 1973.
Vandenbroucke, Lucien. *Perilous Options: Special Operations as an Instrument of U.S. Foreign Policy*. New York: Oxford University Press, 1993.
Vick, Alan. *Snakes in the Eagle's Nest: A History of Ground Attacks on Air Bases*. Santa Monica, CA: RAND, 1995.
von Caemmerer, Rudolf. *The Development of Strategical Science During the 19th Century*. Translated by Karl von Donat. London: Hugh Rees, 1905.
von der Goltz, Colmar. *The Nation in Arms: A Treatise on Modern Military Systems and the Conduct of War*. Translated by Philip Ashworth. London: Hugh Rees, 1913.
von Senger, Harro. *The Book of Strategems: Tactics for Triumph and Survival*. Translated and edited by Myron B. Gubitz. New York: Viking, 1991.
Walker, Greg. *At the Hurricane's Eye: U.S. Special Operations Forces from Vietnam to Desert Storm*. New York: Ballantine, 1993.
Wallach, Jehuda. *The Dogma of the Battle of Annihilation: The Theories of Clausewitz and Schlieffen and Their Impact on the German Conduct of Two World Wars*. Westport, CT: Greenwood Press, 1986.

Bibliography

Waller, Douglas. *The Commandos: The Inside Story of America's Secret Soldiers*. New York: Simon & Schuster, 1994.

Walton, C. Dale. *The Myth of Inevitable U.S. Defeat in Vietnam*. London: Frank Cass, 2002.

Warden, John. *The Air Campaign: Planning for Combat*. Washington: Pergamon-Brassey's, 1989.

Warner, Philip. *The Special Air Service*. London: Sphere Books Limited, 1971.

Warren, C.E.T. and James Benson. *Above Us the Waves: The Story of Midget Submarines and Human Torpedoes*. London: George G. Harrap & Co. Ltd, 1953.

Watson, Bruce, et al. *Military Lessons of the Gulf War*. London: Greenhill, 1991.

Watts, Barry. *Clausewitzian Friction and Future War*. McNair Paper No. 52. Washington: National Defense University Press, 1996.

Weale, Adrian. *The Real SAS*. London: Sidgwick & Jackson, 1998.

Wells, H.G. *The History of Mr Polly and The War in the Air*. London, Odhams Press, 1936.

Westermann, Edward. *Hitler's Police Battalions: Enforcing Racial War in the East*. Lawrence, KS: University Press of Kansas, 2005.

Wheldon, John. *Machine Age Armies*. London: Abelard-Schuman, 1968.

White, Terry. *Swords of Lightning: Special Forces and the Changing Face of Warfare*. London: Brassey's, 1992.

Whiting, Charles. *Skorzeny: The Most Dangerous Man in Europe*. London: Leo Cooper, 1998.

———. *The Battle of the Ruhr Pocket*. New York: Ballantine, 1971.

Wilkinson, Spenser. *The Brain of an Army: A Popular Account of the German General Staff*, 2nd edn. London: Constable, 1895.

Williams, Maxine. *Death on the Rock: How the British Government Got Away With Murder*. London: Larkin, 1989.

Williamson, Tony. *Counter Strike Entebbe*. London: William Collins, 1976.

Winterbotham, F.W. *Secret and Personal*. London: William Kimber, 1969.

Woodward, Bob. *The Commanders*. New York: Simon and Schuster, 1991.

Woodworth, Steven. *Jefferson Davis and His Generals: The Failure of Confederate Command in the West*. Lawrence, KS: University of Kansas Press, 1990.

Wragg, David. *The Offensive Weapon: The Strategy of Bombing*. London: Robert Hale, 1986.

Wylie, J.C. *Military Strategy: A General Theory of Power Control*. New Brunswick, NJ: Rutgers University Press, 1967.

Young, Darryl. *The Element of Surprise: Navy SEALs in Vietnam*. New York: Ivy Books, 1990.

———. *SEALs, UDT, Frogmen: Men Under Pressure*. New York: Ivy Books, 1994.

Zaffiri, Samuel. *Westmoreland: A Biography of General William C. Westmoreland*. New York: William Morrow, 1994.

Zedong, Mao. *Selected Military Writings of Mao Tse-Tung*. Peking: Foreign Languages Press, 1966.

———. *Mao Tse-Tung on Guerrilla Warfare*. Translated by Samuel Griffith. New York: Praeger, 1961.

Zetterling, Niklas. *Normandy 1944: German Military Organization, Combat Power and Organizational Effectiveness*. Winnipeg, MB: J.J. Fedorowicz, 2000.

Zhang, Xiaoming. *Red Wings Over the Yalu: China, the Soviet Union, and the Air War in Korea.* College Station, TX: Texas A&M Press, 2002.

Articles

Bassford, Christopher. "John Keegan and the Grand Tradition of Trashing Clausewitz." *War in History*, 1:3 (November 1994): 319–36.

Bellamy, Chris. "Red Star in the West: Marshal Tukhachevsky and East-West Exchanges on the Art of War." *Royal United Service Institute Journal*, 132:4 (December 1987): 63–73.

Betts, Richard. "Compromised Command," *Foreign Affairs*, 80:4 (July/August 2001): 126–32.

———. "Is Strategy an Illusion?" *International Security*, 25:2 (Fall 2000): 5–50.

Biddle, Tami Davis, "British and American Approaches to Strategic Bombing: Their Origins and Implementation in the World War II Combined Bomber Offensive." *The Journal of Strategic Studies*, 18:1 (March 1995): 91–144.

Bingham, Price. "Revolutionizing Warfare Through Interdiction." *Airpower Journal*, 10:1 (Spring 1996): 29–35.

Boot, Max. "The New American Way of War." *Foreign Affairs*, 82:4 (July/August 2003): 41–59.

Byman, Daniel, and Matthew Waxman. "Kosovo and the Great Air Power Debate." *International Security*, 24:4 (Spring 2000): 5–38.

Copp, Terry. "Scientists and the Art of War: Operations Research in 21 Army Group." *Journal of the Royal United Services Institute for Defence Studies*, 136:4 (April 1991): 65–70.

Corum, James. "The Myth of Air Control: Reassessing the History." *Aerospace Power Journal*, 14:4 (Winter 2000): 61–77.

Dwyer Christopher S. "Raiding Strategy: As Applied by the Western Confederate Cavalry in the American Civil War." *Journal of Military History*, 63:2 (April 1999): 263–82.

Echevarria II, Antulio J. "Borrowing from the Master: Uses of Clausewitz in German Military Literature Before the Great War." *War in History*, 3:3 (Summer 1996): 274–92.

Farrar, Jr., L.L. "Peace Through Exhaustion: German Diplomatic Motivations for the Verdun Campaign." *Revue Internationale d'Histoire Militaire*, no. 32 (1972–1975): 477–94.

Fuller, J.F.C. "Correspondence: Scientific Soldiership." *The Royal Engineers Journal*, 42:4 (December 1928): 743.

———. "Scientific Soldiership." *The Royal Engineers Journal*, 42:2 (June 1928): 198–204.

———. "Principles of Defensive Warfare." *The Royal Engineers Journal*, 39:2 (June 1925): 226.

———. "The Application of Recent Developments in Mechanics and Other Scientific Knowledge to Preparation and Training for Future War on Land." *Journal of the Royal United Services Institution*, 65:458 (May 1920): 227–74.

[Fuller, J.F.C.] "The Principles of War with Reference to the Campaigns of 1914–15." *Journal of the Royal United Services Institution*, 61 (February 1916): 1–40.

Gat, Azar. "British Influence and the Evolution of the Panzer Arm: Myth or Reality? Part II." *War in History,* 4:3 (Summer 1997): 316–38.

———. "British Influence and the Evolution of the Panzer Arm: Myth or Reality? Part I." *War in History,* 4:2 (Spring 1997): 150–73.

Gray, Colin S. "Why is Strategy Difficult?" *Joint Forces Quarterly,* no. 22 (Summer 1999): 6–12.

———. "Handful of Heroes on Desperate Ventures: When do Special Operations Succeed?" *Parameters,* 29:1 (Spring 1999): 2–24.

Hart, Russell A. "Feeding Mars: The Role of Logistics in the German Defeat in Normandy, 1944." *War in History,* 3:4 (1996): 418–35.

Howard, Michael. "The Forgotten Dimensions of Strategy." *Foreign Affairs,* 57:5 (Summer 979): 976–8.

Hutchings, I. "Bouncing Bombs of the Second World War." *New Scientist* (2 March 1978): 563–7.

Jervis, Robert. "Complexity and the Analysis of Political and Social Life." *Political Science Quarterly,* 112:4 (Winter 1997–1998): 569–94.

Jones, Clive. "Israeli Counter-Insurgency Strategy and the War in South Lebanon, 1985–1997." *Small Wars & Insurgencies,* 8:3 (Winter 1997): 82–108.

Katz, Samuel J. "Incident at Ansariya." *Jane's Intelligence Review,* 10:1 (January 1998): 24–8.

Keegan, John. "Please, Mr Blair, never take such a risk again." *Sunday Telegraph* (6 June 1999).

Kibbe, Jennifer. "The Rise of the Shadow Warriors," *Foreign Affairs,* 83:2 (March/April 2004): 102–15.

Kiras, James D. "The Strategic Utility of Special Operations in the Conflict in Afghanistan." *Defence Review* (December 2001): 45–7.

Lawrence, T.E. "The Evolution of a Revolt." *Army Quarterly,* 1:1 (October 1920): 55–69.

Liddell Hart, Basil H. "The 'Man-in-the-Dark' Theory of Infantry Tactics and the 'Expanding Torrent' System of Attack." *The Journal of the Royal United Services Institution,* 66:461 (February 1921): 1–22.

Lambakis, Steve. "Forty Selected Men Can Shake the World: The Contributions of Special Operations to Victory." *Comparative Strategy,* 13:2 (Summer 1994): 211–21.

Mack, Andrew. "Why Big Nations Lose Small Wars: The Politics of Asymmetric Conflict." *World Politics,* 27:2 (January 1975): 175–200.

Meilinger, Phillip. "The Historiography of Airpower: Theory and Doctrine." *The Journal of Military History,* 64 (April 2000): 467–502.

Mendel, William and Lamar Tooke. "Operational Logic: Selecting the Center of Gravity." *Military Review,* 73:6 (June 1993): 2–11.

Metz, Steven, and Frederick Downey. "Centers of Gravity and Strategic Planning." *Military Review,* 68:4 (April 1988): 22–33.

Miller, Sergio. "Special Forces—A Future?" *RUSI Journal,* 138:4 (August 1993): 70–4.

Rosinki, Professor, trans. "The Failure of the War of Exhaustion." *Army Quarterly,* 35 (October 1937 – January 1938): 117–22.

Ryan, Steve. "Special Operations: Is Light Right?" *Asian Defence Journal,* 108 (May 1995): 44–7.

Scarborough, Rowan. "Myers says 'annihilation' of Iraqi army wasn't goal." *The Washington Times* (30 June 2003).

Schneider, James. "A New Form of Warfare." *Military Review*, 80:1 (January–February 2000): 60.

Searle, Alaric. "J.F.C. Fuller, Tukhachevsky and the Red Army, 1923–1941: The Question of the Reception of Fuller's Military Writings in the Soviet Union." *The Journal of Slavic Military Studies*, 9:4 (December 1996): 848–84.

Strachan, Hew. "Essay and Reflection: On Total War and Modern War." *International History Review*, 22:2 (June 2000): 341–70.

Tilford, Jr., Earl. "Operation Allied Force and the Role of Air Power." *Parameters*, 29:4 (Winter 1999–2000): 24–38.

Tooke, Lamar. "Blending Maneuver and Attrition." *Military Review*, 80:2 (March–April 2000): 7–13.

Turner, Robert. "Killing Saddam: Would It Be a Crime?" *Washington Post*, (7 October 1990): pp. D1–D2.

Twohig, J.P.O. "Are Commandos Really Necessary?" *Army Quarterly*, 57:1 (October 1948): 86–8.

Vego, Milan. "Center of Gravity." *Military Review*, 80:2 (March–April 2000): 23–9.

Vigor, P.H. "The Soviet View of Fuller and Liddell Hart." *Journal of the Royal United Services Institution*, 123:1 (March 1978): 74–7.

Vogel, Robert. "Tactical Air Power in Normandy: Some Thoughts on the Interdiction Plan." *Canadian Military History*, 3:1 (Spring 1994): 37–47.

Wallis, Barnes. "The Man and His Bomb: The Dam-Busting Weapon." *Aerospace Historian*, 20 (1973).

Warden, John. "The Enemy as a System." *Airpower Journal*, 9:1 (Spring 1995): 40–55.

Watts, Barry. "Ignoring Reality: Problems of Theory and Evidence in Security Studies." *Security Studies*, 7:2 (Winter 1997/98): 115–71.

Woodward, Bob. "CIA Told to Do 'Whatever Necessary' to Kill Bin Laden: Agency and Military Collaborating at 'Unprecedented' Level; Cheney Says War Against Terror 'May Never End'." *Washington Post* (21 October 2001).

Zuber, Terence. "The Schlieffen Plan Reconsidered." *War in History*, vol. 6, no. 3 (July 1999): 208–32.

Unpublished reports, theses, and transcripts

Boyatt, M.D. "Unconventional Operations Forces of Special Operations." Unpublished thesis. Army War College (1993).

Boyd, John. "Patterns of Conflict." Unpublished briefing (December 1986).

———. "Destruction and Creation." Unpublished article (3 September 1976).

———. "New Conception for Air-to-Air Combat." Unpublished briefing (4 August 1976).

Brown, H.S. "Command and Control of Special Operations Forces." Unpublished thesis. Naval Postgraduate School (1996).

Carter, Sue. "A Shot to the Space Brain: The Vulnerability of Command and Control of Non-Military Space Systems." Unpublished thesis. Air Command and Staff College (1997).

Cowan, Jeffrey. "From Air Force Fighter Pilot to Marine Corps Warfighting: Colonel John Boyd, His Theories on War, and their Unexpected Legacy." Unpublished thesis. Marine Corps Command and Staff College (2000).

Eikmeier, Dale. "The Center of Gravity Debate Resolved." Unpublished thesis. Army Command and General Staff College (1999).

Flavin, William. "Concept for the Strategic Use of Special Operations Forces in the 1990s and Beyond." Unpublished thesis. Army War College (1991).

Fondacaro, Steve. "A Strategic Analysis of US Special Operations During the Korean Conflict, 1950–1953." Unpublished thesis. Army Command and General Staff College (1988).

Garner, Robert. "Ethical Guidelines for Military Covert Operations." Unpublished thesis. Army War College (1990).

Giles, Kevin. "Center of Gravity: Determination, Analysis, and Application." Unpublished thesis. Army War College (1996).

Gray, Colin. "Special Operations: What Succeeds and Why? Lessons of Experience, Phase I." Unpublished report. National Institute for Public Policy, 1992.

Haselton, M.A. "Role of Special Operations Forces in Counter-Narcotic Operations." Unpublished thesis. Army Command and General Staff College (1990).

Hestermann, Jennifer L. "The Erosion of the Enlisted Force: A Study of Attrition." Unpublished thesis. Air Command and Staff College (1999).

Ignatieff, Michael. "Future War, Part One: The Revolution in Military Affairs." Unpublished transcript. British Broadcasting Corporation, 15 April 2000.

Johnson, Darfus. "Center of Gravity: The Source of Operational Ambiguity and Linear Thinking in the Age of Complexity." Unpublished thesis. Army Command and General Staff College (1999).

Jones, Gregg. "A Historical Perspective of Special Operations Forces as an Instrument of Strategy." Unpublished thesis. Army Command and General Staff College (1991).

Kiras, James. "Viet Cong Organization and Operations: A Critical Assessment Based On Rand Documents." Unpublished thesis. University of Toronto, 14 December 1990.

Lee, Seow Hiang. "Center of Gravity or Center of Confusion: Understanding the Mystique." Unpublished thesis. Air Command and Staff College (1999).

Lindemann, Timothy. "Decapitation: Contemporary Air Power Countercontrol Strategies." Unpublished thesis. School of Advanced Airpower Studies (1998).

Luttwak, Edward N., Canby, Steven L., and Thomas, David L. "A Systematic Review of 'Commando' (Special) Operations, 1939–1980." Unpublished Report. C&L Associates, 24 May 1982.

McCarthy, Michael. "Strike Operations: Contingency Operations with Light-Heavy-Special Operations Forces." Unpublished thesis. Army Command and General Staff College (1991).

Riley, C.A. "Role of Special Operations Forces in Operations Against Theater Missiles." Unpublished thesis. Naval Postgraduate School (1996).

Smith, Bradley. "Parallel Attack and the Enemy's Decision Making Process." Unpublished thesis. Air Command and Staff College (1998).

Watson, Douglas. "Countering the North Korean Special Operations Threat: The ROK/US Response." Unpublished thesis. Naval War College (1989).

Wilson, Gregory R. "Modeling and Evaluating U.S. Army Special Operations Forces Combat Attrition Using Janus(A)." Unpublished thesis. Naval Postgraduate School (September 1995).

Winters, E.G. and Paro, Kia. "Misuse of Special Operations Forces." Unpublished thesis. Naval Postgraduate School (1994).

Index

487 Squadron (RNZAF) 98
617 Squadron 14, 38, 58, 109, 156 n124, 156 n127; attack on dams 53; establishment of 52–3, 156 n123; precision bombing and 157 n142, 193 n167
Afghanistan 16, 61, 98, 116–7
AFSOC *see* Air Force Special Operations Command (AFSOC)
Aideed, Mohamed Farah 79
Air Attacks on Dams Committee 49
Air Force Special Operations Command (AFSOC) 37
Air Ministry 46, 155 n114, 155 n118
air policing 36, 39–40, 133 n65, 144 n11, 147 n29, 147–8 n33
airpower 13, 48, 85–6, 98, 107, 109, 113, 117; advocacy of 37–9; British expectations of 36, 40–3, 151 n60; criticisms of 38–9; and moral effect argument 40, 148 n34–5; moral effects of 145 n21, 147 n30, 148 n39, 151 n64, 154 n101, 155 n107; in the Normandy campaign 106; and raids 37–8; strategic utility and definitional problems of 37–8; Warden's theory of 23–8
Air Staff 3, 16, 36, 39–43, 45–50, 52, 54, 57–8, 109, 150 n56, 150–1 n57, 156 n120
Air Targets Sub-Committee of Bombing Committee 45
Alcibiades 67
al-Majid, Ali Hassan ("Chemical Ali"), 17
Amiens prison raid *see* 487 Squadron (RNZAF)
Amin, Hafizullah, assassination of 16
annihilation 14, 38, 58–9, 61–3, 65–72, 74, 77–8, 92–3, 115, 170 n85; Boyd and 28; Clausewitz on 63–5; Delbrück on 65–8, 165 n37, 165–6 n48; Fuller and Liddell Hart on 160 n7; Mao on 71–3, 170 n85; morality of 174 n114; Stalin and 166 n49; strategic paralysis and 3, 23, 27–8, 69; strategy of 13–4, 65–6, 69–70, 114, 165 n37, 165–6 n48; Tukhachevskii and 166–7 n51; war of 59, 65, 72
Arnhem 111
assassination 16, 110, 136 n105, 171 n89, 177 n12, 184 n68
atomic bomb 1, 183–4 n66
attrition: Boyd on 140 n155, 141 n157; Clausewitz and 160–1 n7; Delbrück and 65–8, 165 n37, 165–6 n48; Fuller and 20, 160 n7; Mao and 72–3, 169 n76, 170 n83–5; moral and material aspects of 14, 35, 59–61, 66, 70–1, 74, 76–7, 83, 102, 112–15; relationship to non-linearity 77; special operations and moral 75–7; strategy of 59, 66–8, 70, 83, 85, 113, 150–1 n57, 165 n37, 166 n49, 176 n3; war of 59, 65, 72, 170 n85; Warden and 23, 25, 27
Auchinleck, Claude 86, 96, 177 n11–12
Aucun, SAS attack upon 80, 175 n120.

Baldwin, Stanley; on utility of airpower 42, 150 n52, 150 n54
Beaufre, André, definition of strategy 7, 121 n30
Beddell Smith, Walter 96, 103, 185 n85
Bidwell, Shelford 102
Blackburn, Donald 74, 171 n90
Bomber Command 42, 52, 56, 58, 150 n51–2, 151 n62, 152 n74, 157 n142
Boyd, John 13, 17, 113, 139 n133; and annihilation 28; on attrition 140 n155, 141 n157; and fast transients 30; and fighter acquisition 29, 140 n142; and fighter tactics 29, 139 n140; OODA loop of 30–1; scientific basis of theory

31; SOF and 31–2; on strategy as a competition 29–31; strategic paralysis and 31–2
bouncing bomb *see* Upkeep
Bourges-Orleans 95
Bradley, Omar 93, 183 n62
Brest 93
British Army formations: Eighth Army 86, 90, 117 n12; 21 Army Group 84–5, 90, 92, 95, 98, 101–4, 108, 110, 116, 188 n113, 189 n120, 189 n125; 1 Airborne Corps 95, 101; 2 Canadian Corps 93; SAS Brigade 14, 84–5, 89–91, 95–6, 98–9, 102–3, 110–11, 116, 179 n34, 180 n39, 185 n82, 189 n125, 192 n159, 192 n160; 8 Commando 86; SAS Regiment 60, 76, 89, 123 n48, 173 n110; 1st Regiment SAS 90, 178 n21, 179 n30, 179 n34; 2nd Regiment SAS 179 n34; "L" Detachment SAS 86–7, 89, 177 n12, 177 n15; LRDG 6, 86, 179 n22, 179 n23, 180–1 n46; Phantom 192–3 n160; PPA 87, 179 n22; SBS 87, 178 n 21, 179 n22
Browning, Roy 101
Builder, Carl 23
Bush, George H.W. 26, 163–4 n28

Caen 93
Casablanca Conference 91
center(s) of gravity 2, 14, 16, 24, 32–3, 36, 142 n173, 142 n175; Clausewitz on 32–3, 65, 142 n176; and friction 33; Fuller and 19–20, 22, 160 n7; strategic paralysis theory and 3, 17, 19–20, 24, 26–7, 33, 35, 65, 77; Warden and 24, 26–7, 135 n87, 135–6 n92–94, 137 n114; will and 22
CFLN *see Comité Françis de la Libération Nationale* (CFLN)
Châtellerault, example of SOF and precision airpower in Normandy 98, 193 n162
Checkmate 23, 26
Cherbourg 93, 107, 189 n119
Chiefs of Staff Committee 94, 125 n67, 158 n150
Chiefs of Staff—Joint Planning Committee 43
Churchill, Winston S. 50; and American public opinion 54; appointment of Montgomery to command Eighth Army 90; and RAF 147 n31; relationship with Henry Tizard 155 n105; and speech to US Congress after Operation Chastise 55; and support for special operations 51
Clarke, Dudley 85
Clausewitz, Carl von Maria 12, 14, 27, 59, 61–4, 70, 73, 112, 114, 163 n27, 164 n29, 164 n31, 171 n94–5; attrition and 160–1 n7; Boyd and 31; on center(s) of gravity 32–3, 65, 142 n176; on *coup d'oeil* 165 n43; and culminating point of victory 64, 165 n40; and flanking operations 81; and forms of war 65, 67–9, 164 n34; on friction 11, 32, 79, 121 n31, 141 n163; on moral and material aspects of strategy 74; on the nature of war 66, 121 n30, 140 n144, 140 n148; non-linearity aspects of 62, 121 n31; on offense and defense 63, 65; principle of continuity 64; pure concept of war 143 n179; pure defense 162 n23; translation of 59; Warden on 138 n119; Wylie on 167 n57
Comité Françis de la Libération Nationale (CFLN) 94, 183 n65
Comitato di Liberazione Nazionale Alta Italia 94
Committee of Imperial Defence 39
Connor, Ken 9, 123 n48
corps d'elite, distinction with special operations 6
counterterrorism, definition of 5
coup de main 21
coup d'oeil, 22, 121 n33, 165 n43

Dambusters raid *see* Operation Chastise
dams, Ruhr valley; Bever 53; Diemel 50, 151 n67; Eder 45, 48, 53–4; Ennepe 53, 151 n67; Möhne 45–51, 53–6; Sorpe 45
decapitation, and strategic paralysis 2, 126 n11, 134 n73, 137 n112, 144 n10
de Gaulle, Charles 95
Delbrück, Hans 59, 61–2, 69, 114; and attrition and annihilation 65–7, 70; Clausewitz and 66–8, 165 n40; on command 67, 165 n43; and forms of war 65, 67–9, 165 n37, 165–6 n48; Mao and 72; and *Sachkritik* 65, 164 n36; Svechin, similarities to 68
direct action, definition of 5
Dornberger, Walter 56; meeting with Hitler 158 n160
Dortmund 56
Dortmund-Ems Canal 58, 157 n142
Doubs 95
Dyle Plan 10

226 Index

Eben Emael: importance of 9–10, 124 n58–60; special operation to seize 6, 9–10
economy of force 13, 21, 36, 46, 77, 114; law of 66–7; as principle of war 18, 21, 76, 131 n47, 131 n49
Eisenhower, Dwight D. 84, 91–2, 111, 116; authorizes SAS for Normandy 104, 181 n47; Beddell Smith and 96, 103; civil affairs and 103–4; command style of 102, 185 n85, 190 n131; leadership qualities of 91; decision to halt major resistance 104, 190 n133; Montgomery and 84, 92, 102, 182 n57, 190 n142; planning for invasion of Europe 96, 102–3, 182 n52; SFHQ and French resistance 95; on SOF 189 n123
EMFFI *see Etat-major des Forces Franqis de l'Intérieur* (EMFFI)
Enigma 106
Entebbe raid *see* Operation Jonathan
entropy, concept of, and relationship to strategy 31
Etat-major des Forces Franqis de l'Intérieur (EMFFI) 95, 183 n65, 185 n78, 185 n82
Evreux 98
Explorations in Strategy 11

Falaise Gap 93, 105, 111, 183 n64
Ferris, John 43
Finch-Noyes, C.R. 47, 153 n82–4
French resistance 14, 93–5, 108, 185 n73, 186 n90, 192 n156; *maquis* and 90, 94, 99; and *Armée Secrète* 94; and *Franc Tireurs et Partisans* 94; and *Groupe de l'Armée* 94
friction 3–4, 7, 11, 15, 17, 24, 28, 31–3, 35, 59, 62, 64, 67, 70, 77–9, 83–4, 88, 91, 93, 95, 101, 113, 115, 121 n31, 141 n162
Fuller, John Frederick Charles 13, 17, 39, 113; aeroplanes and 21, 131 n46, 132 n55–6, 132 n61; attrition and 20, 160 n7; beliefs of 18–19, 128 n 19–20; career of 18, 127–8 n18, 128 n23, 132 n63–4; center of gravity and 19, 22; compared to Boyd 28–9, 31; and concept of body and brain warfare 20–1, 131 n49–50, 132 n53; correspondence with Liddell Hart 131 n44, 131 n49, 132 n51, 133 n69; decapitation and 126 n11; influence of 17–18, 126 n12–13, 127 n14–15; and moral effect argument 40; on offense and defense 20, 130 n40; and Plan 1919 19–20, 129 n28; and principles of war 18, 131 n47; similarities with Warden 23–6, 28–9, 135 n93, 138 n129; strategical paralysis and 19–22, 132 n58, 133 n69; tank and 19–21, 129 n36, 130 n43, 131 n44, 132 n55–6, 132 n61; and Tuchachevskii 68

Gazala 86, 177 n15
German army, or *Heer* 25, 56; formations: *Westheer* 83, 85, 87, 89, 91–2, 98–9, 102, 105–11, 116; *OB West* 106; *Army Group B* 93; *Panzer Group West* 110; *Deutsche Afrika-Korps* 55, 84, 86–7, 90, 110; *Seventh Army* 14–15, 99, 105, 110; logistics of 84, 87, 100, 105–11, 191 n149, 192 n152, 193 n164, 193 n167
Gestapo 94, 99, 154 n101, 184 n69
Gibson, Guy 52–3, 145 n17,
Goebbels, Josef, assigns blame for dams attack 53, 157 n135
Gordon, John 110, 120 n22, 176 n5
Göring, Hermann 56, 157 n135
Graf Zeppelin 52
Graham, Dominick 102
Gray, Colin S., 7; definition of SOF 118 n8, 119 n16, 125 n76; and dimensions of strategy 121 n32; on developing strategy 173 n105; on strategic effect 121 n36, 125 n75; on strategic utility of SOF 11, 125 n69
great raids 2, 4, 67, 85, 90, 115
Green Island, Israeli raid upon 75, 172 n97

Habr Gidr, militia 79
Hamburg 56
Harris, Arthur; on bombing accuracy 152 n73; on strategic bombing 49, 154 n101; on Operation Chastise 51–2, 155 n106; on panacea targets 50, 154 n102; on Upkeep 51, 154 n103
Heisenberg, Walter 1
Hitler, Adolf 2, 10, 13, 33, 36, 41, 43, 53–4, 56–8, 91, 93, 110, 122 n41, 128 n20, 138 n127, 157 n135, 158 n160, 159 n165, 184 n68, 184 n70, 188 n115, 191 n145
hostage rescue raids; attempt, Tehran, Iran 1980 *see* Operation Eagle Claw; Iranian Embassy, London, 1980 *see* Operation Nimrod
Hurtgen Forest 111
Hussein, Saddam 16–17, 26, 117, 136 n103, 136 n105, 161 n15
hyperwar 27

"Instant Thunder," air campaign plan against Iraq 23, 133 n70, 136 n102, 137 n107
Iraq 16, 25–7, 29, 117

Jones, Gregg 10

Kemp, Anthony 107
Kissinger, Henry 74
Koenig, Pierre Joseph 95
Kriegsmarine 25

Lake Tinn 1
Lawrence, Thomas Edward 62, 70, 84, 114; attrition and 70–1; Arab culture and 70, 169 n69; maneuver without battle 70, 169 n73; success in irregular warfare 71, 168 n66
Lewes, John "Jock" 89, 176 n9, 179 n32
Liddell Hart, Basil Henry 18–19; airpower and 148 n36, 149 n43; on annihilation and maneuver 160 n7; on Eben Emael 124 n60; correspondence with Fuller 131 n44, 131 n49, 132 n51, 133 n69; Fuller's influence upon 127 n15; and Lawrence 169 n73; reputation of 126–7 n13, 127–8 n18, 129 n24, 129 n26; similarities to Boyd 141 n158
Limoges 98; 617 Squadron bombing of engine factory in 157 n142
logistics 8, 15, 59, 84, 87, 92, 100, 105–11, 191 n49, 192 n52, 193 n67; as dimension of strategy 121 n32; of SOF 120 n26; Warden and 135 n92
London 12, 41, 57, 99
Long Range Desert Group (LRDG) 6, 86, 179 n22, 179 n23, 180–1 n46
LRDG *see* Long Range Desert Group (LRDG)
Luftwaffe 25, 56, 139 n136, 152 n72, 157 n135, 158 n160, 186 n92, 191 n146,

Magic 106
Malcom, Ben 73, 171 n88
Manor, Leroy 74, 171 n90
Mayne, Blair "Paddy" 179 n34
McLeod, Roderick 89, 96, 101, 104, 109, 193 n163
McNab, Andy 8
McRaven, William 9; on Eben Emael 124 n59; principles of special operations 125 n69; on relative superiority and friction 11
Metz 93, 111
Milice 94, 99, 101, 104

military revolutions 63, 65
Ministry of Economic Warfare 49–50, 94, 154 n102, 156 n122
Mogadishu 79
Montgomery, Bernard Law 84, 89–93, 102, 109, 111, 180 n44, 180–1 n46, 182 n53, 182 n57, 182–3 n59, 189 n127, 194 n170
Mrazek, James 9

NATO *see* North Atlantic Treaty Organization (NATO)
non-linearity studies 62; relationship to special operations 73–7
Norsk Hydro 1
North Atlantic Treaty Organization (NATO) 16

Office of Strategic Services (OSS) 84–5, 89, 94, 101, 108, 183 n65, 184 n68; Jedburghs 102, 188 n110, 188 n115; Operational Groups 101–2, 188 n115;
Operation Agreement (Tobruk/Benghazi raid, 1942) 88–9, 179 n29
Operation Anvil (invasion of Southern France, 1944) 96, 102, 182 n52, 189 n127
Operation Chariot (St. Nazaire raid, 1942) 10–1, 75, 172 n96
Operation Chastise (Dambusters raid, 1943) 35–6, 58; 617 Squadron and 52–3, 156 n127, 156 n131; Air Staff planning for 47–51; Cochrane and 52; Churchill and 50–2, 54–5; Gibson and 52; Harris and 49–52; Hitler and 56–7; material aspects of 52–3, 156 n126; physical damage caused by 53–4, 56; Portal and 47, 49, 50, 52, 156 n122; Saundby and 52, 156 n120; as a special operation 38; Speer and 56; strategic effects of 54–7; Tizard and 50; Upkeep and 48, 50, 52, 115 n118, 145 n16, 156 n121, 158 n150; Wallis's influence upon 48–51, 154 n96; Winterbotham and 50
Operation Crusader, special operations planning in support of 86, 177 n12
Operation Eagle Claw (Iran hostage rescue attempt, Tehran 1980) 12, 75, 172 n98
Operation Enduring Freedom 98, 117
Operation Fortitude (Normandy deception plan) 85, 190 n133
Operation Iraqi Freedom 16, 117, 161–2 n15
Operation Jonathan (Entebbe raid, 1976) 12, 75, 119 n18, 172 n101

228 Index

Operation Neptune (amphibious portion of invasion of Europe, 1944) 89, 96, 98, 181 n50, 182 n54, 185 n73
Operation Nimrod (Iranian Embassy hostage rescue raid, London 1980) 12, 119 n18
Operation Overlord (invasion of Europe, 1944) 85, 92, 95, 101–2, 104, 107, 125 n76, 179 n34, 182 n57
Organisation Todt 55; Fuller's comments on 128 n20
OSS *see* Office of Strategic Services (OSS)

panacea targets 24, 34, 36, 50, 135 n91, 154 n102
Paris 10, 93, 106, 109
Patton, George S. 93, 99; and French resistance support to Third Army 187–8 n108; purported influence of Liddell Hart upon 129 n24
Pemberton, Noel 47
Peenemünde 56
Popski's Private Army [1st Demolition Squadron] (PPA) 87, 179 n22
Portal, Charles 36, 47, 49–50, 52, 156 n122
PPA *see* Popski's Private Army [1st Demolition Squadron] (PPA)
principles of war 18, 21, 120 n33, 131 n7, 167 n56

RAF *see* Royal Air Force (RAF)
RAF Scampton 53
relative superiority, and theory of SOF tactical success 11
Revolution in Military Affairs 23, 27, 163 n25
Ritchie, Neil 86, 96, 176 n5, 177 n11–12
Rommel, Erwin 7–8, 122 n41; British attempt to assassinate 177 n12; Liddell Hart's influence upon 126–7 n13, 129 n24
Royal Air Force (RAF) 1, 33, 36–7, 39–40, 42–7, 50, 54, 88, 99, 114, 116, 133 n65, 147 n31, 148 n36, 150 n51, 150 n56–7, 151 n60, 151 n62, 151 n64, 152 n73, 155 n116, 156 n123, 187 n101
Ruhr Pocket 93, 183 n61

Salmond, John 40, 148 n38–9
SAS *see* Special Air Service (SAS)
Saundby, Richard 36, 52, 149 n42, 156 n120
SBS *see* Special Boat Section (SBS)
Schlieffen Plan 10, 162 n18, 164–5 n36
Schwarzkopf, Norman 26
SD *see Sicherheitsdienst* (SD)

SFHQ *see* Special Forces Headquarters (SFHQ)
SHAEF *see* Supreme Headquarters Allied Expeditionary Force (SHAEF)
Sicherheitsdienst (SD) 94
Simonds, Guy 93
Skorzeny, Otto 16
Smith, Malcolm 41, 143–4 n6, 150 n56
SOE *see* Special Operations Executive (SOE)
SOF *see* special operations forces (SOF)
Special Air Service (SAS) 2, 6, 8, 12, 14–15, 123 n49; 1st Regiment 90, 178 n21, 179 n30, 179 n34, 177 n16, 178 n20, 180 n36,; 2nd Regiment 179 n34; Brigade 14, 84–5, 89–91, 95–6, 98–9, 102–3, 110–11, 116, 179 n34, 180 n39, 185 n82, 189 n125, 192 n159, 192 n160; Claret operations 119 n17; commitment to Northern Ireland 76, 173 n110; creation and initial use of 85–7, 176 n5; Eisenhower and 102–4, 181 n47; expansion of 15, 84, 89–90, 179 n30, 180 n39; friction in Falklands 60, 141 n166; friction in Normandy 84; impact of David Stirling's capture upon 89; initial raids on Gazala and Timimi 86, 177 n15, 178 n18–19; "L" Detachment 86–7, 89, 177 n12, 177 n15; Montgomery and 90–3, 102; in Operation Agreement 88–9; Operation Bulbasket 98–101, 104, 187 n97, 187 n106; in Operation Crusader 177 n12; Operation Dingson 96, 186 n88; Operation Dunhill 104; Operation Houndsworth 99, 104, 188 n118; Operation Loyton 104; Operation Nelson 100–1, 188 n109; Operation Titanic 4 91, 181 n47; Operation Wallace 104, 189 n119; planning and operational aspects in Normandy 95–105, 180 n41, 185 n84–5, 187 n107, 188 n112, 188 n115–16, 189 n119–20, 189 n125, 190 n132; Republican image of 76; role in delaying 2nd SS Panzer Division 98–9; SFHQ and 95–6, 101; SHAEF and 95–8, 102–3; as strategic troops 8–9; suggested use of in Normandy 105–10, 192 n154, 192 n159–60, 193 n161–3
Special Boat Section (SBS) 87; formation of 178 n 21; effectiveness of 179 n22
Special Forces Headquarters (SFHQ) 84–5, 95–7, 99, 101, 103, 111, 185 n84, 188 n112–13, 189 n119–20, 192 n154

Special Interrogation Group 87, 179 n23
specially designated units 5–6
special operations; definitions of 4–5, 119 n16; direct effects of 73–4; misuse 2–3, 8, 37, 61, 81, 84, 112, 115–16, 121 n27, 123 n43, 180 n36; moral effects of 14, 54–5, 61, 75–8, 80, 105, 107, 110, 112–13; non-linear aspects of 75–7; strategic aspects of 8–11, 123 n47–9, 124 n64–75; strategic enabling value of 79–81; utility of 199 n17
Special Operations Executive (SOE) 84–5, 89, 93–6, 98–99, 108, 111; circuits delay *2nd SS Panzer Division* 98–9; competition between SOF 189 n119; counterintelligence success against 184 n69; planning staff in SHAEF 96; resolve disputes with SAS 101–2; responsibilities for resistance 93–5, 183 n65, 185 n78; Section X and targeting Hitler 93, 184 n68; suspicions of SAS 95–6, 192 n159
special operations forces (SOF) 2–3, 12, 15, 67, 78, 101, 108, 111–2, 117; 617 Squadron as 38; airpower and 98; attrition and 60–1, 73; Boyd on 32–3; competition between 84, 87, 101, 189 n119; definition of 6–7; familiarity of Eisenhower and Montgomery with 84, 90, 102, 180 n44; 180–1 n46; and friction 79, 141 n166; ineffectiveness in Normandy campaign 102–4, 116; literature on 8, 123 n43–6, 178 n20; misuse of 2–3, 8, 37, 61, 81, 84, 112, 115–16, 120 n25; 121 n27, 123 n43, 180 n36; non-linearity studies and 75–7; in North African campaign 87–90, 110; in Operation Enduring Freedom 117; in Operation Iraqi Freedom 16; in Somalia 79; Soviet use of 16; strategic aspects of 8–11, 123 n47–9, 124 n64–75; strategic enabling value of 79–81; utility of 199 n17
special reconnaissance, definition of 5
Spetsnaz: role of against NATO 16; use in Afghanistan 16
Speer, Albert 53–4, 56; and V-2 158 n160
St. Nazaire, raid upon *see* Operation Chariot
Stirling, David 85–9, 95–6, 176 n9, 177 n11, 179 n23, 179 n30; capture of 89, 116; creation of SAS 85–7; Montgomery and 90, 180 n44
Stirling, William 179 n34
strategic bombing 36, 39–41, 43, 45–6, 50, 114, 116, 137 n108, 114 n10, 151 n60, 151 n62, 152 n71, 172 n101

strategic paralysis 3, 12–3, 17–18, 22–3, 26, 28–9, 32–36, 48, 58–9, 65, 67, 77, 113–14, 117, 126 n7, 133 n69, 151 n64, 167–8 n62
strategy: of annihilation 13–4, 65–6, 69–70, 165 n37, 165–6 n48; art of 4, 81; of attrition 59, 66–8, 70, 83, 85, 113, 150–1 n57, 165 n37, 166 n49, 176 n3; chance in 7, 32, 62, 115, 121 n31; choice in 62, 66–7, 80, 117; competition as element of 7, 13, 29, 36, 59, 62, 112, 114, 117, 121 n30; cumulative 69, 76–7; dimension(s) of 2, 7, 61, 77, 115, 121 n32, 169 n76; as distinct from operations and tactics 162 n20; forms of 65, 68–9, 77, 165–5 n48, 167 n57, 167 n61; logic of 77, 82; grammar of 82; as a method of thought 7; nature of 3–4, 7, 12–13, 112, 165 n37; non-linear aspects of 61, 75–7, 114; offense and defense in 62; and "paradoxical logic" 7; paradoxes of 64; in practice 35, 61, 68, 77, 83–4, 113–4, 168 n65; principles of war and 121 n33; pure 68–9; science of 81; sequential 69, 77; in theory 35; uncertainty in 4, 7, 33
Sturmabteilung Koch 6, 10
Supreme Headquarters Allied Expeditionary Force (SHAEF) 84–5, 89, 93, 95–6, 98–9, 102–4, 108, 110–11, 116, 185 n82–3, 185 n85, 185–6 n86, 189 n120, 189 n125
Svechin, Aleksandr A. 61, 68–9, 166 n49; on nature of war 121 n34

Tarawa 6
technology
Telemark raid *see* Vemork
thermodynamics, second law of, as explanation for strategic interaction 31
Timimi 86, 177 n15
Tirpitz 11, 52, 183 n66
Tissaphernes 67
Tizard, Henry 50
Torigni-sur-Vire 99
Toulouse 98–9
Tours 98
Triandafillov, Vladimir K. 68, 166 n50
Trenchard, Hugh 36, 40–3, 48, 148 n36, 149 n41; and Churchill 147 n31; on failure of disarmament 150 n55; and moral effect of bombing 40–1, 148 n34–5, 149 n40; and Salmond 148 n39
Tukhachevskii, Mikhail 68, 127 n14, 166 n49, 166–7 n51
Tulle 98

230 Index

Tzu, Sun 31, 33, 126 n8, 140 n151, 171 n95

Ultra 98, 106, 183 n63, 186 n93, 187–8 n108
Upkeep 38, 49–50, 52–3, 155 n114, 156 n121, 158 n150; Admiralty pressure to use 52; delivery of 145 n16; Harris and 154 n103; idea for 48; naval variant Highball 52, 154 n94
unconventional warfare 73–4, 90, 99, 101, 103, 118 n8, 123 n45; anti-partisan activities 119 n11; definition of 5–6; opinions on effectiveness of 123–4 n50, 171n88, 171 n92, 173 n108, 184 n71; partisans in 73, 94–5, 111, 117, 171 n88, 184–5, n71
United States Air Force 23, 26, 28–9, 133 n71, 134 n74, 134 n78,
United States Army Air Force (USAAF) 1, 139 n136, 149 n45,150 n54, 171 n90
United States Special Operations Command (USSOCOM) 5, 123 n45
United States Strategic Bombing Survey; on damage from dams raid 54
USAAF *see* United States Army Air Force (USAAF)

Vemork, attack on German heavy water supply 1–2,
Versailles Treaty 42
Vietnam: North 23, 33, 73–4, 134 n77, 142 n177, 161 n8, 170 n79; South 23, 142 n177, 170 n79, 173 n108; special operations and 122 n42, 123–4 n50, 173 n108, 173–4 n123
Von Braun, Wernher 56; meeting with Hitler 158 n160
von Schieffen, Albert Graf 62

Waffen-SS 98, 186 n92; units of: *1st SS Panzer Division (Leibstandarte Adolf Hitler)* 98; *2nd SS Panzer Division* (Das Reich) 98–9, 187 n100–1, 187 n103; *12th SS Panzer Division (Hitlerjugend)* 98, 186–7 n95; *17th SS Panzer Grenadier Division (Götz von Berlichingen)* 98; *schwere Panzer Abteilung* (sPzAbt) 101 98, 186–7 n95
Wallis, Barnes 52–3, 114, 155 n104, 156 n121, 156 n131, 157 n142, 193 n167; advocate of strategic paralysis 48–9;
idea for Upkeep 48; influence on Harris 50–1, 154 n103, 158 n160; suggests Eder Dam as a target 48, 50, 154 n96
war(fare): absolute 59, 65, 69, 72, 77; of annihilation 59, 65, 72, 170 n85; of attrition 59, 65, 72, 170 n85; chance in 67, 70, 115, 121 n31, 165 n43; form(s) of 12, 20, 28, 59, 63–5, 67, 71–2, 148 n37 ; irregular 14, 23, 59, 62, 68–70, 118 n8, 123–4 n50, 129 n24, 163–4 n28, 168 n66; limited 59, 70, 72, 76–7; in practice 64; preemptive 2; real 65; in theory 64; uncertainty in 67, 78
Warden III, John 13, 17, 113, 135 n91; and *The Air Campaign* 24, 135 n86; and attrition warfare 23, 25, 27; Boyd and 31, 33; career of 23–6, 133 n70, 134 n74, 136 n99, 137 n109; center(s) of gravity and 24, 27, 135 n92, 136 n94; and decapitation 126 n11, 137 n112; and five-ring model 24–7, 137 n113; on offense and defense 28, 138 n119; and parallel attack 23, 136 n95, 138 n124; similarities to Fuller 23–6, 28–9, 126 n11, 134 n81, 135 n93, 138 n129; technology and 27–8, 138 n119
War of Attrition, use of SOF in 76
War Cabinet 42, 55, 94, 184 n68, 185 n75
Wavell, Archibald 85
Wells, H.G. 38, 145 n18–21
Western Air Plans 43–4
Wilkinson, Spenser 21, 131 n48
Wilson, Harold 76
Winterbotham, Frederick W. 50
Wunderwaffen: Dornberger and 56, 158 n160; He-177 56; Hitler and 56–7, 158 n160, 158 n164, 159 n165; Me-262 159 n165; Speer and 56, 158 n160; V-1 flying bomb 56, 159 n166; V-2 rocket 56, 145 n15, 158 n160, 158–9 n164, 159 n166; von Braun and 56, 158 n160
Wylie, J.C. 69, 76, 167 n57

Zedong, Mao 62, 70, 169 n75, 170 n82; attrition and annihilation 72–3, 169 n76, 170 n83–5; career of 70–1, 168 n67; differences with Delbrück 72; forms of war 71–2; offense and defense 72; similarities with Clausewitz 73; similarities with Lawrence 70–1; stages of revolutionary warfare 71, 170 n79